FOULA

The Time of My Life

18 months in 1954–55 with the most isolated
human community in the British Isles, on an island
fifteen miles off the Atlantic West coast of Shetland.
The first stage in my transition from teacher to
wildlife film-maker in my search for the
meaning of the word 'Insularity'.

by

Christopher Mylne

THE ISLANDS BOOK TRUST

Published in 2011
by The Islands Book Trust

www.theislandsbooktrust.com

ISBN: 978-1-907443-15-2

Typeset by Erica Schwarz (www.schwarz-editorial.co.uk)
Printed and bound by Bookwork PL, Warsaw, Poland
Cover design by Jim Hutcheson

The Islands Book Trust
Ravenspoint Centre
Kershader
South Lochs
Isle of Lewis
HS2 9QA
Tel: 01851 880737

Contents

About the Author

Christopher Mylne was born in 1927 at Dalhousie Castle in Midlothian, where his boyhood home was his father's Preparatory School for boys. At 8 he won a Major Scholarship to Cargilfield School, and at 13 another to Sedbergh School where he spent the war years studying Classics and exploring the bird-life of the Yorkshire fells. As the top pupil in the Upper Sixth, after achieving both School and Higher Certificates by 16, his academic success was marred when he nearly died from cerebro-spinal meningitis and found his memory seriously impaired. However in 1945 he won an Exhibition to St John's College, Cambridge; and then joined the army – on VJ Day! To make sense of post-war conscription he followed his interest in field radio in the cadets and opted for the Royal Signals. The tempting bonus was a science course in Maths and Physics at Oxford, but this meant starting almost from scratch in both subjects in only two school terms. He found his Army training – learning how to kill the enemy – a culture shock but was still able to earn Best-all-round Cadet status at both Aldershot and Catterick Training Units. After demobilisation at 21 he took up Classics again at Cambridge, changing to English in his third year before graduating with Honours.

After gaining his Diploma in Education at Edinburgh University his first job was teaching Classics at John Watson's School in Edinburgh, a unique co-educational boarding school for fatherless children for which he was admirably suited by both his home and school background. Health problems, in the form of acute duodenal ulcer trouble during army service and at University, did not prevent him leading expeditions to Norway, as President of the Cambridge Bird Club, to study the autumn bird migration. This had included a visit to Utsira in 1950 with scientists from Stavanger Museum. Bird Observatory work, mostly at the Isle of May in the Firth of Forth, taught him the value of islands for migration studies. So a turning point in his life came with an advertisement for a job in Shetland as Head Teacher of a primary school with only 5 pupils, on Foula, the 'island of birds'. As the first person to take on both jobs as Teacher and Lay Missionary, he found himself in a community of 70 islanders, with an average age of 60, living as subsistence crofters with virtually no contact with the outside world except one mailboat a week – weather permitting, which it often didn't. A house came with the job, but no electricity, phone or transport and only one family of neighbours. He had hoped for a healthier way of life than in the city to cope with his health problems, but found a six-day week and the busiest schedule he had ever known very stressful in that it involved much the same struggle for survival that everyone else shared. But the rewards were deeply satisfying and living so close to nature a revelation that changed his whole philosophy of life. Sadly his health once more let him down when medical advice on the probability of fatal ulcer perforation forced him to resign after only eighteen months, but not before the lessons of how to live happily with one's fellow men had bound him emotionally to Foula for life.

Foula's wildlife and natural beauty started his career in photography, and prompted his first movie as a record of his life there. This short film earned him the lucky chance of filling a vacancy in the RSPB's new Film Unit, a pioneering opportunity when the BBC had no natural history film on its shelves. In seven years as a one-man Film Unit he filled the Royal Festival Hall in London 13 times without an empty seat, and also produced eight network TV programmes for BBC on British wildlife subjects. Two of these earned him his Fellowship of the Royal Photographic Society, his films being unconventional as devised, scripted, filmed, edited with picture, sound effects and often commentary both written and spoken, all the creative work of only one film-maker. The trade unions made life difficult but it is no co-incidence that the RSPB membership rose from 20,000 in 1957 upwards towards its present total of over a million, with a succession of brilliant cameramen.

In 1963–65 he spent two years as Principal Field Officer with the National Trust for Scotland organising Adventure Camps for young people and running their highly popular Adventure Cruises for the young in heart of all ages. In 1966 he went free-lance, starting a career in island films with St Kilda, and later Fair

Isle, Rum, and especially wildlife topics for schools programmes – ospreys, the Scottish albatross, owls, "Proud Predators", and animal welfare subjects for several charities.

His final island was Karlsoy at 70°N, to tell the life story of "The Remarkable Willow Grouse".

Islands remain his first love. This book was written to enable others to catch a glimpse of the magic of an island home; the beauty of birds; the miracle of migration; the stars at night in black winter; the joy of a workable human community; and last, but not least, the companionship of a collie dog.

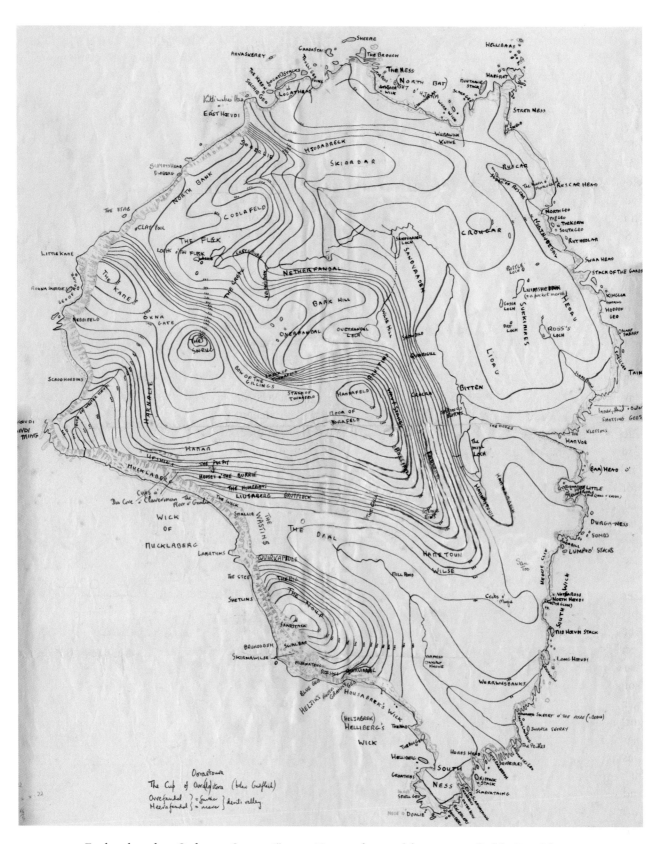

Foula – based on Ordnance Survey 1″ map. Names of natural features supplied by Eric Isbister

By Way of Introduction

It was January and very cold on the platform of Oxenholme station, on the border of the West Riding of Yorkshire. In 1945, at the end of five years of World War II, with petrol rationing and troop movements clogging up the railways, the prospect of a long train journey to Oxford was not very attractive. I was 17 and in my last year at Sedbergh School, and had entered for a Scholarship to St John's College. The prospect of the exams involved was daunting. The papers were set for a group of Oxford Colleges which included Balliol, the ultimate goal of any Classical student, so that one knew the standard would be high. I should have been one of the most favoured candidates. My name was at the very top of the school list, the most senior student academically in the Upper Sixth Classical in a public school with over 400 pupils and fairly high expectations. On paper it must have looked as though I had a good chance. I had after all won a Major Scholarship to Sedbergh in 1940, a year after war was declared, gone straight into the Upper Fourth at the tender age of 13, and been promoted to the Fifth Form after one term. I remember finding school work easy. I enjoyed using my brain and just seemed to waltz through exams. I sat School Certificate in my first year aged just 14 and achieved five Credits and two 'Very goods', equivalent to A Grades nowadays. From 1942, I had consolidated my position in the top form, the Upper Sixth Classical. There was no hurry to take my Higher Certificate as it was obvious by then that I would have to do my National Service before going to university. But it was equally obvious that the best course was to secure a university place before leaving school for the army. My father had been the middle son of Bishop Louis Mylne's seven sons, and so had studied Classics at Keble College where sons of the cloth had priority. Not surprising therefore that, as he had nurtured me in the classics to scholarship standard, it was to Oxford that I was heading in January 1945. But by 1945 my position in the scholarship stakes had changed and become suddenly precarious. Between my precocious successes in my early school years and my achieving my Higher certificate in 1944, I had suffered a setback which was to dog me all my life and the effect of which was only really apparent to me – from the inside.

It happened like this. Towards the end of the summer term of 1943 when exam pressures slackened, we were blessed with an unusually fine day, a comparatively rare event in the rain-swept Yorkshire fells. The Headmaster declared an 'Extra Half', which meant that the afternoon classes were cancelled. On such occasions anything went for recreation, but within strict rules of course, especially where river bathing was concerned. We persuaded our friendly music master to take responsibility for half a dozen of us to go down the river Lune to a favourite pool. It was a day to remember; exams were over, the long summer holidays were just ahead of us, and we had fitness, friendship and frivolity to enjoy. An extra dimension was created by a small party of local girls who hid behind the bushes on the far bank and giggled and wolf-whistled, especially when we came out of the pool and towels slipped carelessly as we dressed – to their audible delight. It was a fitting end to a hard-working term and I for one never gave a thought to the potential hidden menace in the water. We were several miles downstream of the town, and there were several farms with byres and probably muck-heaps beside the streams running into the river. Perhaps we should have recognised the risks but all we thought about the water was that it was rather cold.

A week after arriving home for the long summer holiday, I seemed to develop 'flu. My family departed to the Solway, to our traditional holiday venue, though rather more difficult to reach with petrol rationing at its worst. I was to follow when my headache cleared and my temperature went down. I was left to recover in my fourth-storey bedroom in the Scottish baronial castle which my father rented from the Earl of Dalhousie to run his 75 pupil preparatory boarding school. His pupils had also gone home and the huge building was empty. My father had a heart condition and was confined to the ground floor, four flights of stairs below. An old retainer had stayed on to look after us both and brought up my meals on a tray. She was very kind but my headache got worse, my temperature remained high and I neither ate nor slept for three days and nights, by which time my mother had been alerted and rushed home to the rescue. Just in time! I had been brought a cup of Ovaltine, and when she tried to get me to take some I couldn't bend my neck forward to drink. From previous experience as a Headmaster's wife – thank God! – she recognised one of the tell-tale symptoms of the dreaded disease, cerebro-spinal meningitis. Our doctor was on holiday but within hours a specialist had arrived from Edinburgh and prescribed the latest May & Baker drug. I gather it was touch and go for a few days; and then after weeks of long, slow convalescence I learnt to walk again and gradually got back to normal food and some exercise. I read a lot as soon as my brain had recovered from the shock but it was clear to me, though hard to explain to anyone else, that concentration and the ability to assimilate knowledge or experience from the written word was on a different plane from before. Most especially my memory, the basis of learning and the most vital prerequisite of all scholarship, was sorely impaired. I could comprehend but not retain what I read.

I finally returned to school more than halfway through the next term, to the Upper Sixth and the curriculum leading to Higher Certificate, acutely aware within days that my academic life was threatened by a new word – 'failure'. Everything seemed to be that much harder and more time-consuming than before. The old facility and enjoyment had gone. From now on all schoolwork was hard slog. Only one thing seemed to remain unchanged. The old joy in creativity, in writing good prose – or verse – in playing a piece of music well on the piano, anything where activity rather than assimilation was the keynote, still brought me as much pleasure and contentment as before.

I had one shining hope for any looming exam. At least I could look forward to the English Essay paper. This did not rely on memory or creativity dependent on recall. There surely I could shine. Although I had led a sheltered life and my experience of travel or adventure had been seriously limited by wartime conditions for five long years, I had new interests, especially in natural history. The Dalhousie Castle estate, full of unspoiled woodland, with the River South Esk running close by, was a fertile training ground for my inquisitive mind. Jock Clark, the groundsman, a born naturalist, had opened my eyes to the countryside I lived in. In 1944 I started keeping a nature diary for the year, covering my observations both at home and at school. I submitted it for the school Natural History Prize and won it, to add to a whole list of prizes I had won for Classical and literary subjects. So although I knew I was no expert, I felt I would always have a world of first-hand experience in the field to draw on when it came to creative writing.

The journey was a bad omen. I had to change at Birmingham. There was a huge crowd waiting on the platform there for the Oxford train. When it came in it was crammed to the doors, mostly with servicemen. The crowd surged forward, my flimsy night-bag was nearly swept from my hand; only a few at the front squeezed in to the carriage. A guard blew a whistle and the doors of a guard's-van were flung open. About a hundred of us crammed into the almost empty van; the lucky ones went to the sides or found a seat on a few packing cases, but most of us stood, propped up in the middle of the swaying crowd as the train pulled out, with no alternative until we reached our destination except to

Dalhousie Castle, near Bonnyrigg, Midlothian; my birthplace and my home for 25 years

stand and think and try to stay awake until we got there. It was a long night.

St John's College was welcoming in its way but the rooms I was allocated were unheated and the fire totally inadequate. We ate well enough in the College Hall, made a few temporary friends, commented on the cold and sat 5 or 6 hours a day of exams during which my spirits fell lower and lower. At night I collapsed into bed to try to get warm and recover some mental energy. On the third day I was at a rather low ebb but buoyed up by the prospect of the English Essay paper. So far as I can remember some 65 years later, the paper was the first of the morning so I was as alert as I was likely to be. I was raring to go. We filed into the exam hall, and sat waiting for the invigilator to put the papers face-down on our desks. Then as the clock struck I turned mine over. At first there seemed virtually nothing on it – the Examination Board title at the top, the list of colleges in the Scholarship group – and then 'English Essay Paper' and, halfway down the empty page, one single, lonely, threatening word – INSULARITY.

I think I was not the only candidate who, with furtive glances at fellow sufferers, turned the paper over in the vain hope of some alternative to this unknown, uninspiring, deadly word on the front of the page. Nothing. Panic started to well up. What did the word really mean? Of course for Classic scholars it was perfectly obvious what it meant literally. But what were we expected to write about? We were all British, all islanders in that sense, though probably few of us had had the chances to travel (as undoubtedly the examiner would have had) and to meet other people who lived on islands or who were able to form views about how different living on an island made one.

Every summer of my childhood our family spent the month of August on the Solway coast at Rockcliffe. And every holiday we had to have the traditional picnic on Rough Island, a few hundred yards off-shore. We walked across the mud at low tide and then let the sea come in round us. We collected driftwood, lit a fire and cooked sausages. We played at Robinson Crusoe. It was always a highlight of the holiday, the primitive excitement of being marooned until the tide turned; but it taught us nothing of insularity. At that stage in my life I don't think I had ever travelled to an island that gave any sense of remoteness, even though my home country Scotland abounds with such islands and has thousands of its citizens whose history and total experience of life are all insular. But I had no experience of this nor did I ever use the word in the common parlance in which one

discusses the philosophies of life; either those created and forged by island living or those imposed by the narrow-mindedness of people whose lives are limited by natural boundaries. Do mainlanders see in islanders an insularity of thought and culture from their proscribed circumstances? Is physical insularity without choice a handicap leading to narrow-mindedness or the way to the contentment that comes from limited choice and a culture of self-help and social harmony. Insularity could imply the frugality which leads to contentment or the bitterness which results from deprivation.

All these thoughts raced round in my head as I stared in disbelief at this one-word exam-paper. I can't remember now how I filled those two hours or what rubbish I wrote trying to satisfy the examiner. Bang went all my creativity. When I got back to school I looked the word up in my Concise Oxford Dictionary and found only the dry definition of an attitude of mind developed by isolation from the worlds of experience and culture and so deemed to be 'narrow' in a pejorative sense. At the time I think I probably mused that the definition of insularity is like the alternative definitions of freedom as either the acquisition of sufficient power and wealth to do what you like; or as the voluntary limitation of what one wants to do to match whatever power one already has.

The moral of this tale, and indeed of this book, is that happiness, which always depends to some extent on fulfilment of the human spirit, can be found more easily in human terms within the confines of a limited physical and social environment. Perhaps that is how man is designed to live, where the rewards to be derived from hard work, service to the community and love of one's neighbour are more immediate and easier to come by than in the confusion and turmoil of our over-crowded world. Perhaps man's ingenuity in such masterstrokes as the invention of the wheel, the spinning jenny, the jet engine, and now even of the Internet, were all in the ultra-long term disasters for the human spirit. Perhaps the strict limitation of an island's shores, and especially a fairly small island, makes one of the best scenarios for a happy life. Perhaps small really is beautiful?

The tragedy of that Oxford exam was that the subject was for me, as a Scot, so ill-timed. Scotland has a wealth of islands and a population whose insular lives bring new dimensions of contentment and culture to our national life. Insularity offers the perfect training ground for understanding one's fellow men and enjoying life. If I had had then the knowledge and experience of so many islands – especially of my favourite of them all,

Foula in Shetland – that I have now I could have written my essay for two thousand hours and never reached the end of the story. But I didn't; and I failed to win a place at Oxford.

In the end I went to Cambridge instead. But that was after army service, and after my education in islands had really started. Captivated by the discovery of the mysteries of bird migration, in 1946 my closest school friend John Hyatt and I plotted to spend a few days of precious army leave together manning the Bird Observatory on the Isle of May in the Firth of Forth. We exchanged dates. The only leave period which offered a common opportunity was in February, not the best month for migration studies; but we organised the visit and spent our first magic days completely cut off from the post-war world and totally engrossed in a barren, rocky outcrop full of life and movement and the sound of the sea. We were hooked. Yet we had only savoured one aspect of the value of islands, their suitability for the study of natural history and especially birds and their migration. I had yet to discover the real meaning in human terms of the word – INSULARITY.

Fishing boat SV1960 – drawing by Eric Isbister

Chapter 1: The Turning Point

Looking back on it, I seem to have made one of the biggest decisions in my life quite casually, in the staff room of John Watson's school in Edinburgh at the end of a stressful day. To understand why such a momentous decision was so clear-cut, you need to know the background. John Watson's was my first job after three years at Cambridge graduating with a degree in Classics and English, followed by a further year at Edinburgh University and Moray House Training College. It was a strange school. I liked it because it was different in almost every respect from other schools in Scotland. It was a Foundation, started with a legacy left by one John Watson WS, to be administered by the Writers to the Signet for the benefit of the widows of professional men. It was a god-send for mothers who found themselves unable to afford the kind of education for their children that their husbands would have chosen for them had they lived. As was possible in the late 19th century, John Watson's legacy of a few thousand pounds had been skillfully invested by successive Treasurers of the WS Society until sufficient capital had been amassed to allow for a splendid neo-classical building to be built as a co-educational boarding school designed to house about 100 pupils. In 1952, when I arrived there, the school still stood in its own grounds above the Water of Leith, no

distance from the West End, Edinburgh's city-centre. In 1820 when it first opened, the site had been truly a green field on the outskirts of the capital. Now, if you're lucky, you can still see the azure of a passing kingfisher down by the river, like a knife glinting in a flash of blue light; but the building has found a new identity as Scotland's National Gallery of Modern Art. In the field in front of it is a prize-winning landscape sculpture of terraced banks, enclosing in sinuous curves a graceful water feature. That used to be the playing field where once a year the girls' hockey team was able, with impunity, to batter our ankles during the traditional match against the staff.

Originally the Foundation provided not only free education but free clothing and, during term-time, free board and lodging as well. So the school fulfilled a vital role for many war widows, but in the Second World War when the pupils were evacuated to the Borders, the buildings were commandeered by the army and things were never quite the same again. When the pupils eventually returned to a refurbished school, both numbers and funds were low and the prime necessity was recruitment. So for the first time fee-paying day pupils were welcomed, regardless of qualifications, to swell the numbers to 150 and keep the school afloat. Quantity prevailed over quality, the academic reputation was low and my role as a Classics

The classical façade of John Watson's School, Edinburgh, where I taught Classics from September 1952 to March 1954

graduate an anachronism. However the pioneering idea of a co-educational boarding school appealed to me as my own education had been solely in single-sex boys' schools, with all their drawbacks. John Watson's was organised to have segregated dayrooms for recreation on the ground floor and dormitories on the first floor, where three of each sex of residential staff also had their living quarters. So the boy boarders occupied one end of the building, the girls the other. The central block housed the Assembly Hall on the ground floor and the ablution rooms on the first floor. This allowed access from one end only, for baths and showers on alternate nights. One of my first disciplinary exercises was to dismiss the little queue of boys waiting for a peep through the keyhole of the locked door on their side of the bathroom on the girls' bath night. The querulous tone of the inevitable "Oh but, please Sir!" that greeted my censure was only evidence that they detected from the smile on my face that though discipline came first, I was really unfazed by such delightful innocence.

Generally it was a happy school; though, with only three male staff living in, it was hard work for all of us being as it were substitute fathers for 50 fatherless boys, especially for recreational activities for which there was hopelessly inadequate provision. From line-up for breakfast at 8 a.m. to lights-out at 9 p.m., the day was divided into three so that we took it in turns to be on duty either from reveille to mid-day; or from lunch to supper; or for the evening and overnight. For roll-calls, supervising meal-times, recreation periods and the occasional emergency, morning and afternoon duties seemed just part of the daily school routine, a tie but not arduous. But every third week I found myself, after a normal day in the classroom, solely responsible for overseeing the evening meal for all the boarders, boys and girls, their 'homework', and then, for the boys, their ablutions and seeing them off to bed. At the end of such a tiring week, there followed weekend duty, including morning service at the local Presbyterian church and the Sunday walk. No wonder that I looked forward so much to the blessed relief of Monday afternoon, when the first morning duty of the new week was over, and at last I got a break from the constant noise and the insistent demands of "Please Sir....Please Sir," all day long. Boarding school life is no sinecure.

At the end of a thirteen week term I was exhausted and yet I felt buoyed up by a sense of achievement. At least some of the boys for whom I was *in loco parentis* had done me the honour of sharing with me their worries and personal problems. It was hard going with some but others made it clear that my own fondness for them was rewarded by their genuine trust and affection.

I began to understand the first inklings of what it feels like to be a real father. Having been brought up in a boarding school as my home, I had always enjoyed the vivacity and enthusiasm of young boys, but now I began to understand what had kept my father going for so long in the arduous business of being a boarding school Headmaster. Academically the rewards at John Watson's were few but there were a small number who appreciated their progress in the classroom towards their next promotion or exam and seemed genuinely to enjoy my teaching. I can remember to this day, over 50 years later, how I looked forward to 'classes' with my two Greek pupils, David Bruce and Tommy Quinn, who responded with such enthusiasm to what amounted to individual tuition. Sharing the window of discovery into a new language, especially one as rich and versatile as Greek, is a revelation and a joy. However the school only catered for education to the third year of Secondary. They left at 16 to look for jobs, which in those post-war days were not difficult to find.

Since 1925 my father had managed his own boys' boarding school, a fee-paying Preparatory School for 60 boys. He had always wanted to establish a school dedicated to non-competitive achievement. Every boy worked in classroom and sportsfield for his team and not himself, and no individual prizes were ever allowed. It was like a large family with high ideals of physical fitness and recreational freedom. My father's venture was made possible because of Dalhousie Castle in Midlothian, the Scottish baronial seat of the Earls of Dalhousie, which my father rented for £150 per annum because it was huge and nobody else wanted it. Dating back to the 12th century and built of glowing red sandstone from a local quarry by the river South Esk, it stood in a picturesque estate with wide lawns and magnificent cedar trees and showpiece rhododendrons. I was born there in April 1927 and lived my whole boyhood amongst its woods and parks, where my mother taught me to name and love the flowers and trees and wildlife. I flourished in the atmosphere of a school where an unexpected item for most parents on the Clothing List was a pair of dungarees. Most of the boys' recreation time was spent out of doors where dungarees were the order of the day, to protect their normal school clothes and to enable them to build the tree-houses which absorbed so much youthful energy and enthusiasm. We lived our whole life as a family in the boarding school atmosphere, our daily timetable punctuated by bells for lessons, the dinner-gong for meals and the shrill sounds of young boys' voices and beginners torturing pianos.

Dalhousie boys left the school at 13, so I had long experience of that magic age when boys between the ages of eight and twelve, in the right educational atmosphere, scarcely need to be disciplined, and where esprit de corps and enthusiasm are sufficient incentives to progress and achievement. I found there a wonderful outlet for my own growing enthusiasm for nature and especially for birdlife, and discovered too an innate desire to communicate this to others. So I developed a particular satisfaction in trying to provide opportunities for youngsters to share my enthusiasm and to develop into budding naturalists. My other hobby was photography though I never had enough money to afford a proper camera and yearned to emulate those who could capture images of natural beauty on film. I can remember quite clearly, seventy years on, a red-letter day at Cargilfield, the old-established Prep. School in Edinburgh my father sent me to at the age of eight. (He deliberately sent both my brother and me to other boarding schools and not his own.) A former pupil had come back to talk to us about how he photographed birds in his own garden. I was only nine but I was thrilled by the intimate shots he showed us in close-up of common species like blackbirds and robins. "That's what I'm going to do when I grow up," I vowed. I also remember, as clearly as though it were yesterday, giving as my excuse for gross inattention in a history lesson – "But please Sir, I was watching two bullfinches eating the buds off the apple tree just outside the window." This was of course of far greater importance than the date of the battle of Hastings; and all credit to Mr Cranmer, our history teacher, that he not only accepted my excuse but even commended me to the Headmaster for being so observant. My father's ambition for me was Eton, but as I was 12 in 1939, fate and air-raid phobia diverted the course of my education to Sedbergh amongst the Yorkshire fells. I often felt I was totally unsuited to a boarding school with the Spartan motto of 'Dura Virum Nutrix' – the Stern Nurse of Men. There were compulsory cold baths, runs and rugby and at that time, among the majority of pupils, a fairly hearty disdain for most of the things I was good at – natural history, literature and music. I was a 'swot' in a world of rugby heroes. Organised games called for skills and courage I just didn't have, so bird-watching with a select group of enthusiasts became our escape-route from competitive sports. Luckily the regime was liberal enough to give us scope and in my final years there I abandoned the claustrophobia of the cricket field for the open fells and the search for rare peregrine falcons and buzzards nesting on high crags within running distance of the school.

My formal school education was almost entirely Classics, which meant the language, literature and history of ancient Greece and Rome. I capped it with an Exhibition to St John's College Cambridge. In only one respect was I a scientist through my hobbies and interests. With a chosen group of friends we took part in the Bird Ringing Scheme run by the British Museum, which was a technique of marking individual birds, either nestlings or captured adults, with a metal ring designed to be lightweight but permanent, clipped round one leg and inscribed with a unique number and the legend "Inform British Museum, London". This was enough to reach the Natural History Museum in South Kensington from anywhere in the world. This meant keeping accurate records and occasionally enjoying the rare reward of a 'Recovery', when notification was received of the fate of some migrant species which had been found perhaps in a foreign country. Suddenly one's knowledge of the life of birds was enlarged, not from books written by others but from one's own efforts. This was first-hand knowledge and an entirely new experience, the genuine discovery of real facts and a sense of contributing to science in a field where clearly there was so much we did not yet know or understand. Bird migration became not just a fascinating feature of the natural world but a mystery waiting to be solved, and for me my only real experience of practical science.

A favourite pastime was visiting the barns of all the local farms and ringing broods of young swallows. Of course much was known about swallow migration but among the school's recovery records was hard evidence of journeys to South Africa and of birds returning six thousand miles to nest in precisely the same barn they had used the previous year. How did they do it? Our minds were enlarged not by the meagre facts we had uncovered but by the thousands of questions those facts aroused as we marveled at the feathered perfection of a nestling swallow, a miracle of navigational skill in such a tiny morsel of life. Everything I looked at in the natural world, typified by the perfection of the feathering of a swallow's wing only a few weeks after the naked nestling had hatched from the egg, was clear evidence that natural selection worked. It produced life forms of incredible complexity but with that vital capacity of survival because they had been forged in the fiery furnaces of time through an unimaginable number of tiny changes, all designed to make them the fittest possible for their niche in the environment.

In this way I learnt from first-hand experience that the origin of species is a constant miracle. Evolution to us was not just a theory taught in school, but a rational, observable explanation of facts of daily life we encountered every time we went exploring in the local river valleys or up on the fells. We just took it for granted and it didn't seem to conflict too seriously with traditions of worship in the school Chapel and the idea of a spiritual Creator. It was science. Because of my upbringing as the grandson of an Anglican Bishop, I was confirmed, along with perhaps the majority of my schoolfellows, into the Church of England, and attended chapel and sang with enthusiasm in the choir; but I distrusted the rather precious piety of the ordained members of staff. I began to feel that perhaps the world was better ordered the way it was by the forces of time and change on a lonely planet than by an interfering God. Darwin began to be my greatest hero, but it was only later at University that I realised that my definition of his genius was his ability to demonstrate and prove the blindingly obvious, in the face of religious prejudice based on ignorance of the scientific truth. At school out of family loyalty and to some extent patriotic hatred of Nazism, I clung doggedly to my belief in the moral code and philosophical priorities of Christianity. Love not hatred, peace not war must be the future for mankind as we celebrated VE day in May 1945. Apart from family ties my own personal experience of love in an almost all-male world was wrapped up in my deep feelings for special friends of my own age, and sometimes, perhaps a little too romantically, in the attractiveness of the more personable younger boys in my house, all of which was partly an escape from the horrors of war in our daily news, and in my later 'teens, the inevitable pressure of the hormones of adolescence. My love of children made my ultimate goal seem natural, almost inevitable, to become a teacher in the footsteps of my father, who had dedicated his whole life to boys. However such long-term goals were only dreams when faced with the realities of war-time Britain. Among the peaceful hills of Yorkshire, my schooldays were often almost too isolated from the horrors of Nazism and the hardships of those fighting on our behalf. My sheltered life was soon to change.

In the second half of 1945 the war against Japan was grinding on towards an Allied victory but I still had conscription to cope with. I went for an Army Selection Board and passed with flying colours. I wanted to get value out of my army service as the idea of fighting and killing people was anathema, so I opted for Royal Signals. I had joined the Signals Section of the Junior Training Corps and become fascinated by using wireless sets on Field Days where technical skill was valued as an essential component of military operations. I was accepted by the Board as 'potential officer' material provided I studied some science before I left school. But I had never done a Physics or Chemistry lesson in my whole school career. My Housemaster was also my Maths teacher at one stage. After glowing reports from my Classics and English masters, his report for my year's Maths results was, "He is woefully weak at this subject." But when I was faced with catching up four years of missed science in only two terms, he took me under his wing and master-minded my individual efforts in Physics to enable me to seize this chance to broaden my education beyond anything I had ever dreamed possible. The scheme was that after Primary Training, those of us who were classed as potential officers would spend an academic year at University reading Maths and Physics to enable us to cope with the technical training. It was an exciting but daunting prospect for a student who for three years had been immersed in the exclusive study of ancient Greece and Rome. I found the revelations of Physics fascinating, but I was still never going to be a mathematician. Finally, in 1945, as my first step into the real world, I went to the Recruiting Office and volunteered to join the army in the Royal Corps of Signals.

Then, a week after I left school for good, America dropped two atom bombs on Japan. At first I thought the newsreader had said an 'automic' bomb. I had no idea what an atomic bomb was, and I was not alone. I was completely mystified but then the fearful explanations and revelations about a new era in human history followed. Ten days later I left home on VJ Day to join my Primary Training Centre, for the technical branches of the army, at Bodmin in Cornwall. My role in all this was now completely ridiculous. The life I had led at school now seemed a haven of sanity in a mad world. Home and the freedom of the countryside now became infinitely precious. Fortunately, good friends and a very active life just kept me sane. While the rest of the world was rejoicing at the end of conflict, I went to learn how to kill people with rifles, machine-guns, and bayonets. After three years in the Royal Signals, which included the six month army course at Oxford University, studying degree level science for the first time in my life, I was demobilized in 1948 and returned to University to take up my Exhibition in Classics at St John's College, Cambridge. After a three-year gap and with serious memory problems following my meningitis episode at school, this was an even tougher assignment. I took up rowing, disillusioned by my fading interest in Classics, and then changed to English in my final year, but more significantly ended up as President of the Cambridge Bird Club.

This is where islands started to take over. My baptism had been the Isle of May visit with John Hyatt in 1946, my first ever visit to a Bird Observatory. In Edinburgh I had joined the Scottish Ornithologists' Club and met up with its founder George Waterston who owned Fair Isle and Kenneth Williamson who was leading the fieldwork on bird migration on the island. In the summer vacations from 1950–54 the Cambridge Bird Club pioneered research expeditions to south Norway, the first three of which John Hyatt and I organised, studying bird migration in liaison with Kenneth Williamson's research on North Sea migration from the Fair Isle Bird observatory. He had pioneered the concept of 'drift migration', where birds lost in adverse weather over the sea seemed to fly downwind to achieve the highest possible ground speed in order to reach land. This instinctive behaviour made seasonal bird migrants dependent on the compass direction of N. Atlantic wind patterns over Britain. On the 1950 expedition we included a visit to the island of Utsira off the west coast of Norway, not so strategically placed for drift migrants as Fair Isle and unheard of then, but now a household name delineating two of the sea areas in the daily BBC Shipping Forecasts. There we were storm-bound for several days in the company of two Norwegian ornithologists from Stavanger Museum. We were surprised to see a shot-gun amongst their bird-recording equipment, rather like the old pictures of Dr Eagle Clark on Fair Isle. We marveled at the fury of the storm, and at a hardy population of islanders where the men only needed to work for six months of the year to earn a living from the rich fishing grounds within easy reach. We stayed in the house of a widow who cooked for five of us with hearty appetites on two Primus stoves, and we learnt to enjoy tinned fiske-kake, hot and tasteless for supper, but not the left-overs sliced, cold and tasteless for breakfast the next morning. I met the teacher in the little school where I found a contented man and a happy crowd of youngsters. It was a scene I never forgot as a potential reward of island living. If the Isle of May had been my baptism, Utsira was my confirmation. Islands were magic. Good weather was a bonus, though the major snag for me was always the crossing as I had yet to discover a reliable antidote for sea-sickness. However the lure of islands was by this stage sufficient incentive.

Within a few years I had the highest total of visits to the Isle of May of anyone in the Observatory Visitors Book. I was now not only an ornithologist but I had

the island disease. The next addiction was photography, which came as a result of the need to have a record of our exploits in the field, as much as any desire to make pretty pictures. It had all started very humbly at Dalhousie when I was still a student. I had rigged up a makeshift darkroom in a cupboard under the stairs. As I couldn't afford a decent camera I had few negatives worth very much; but even so I quickly learnt the magic, in the red glow of the safelight, as the piece of white paper in the dish gradually darkened to reveal the image as the exposed silver in the emulsion was developed. With a few selected pupils who shared my interests, I was able to watch their faces light up as they too watched the magic unfold. Soon we were into the skills of choosing the correct exposure time, the right paper, the best chemicals. Often pupils from well-to-do homes had better equipment than I had in my student days, but by trial and error and constant practice we started to get results. Serious photography with anything like professional equipment was still way beyond my wildest dreams. I had never owned a Single Lens Reflex camera nor did I for many years to come. But I still took photographs.

Pursuing hobbies which cost money was frustrating with my pupils at John Watson's. Many came from comparatively poor homes. The WS Society could barely afford the basics, let alone provide meaningful recreation beyond ping-pong or the gym. I was able to indulge one or two of my pet theories of informal education like reading to children at bed-time. The senior dormitory was last for 'lights out' at nine o'clock, and often needed something to settle them down after the excitements of the day. The bribe of a book at bedtime provided they were in bed by 8.45 worked for the vast majority. One term I read Jules Verne's complete trilogy – *Dropped from the Clouds; Abandoned; and The Secret of the Island* – as romantic an island story as Robinson Crusoe. The magic of islands extended to literature. In theory I read for half-hour sessions though sometimes it was 10 o'clock before they would let me stop. Sometimes I think some of them learnt more of science and survival from those books than all their Science classes, judging by the questions they asked in their attempts to delay the lights-out ritual. And my misdemeanours with the timetable remained a well-kept secret.

As a first job John Watson's was a challenge and a valuable experience. But I felt cooped up in a city and starved of the joy of quiet places and the eternal mysteries of the natural world. One break came with the special Coronation holiday when for once schoolteachers got a chance to escape the confines of the curriculum in June, the best month for observing breeding birds in Scotland. So with the help of Ian Balfour Paul, a housemaster from Merchiston School, where my grandfather had been educated and my father had held his first headmaster's post, we escaped in his vintage Austin to Speyside. Within minutes of arrival we watched an osprey being harried by a bevy of oystercatchers in noisy pursuit. This was the exciting confirmation of endless rumours of sightings of ospreys, dramatic fish-eating raptors which had been made extinct in Scotland 50 years before by the activities of Victorian egg-collectors. Little did we realise that this bird was to be the forerunner of the first pair to breed in the following years, or that by 1957 I was to be the only bird photographer permitted to work at their nest at Loch Garten.

That three-day holiday in the Old Caledonian pine-forest area was unsettling to my status as a city-bound teacher in a busy, noisy school. And so it was, in a strange sort of way, the moment I had long been waiting for when, in the winter of 1954, picking up the Scotsman in the staff-room one afternoon at the tea-break, I glanced as one often did in a detached way at the advertisements for teaching jobs, and there jumped out at me from the Situations Vacant page a short announcement. I can remember still that feeling in the pit of my stomach that this was a deciding point in my life. It stopped me in my tracks, for what I read seemed to make John Watson's seem like the urban, conventional, boring job which it truly wasn't:

Zetland Education Authority.
Teacher and Lay Missionary, Isle of Foula.
Single-teacher primary school; school roll five.

I went straight to my room to write to the Director of Education for Shetland in Lerwick for an application form. There was no looking back. This really seemed like an answer to a prayer. But how could I possibly qualify when I had never been to Shetland in my life, and knew nothing about Foula except that it had been the first site after St Kilda for the breeding of the fulmar petrel when it started its amazing spread to every rocky coastline in Britain.

What use would my Classical qualifications be to the children of crofters? As I waited in the hope of an interview, I started to do some urgent research into Scottish islands. When I looked at that tiny dot on the map off the Atlantic coast of Shetland, I began to realise what a fundamental change this would make in both my daily work and my whole way of life. Was I really prepared to cut myself off from friends and family, to desert the pupils I had become so fond of and the staff I enjoyed so much working with? Was I quite mad? And yet at the same time a strange ache developed in my mind which brought me a tingle of excitement, a longing to be part of the adventure of living close to nature, of breaking free from the stresses of crowds and traffic, of testing my survival skills beyond the shield of the welfare state and the residential establishments I had grown to depend on. Was I up to the challenge? Did I really want to have to face my horror of sea-sickness on every journey to an island? Would I have the faintest chance of landing the job anyway?

As I sealed the envelope, the bell rang for my Latin class with SII, which was always a bit of a struggle against negative apathy, and some positive resistance. Why should they bother with a 'dead' language for which they had no practical use and little interest? As luck would have it my star pupil, the fair-haired charmer Tommy Quinn was sitting in the front row of desks, with his blue eyes as bright as his quick intellect. How could I secretly entertain plans to deny him the magic of a language invented three thousand years ago, the gateway to our understanding of all literature and drama? Was I being intrinsically selfish to deny him the truths of Socrates in my private quest for the truths of the natural world I was so eager to explore? "*Let's see if you've done your homework. Page 54, 'Julius Caesar's conquest of Germany'. Sally, will you start please*?" Sally was a responsible pupil with a wicked sense of humour. I had just returned from my school holiday, which had ended with a visit to the Isle of May Bird Observatory where there were few facilities for shaving. So I'd grown a beard – of sorts. I fully expected nicknames like 'Beardie', to replace 'Baldy-nut' which I had no doubt deserved in the past. However when Sally put her hand up in that Latin class with the good manners and keenness I expected from such a promising pupil, I did not expect the question she posed ever so politely – "*Excuse me, Sir, but I think your hair has slipped*?" The outburst of merriment from the whole class at my discomfiture was something to remember – and treasure. The joys of teaching! Was I really going to give up all this?

Chapter 2: Preparations

I had a flurry of questions buzzing around in my head. I now faced the possible task of making the necessary preparations for the big adventure of changing my job from a bustling boarding school near the centre of Edinburgh with ten staff, to Head Teacher of probably the smallest primary school in Scotland in the remotest, most isolated community in the country. Foula is an island fifteen miles west of the Northern Isles of Shetland, an Atlantic outpost completely unprotected by any sort of barrier from the full power of over two thousand miles of open Atlantic between it and the next landfall, Newfoundland. As soon as I looked at the map I began to realise the difference between this sort of remoteness and the other outposts on the mainland or on offshore islands where the human race had battled for a living against the elements. Historically islands were attractive to human settlers for security in dangerous times or simply because there was a living to be made there from the sea or from fertile land. The only other place in the British Isles with the same degree of remoteness was St Kilda, 50 miles west of North Uist in the Outer Hebrides. St Kilda was then a deserted island, evacuated by an ageing population in 1930. I knew very little at that stage in my life about the early history of either outpost except that St Kilda was Celtic by tradition and the people had spoken Gaelic, and Foula by contrast was Norse and one of the last places in Britain where the Old Norn language was remembered and the Lord's Prayer recited in Norn.

Both islands were well known in ornithological circles as huge seabird sanctuaries. St Kilda provided a nesting-place for over a million seabirds, and was most famous for its gannets, fulmars and puffins, which along with other cliff-nesting species like the noisy guillemots and razorbills, and the gentle kittiwakes, found space on its cliffs which at a quick estimate I reckoned to offer about 150 acres of vertical rock. Until 1854 St Kilda had a special claim to fame as the only breeding site of the fulmar in Britain, but in that year fulmars nested for the first time on Foula, probably as a spread south from the Faroes. The subsequent gradual invasion by fulmars of almost every cliff in the British Isles was a 100 year mystery, finally explained by James Fisher in his monograph 'The Fulmar', which had just been published by Collins in 1952. Both islands had seldom been visited or studied by scientists but the fulmar saga helped to establish in my mind at least the status of Foula as second only to St Kilda, and in one respect it was way ahead. Foula was well known as holding the largest colony of skuas in the Northern Hemisphere, especially the Great Skua or 'Bonxie', aptly described as 'a pirate and predator, the scourge of Foula'. So here was an ornithological treasure-house awaiting detailed study. Could there perhaps also be potential for a bird observatory?

The name Foula was derived from Fugl-Øy, or Bird Island in Norse, named by the Vikings probably 1000 years ago. It was by definition therefore my kind of place. It had no official status as a nature reserve or sanctuary, having to date no need for special protection beyond that offered by its extreme remoteness and the sheer difficulty of getting there, or finding anywhere to stay when you did. This factor alone was an appealing prospect, the promise of a home that would offer a real difference. There I could perhaps be as close to nature as anywhere in Britain, and able without interference from human intrusion to observe just how the forces of the natural world worked to ensure the survival of the fittest. After all it was on the Galapagos islands far out into the Pacific that Darwin had really confirmed in his mind the theory of the slow evolution of species through an infinite number of small but progressive changes. He had detected it through the many similar species of small finches, each adapted, mostly by bill size, to one island or one specialized habitat, but all, as he assumed, derived from a single progenitor species. Small remote islands were the key which unlocked the secret. The isolation of a few stray migrants aeons in the past had been the trigger to the formation of new differentiated species. All Darwin did was to observe the facts, study the adaptation to food sources on the different islands, and then extend their story to explain the development of all the multifarious species which now survive on our planet. Millions of species had gone; millions more would go by the process of natural selection to which all life was subject under the natural pressures of an ever-changing environment.

In the 1950s I was only starting on my own journey of understanding. But I felt sure Foula would help me on that journey by enabling me to get to grips with the study of any of the species that were special to 'the island of birds'. I had heard about the St Kilda Wren and there were rumours of a Foula Fieldmouse. Could such sub-species be on their way to becoming proper species? Then there would be the human history and the present community as an added bonus, a subject for study beyond my primary interest in the bird-life.

In 1954 Foula was the property of the Holbourn family, having been bought at the turn of the century by, of all unlikely owners, the Professor of Fine Art at Edinburgh University. Iain Stoughton Holbourn was a romantic who had proclaimed that his life's ambition was to own the most beautiful house and the most beautiful island in the most beautiful country in the world. He felt he had achieved this by living in Penkaet Castle in East Lothian, as perfect an example of a Scottish baronial mansion in traditional style as one could find, and by taking ownership of Foula whose beauty in terms of raw wildness and stark, awesome grandeur could hardly be challenged. Professor Holbourn's book 'The Isle of Foula' published in 1938 by Johnson & Greig of Lerwick in Shetland, was clearly a must. It was sub-titled 'A Series of Articles on Britain's loneliest inhabited island by the late professor Ian B. Stoughton Holbourn, Laird of Foula for thirty-five years.' It is full of legend and history, with fable and fact inextricably mixed, and dwells at length on the Udal system which owes no allegiance to the Crown and gives the landlord ancient Scandinavian rights. It has only a few black-and-white photographs of cliff scenery and dignified peasant people in primitive garb living primitive lives. Perhaps the most interesting parts of the book are the long memoir of her husband by his widow Marion Holbourn, and the foreword by film producer Michael Powell. His film 'The Edge of the World' put Foula on the map in 1936 and achieved world-wide publicity both for the film and the island when the whole cast of famous film-stars were marooned there by the autumn storms in dramatic fashion. Michael Powell's own book '200,000 ft on Foula' is a racy account of the problems of filming on such a remote location with all sorts of delays, largely caused by technical problems (hence the inordinate expenditure of film footage reflected in the title of his book) which resulted in the best publicity any such film could have achieved without costing a penny extra. The film was in fact the story of the evacuation of St Kilda, in a roughly equivalent geographical position off the west of the Hebrides as

Foula is off Shetland, because Powell could not obtain permission from the owner, Lord Dumfries, to make it on St Kilda itself. The story was too good to miss so he chose Foula, whose landlord was delighted to comply. Sensibly the film does not attempt to conceal the fact that Foula was used but as a result it is something of a compromise and confusing in that it appears that Foula has the same problems as St Kilda which was never so. But it was the final paragraph of Powell's foreword to Holbourn's timely book which alerted me to the very special nature of the job I had taken on:

My film tells the tale of the defeat of a people. It was created and brought to life by the help of the people of Foula. They one and all proved more helpful, more sympathetic, and more truly intelligent than any men and women with whom I have worked. Whatever the critics say, the real star of my film is the lonely island of Foula – and the real makers are its people.

This is a pretty astonishing statement by one of the most successful and dynamic film producers of his time. In the same foreword he asked a question I soon became desperate to answer: "*Why has an island an irresistible appeal to us all?*"

I went for interview to the offices of the Church of Scotland at 121 George Street, Edinburgh where I understood I was one of six candidates for the job. I knew very little about the S.P.C.K., the Society for the Promotion of Christian Knowledge, which apparently, along with the Church of Scotland, jointly financed these appointments of lay missionaries in the Northern Isles. It had also played a key role in providing ministers for the Kirk on St Kilda. Clearly in a community of 70 souls like Foula there wasn't enough to employ a full-time minister of the Kirk who in an equivalent mainland post would have had responsibility for two, if not three, small rural parishes. Now there is a quaint Scottish tradition that a minister of the Kirk is a liability on a boat, a 'Jonah' to the superstitious, which would have been awkward to say the least if the island depended on him for frequent journeys by sea.

So lay missionaries were the order of the day, and the church was undoubtedly delighted to share the cost with a long-established charity. For me, a former College secretary of the S.C.M. – the Student Christian Movement – but with no experience of occupying any pulpit, the S.P.C.K. was a less intimidating employer than the General Assembly of the Church of Scotland. By upbringing I was an Anglican, a member of the Scottish Episcopal Church, and virtually my only experience of the Presbyterians was taking the John Watson's pupils to Sunday services. There I had found the building bleak, the congregation conventional, and the sermons uninspiring. I was also at a very transitional stage in my beliefs, struggling still with the turmoil of student religious debate and the conflict between my love of people and especially children, which was a real gut-feeling, and my love of 'God' which seemed to have no substance. And then what about my love of nature and wild places where I felt closer to whatever God there was than in any church, and my sense of vocation to wake the world up to the beauty and value of the natural world? We seemed to be destroying it all by neglect in our pursuit of economic and political ends which presumed that the world of God's bounty – land and sea, forest and field, vegetables, fruit, cereals, roots, and more significant in our new industrial era, coal and oil – all free for the taking, were ours to raid and utilize, or modify and pollute as we willed, without penalty or control. I had a faith of a sort, ideals a-plenty, love for everything beautiful and simple and innocent and for almost anyone worse off than I was; but I was not at all sure of my love for humankind as a whole. I loathed war, violence and almost everything macho, and as a means of preaching peace I found teaching an inspiring vocation. In spite of all my classical training, I found that my favourite subject was Nature Study which I had taught to Primary 7 at John Watson's, the 11-year-olds whose enthusiasm I found entrancing and inspiring. The opportunities Foula seemed to offer were obvious and right up my street.

So far as I remember there were three members of the interview panel, one each from the Church of Scotland, the S.P.C.K., and the Zetland Education Authority. I expected my educational qualifications to be adequate and I put my rather scanty hand of religious cards on the table with as much honesty as I could muster. I felt I must appear patently desperate to secure the post. In that spirit I answered their questions and declared my humility at the prospect of spiritual responsibility for such an island community; and got the job. I heard years later from a friend who knew well one of the triumvirate who interviewed the six candidates, that I was the only candidate seriously considered for the post. I suspect that they were as desperate to appoint someone as I was to get the job, and aware that it was almost designed to attract eccentrics. Apparently it did; five of them! Or should that really be six?

I was at first rather horrified by my own success. What had I let myself in for? The prospect of 1) working in such exciting and wonderful surroundings; 2) being paid more for teaching only five children than I had been paid in Edinburgh for taking classes of twenty-five; 3) of getting a two-bedroom, slate-roofed house that went with the job for a rent of only £10 per annum; 4) of living close to the sea for the first time in my life; and 5) of sitting with a potential landfall for North Sea migrant birds right on my doorstep – all these seemed like golden compensation for the responsibilities involved. But I was also daunted by the thought of being entirely on my own, and having to look after myself in a way that in the army, in college, at home and in boarding school I had never had to do in the sheltered life I had led up to that point. In fact I was both excited and apprehensive, in exactly the same way as I had felt leaving home in 1945 to join the army, at the unknown life that lay ahead of me.

My family were I think pleased for me but also naturally apprehensive, especially in view of my medical history. I had come out of the army with a crippled digestive system which, at university, revealed itself as chronic acidity. This resulted in duodenal ulcers, which was rapidly becoming one of the most fashionable ailments of the post-war period. The only really effective treatment in those days was as bland a diet as possible. So I had undertaken much of my academic work on a diet of egg-flips and orange juice and food specially minced and prepared by the college kitchens. No roughage was the order of the day, and this diet produced a welcome respite from periodic bouts of crippling pain. By 1954 I had that problem more or less under control. However Foula would offer little opportunity for fancy diets, and all aspects of the job description seemed to call for a fairly tough constitution. Would they want someone whose recent past had been dogged by digestive problems? My doctor did not disapprove of my going to a quiet and stimulating environment, giving me much food for thought along the lines that stress – of which there was plenty in my John Watson's timetable – was also a likely cause of my problem of acidity, and fresh air and exercise could be as good a cure as any for my medical complaints. However the thrill of getting the job and the anticipation of such a complete change in the direction of my career was compelling. I could think only about what to take to my island home, and how to make what would undoubtedly be a much tougher life as tolerable as possible.

The church was helpful over those aspects in which I was most competently ignorant. I had not concealed my unfamiliarity with matters Presbyterian at the interview – and so they had furnished me with their Prayer Book. This included the forms of service for funerals, which I had been reminded I might well have to conduct as the only representative of the church on the island. By contrast weddings or baptisms could clearly wait for the arrival of an ordained minister as weather allowed. I was acutely conscious that at the age of 26 I had never in my life attended a funeral, let alone conducted one, nor so far as I was aware ever seen a dead human body. Had I been born only a year or two earlier than 1927, I might well have witnessed some of the carnage and slaughter of the closing stages of World War Two. As it was I had spent three years in the army without the sight of anything more belligerent than a rifle-range, and no place more dangerous than Aldershot and Catterick Camps. So I just had to presume that by force of circumstances I would cope with a death on Foula as well as (and probably much better than) I could ever have coped with the deaths of companions on the battlefield. Anyway such possibilities seemed hopefully remote. Of more immediate concern was how I was going to cope with domestic problems like doing my own laundry, baking bread, DIY, gardening etc., in a situation where there were no tradesmen, no labour for hire, no electricity, virtually no phone contact, no doctor, no hospital, no dentist, no library and only one shop open three afternoons a week. The fact that there was no pub and no policeman seemed a mixed blessing, while the lack of motorized transport merely made me add a bicycle to my list of requirements.

All these things I quickly found out to be the realities of the situation from the Holbourns, whom I was strongly advised to contact by the church authorities. I found them as eager to meet me as I was to meet them. So during my final term at John Watson's, in the spring of 1954, I went to Harmony House to meet Alasdair Holbourn, an Art Master at Edinburgh Academy, and his wife Betty. It was one of the most fascinating and compelling evenings I have ever enjoyed, an enthusiastic introduction to a totally new subject of enquiry. Foula to them was a way of life. The islanders were clearly both tenants and friends, technically subordinate and yet people they respected, almost revered in many cases. They made no bones about the problems of feuding between crofts, and the tensions between original islanders and incomers, but also sung their praises for their generosity and gallant ability to cope with the hardships of their lives.

They also expressed the need for patience with the islanders' insularity, their tardiness, their frustrating nonchalance in completing jobs or meeting deadlines. They described clear family characteristics, some much more hard-working and efficient than others, some

quite hopelessly disorganized and slovenly even about simple time-keeping, most of the elderly not really able to maintain adequate standards of cleanliness in their houses, without more help than was reasonably available in such a small community. I was warned not to expect too much and to be prepared for a culture shock in a world where simply to get light and warmth in your house entailed diligence and know-how. For instance both Tilley Lamps and peat seemed to demand skills I had never even heard of in managing paraffin and peat as the only available fuels. The islanders were experts in all this and would soon put me right. They would love to demonstrate to me how to cut peats and how to stack and then store them; but nobody would even offer to do this for me given their own commitment to the labour and time needed to look after relatives or neighbours if they were too infirm to do it for themselves.

The main problem of the community was old-age. There were 71 people of whom 19 were 70 or over, so that even with 9 children of 11 or under, the average age for the whole population worked out at 60. The crucial shortage was of able-bodied people of working age with only twelve between 15 and 50. Alasdair had prepared for me a complete list of all the crofters with ages and abilities and needs all written down. Many couldn't manage their own peat cutting or carrying, their own house maintenance or cleaning, even cooking or shopping. In emphasizing the statistics of the numbers aged over 70, they issued a warning, several times repeated, that I was not to feel that, just because I was there, it was my responsibility to risk either my job or my sanity by trying to solve all their problems or help out physically with all their needs. In the first place I would be the first ever incumbent to tackle both jobs, school and church, on my own. Most previous teachers had been married not single, and with the church as a separated responsibility. I would have my time cut out to cope.

They raised some points I had not anticipated. I had to realise that books were a lifesaver to many of the old folk and that with no money to buy and no library to borrow from, one of the most important parts of my 'ministry' would be to distribute books sent in by the Lerwick Library. I should run a bookcase in my porch from which the islanders could come and help themselves when I was teaching, but books for the elderly would have to be taken round. It looked as though my Saturdays were going to be pretty busy, quite apart from preparing my church services – two every Sunday – which being unfamiliar territory would undoubtedly take time. And they advised me never to neglect my need for winter peats. Starting in April I would have a flying start with the whole summer to bring a supply home to store at 'the Manse', which they strongly advised me to make my home. The Schoolhouse was also mine by right; it went with the job too. But the Gear family were already installed there (at an even lower rent than my own!) and that meant seven adults and two children until John Henry got his house built, which was over 12% of the island population dependent on my not living in the Schoolhouse – one of whom was the Skipper of the mailboat and so, in one sense the most important able-bodied male on the island. Some decisions were clearly being made for me that night.

All in all my evening of enlightenment with the Holbourns was a revelation in many ways. I had an obvious source of advice from friends totally dedicated to the island's cause and the welfare of its people. Their knowledge of the crofters' every need and their understanding attitude towards their problems showed real empathy and care. Their outspoken criticism of their insularity was a warning rather than a disaffection. It was obviously frustrating but they expected me to cope with that as they had learned to. They pulled no punches. If I didn't get my peats home in adequate quantity to fuel my Rayburn cooker and my open fires, I would be cold and miserable. And there was nobody to come to my rescue if I wasn't efficient. If I planted tatties and carrots, they would grow and I would have winter supplies. The islanders would grow kale (i.e. cabbages) in their special enclosures, called plantie-crubs, better than I could, so I could have vitamins, carbohydrates and calories. But other supplies for school dinners, for instance, I MUST order months in advance to ensure they came in time, in competition with all the other supplies being imported and with the vagaries of the weather. There were some bonuses, to fill needs I had not even anticipated. Alasdair had himself built the house I would live in, and had ensured an adequate water supply from a well on the opposite hill. So I had a flush toilet and one of only two baths on the island, the other being in the Nurse's house. My predecessors had been the Chedburns. She had been the teacher and he, having been a lay missionary in China, had filled that role on Foula. They would leave me their five hens which would give me eggs all year, and the islanders would feed them till I arrived. Poultry-food was available at the shop but household scraps and potato peelings would supplement what they would get from scratching around in my garden. I would need waterglass if I wished to preserve my fresh eggs. I must take reliable torches

with plenty of batteries for the winter. I would inherit two home-made barrows, essential for getting my peats home from the peat-banks fully a mile from the house. There were long hills down to and up from the Ham burn in between. An ordinary wheelbarrow would wear me out in a week. A Foula barrow balanced all the weight on the wheel not on my arms and shoulders. There were of course no tarmac roads and no vehicles at all, except an ancient motorcycle belonging to Harry Gear, the Postmaster.

As part of the run-down on the population I also got a précis of Harry the postmaster's life and antecedents, including an account of how Michael Powell had come to depend on his mechanical wizardry to repair his complex cine-cameras when his professional cameramen (who were not fully qualified maintenance engineers) failed. Harry was entirely self-taught apparently. The mail crew depended for their lives on his maintenance of the mailboat's diesel engine. The postal run was once a week on Mondays, weather permitting. Telephone communication was by radio connection to Lerwick exchange for a limited time at 6 p.m. daily. There were no 'local' (i.e. cheap) calls. Advice on clothing was not to under-estimate the chill factor of the wind, which was more or less constant and often violent. Nearly everyone had at one time or another been blown over by the 'flans'; miniature whirlwinds caused by the hills and especially prevalent with gales from the N.W. One of these had caught Mrs Chedburn by surprise, knocked her over and scattered her barrowload of peats across the moor. The recommended technique was to set the barrow down on its legs when one heard the flan coming, and sit on them in the hope of weighing it down enough to avoid disaster. If caught walking in the open, one should crouch low and hang onto the grass or heather to avoid being blown away! It all sounded rather terrifying.

It was a long and fascinating evening and I came away with a notebook full of facts and life-saving advice. I also had a heart full of gratitude and exhilaration that others before me had found Foula not just a wonderful challenge but a fascinating experience of real life. From then on my preparations became a hectic round of shopping for what I felt I needed in the light of all this new knowledge, and packing – some of which I was soon to realise was hopelessly optimistic. Perhaps books were my biggest mistake. I thought about the Shetland winter, dark by 3.30 p.m., and all the time I would have for reading. So I procured some large wooden boxes from a second-hand merchant and spent several evenings selecting what to take. It took two to lift each box when I was finished, and

I congratulated myself for my foresight in looking after the need to enjoy some culture and escapism in my new life. What a dream! If only I had known what it would really be like.

I made two other contacts before leaving home. I met the Chedburns in Edinburgh and picked up plenty of practical advice about the school and the house where I would live, and yet more information about the crofters and their families. And I made an appointment at the office of the Fair Isle Bird Observatory Trust in India Street where I had a long conversation with my friend Kenneth Williamson, the Director, who agreed to my running a Foula sub-station of his world-famous Bird Observatory and, if feasible, building a Heligoland trap on the island for catching migrant birds. He would supply wire-netting and the rings I would need. These were supplied by the British Museum in London, each ring, however tiny, carrying their address in case of recovery. He was also anxious to supply me with equipment for collecting bird parasites (fleas, feather-lice, flat flies etc.) from any birds I trapped as part of a new research programme he had instituted on Fair Isle. I felt honoured to be allowed to take part in his scientific programme of research on migration, my favourite subject in ornithology, and for the first time I began to see some real value in the scientific studies I had so laboriously undertaken at Oxford. At the time they had merely been the means of making part of my military service more useful than learning how to kill people. I still didn't really feel I was a scientist at heart, but I was prepared to take advice from a brilliant one and ready to subject myself to the disciplines involved. It would give more meaning and purpose to my bird studies and to my enjoyment of the island environment. But I was not going, I reminded myself, on a holiday or for any sort of entertainment. I aimed to invest part of my life in an experience which I hoped might benefit me, the community of 70 complete strangers I was to serve and those five very special pupils who had caught my eye in that Scotsman advertisement. I was ready to go.

Chapter 3: Arrival

By a strange co-incidence my departure from John Watson's School to Shetland at the end of the Spring Term in 1954 was matched by the departure of the Headmaster, Robert Mack, to become Director of Education for the Orkney Islands. We were both taking on a challenge though his was way ahead of mine in responsibility. In terms of career structure his move was more conventional, whereas mine could have been considered more adventurous, even reckless, though with Shetland Allowance and Remote Island Allowance I would actually earn more on Foula than I had in Edinburgh. I think we had both enjoyed our experiences at John Watson's, though mine had been more carefree than his. Surprisingly, apart from myself no other member of staff had had any previous experience of boarding school life. Robert had several times sought my advice on the social and recreational problems of a residential community of a hundred children and adults living and sleeping under one roof. However I am sure that I learnt far more from his calm and efficient ways of handling both staff and pupils than he ever learnt from me, and I was sorry to say good-bye. We wished each other well in our respective adventures.

There was little time between the end of term at the beginning of April and the start of the summer term in my new location. All I remember now was a hectic rush of packing from the list I had compiled as a result of all the advice flung at me by well-wishers and a rather anxious family. Since leaving university and when not in residence at the school during term, I had lived with my parents in a quiet corner of Edinburgh's south side. They lived in the last house in a Victorian cul-de-sac called Glenisla Gardens, which had attracted a close-knit community of delightful neighbours, all of whom seemed to be taking an interest in my rather bizarre new job in the far North. The more I talked with people, the more I discovered how fragmentary was the normal urban dweller's knowledge of the remoter parts of his own country, and especially of the way of life of such people as crofters. I knew that I knew very little about them myself, but by now I was beginning to have some understanding of both the distance involved in reaching Foula and the difficulties of the journey. My first problem was the transport of the larger items of luggage such as my boxes of books, and various items for the Manse which were not provided and which the Chedburns were not leaving behind. These included floor coverings for the main rooms. Following all the dire warnings I had received about the unreliability of the mailboat, I tried to ensure that I would take all these with me on the crossing from Walls, but the first stage was to get them all to Leith Docks for the sea journey to Shetland. Word of my need soon got around our neighbours and the offer of the use of his van came from Eric Lucey, a brilliant scientist whose specialized work filming through microscopes at the Genetics Dept. of the university had already attracted my attention. Little did I know then how closely our career paths would be intertwined in the future, but I was delighted to weigh down his springs with a hefty load of my domestic bric-a-brac and commit them to the care of the shipping company at Leith.

Eventually the day dawned for my journey to Aberdeen by train and then on the P&O ferry to Lerwick overnight. In the morning I had my first excited view of Sumburgh Head with its lighthouse perched on dramatic cliffs, and the gentle, sleepy aspect of the Shetland Mainland with its misty hills and secret valleys. There were small groups of houses and sheltered bays full of boats, interspersed with long stretches of bare moorland showing little evidence of the hand of man on the landscape. I have many times since seen it looking a lot more bleak than it did on that sunny April morning as we headed up the long low coastline which, perhaps because of my mood of expectancy, seemed somehow so welcoming. And then we were into the channel with the island of Bressay on our right – sorry, starboard – and soon entered the bustle of Lerwick harbour, full of fishing boats and noisy activity. With so much to look at that was new, it was difficult to concentrate on a tight timetable leading up to my departure by bus for Walls on the west side of the Mainland. I was to stay there for the weekend with the minister, ready for catching the weekly Foula mailboat on the Monday afternoon. Already I had been diverted by watching from the deck rail the Great Skuas and the hordes of gulls round the fishing boats, with the occasional stiff-winged fulmars among them. Now however it was time to keep my appointment at the Education Offices where I received a warm welcome from the Director and helpful answers to my questions. I needed to know about communications with his office from a place with one mail delivery a week and no telephone link during working hours. There would be one visit of inspection at the school in the summer to coincide with the annual visit of the school dentist, an event which I was told was welcomed by the whole island, anxious to seize the opportunity of curing present toothache or avoiding future trouble. Their alternative would be to organise a whole day or more away from home and the croft, a two-hour crossing on the mailboat and then the bus into Lerwick, solely to keep a half-hour appointment. This had been one of several warnings I had been given by the Holbourns. Having myself had a bad dental history following three years of gross neglect by army dentists, I had been careful to fit in a precautionary visit to my dentist in Edinburgh before departure. The school inspection however would be a red-letter day to note in the diary, a day to be thoroughly prepared for.

The bus journey to Walls was another eye-opener for me. Everyone seemed to know about 'P.I.'s bus', which Peter Isbister had clearly been driving to Walls as far back as anyone could remember. It was a small, brown bus which seated about 25 passengers and every kind of parcel and freight one could imagine piled up on spare seats ready for delivery at the frequent stops the tireless P.I. made for the purpose. The road was twisty but there was a new seascape round every corner as we descended

a hill to meet the head of a long inlet or climbed up another long pull to cross over, past enticing lochans, large and small, to the next arm of the sea. Shetland seemed to be all water. And where the longer views opened up like that down Whiteness Voe to the south, it was all islands, some just rocks, others long low islets with the outline or silhouette of a house occasionally breaking a skyline. In places like Weisdale Voe there were long cultivated slopes running down to the sea below a line of houses, where the narrow rigs belonging to each house made ribbons of different colours, defined by the crop they were growing and marked by walls or fences, so that the history of ownership was written into the landscape. And everywhere there was a peat-stack outside each house, and a smoking chimney, and washing blowing on a line, never still. As soon as we got to Walls and I was walking on Shetland paths, I discovered that evocative smell which comes as a result of those smoking chimneys, the inevitable peat-reek which is the symbol of civilized life in a bleak landscape, the smell of warmth and welcome in a cold environment. Once savoured it is never forgotten and on one's first day in Shetland it becomes that part of homeliness which fits with, and is thenceforth inseparable from, the open door, the warm handshake, and the inevitable cup of tea.

All these I got at the Manse in Walls where Mr Mackintosh and his wife made me very much at home, and where the second, more intimate stage of my knowledge of the ways of the island and its unique mix of people – parishioners in this case – started to come to life. I had deliberately allowed a weekend before my crossing to acclimatize to the new way of life and

My first view of Foula, from a croft near Walls; the closest view most Shetlanders ever get

The Foula mailboat, the Island Lass, *at Walls pier (furthest right, green with a brown wheelhouse), 1954*

to allow time for discussion of and advice about the parochial aspect of my new job. As it turned out there was more than enough time as there was a fresh wind on the Monday and word came through that the boat was not crossing that day. Nor on the Tuesday either, and I began to realise how much my timetable was now going to depend on this unpredictable factor of the mailboat crossings. And it wasn't only the wind that was to blame, for the Wednesday dawned a fine, calm spring day, much to my relief. Yet by lunchtime the boat, due out of Foula at 10.30 a.m., had still not left – some mechanical problem with the engine apparently. However our time was not wasted. We had plenty to talk about and I was glad of the chance to sort out some of my own ideas as well as tapping my host's local experience. I still wonder what my minister, under whom I was to be entrusted with the spiritual care of 70 of the people of his parish, thought of this young, inexperienced Anglican teacher who was venturing into the politics of the Foula vestry. Foula clearly had more than its fair share of personalities and eccentrics. My old enemy 'Insularity' had seen to that. I received timely warning of a number of problems between crofts, especially between those representing families whose progenitors went back many generations as 'Foula folk', born and bred, and those considered as incomers, which might mean families which had lived there for several generations or those like me, newly arrived for one reason or another. Patience and tolerance were the two virtues Mr Mackintosh extolled in this respect. He made no bones about the need to listen and not to take sides, and of the need for humility in the face

of the hardships many of the Foula families had endured over years of battling against the elements.

One of the first things he asked me was whether I was a good sailor. I told him about my trips to Norway and my experience of seasickness on the North Sea in an ocean-going liner or on a fishing boat going to the Isle of May. I had learnt which tablets suited me and I had a stock of Avomine ready as there was no way I felt confident that I had the sea legs for a two-hour trip on the *Island Lass* on the open Atlantic. I found myself talking to a man who confessed to being himself the worst sailor he had ever known. At first he was clearly unwilling to discuss his own weakness in this respect for fear of putting me off the journey I was due to make on Monday. But in the end he couldn't resist telling me the story of his predecessor in the parish who regarded his trips in to Foula once or twice a year to take Communion in the Kirk, as the greatest trial of his ministerial duties, a real penance he just had to endure in the course of his duty to his Maker. He had described his first experience of the Foula mailboat on a typically stormy day as follows: "*For the first half of the journey I became increasingly afraid, in my wretchedness, that I was really going to die. During the second half of the journey I felt so ill that I was afraid I wasn't going to die.*" Oh dear! I knew only too well how I hated any form of sickness, which tended to take over both my mind and my body. But I knew a few of the tricks of the trade – keep on deck if possible; keep your eye on the level horizon, and if that doesn't work, lie flat on your back and keep your head down. The *Island Lass* apparently had few comforts, so he suggested that if the worst came to the worst, the best place was down in the hold amongst the mail-bags. That was about the only place he had found where one could rest one's head and try to sleep it off, but a sick-bag would be an essential in the circumstances – just in case.

From the coast of Mainland Shetland Foula looks like a great humped whale lying out in the ocean, often with a cap of cloud, often shrouded in mist, distant, mysterious, remote. The outline of her hills is distinctive and I was to come to learn its shape from the habit the school children had of drawing it on the front of their exercise books with the words 'Hame Sweet Hame' written underneath. The island is roughly 5000 acres, broad in the North, narrowing down to a point at the south, almost heart-shaped, about three miles long north to south and a couple of miles wide. Most of it is hill, from the isolated mass of the Noup in the south to the three-humped range of hills leading up to the great wall of the west cliffs where the whole two-mile range of hills cuts off abruptly into the Atlantic, a vertical wall of rock. I don't remember being able to see the island from the Manse in Walls but we walked out to a point beyond the village where we could look right down the length of Vaila Sound, a long winding inlet blocked at its entrance by the isle of Vaila. There on the horizon lay the grey shape of my future home. The sight of it, at last within reach, a reality not a dream, was exciting in a way I had seldom felt before. There was a tingle of expectation, damped by a fair measure of apprehension about what to expect, how I would cope, what would it be really like. On the final day the waiting time passed slowly and I was impatient to be off. When the boat did come into the harbour at Walls, they too seemed in a hurry for it was getting late in the day and they needed to cross in good light. As I was later to discover the mailboat was seldom punctual. But that day they had set off from Foula even later than usual and were anxious for a rapid turn-round. There was no attempt to inform us of their intended departure time. We were expected to make our own plans. The boat was tied up at the little jetty opposite the shop, A.K. Reid, General Merchant, where all the islanders' boxes and orders for groceries were taken. Mr Macintosh allowed a measure of time for this vital procedure of fulfilling the orders from a dozen or more crofts and we headed for the jetty. The *Island Lass* was heading out down Vaila Sound and the dreadful thought crossed both our minds that they had deliberately left me behind. I was not reassured by him saying he wouldn't put it past them if they just felt like being bloody-minded. However the boat was heading

for the old pier, a high wooden structure across the other side of the bay. The word came that they had to call in there to load up some unexpected baggage. I immediately reached the conclusion that this must be my luggage and boxes forwarded from Leith. We both got the distinct impression that the crew had not been pleased at this diversion from their normal routine, especially as they were already running late, and perhaps out of pique they had not informed us, so that we also had to make the diversion but on foot, by walking right round the bay to the further pier.

It was not an auspicious start. When we got there, nothing was said and Mr Macintosh soon smoothed things over by introducing me to the crew. They said little but were polite and gave me a formal sort of welcome. I shook hands with my host, my last physical contact with my employers so to speak, and got aboard. I was amazed at how small the boat seemed, an impression made even more significant by the impressive scenery as we chugged down Vaila Sound which is lined at its outer end by impressive rock stacks and skerries. There we passed Vaila with its huge mansion, round which I later discovered there were many stories to be told. And then there was nothing but sea and a slow swell which made our little boat seem even more dwarfed by the scale of the elements – smooth enough but with a massive lift of water up which the thudding of our Kelvin diesel engine pushed us almost reluctantly until it turned into a downhill slope and our round-hulled tub suddenly came to life and chugged cheerfully down the other side. In the long troughs the island almost disappeared from sight, but as we lifted the whole coastline of Shetland gradually appeared as we got further out into open water. Soon I realised that Foula was getting visibly closer and details were appearing. That first approach to the magic isle and the oh! so gradual revelation of its green hills and grey cliffs, the white surf and tiny dots that became sheep and shapes that grew into houses, was a never to be forgotten experience. It was the gradual realization of a dream that slowly and inevitably now was turning into a real experience. Foula was starting to possess my soul.

My memories of Foula crossings are now muddled, nor can I offhand remember exactly how many I made. Others were memorable, like another really calm one, but on a flat but foggy sea. On that occasion I noticed how much care the crew took to record the time of departure and to consult the compass. There was much discussion en route too about the state of the tide in the kind of seaman's jargon that means little to a landlubber like me. The tidal flow between Foula and the west coastline of

Foula on the horizon, from the stacks in Vaila Sound; 2½ hours to go

the Mainland changes direction four times a day and changes speed according to the date and the phase of the moon. Knowledge of the surface condition of the sea at any one time depends on a lifetime of experience of such a crossing if one is going to tackle it in fog. After two hours the mist thickened and things fell quiet and clearly everyone was listening. Conditions were ideal as the day was so still, except that there was little swell and so the sea on the shoreline was also much quieter than normal. The compass and the corrections made to compensate for the tidal flow were vital. After two hours and fifteen minutes of a journey normally reckoned to take two hours and twenty and with visibility of about a hundred metres, things become critical. Foula is a very small speck in the Atlantic even if it is about three miles long. If one misses it altogether, there is only one sensible course, which is to turn round and head back for the Mainland, which being a hundred miles long can hardly be missed. Nobody wants to start an Atlantic crossing instead of visiting Foula. But no sooner had I been made wise of these calculations than someone heard the sound of waves on a shore, and through the

mist appeared a familiar coastline, and there we were right opposite the entrance to Foula's tiny harbour. One slight correction to the rudder and we were home – no fuss, no panic, just the quiet confidence of men who can read the surface of the sea like a book and get it right when it really matters.

My first ever crossing was of course special in several ways. It was my first meeting with real Foula folk and the opening encounter had not been auspicious. At first they were shy to talk much. After all we didn't have very much in common – yet. I expect they were thinking who on earth is this student coming to tell us how to run our lives? What does he know about island life? Naturally I was everything that inhibits conversation – a beginner, a stranger, an intruder. And then there was the old Scottish tradition of the minister being a Jonah and bringing bad luck on the sea. But I tried the oldest trick in the book, asking questions they couldn't resist answering because I pleaded ignorant and anxious to be informed – and they of course had the answers at their fingertips. Of course I risked being thought of as naïve and ignorant, though I was careful to choose topics I wasn't likely – as a 'Sooth-moother' – to be as well versed in as they were. It worked well enough to become a pattern for the next few weeks in meeting up with those who were to be my neighbours for the foreseeable future. By halfway across, by which time I felt reasonably sure that my seasickness tablets had worked well enough, I had managed not only to see the practical importance of being a good listener as Mr Mackintosh had recommended, but I had learnt a good deal about the mail service, the boat, the vagaries of its performance of that service, and a host of island topics on which I was desperate for their views and information. Surprisingly we hardly touched on that most dependable of all topics of conversation, the weather. I was soon enough to discover that a factor which completely controls one's life in such a place as Foula, is more than ever the favourite topic of most conversations. At least on my introduction to the island the weather was kind and although frozen (being on the sea in April is always colder than one expects) I arrived in good shape and safely over the first dreaded hurdle.

It was 11.30 p.m. and pretty dark when we arrived. If my welcome from the crew had been a little tentative and the conversation slow to get started, the welcome party organised by the womenfolk and the elder of the Kirk, Peter Gray, was overwhelmingly kind. I had seen photos of Ham Voe, (a voe is just a harbour and this one is next to the croft of Ham) and of the pier, but the scale of it was still a surprise. A small jetty protruding from one side of a very narrow inlet, the mouth of which was wide open to the East, was the only shelter for a returning boat. As a consequence of this lack of protection from any easterly wind, the boat had to be lifted clear of the water most of the year on a couple of davits by a slow method of gearing, an endless chain pulled through a block and tackle system. It took a long time to lift several tons of boat onto the jetty. There it was secured on a cradle on rails, which then had to be hand-winched to the top of a long, sloping concrete slipway. None of this I saw that first night. It was nearly midnight and it would be long after dark before any of the crew reached their homes, some of them after trudging a mile from the pier carrying their grocery box over one shoulder or wheeling anything heavier in a barrow. I had so much to take in. All I can remember now was that within minutes of stepping ashore for the first time, I was in the warm kitchen at Ham. There was of course that wonderful smell of the peat 'reek', with tea and biscuits laid out ready and everyone anxious to be helpful – and no doubt to get a good look at the new

teacher and missionary. I was aware at once of those island surnames which the Holbourns had told me so much about; Mary Umphray, a Glasgow girl originally, with a little daughter of three, and an absent husband, Willie Umphray, who was out working on the Mainland; Mima Gear from the Schoolhouse family, mother of one of my older pupils and grandmother of the youngest, as she was at pains to point out to me that night with some pride. Mima was immediately a striking personality, both her posture and her smiling, courteous manner. Perhaps even more so was the portly figure of Peter Gray, Factor for the Laird and Elder of the Kirk, member of one of the ancient families in Foula's history. These were all going to be important people in my life but now, suddenly, they were real, human, friendly, anxious to make me feel at home. I enjoyed the tea and the warm stove but I enjoyed even more their caring that I had arrived safely and their willingness to put themselves out for my sake. Foula was already seeming like home.

Peter was a big man, stout and with a round, smiling face. He was, as the representative of the church, anxious to see me into my house, the Manse. What could he help me with? He had a barrow handy and somehow had loaded one of my big wooden boxes of books into it. If I could carry my case with my night things, perhaps he would make a start to bringing my baggage up from the pier by wheeling this box up? I winced at the thought. Those boxes were really heavy and Peter was surely in his 60s? He insisted and we set off down the steep little hill to the Voe, along to the bridge over the Ham burn, and up the even steeper little hill to the flat ground by the nurse's house. We were facing south-west and the sun had long gone down below the horizon, and I was already captivated by the distant views across to the Shetland coast, now only a shadow to the east, and by the dark hill looming above us to the west. It was a good path, almost a road, but the stone surface was loose and it was hard to avoid slipping when taking the strain of a heavy barrow. From the nurse's house it is a long steady haul to the top of the hill and the level road along to the Manse. As we trudged on through the dark with the sounds of gulls down by the harbour and that mysterious, plaintive 'cheeka, cheeka' call of the common snipe from the foot of the hill, I was suddenly all too aware of the almost desperate wheezing of my companion as he plodded behind his heavy load, getting steadily more and more breathless as we went. He insisted on pressing on to the gate at the top of the hill, where I suggested he take a rest as I was genuinely afraid that his good manners and his eagerness to help were getting the better of his common sense. Also I knew he lived fully halfway up the island by the road to the North end and still had a fair way to go home. If this was how the islanders treated a complete stranger, even if he was their new preacher, it boded well for the future. I have seldom felt more of a sense both of gratitude and of genuine humility as I felt towards Peter Gray that night.

Soon we were along the road, through the gate of the croft of Mornington, where my next-door neighbours, the Beagries from Aberdeen lived with their three children, and at the door of the Manse. There was a wooden porch, a front door into a lobby and to the left a sitting-room with a cheerful peat fire burning in the grate and best of all a lighted Tilley lamp on the table, casting its warm cheerful light over the empty room with a comforting hiss. Peter asked whether I was familiar with Tilley lamps and made sure I knew how to turn it off safely and release the pressure. I felt reasonably happy I remembered it all from Isle of May days, but was glad to be reminded and reassured by his expertise. At the rear of the house was a kitchen with a Rayburn cooker glowing with heat and a kettle on the hotplate. On the kitchen table was home-baked bread, fresh butter and a bowl of the fresh eggs from my own hens. I felt I was off to a good start. We lifted the big box of books in together and then Peter shook my hand and bade me goodnight. It was late and anyway I had a great deal to do before I could get to bed for my first night on Foula. I sat down on the wooden box and wondered what to do first, and how long it would take me to get everything done. The list seemed endless and within a few days I would face my first Sunday in the Kirk, and then my first day at the school. I had a house to get organised, new carpets to lay, food to store, hens to feed, clothes to unpack, meals to cook, parents and pupils to meet, and nearly 70 islanders still to meet or to visit in their homes. Just what had I let myself in for and how was I going to find enough hours in the day to get through it all unaided, entirely on my own? I went outside and listened. It was well after midnight but there was still a glow in the sky behind the hills to the west. I could still hear snipe calling and as a background accompaniment the slow muffled wash of the sea at the base of the cliffs out to the east. It was then that I suddenly realised I couldn't see the sea from my house, though here I was completely surrounded by miles and miles of it. As it got darker I began to see the stars as I never remembered seeing them before, bright companions in a black sky. The outline of the hill was just another shade of black now but somehow friendly, a protection to the west from the winter gales. But now I had the spring and summer to look forward to. The experience I had opted for had begun – and best of all I had been made to feel welcome and wanted. I reckoned I would survive.

Chapter 4: Early Days

I arrived on Foula on 21st April 1954, eight days before my 27th birthday, an ex-serviceman, a graduate, a teacher of less than two years' experience, an enthusiastic bird-watcher (aspiring to be an ornithologist) and a complete novice at domestic science and island life. I knew far more about birds and their habits, and especially the mysteries of their migration, than I did about cooking or sewing or gardening. But I had had a wise and practical mother and a keen scoutmaster-cum-headmaster for a father, and as a student I had discovered that 'the mother of invention' in these arts is when there's nobody else to do them for you. I just hoped I had enough know-how to see me through. Managing a Rayburn stove with peat as my only fuel looked like being a bit of a challenge. Would I remember the tips Betty Holbourn had tried to impress on me, like how to bank it up at might with damp peat 'mould'? I would soon see.

I cannot remember, well over fifty years after the events, exactly how I spent my first days on Foula. I seemed to have an overwhelming number of things to attend to and to find time for, but several priorities had formed in my mind as to how I should go about coping with the demands on my time. The first was the school, which was both the job I was paid to do and the work by which I would be judged by the community and especially the three families whose children were my pupils. The second was the church which also contributed, through the S.P.C.K., towards my salary, but which gave me my best opportunity to meet first the families which supported the church, and then all those who needed a bit of my time in such voluntary tasks as distributing their library books or visiting the elderly or housebound. In such a small community I saw no reason to make any distinction between those who actually came to church and those who chose not to. But the crofts were scattered and I would have to walk, so I had decided from the outset that getting round them all, and then sustaining visits on a regular basis, would take some weeks to sort out, and would discover its own priorities.

When I first stepped outside the house on my first morning, the bird-watcher took over. There was a row of birds sitting on the fence which I took to be house sparrows. But were they? I grabbed my binoculars and found myself looking at a row of twite, daintier than sparrows with attractive yellow beaks and streaky brown backs. Wow! I never saw those on the fence at Glenisla Gardens. I was going to have to revise all my ideas about even the everyday birds and get to know them well, before the migrants arrived to test my skills in identification. It was quite a relief to note that the other birds sitting on the wall over by the gate were just starlings – except that I remembered that the Shetland Starling was a subspecies recognised primarily from the fact that their young were dark plumaged and quite unlike the sandy-brown juveniles of *Sturnus vulgaris*. I would have to take time to see if I could distinguish the adults by their plumage as well? There was going to be a great deal to learn here and not just the thrill of species new to me at migration time, with perhaps the daily possibility of adding species to my 'life list' – 'lifers' as we called them. Already on my first morning I was experiencing that tingle of excitement I had known so often on the Isle of May, the feeling of being engaged in a sort of avian treasure hunt, looking for gold amongst the dross.

All my friends knew that this was a major incentive for me in applying for the Foula vacancy. The idea of being paid to work in a place where I was also planning to run my own Bird Observatory on my own doorstep very much appealed to my bird-watching friends. The current jargon at that time for such a move was 'jammy', so far as I remember. I rather resented the implication that I had opted for anything easy. The job may have had jam on it, but it certainly didn't look like being a 'skive'.

In the post-war years Bird Observatories had blossomed at strategic points on the east coast of Britain offering unique opportunities to study all those exotic continental species we seldom or never encountered at home. Visiting them at migration time was always a risk which could turn into intense excitement and success or intense frustration and failure. Dependent on the weather and especially the wind direction, each day was an unknown quantity and if conditions were 'right' for bringing in unusual species, there was always a sense of heightened expectation. This sharpened the senses and made continuous detailed observation of the landscape a basic habit, an added sensitivity to movement. I had always emphasised to my pupils that they would never be good at detecting the rare birds we all wanted to find until one knew the common ones really well. As an aid to understanding the birdlife of wherever I happened to be and of recording everything of interest that I found or which added to my knowledge, I had for years kept a bird diary. When I was away from home the need to keep notes on my observations was far greater but the time much shorter, and keeping the diary up to date became a discipline. And notes and especially descriptions must be written up soon after the event to be of any value as observations. Writing up with accuracy what one had seen only a few days back became impossible, especially at migration time when valuable records of unusual species could occur daily. Identification details must be written down on the spot, so that a field notebook (and pencil) were as vital as binoculars.

I arrived on Foula with several years of this discipline behind me and I have on my desk as I write the daily typewritten entries for the first exciting days after my arrival. A transcription of the first few days will reveal several factors. The time I had to devote to bird-watching was, under the pressure of my settling in period, very limited. On the other hand this is the only day-by-day record I have now of that time. As a result I can easily present an impression of being only interested in the bird-life of Foula, whereas the truth is that I was so busy that only this learned discipline, which I was determined to keep up during my stay on the island, enabled me to make the time to record my observations. Typing was always my last activity before going to bed. Once or twice when vital correspondence on island affairs competed with an eventful period of migration watching, I never got to bed at all before mailboat days.

For me of course, reading those rather brief records of the first days on the island brings back very vividly the sense of wonder that instead of seeing a few sparrows and starlings in the school grounds in Edinburgh, now my sparrows were twite, my rooks were fulmars and my whole world was different and intensely exciting. There were of course no trees or hedgerows at all because of the wind, so I needn't expect blue-tits or finches, rooks or jackdaws, in fact very few perching birds – the passerines which make up our normal song-bird fauna on the mainland. But there were a few as my first four days of brief entries in my diary reveal:

FOULA, SHETLAND

April 21st *Crossed at last from Walls leaving about 9.30 p.m. so that we saw very little from the boat except an occasional gannet or fulmar. Arrrived about 11.30 p.m. very cold and glad of the cup of tea at Ham.*

April 22nd *Fulmars seem to be everywhere and are all displaying very noisily both on the cliffs and inland on the hillsides. Several first thing this morning on the ruined chimneys of Mornington and in fact my first bird for the island. Twite also apparently common. A small party of waders in Ham Voe, when I was fetching some of my luggage, included 6 Purple Sandpipers and 10 Turnstone. There were 1 Robin and 2 Redwing in Ham garden.*

April 23rd *Two Red-throated divers on Mill Loch early this morning. About 30 Bonxies (Great Skuas) bathing there later in the day. Saw my first Arctic Skua today, a single light-phase bird flying idly over the southern breeding ground. Three wrens singing at the south end tonight at Dykes, Punds and the Old Kirk, all apparently tied to stone wall areas and away from the cliffs. Robbie Isbister at S.Biggins says that the Manx Shearwaters have been in for a day at least and have been heard at night.*

April 24th *On the cliffs at the back of the house were many shags and the inevitable tysties (Black Guillemots). Several of these flew out of holes or gaps in the rocks and looked to be well-established in their territories.*

My house was called 'The Manse' and stood on the croft called Mornington. It had been built under the direction of Alasdair Holbourn and largely, so I understood, by the work of his own hands, to house the lay missionary in a more modern and easily managed house than the 'Old Manse'. All the houses were on the more sheltered east side of the island, almost the whole of the west side being steep, grass-covered hills terminating abruptly in precipitous cliffs. The croft lay in a reasonably sheltered depression close to the road before it started to climb up the long hill to the Kirk which stood on a ridge looking south over the Hame Toun, the largest walled area of crofting land at the south end. The original croft house called Mornington, where I recorded the first sighting of fulmars from my bedroom window on that first morning, was just a ruin, as were so many of the original houses marked on the 1902 6-inch Ordnance Survey map which I hadn't yet unpacked. In fact most of my luggage was still down in the big hut by the harbour, so that much of my first day was spent barrowing my bags and boxes up to the house, a sobering introduction into how long ordinary jobs take on an island with no motorized transport. I had inherited from my predecessors in the job a very valuable asset in the form of two wheelbarrows, both Foula-made but each quite different in design and use. I quickly discovered which was the best, a deep capacious wooden box with the front wheel not out in front of the box structure but inset into a recess so that the weight of the contents of the box was more directly over a large wheel and so transmitted through the wheel to the road rather than on the handles which I was holding. This subtle but practical design made a marked difference to the effort required to push a full load of books up from the Voe or, within a few days of my arrival, my first load of peats from the peat-bank. As peat is light compared with coal, there were spare boards, which fitted neatly round the top edge of the barrow to increase the depth of the box to take a greater volume of peats. The increased weight was fine on the level, but it took practice to push a fully loaded barrow up the long hill from the Ham Burn below the Post Office to the top of the hill, where it levelled out along the moor called Hamnabreck. As the road dipped down towards the Manse there was a wooden gate across it, to keep the sheep out in summer and if necessary inside in winter. A second gate three hundred yards further on marked the other side of the 'toun'. This was the smallest enclosed area on Foula, separated from the open hill partly by stone walls, partly by stob and wire fences. Small strips of cultivation here and there had potatoes or oats. At the back of the Manse and sheltered from the west winds was my small vegetable plot, which I fully intended to make use of and had brought seeds for the purpose. At my back door was a hen-house with a small wired run for my five hens, and in the end gable wall a door opening into my peat cellar. I had been advised to fill this first with really dry peats and for further storage I would have to build a peat stack, covered with a roof of turf, a feature of virtually every house in Shetland. I did not intend to be cold in my first winter.

I had crossed late on a Wednesday and it was planned I should open the school the following Monday. In between, of course, came my first Sunday with two services to take at the Kirk. I had my time cut out. The school was half a mile north, the Kirk half a mile south. I had three lots of parents to meet. Two children were my next-door neighbours in the 'Old Manse' to which the name Mornington had been transferred from the original ruined croft-house. Two lived in the Schoolhouse where I had to go anyway to sort out the schoolroom, which was simply a large downstairs room with an outside door into the walled playground, and a connecting door through into the Schoolhouse kitchen. There were records to prepare, the School Log to make up, the meals to organise, the available books to be sorted and studied. The church was clean and tidy though with that inevitable musty smell which all buildings acquire which are only used one day a week. But I needed to pay courtesy calls on my elders at least and to arrange

The Manse, below the steep slopes of Hamnafield – out of sight of the sea!

The North 'grind' of the croft of Mornington, where the road passes the Mill Loch

an organist for Sunday. I could – just – have managed to play the hymns myself with a bit of practice. Using this as an excuse I enjoyed half an hour learning how to work the bellows with my feet while working the stops and keys with my hands. Not so easy as it looked, for I had to remember to use my hands to sustain the notes, my pianist's instinct being to use my right foot for this purpose. Unlearning such an instinctive movement was quite hard but a chance to sit at a keyboard was always welcome. Later I would often drop into the church to play as a relief from stress. Not surprisingly there were no pianos in Foula but there were other pedal organs in some houses and musicians to go with them.

The first musician I came across was Bobby Isbister, who ran the shop. His only son Eric, aged 11, was my fifth pupil. Their house, South Biggins, was the southernmost croft on the island and a visit there was one of my top priorities before school started. This was not just to meet Eric's grandfather, old Robbie, who was well known as the self-appointed 'keeper' of the Manx Shearwaters which nested in a straggle of boulders at the back of the Noup. More urgently it was because I had been warned both by the Holbourns and the Education Office in Lerwick, that Eric had not attended school for many months. Something had to be done.

It was a delicate situation but I was determined to solve it. Bobby's elder brother Jimmy had had two sons who had also lived all their lives on Foula and who like all isolated islanders had limited resistance to infections they had never encountered – like 'flu. Jimmy decided there was no future for his family crofting on Foula, and

so, partly for the boys' benefit and to give them a better chance in life, he offered his services as a lay missionary. Alfred, the elder boy, aged 14, said he wanted to stay in Foula with his grandfather because, as he put it, if he left he would *"surely die of the 'flu"*. However the decision was made and the family left, staying for the first few weeks at the Manse in Walls. It was there that Alfred did fall ill and within a few weeks of leaving Foula was dead. The younger son Ivor, when Jimmy was working as missionary on the island of Papa Stour just across the water from Foula, joined the army towards the end of the Great War and so he also caught an infection and died in the Mediterranean aged 18. No wonder then that Bobby remained firmly ensconced in Foula and vowed that his only son Eric would never leave the island. When I arrived he never had. But because the Schoolhouse family had two and sometimes three members of the mailboat crew, and so had more contacts with outsiders than any other family, they were regarded as a primary source of possible infection, Bobby had become almost paranoid about his son's health and refused to let him go to school in spite of all the protests of my predecessors and the Shetland education authorities.

I personally had every sympathy with his stand. In my own family in autumn 1926, the eldest son had contracted diphtheria at the age of four and died, just before I was born in spring 1927. It was almost as though one cause of Foula's backwardness in the modern world of the 1950s was to belong still to the age when infectious diseases regularly took lives before the advances in medicine and hygiene started to make such deaths preventable. After reassuring the Isbisters that neither I nor, so far as I could tell, anyone else in the Gear family had any infection at that time, there seemed to be a good opportunity to break the deadlock and for Eric to start again. I promised that as an incentive for them I would agree to come down to their house and fetch him every morning if this would help, and I guaranteed to watch out for and notify them of any cold or other infection should it affect anyone who might be in contact with Eric on his schooldays. We shook hands on this deal and I was then able to change the subject and discuss other important matters like the return of the Manx Shearwaters, with Eric's lively and likeable grandfather, old Robbie.

If my first encounter with school parents was unusual and for me a unique experience, my first official encounter with my church Elders (after my initial welcome from Peter Gray) was even more memorable. While visiting the Hametoun it seemed rational to drop in on James Ratter at Broadfoot. I knew he was a cripple, so severely bent in his old age from arthritis that he could only with difficulty reach the Kirk on the ridge behind his house, which I had been told he did manfully and without complaint every Sunday. So I could hardly expect him to call on me, nor was there any easy means of notifying him when I would come. So on my way home from South Biggins I turned left off the road and took the path which leads west towards the Daal, a great U-shaped valley sweeping across between the Noup and the main group of hills. Through this gap was revealed, far off against the western horizon, the dramatic outline of the Wester Hoevdi, the southern buttress of the great line of cliffs which face up to the Atlantic gales and create such turbulence in the atmosphere in times of storm.

My mind had been full of awe at this majestic view as I approached the back door of Broadfoot and knocked. No answer; but there were sounds of life within. I knocked again on the outer door but then, surmising that the old folk might be deaf, opened it and approached the inner door into the house. It was dark in the porch and as I stepped cautiously forward the door opened and a lined face, with rather straggly grey hair, peered up at me. It was old Lily, James' wife, who took one look at me in the gloom and with horror in her voice exclaimed loudly, "*My God! The Minister!*" turned abruptly and disappeared into the room, shutting the door rather firmly behind her. I had seldom heard a more fervent prayer for divine assistance in my life. But I was too upset at the idea of her confusion at being caught unprepared for my visit to worry about being left standing outside on the doorstep. There were urgent

voices inside, a short period of domestic noises, chairs being moved, the clink of china, and then while his wife hastened to tidy up her appearance to match such an austere occasion as the first visit of a new 'Meenister', the bent figure of her old husband in his carpet slippers appeared at the door, shook me warmly by the hand and ushered me in to a chair by the stove.

As I had just found at the Isbisters there was an old-world courtesy about their manners, and always a tradition of hospitality expressed in terms of cups of tea, usually accompanied by Black's Biscuits. These were bland but wholesome, thick, flaky biscuits baked by the firm in Lerwick which cashed in on the simple fact that bread is a difficult commodity in remote places with infrequent deliveries of goods. It goes stale, or worse still mouldy, whereas dry biscuits kept in a tin can stay crisp and palatable for weeks. They were floury and made from exactly the same ingredients as a white loaf – but were so much more rational and palatable than bread. I grew to like them very much and when spread with freshly churned butter, slightly salted, were a luxury food as well as a symbol of the genuine warmth of a Shetland welcome. After discussing church matters, which was mostly a case of James answering my many queries about the style and form of their services and what their customary procedures were, he suggested I might like to meet the other members of his family at Broadfoot.

His son James Andrew (I was quickly learning that most boys in Foula were given two Christian names, both of which were always used) was out of the island, working in fact in his professional role as a diver on the foundations for a new pier on Fair Isle. His wife was Ena Beagrie, the daughter of my next-door neighbours at Mornington and I met their daughter Andrea Joyce, aged 4. But it was when they took me across to the older house called Broadfoot East, at the back of Broadfoot West to meet the two elderly Robertson sisters that I had another new experience, a sort of mini-revelation of domestic customs which altered for the rest of my life the way I ate my porridge. The elder sister Mary had had a stroke and was not able to talk to me, but her younger sister Liza, aged about 70, was just starting her supper and I asked if she would mind if I sat and talked to her while she ate it. She was not in the least put out by this suggestion and we chatted on the sort of subjects I quickly learnt to raise on my visits to the crofts – sheep, cattle, peat, the weather, the mailboat etc. etc., all subjects on which I pleaded genuine ignorance and they were only too delighted to impart some of their inherited or learned wisdom on these important matters. All the while I couldn't help noticing the ingenious way Liza ate her porridge. It was clearly steaming hot in the bowl on the table, but she held in her left hand a teacup full of cold milk. Each spoonful taken piping hot from the bowl was then dipped into the cup and eaten without burning herself and with obvious relish. At the risk of being personal beyond politeness, I commented what a sensible way to eat hot porridge. She seemed genuinely astonished that I could think of eating it any other way. She had always eaten her porridge like this as she liked it hot but with fresh cold milk. So do I but usually ended up with tepid gruel in tepid milk as I neared the end of my helping. Looking back over fifty years to that moment I can't remember a word of what we talked about, but I can see her now enjoying her porridge – as she always had – and rather relishing instructing this ignorant young 'Meenister' in the right way to do things. I seem to remember also how impressed I was that such a simple meal, for that seemed to be all she was having, in the unpretentious surroundings of her cottage kitchen, seemed to offer her such contentment with her lot. She also expressed her great gratitude to the folks next door, who clearly looked after the two old sisters, which must have entailed no end of daily chores, as though it was the most natural thing in the world.

There was one other inmate at Broadfoot who was never discussed and who also seemed to be just accepted as someone needing constant care but without much return except family pride and family love. This was 'Pirie Walter' whom I met occasionally wandering about in the vicinity of Broadfoot and who occasionally came further afield – to the shop for instance. He must have been in his twenties, a little uncouth in appearance but quite harmless. In the parlance of the day, the Holbourns had described him as 'M.D.' though now he would probably be described as having severe learning difficulties. I know nothing of his origins but in a very small community such offspring of too closely related parents (usually a brother and sister) will sometimes crop up proving the severe effects of in-breeding. Conversation with Walter was not really possible as he had no speech except an emphatic "*Yah!*" to almost anything you said or asked. But I always tried to include him among those with whom I stopped for a yarn on my way around the island. Sometimes it was a blessed relief to meet a good soul like Walter, who at least didn't go on forever like Tom o' the Gravins.

Tom and his sister Janie were two members of the Umphray family who had never married. They lived in a rather run-down croft-house half way along the road from the school and the Post Office to the pier. This presented me with one of my first problems; it was a road I had to walk down often. Here I found a real example of insularity, two people of very limited education, yet with a fundamental knowledge of the island and its past history which was clearly of great value for any archive. They had a very poor croft and the only house into which I was never invited. This was simply because they knew it was well below any reasonable standard of cleanliness, and they were ashamed to let anyone else inside. And they loved talking. Waylaying visitors was

Fulmar on the chimney of the ruined croft of Mornington; the first bird identified on my first morning on Foula from my bedroom window

a way of life for them both and they had all the time in the world to spend at it. So it became a major hazard in my timetable how to slip past 'the Gravins' without being intercepted for an hour's chat – or longer. More than once, after many attempts to move on, I just had to walk away leaving Tom telling his long, fascinating stories about generations past to an empty road. Now, sadly, I can't remember a word of it.

Chapter 5: My Neighbours

In a community as small as Foula everybody is in a sense your neighbour. But we had no telephones and no transport so that in terms of walking time, I was still quite far from a number of the crofts. I was going to have to make a conscious effort to get to know many of the islanders. My immediate neighbours; the crofters on whose land my house was situated and the Schoolhouse family whom I would see every working day, were in a different category. It was easier with people whom I was meeting just as neighbours rather than in any official capacity, where I had so far been impressed already by their natural courtesy and helpfulness. Looking back on those first encounters now, I can't help feeling that they were probably rather sorry for me, as well as being curious to know why anyone should want to exchange the comforts and advantages of life in 'the South' for their isolated and restricted environment. Perhaps this was why I had such an easy landing, and not just when I stepped ashore for the first time onto the jetty. It had certainly helped that my first sea crossing had been so smooth, even if rather later than expected. That was always one of my worst anxieties about island life; the getting there, knowing that I was so prone to sea-sickness. But having got over that hurdle for the meantime, it seemed that everyone went out of their way to make my entry into their circle just as smooth and relaxed as the crossing had been.

Perhaps this was because they really were rather sorry for me. They knew what island life was like and were used to it. I, poor soul, had it all to learn. Most of them probably thought I was plain daft to have given up so many home comforts and cultural contacts to choose such an isolated life among them. Not that they didn't truly appreciate their homeland. They were fiercely proud of their lifestyle, however simple, however harsh at times and I was soon aware of their determination against all the odds to show the world outside not just that they could manage, but that they could make a good job of it. To do so they needed rules, both for their individual lives and for their communal lives, and I very soon discovered how inflexible and overpowering were some of their traditions and customs. Naturally I knew little of any of this traditional background, and, as in many

other aspects of our relationship, I found them tolerant and eager to instruct me. I was of course just another incomer and they were to that extent sorry for me. But having chosen to come I seemed now to be accepted as one of them. On thinking it over this must have been due in very large part to the sense of interdependence and co-operation which were two of the most striking aspects of this tightly knit community of very diverse people. We were all bound by common challenges and the same sobering conditions. We all had our own job to do and there was an atmosphere of trust that we would just get on with it. I never coerced anybody to fit in with my plans or do it my way. And so I very seldom met any opposition to the way I led my life or did my jobs.

Luckily in my own spheres of the school and the church, I had both some official authority and the edge over them in experience. Of course had they known that I had never preached from a pulpit in my life – and, particularly, had never conducted a funeral – they might have been less sure of giving me such a wonderfully warm welcome. But it gave me great confidence to keep very quiet on that score and to start right away being the schoolmaster who knew what he wanted from and for both parents and pupils. I admit that my confidence was tinged with quite a dose of nerves and humility at the thought of all the new things that awaited me in those first few anxious days. But my apprehension was softened by a genuine eagerness to convert names into faces, and crofts into homes housing real people who seemed to have inspired their landlord at least with so much interest and affection. Here I was amongst a batch of complete strangers and yet already I felt a real affinity with them.

At my meeting with the Holbourns in Edinburgh they had made me out a hand-written list on a few pages of an exercise book, (which I still have before me as I write) of all the crofts and their inhabitants, giving their ages, either known or guessed, and some of the many close relationships of an island community with only seven basic surnames – Isbister, Gray, Ratter, Umphray, Gear, Manson, and Henry. In a community of only 70 people in twenty-one households it is probably worth reproducing the whole list, namely with little written comment except the occasional word to remind me of special points they made as we went over it, to clarify their occupations and some of their complex inter-relationships. For legal reasons, as a result of legislation introduced since the 1050s, it has been thought better to omit ages except in the case of infants and the schoolchildren:

LIST OF CROFTS AND TENANTS AS COMPILED BY ALASDAIR HOLBOURN IN SPRING 1954

The five schoolchildren are underlined.
The crofts are listed geographically from South to North

HAME TOUN:

South Biggins	Robert Isbister	Crofter – interested in local birds
	Jessie Isbister	Robert's wife
	Bobbie Isbister	Son, shopman (R & J Isbister), crofter
	Aggie Jean Isbister	Bobbie's wife (née Gray)
	<u>Eric</u> (age 10)	Their only son
North Biggins	Mrs Henry	Widow, crofter
	John Thomas Ratter	Son, metal-worker; mailboat crew, crofter
	Jessie Ratter	John Thomas' wife (née Henry)
Broadfoot, East	Mary Robertson	(Stroke patient)
	Liza Robertson	Mary's sister
	Walter Ratter	
Broadfoot, West	James Ratter	Crofter; Elder of Kirk
	Lily Ratter	James' wife
	James Andrew Ratter	Son; professional diver
	Ena R.	J.A.'s wife (née Beagrie)
	Andrea Joyce (age 3)	Ena's daughter
Breckans	Robert Isbister	Last 'black house'; retired crofter
Niggards	Teenie Henry	Crofter
	Sweetie Henry	Teeny's sister
Dykes	Tammie Gray	Retired crofter
	James Andrew Gray	Son; watchmaker/joiner/crofter
	Anna	J.A.'s wife, from Leith, Edinburgh
	Marion Jane (age 3)	Anna's daughter
	(Baby due)	
	Louis Gray	Tammy's unmarried daughters
	Edith Gray	
Quinister	James Henry	Crofter
	Magnie Henry	James' brother; married to Betty of S. Harrier
Punds	Meggie Ratter	Widow of Walter, late mailboat skipper/crofter
	Jeannie	Meggie's elder sister
Old Manse	(William Beagrie)	From Stonehaven, employed outwith Foula
	Mrs Beagrie	William's wife, crofter
	Alec	Son, at school in Lerwick
	<u>Norman</u> (age 11)	Son
	<u>Joyce</u> (age 8)	Daughter

HAM TOUN:

Leraback	Dodie Isbister	Retired crofter, Elder of Kirk
	Robina Isbister	Wife, crofter

	Ada Umphray	Crofter
	Andrew Umphray	Crofter
	Donnie (age 16)	Adopted son; at school in Lerwick
Nurse's House	Oliver Peterson	Nurse's husband
	Mrs Peterson	Nurse – due to leave very soon
	Michael (age 11)	Son
Lower Mogle	Peter Gear	Retired crofter
	Grace Anne Gear	Wife
	Harry Gear	Son; postmaster/engineer/crofter
Schoolhouse	Davie Gear	Mailboat skipper
	Mima Gear	Wife (née Henry), crofter
	Vida	Daughter; married to John Henry, at sea
	Andy	Son, at Aberdeen University
	Ken	Son, recently left school in Lerwick
	<u>Jim</u> (age 11)	Son
	<u>Vina</u> (age 7)	Grand-daughter, daughter of Vida
	Mary Henry	Unmarried sister of Mima
Gravins	Tom Umphray	Crofter
	Janie Umphray	Tom's sister
Ham	(Willie Umphray)	Working in Glasgow
	Mary Umphray	Willie's wife, from Glasgow, crofter
	Sheila (age 3)	Mary's daughter
	Elisabeth Wiseman	Adopted daughter of the croft
Loch	Peter Ratter	Son of James of Broadfoot, roadman
	Bessie Ratter	Wife (née Henry; sister of Mima Gear)
Burns	Peter Gray	Factor, Kirk elder/crofter
	Muriel Gray	Wife (née Gear), sister of Harry
	Jane Gray	(Bedridden)
South Harrier	Scott Umphray	Crofter
	Babbie Henry	Married to Magnie of Quinister
	Betty Umphray	Scotty's sister
North Harrier	Betty Gray	Spinster: open-hearth, semi-black house)
Blobersburn	Peter Manson	Mailboat crew member, crofter
	Katie Manson	Wife (née Ratter); late Walter's sister
	Kittie Manson	Peter's sister

I had this list in my kitchen every mealtime at first, trying to memorise who lived in which croft and what the relationships were. The most noticeable thing about the whole population of Foula was that the average age of the 70 residents at the time was just over 60. With 10 children under 12, this meant that there must be a high proportion of very elderly people. I counted 17 aged 70 or over. Only 20 came into the age range from 20 to 50 years. Here was a dire shortage of able-bodied workers to carry the burden in a situation where labour was at a premium. Part of the reason for this was of course that so many had reached, or would soon reach, the age where they could no longer manage their lives for themselves,

but would need daily help to survive. It wasn't that folk were unwilling to help their neighbours; just that there were too few helpers and too many in need. This was the situation which had brought the end for St Kilda in 1930. Could Foula go the same way? I puzzled of course over the family names and wondered if I could ever build up some family trees to help me understand some of the complex and close relationships within the families.

A welcome exception to this problem was the family who were my immediate next-door neighbours, the Beagries, (the first syllable pronounced as in Bay) whose home base had been Stonehaven in Aberdeenshire. Their house, a solid stone-built two-storey house, originally the

*The Old Manse; croft-house and
home to the Beagrie family,
my nearest neighbours*

'Old Manse', was only two hundred yards across a field from my back door, and my first call was there. There was an immediate problem which they, not I, had to set about trying to cope with by amending their normal way of speaking. I had on my journey already realised that Shetlanders, though they can almost all talk very intelligible English to visitors, will talk a dialect among themselves which can be very hard to understand until one has lived there for many weeks. The Beagries had had to cope with this too but their brand of Aberdeen brogue was so strong and deep-seated that it had hardly suffered a dent from the impact of living in Shetland for a few years. The effect the Norse dialect had had on their Scots speech was to make it even stranger and harder to interpret for the poor innocent teacher, educated almost entirely south of the border in England. I struggled to understand and they struggled to repeat almost every sentence with an interpretation in the best English they could muster. We managed. I only wish I now had a tape-recording of those first encounters.

I was aware that Mrs Beagrie's husband would not normally be at home. He had found, fairly soon after they had arrived on Foula, that it was not possible to move into an empty, unworked croft and expect it to provide a living for a family of five. So he held down a full-time job away from home, taking such opportunities as holidays and the weather allowed him to come in and see his family. Mrs Beagrie held the fort in style. They had the only bull on the island on their croft, a wise move made as soon as they realised that the old bull was at the end

of his days and nobody seemed to have got organised to bring in a new one. This immediately gave them a lever of some power. There was no point in anyone else going through all the hassle of buying from a very distant market and then bringing in a new bull (no easy task in the hold of a small mailboat) when there was already one on the island. So the Beagries immediately had another small part of their meagre income assured. Without the services of the bull, none of the other cows on the island would continue for long giving the milk, butter and cheese which was the reward for the obvious labour of keeping cows throughout the year. Nothing could have introduced me quicker to an aspect of island life I had so far not even thought about, except for receiving a welcome assurance from the Holbourns that there was an ample supply of milk. This was the first of many such factors of daily living which made one think through things one had simply taken for granted in the city. I began to see more clearly than ever before just what was involved in human effort and human interdependence to make daily life tolerable. Within minutes of meeting her, Mrs Beagrie was an ally and a very strong support to me, her newest neighbour, and I had a firm respect for her natural wisdom and ability as a crofter.

I very soon discovered that she was also an excellent mother and a good school parent, though without either the time or the inclination to get too much involved. That was my job and she trusted me to get on with it. I had ample evidence of her capabilities in the little batches of scones or, in the early days before I started baking my own bread, the fresh loaf I would find on my kitchen table when I got home in the evening. I decided straight away to ask for her help in coping with my domestic chores while also trying to tackle both my jobs. So I offered her the use of my hot-water system from the Rayburn cooker for clothes-washing. This would enable her to earn a little extra cash for doing my washing and hopefully make hers an easier task at the same time. She also agreed to feed me on Sundays between the two church services. These were what the islanders were used to, and so what was expected of me. The practical side of this arrangement was not just to relieve me of the chore of housework on Sundays when I knew it would take me all my concentration to tackle the church services. But it was the only time I would wear the 'glad-rags' I had brought with me to make my B.A. gown and hood look slightly less ridiculous by putting them on over a reasonably respectable suit. My lunches at Mornington, in spite of the anomaly of my church dress, were a wonderful break from the mad rush of island life which I soon realised was to be my lot for the foreseeable future. They also saved my few good clothes from the risk of the inevitable splashes and food stains involved in cooking or washing up. Besides it was relaxing to sit down for once and be waited on, especially when the result was a wonderful farmhouse meal and a fresh opportunity to get used to that rich Aberdeenshire accent. And like all Foula folk, the Beagries were experts in island gossip. With a house more or less half-way down the road that runs the three miles from North to South, they were as well placed as any to pick up all the news which was inevitably passed by word of mouth with a rapidity and reliability which never ceased to astonish me. One of the very first lessons of living in a small community is that everyone makes it their business to know as much as they possibly can of everybody else's. Secrecy is almost impossible. The phrase 'bush telegraph', coined perhaps where African drums aided the process, conveys all that is needed of the human skill in being well informed without obvious means of communication. Seldom in all my time on Foula did I arrive at a house unexpected or impart any 'news' to an islander about the movements of people or boats, or even wheelbarrows, that they did not know already. This was especially true of infections such as colds. People isolated geographically from infectious germs gradually lose their resistance to them. Their bodies' defences are weakened. A cold, or worse still a 'flu virus, could be a killer. The older generation were the most vulnerable, having been isolated for longer and so less able to cope with the disease once contracted.

Most remote island histories are marked by disasters such as the smallpox outbreak which killed off all but a handful of the St Kildans in 1724. Four lucky adults, who had been out in a boat at the gannet colonies on the stacks gathering their annual harvests of birds when the disease struck, avoided the infection; but they came back to find 26 surviving orphaned children. The smallpox plague in Shetland was in 1720 and may have followed the Foula outbreak of which Holbourn says that "*tradition, taken in conjunction with the dates on the tombstones of those who were brought in to repopulate the isle after the epidemic, points to an earlier date*". The population at that time was 200, and he also describes how they laid out their dead outside the doors for the survivors to collect and bury until there were hardly enough for the task. Finally there was only one man left with "*sufficient strength to perform this office*". He was the baillie and lived in the croft of Ham in the centre of the island. He was reputed to have been the only man on the island with a gun and to have grown so desperate that he threatened to shoot anyone who came north from the south end crofts. In the end there were only five survivors. As with St Kilda, where the Macleods sent replacements across from Skye to occupy the empty houses, immigrants from the mainland of Shetland, presumably allowing a decent interval after the 'muckle fever' was over, settled in Foula. It can therefore be presumed, and is backed up by a study of the family pedigrees of the present population, that all the members of the seven main island families are descended from these few immigrant families which arrived eight or nine generations ago.

The Gears at the Schoolhouse were not one of those families but much more recent incomers and still regarded as such by most of the islanders. They rented the Schoolhouse from me at such a low rate that I just didn't bother to collect it. Davie had taken over as skipper of the mailboat from the late Walter Ratter who had clearly been highly thought of in that role.

Davie was also a very deliberate man, thoughtful and thorough and sometimes exasperatingly slow to make a decision. He was the head of a big family with a married daughter, Vida, and three intelligent sons, the youngest of whom, Jim, was my oldest pupil in the school. Davie's wife Mima was a true matriarch with an energetic and forceful personality, which I quickly warmed to, not least because she had considerable knowledge of and interest in the bird-life of the island. I was soon aware that my job as a schoolteacher, working daily in their house, was made both easier and more enjoyable because of the presence of both Mima and her unmarried sister Mary, who cooked for both the family and the school. The half-mile walk, or cycle, to the school every morning soon became a routine I looked forward to and enjoyed.

Half a mile to the north of Mornington croft, at the end of a dead straight stretch of gravel road, was the gate into the Ham Toun. At the top of the hill down to the Ham Burn was a branch to the right down to another gate in the fence leading to the nurse's house and Ham Voe. All these roads were at that time made of 'water-bound Macadam'. Historically this had been the best surface possible until the road engineer of that name invented the method of mixing with the gravel the newly imported substance tar, obtained from the tar-pits of Western U.S.A., to make Tarmacadam, or 'Tarmac' for short. There was absolutely no reason to go to the considerable labour and expense of making tarmac roads on Foula when there were only two motorized wheeled vehicles on the island. Harry Gear, the Postmaster, owned them both but only once used his ancient motorbike that I

was aware of during my stay, for an emergency, when the mailboat engine wouldn't start one day and he was summoned, as the mechanical expert of the island, to the pier to help. The other was an equally ancient car, which I never saw and was kept in one of the several sheds at Mogle below the Schoolhouse, hidden away. The story went that advance warning reached Harry's ears one summer that a Customs & Excise man was on his way from Scalloway to check whether there were any cars on Foula without licences. By the time he arrived there was a new peat-stack outside Harry's house, about ten feet long and rather low with a solid roof of 'fells', the cut blocks of turf used to protect the dried peats from the winter rains, thick enough to conceal the hidden centre of the stack. On such occasions, I was told, many a shotgun was hastily stowed under the thatched roof of a lamb-house or byre so that there never appeared to be any need for the overworked taxman to have bothered in the first place.

The Gear family at home in the Schoolhouse. L–R: Mima, Davie (mailboat skipper), Jim (pupil), Andy (home from Aberdeen university), Muriel Gray (sister of Harry, the Postmaster), Mary Henry (unmarried sister)

The straight stretch of road on my way to school every morning went down the long steep hill to the bridge over the Ham Burn and up round the corner past the Post Office outside Mogle, to the Schoolhouse. The only other house I passed was Leraback, which was technically one of the closest to the Manse. There lived another of my elders, Dodie Isbister. His wife Robina, or Binie as she was known, was an expert at growing roses and always had some prize specimens to show me in the summer – just another of the many surprises of my early days. It was she who pointed out to me what she had been told was a Foula speciality in wild flowers, a very pale pink variety of Red Campion which I duly photographed for my collection. The rest of the household were Umphrays, except for Donnie who, as was not uncommon in the island, had been adopted as a youngster and was now a rather rebellious teenager. I could see at once, as indeed many of the islanders acknowledged, that life for the very few young people in such a conservative and elderly community could not be very easy. For instance also living at Leraback was Andrew Umphray, by contrast a very quiet and deliberate character whom I never saw ruffled or inpatient or indeed in any way in a hurry. I can still picture him plodding his way to church, always early as though he never trusted his own slow pace to get him there on time, but as a result one of the few members of my congregation who was never late. The Leraback family worked a number of small fields for hay on either side of the burn at the foot of the steep hill below their house. The house and byre were poised on the edge of the slope, so to make life easier in the summer they had rigged up a simple cable and pulley, by which they hauled the bales of hay across the valley and up to the byre with minimum effort. I soon learnt that this type of ingenuity was typical of the Foula crofter. My early visit to Leraback meant I had now met all three elders of the Kirk in my first week on Foula.

When I opened the school after my first weekend on the island and less than a week after moving in to the Manse, I had met all my pupils informally at their homes; and no doubt they had weighed me up as an individual without the faintest idea what I would be like as a teacher. Any ideas I had dreamt up of what these crofter children would be like on Britain's remotest inhabited island, stuck fifteen miles out into the Atlantic and apparently cut off from all contact with the march of fashion or social change on the mainland, were rapidly dispelled by the five smiling faces and lively characters who sat at their desks in the schoolroom. They very soon showed me that they valued school, and had been well taught by my predecessors. They were of very mixed ability, from very slow to very fast learners, with Mima's son Jim, and more especially her grand-daughter Vina, being amongst the brightest pupils I had ever been privileged to teach. Although the age range from 7 to 11 was, fortuitously for me, not as great as it might have been (even one infant would have doubled my problems) I was quite often able to teach them all together as one class by dint of the fact that the youngest, Vina aged 7, was as bright as a cricket and well able to keep up with the rest. In fact my secret thoughts on this happy situation were along the same lines as my attitude to the whole venture – fancy being paid more than I earned in Edinburgh for living in such a wonderful place with such interesting bird-life, and even more interesting people, to do the things I relish most in life, studying nature at first-hand and enjoying the company of children.

As soon as I got into the routine of term-time, I realised that there just were not enough hours in the day and life was going to be either very frustrating or extremely hectic – or both – if I was going to achieve half what I wanted to. But I always had this daily 'Whoopee!' factor; that glorious sense of elation that things are really going your way and life is hugely worth living, which usually came in two daily doses. First, on arrival at school, the punctual ones would be settling down at their desks, with the usual cheery banter of kids exchanging childish gossip, when the Schoolhouse pair, with only a few yards to come out of one door and into the next, would arrive yawning their heads off as usual but always with a cheerful, if rather guilty, "*Good Morning!*" for their teacher. The second dose came immediately after the last pupil, with homework duly stuffed into a satchel, closed the schoolroom door behind him. Then I would tap on the connecting door through to the Gears' kitchen and be welcomed in to a much-needed cup of tea and a chat before my walk home to the Manse. On a shop day it would be down to the store for some groceries and yet another opportunity to catch up with island news and gossip. In the summer there would be eider ducks in the Voe and noisy oystercatchers down on the beach, and a golden display of marsh marigolds in the burn below the bridge at Ham. By contrast in the winter it would normally be blowing half a gale, making the shelter of kitchen or shop doubly welcome. Then I would have to battle my way along the exposed road at Hamnabrack to the haven of my own kitchen and the glow of the faithful Rayburn stove. How lucky I had been to spot that advertisement in The Scotsman which had so miraculously turned my whole life upside down, to my great advantage!

Chapter 6: Early Exploits with Birds and Children

I had arrived on 21st April and opened the school on the 27th. My first Monday on 26th April saw me starting a weekly routine, on which I had been well briefed before arrival, the delivery to the pier first thing every Monday morning of a stout wooden box with a rope handle. This was my boat box, which I had inherited from the Chedburns, and inside it was my food order for A. & K. Reid, the grocers in Walls who supplied so much of the islanders needs through their weekly orders brought across on the *Island Lass*. The weather was fine and dry that day – in fact the whole island was remarkably dry that spring – and the mailboat went out on time and came back later in the day with a further load of my luggage, and my boat box. These visits to the Voe gave me an opportunity to inspect the possibilities for the first phase of my establishment of a bird trapping station, where Ken Williamson had suggested to me might be the most promising sheltered haven for tired migrants arriving in the autumn. My ornithological diary records the detail:

26th April *First proper look at Ham garden, which looks quite the most promising place for a Heligoland trap. It contained 4 Redwings, some House Sparrows and Starlings, a Blackbird and one or two Twite. Snipe were heard drumming at dusk again; had first noticed a few nights back that this is a very prominent feature of the evening, with many birds taking part and the birds on the ground answering those drumming overhead.*

On returning home about 7.00 p.m., a Black Redstart was sitting on the fence of the hen-run. It seemed attached to the building so that when I returned at 10.00 p.m. with another heavy load of luggage brought in by the boat today and dumped it on the doorstep, I wasn't really surprised to hear it flutter out onto the roof above my head. It went to roost again behind a drainpipe where it was caught with the aid of my beret, duly ringed and placed in the porch for the night. First blood – with my nets and traps not yet unpacked.

29th April *Little seen the last day or two during my first week at school, and with generally anti-cyclonic weather and good visibility. (Migrants occur more often in overcast or wet weather when they are more likely to be disoriented and lost over the sea.) Redwings still about in the Ham area. Up on the moor by the peat-banks tonight, saw four Arctic Skuas together flying over their future nesting territory. The Bonxies are already on the same ground but no fights or display seen between the two species. Bonxies are now proceeding all and every day from the sea up to the hills and have been seen in two lowland localities, Sukkimires and just south of the Manse where one pair at least seem well established and in display. South Biggins described a bird which must have been a Reed Bunting and his mate. They also described a Water-rail caught recently and released again. There are obviously several in the drainage ditches in the Hame Toun.*

Reading between the lines, thanks to the sunny spell of weather I had managed to wheel most of my belongings to the Manse and also fetched my first load of dry peats home after school from the peat banks allocated to the Manse up on the Lioag. This was a stretch of road beyond the gate out of the Ham Toun to the north of the school, from which one got a wide view across the moor to the east, a favourite area for Arctic Skuas to nest. The Great Skuas always arrived first in spring, returning from their winter quarters as far south as West Africa, often as much as a month before the 'Alans' which was the name the islanders gave to the Arctic Skuas. (This species was originally called Alan Richardson's Skua after the man who first identified and named them.) This early arrival gave the Bonxies a flying start over their rivals and any which had already established territories on the lower ground tried to hold it by chasing the smaller, more agile skuas off in noisy and violent aerial chases. Some of the crofters knew to the exact date when to expect their Arctic Skuas back in the spring. At Leraback the resident pair used to perch on the chimneys all through the summer from 15th May, a fixed date so that it was a cause of great concern if they were a day late. Most of the Bonxies nested up on the higher ground where the Alans couldn't compete with such numbers of established birds. But generally about two hundred pairs of Arctic

The Leraback 'Alan' – a semi-domesticated dark-phase Arctic Skua, reputed to have been hand-reared and fed daily with fish by John Henry on his way home from school. It left with the other skuas for the winter but returned every spring to perch on the Leraback lum and usually nested nearby

Skuas held their own eventually over most of the lower moors. They were nearly all sooty brown birds, the 'dark phase' of a dimorphic species. The occasional light phase bird was a much more handsome creature with creamy white underparts contrasting with its dark wings and back, and its white neck and cheeks topped by a smart dark brown cap.

I also deduce from my diary that I had started the daily routine of collecting young Eric from his home at South Biggins and taking him back in the afternoon. It soon became clear that though a little shy and nervous after so long an absence from school, and with a certain diffidence among the other children at the start, he soon settled in and was clearly a quick learner and an artist with considerable skills. His favourite subject for his drawings was the boats he observed through his grandfather's telescope from the South Biggins dyke. When it was quite clear to everybody that all of us at the school were free of 'the cold' and there was no immediate risk of infection, and that he had recovered his confidence, I was able to arrange that he should come on his own to my house and we would then walk together to school in the mornings. His bright chatter and detailed knowledge of all sorts of natural features lightened the start of my day and this rapport helped to restore his confidence that he was a normal part of our school. All the children were experts on the subject of living on a remote island and knowing how to survive in a difficult environment. I soon realised that in that respect I too was a beginner. My education in insularity was just starting.

The 29th of April was my 27th birthday. I had been promised a cake from home, for the rituals of birthdays were always important in our family. On the strength of this I had, some days earlier, invited all the pupils to a birthday tea in the Manse after school on the day. But when the mail arrived on the 26th, alas no cake. I described in the thank-you letter I wrote home after the event, what the result of this was:

> *I invited all the school, all five of them, up to the Manse thinking that one of the many parcels that arrived by the first boat after the one I came on, was sure to be the promised birthday cake. But it didn't arrive until the week later so they had to be content with chocolate 'crispy-cakes' (strictly homemade and a howling success), scones, chocolate biscuits, and tinned pine-apple and orange jelly, all of which went down in remarkably quick time. Of course when the cake came they all had to get a slice each and I had no end of volunteers to help wheel my peats home or carry my parcels from the post office until it was finished. It deserved it all of course. It was a really magnificent effort.*

Looking back on that occasion it seems remarkable that so soon after my arrival I enjoyed a birthday celebration as much as I would have done in the time-honoured way at home. It says a great deal about the kindly welcome I received from all my neighbours. The catalyst was of course the children who invariably love a party and who can be guaranteed, especially on an island where luxuries and sweets were fairly rare, to love anything which indulges a sweet tooth. I soon found on Foula that both the teacher-pupil relationship and the adult-child relationship can be modified without risk to allow a much closer bond than in more crowded and formal situations. A clear example of this occurred on the 1st May, a Saturday and my first opportunity to spend some time exploring the island. When discussing this at his home, it was clear that 11-year-old Jim Gear was only too keen to offer his services as my guide and mentor. He was a great talker and brim full of confidence and I reckoned it would greatly enhance my day to have his company. Luckily for me his parents agreed. I was not disappointed, though I found it quite difficult to stem the flood of information, stories, history, place names, and good island gossip, so that just occasionally we could savour the peace and quiet of our surroundings. It was for me a momentous day, seeing for the first time what must rank as one of the finest cliff seascapes in Britain, which I now know to be second only to St Kilda. It was a privilege to be there and to marvel at the scale of it all. To have an 11-year-old guide who knew it all as though it was his, was the better part of the privilege.

The record of the day in my bird diary reads as follows:

1st May A round tour of the island with Jim Gear started at mid-day. We covered most of the North end and west cliffs. A single Greylag goose near Springs has apparently been there since autumn. Mrs Beagrie who has kept her tame geese there seemed to know of it and although she disclaims ownership it clearly has domestic connections. Although only one Arctic Skua was seen all day the Bonxies are now well established on the breeding grounds. These include some apparently also used by the Arctics later, several pairs being seen near Lumieshedden as well as at least one pair South of the Kirk.

Elsewhere Bonxies were on the breeding grounds everywhere. Display was seen on the ground and in the air all day. Coition was observed in 4 pairs. Most pairs seemed tied to territory but there was no aggressive behaviour at all towards us as yet. Few birds seen not in pairs though occasional single birds still well settled onto a particular territory and would return to it when disturbed. Plumage seems to be extremely variable with all shades from dark to sandy brown. Several darker on the crown. No juveniles distinguished as yet, all birds seeming to be well streaked. One semi-albino bird seen on Brustins had

secondaries on the right wing completely, and on the left wing partly, white. It was a particularly pale bird, sandy brown on the back and mantle with a dark crown. Jim says it is an old inhabitant though not usually on this part of the moor. Nests were found in several places but no eggs yet. The scrapes were well defined and obvious, often marked by the droppings around them.

At Selchie Geo the kittiwake colony, confined to the lower strata, was well occupied but there are clearly not many birds now compared to the accounts given by all the inhabitants of the thousands of Kittiwakes which used to bathe in the Mill Loch and elsewhere. These are about the first I have seen since coming to the island. A few hundred pairs here perhaps, all on nests but no evidence of eggs yet. Guillemots in fair numbers there too and half a dozen pairs of Razorbills. Puffins all up the cliff-tops from there to the Kame which was our next climb, but again not showing signs of nesting yet except the ones at their burrows on the Little Kame. Numbers of these as of Fulmars will be hard to estimate. The latter are everywhere and many were seen prospecting the slopes inland at Selchie Geo (i.e. Soberlie) and Hamnafield where they have been displaying noisily since I arrived. Many seem to be attached to ruined crofts but most fly round the stony slopes. Every corner of the cliffs seems to be occupied, including one pair at the very top of the Kame 1220 ft above the sea. One wren at Soberlie in the wall above the ruins of Logat. It was singing and clearly in territory. Three Snow Buntings up on the Kame. Total population of wheatears remarkably small for the time of year with only 6 or so seen all day.

2nd May First distinct increase in wheatears. Sunday, so not much time for observation. One Arctic Skua seen s. of the Kirk.

3rd May First signs of movement. A House Martin round the house first thing this morning.

It seems to me rather sad now that, because of shortage of time, my diary keeping was restricted to a factual record of ornithological observations. We had covered a lot of ground on that Saturday afternoon. Setting off from the Schoolhouse, the route up the east coastline would anywhere else be a beauty-spot, with the tide flowing past the sloping rocks cut by deep fissures where the storms have forced their way in over millions of years. Just north of Ham Voe are three well-known blow-holes where caves at the tideline end in gaping cracks. At low tide the water laps on hidden beaches of boulders far below, where sometimes one can hear the rumble of stones and the rhythm of the swell. On another day of a fresh south-easterly with white water rushing into every cavern and often up onto the jagged rockfaces, the underground caves fill rapidly with water, compressing the trapped air in the roof with unbelievable force so that it erupts like a Yellowstone geyser in a dramatic spout, not of steam, but of tortured seawater, which emerges as a roaring, hissing monster of white spray some fifty yards inland of the sea's edge below. It is tempting to get close to enrich the experience of the power of the monster, but as the most spectacular displays are always in an onshore breeze, one can only do so at the risk of getting soaked by a cloud of airborne spray which drives inland in gale conditions, disappearing over the moor like horizontal salt rain.

There were two ruined crofts to the north of Ham Voe: Veedal and Sloag. On a later occasion I explored the derelict house at Sloag where the last inhabitant had been found lying dead on his potato patch, felled by a merciful heart attack as he worked. Only the weather had touched his house in the interim, but much of the roof was still intact and many of his possessions, like a pair of boots and his Bible, were still in place where he had left them. I rejoiced for him that he had ended his life busy on the tasks of subsistence crofting so as to be a burden to nobody. But I was sad that no-one else had been willing to follow and to take advantage of those simple pleasures he seemed to have enjoyed. It was one of the few occasions, due to the circumstances of his unwitnessed death, when the police arrived in Foula to investigate and report on the event. It was of course a non-event, in official terms death from natural causes, the end of seventy years of honest toil at little cost to society or his family. I had many long thoughts on this later in my stay on Foula, where I could not escape from the impression that life – and death – there were, in a fundamental way, better than in the sophisticated and expensive procedures of so-called civilized life, where there was far more anguish and pain than in the simple ways and traditions of the Foula community.

I got only a whiff of these sentiments on that tour of the island with Jim. Not that he wasn't a mine of information about the old folk and such recent events as he had been old enough to remember, but his remit was to show me the best bird-life on our route and I didn't divert him from it. Mima, his mother, had told me what to expect and to look for. There were plenty of fulmars

already occupying any rocky outcrop where they could occupy a ledge and lay an egg. There were 'galores of shags' as Mima would have put it in her colourful way of rendering 'shags galore', sleek greeny-black birds busy gathering great piles of driftwood or wrack into untidy nests out on rocks safe from interference by us. Every now and then a whole line of them, decorating a skerry or the edge of a geo, would panic on our approach and fly down onto a patch of green swirl, diving on contact with the water and disappearing from sight, leaving rings of white in the water, their emergency reaction to panic to lighten their load and speed their getaway. All was patterns where the sea, spun by the tide-race into whorls of bubbled water, was suddenly graced by the shapes of shags emerging from below to spin and pirouette on the surface like a troupe of dancers. North of Taing Head we came to a bay of broken rocks and skerries and a short promontory called the Stack of the Gaads. At the top of the cliffs where the turf was green and close-cropped by the sheep, was a hidden depression, almost a cave but still open to the sky. We scrambled through it at Jim's insistence for he was anxious to explain to me the history of 'The Byre of the Gaads', a place where tradition had it that in far-off times, probably when the Vikings were exploring the Shetland coast looking for sites for settlement, the islanders would drive their cattle in haste from the Toun up to this hidden haven. There their animals could all be invisible from the sea and far enough away from any landing place to be reasonably safe.

Further on at Ruscar there was a huge outcrop of old red sandstone, much smoothed by the sea compared with the tougher dark rocks of volcanic origin, hence the name meaning Red Scar. Here we were to look out for terns but it was too early in the year so far north and there were none to be seen. Knowing how many tern colonies in the south had often been raided in May for their delicious eggs, I suspected that this was a place where women with baskets would probably come in due course. Jim almost certainly knew by this time from my conversations with his mother in the Schoolhouse kitchen that I was a member of the RSPB, the Royal Society for the Protection of Birds, whose considerable influence on public opinion had finally achieved its peak of success in the Bird Protection Act of 1954, now awaiting the Royal signature and about to become law. He was coy about discussing such delicate topics but I seem to remember that he knew all the arguments about the rights of crofters to take eggs provided they did so early enough in the season to allow for a successful hatch later on. He did me a good turn here, enabling me to rehearse the rather difficult task of putting the ethical case for upholding this law in the wider interest of birds as a whole. However it was hard, even with one of my pupils, to find a solid case for arguing that on Foula it really mattered. The usual argument that exceptions to the law were dangerous for setting a precedent to others less responsible or more exploitative, would hardly cut much ice in a place where I was perhaps the only purist who would know it was happening anyway. There was no crime on Foula. Yet I smelt trouble ahead.

Beyond Ruscar we came to Stremness – a typical Norse name meaning 'the nose where the tide-race runs'. It was indeed a place of fast-flowing currents and a tremendous show of colours on a sunny day. The water was deep and a rich mixture of blue, azure and turquoise as it swirled between the rock stacks of banded rock, whitened by foam and patterned with miniature whirlpools and eddies. There was red rock interlayered with black, and black cliffs banded with streaks of red, all evidence of the huge upsurge

'The Byre of the Gaads' – a deep cleft in the cliff-top north of Ham Voe, where reputedly cattle could be concealed from Viking raiders

'The Gaada Stack', perhaps the best known rock arch in Shetland

of land which had forced the old red sandstone up to form an island from the steeply inclined sedimentary layers, and then massive volcanic activity which had interleaved it with lava flows. What chaos was recorded there! And then to the west what endless centuries of ordered weathering of that chaotic jumble to create at Wurr Wick a north-facing bay of huge rounded stones, worn down by countless millions of tides into a long boulder beach which ended with Foula's showpiece,

the stacks of The Ness. Of these the Gaada Stack, a giant three-legged stool of rock, supporting a massive tabletop weighing thousands of tons, is the classic goal of all photographers. Some, like Colin Baxter, have at last found the right spot, with infinite patience and planning, to catch the orb of the setting sun framed in the archway. Magnificent! It takes a very single-minded photographer to be both in the right place and at the right moment.

A unique nesting place for a pair of Fulmars at the summit of the Kame, 1220 feet above sea level

And yet the great thing about Foula is that when one approaches the west cliffs, as we did, from Wurr Wick and the sad ruins of the three North end crofts, Ristie, Freyers and Springs, marveling at the scale of these huge stacks still defying the elements in such violent waters, one then has to climb steadily and steeply up Soberlie Hill, above Kittiwakes Haa' and the East Hoevdi, along a steadily rising line of rock to the summit at the start of the North Bank. Now a glance back to where one has climbed from, and the aerial view of the stacks reduces them to their proper scale in this landscape, mere dwarfs like tiny excrescences from a rocky shore, lying far below like little models of rock structures. For this is the landscape of the longest wall of vertical rock, two miles from N.E to S.W., and the second highest vertical, or near vertical, cliff face in the United Kingdom. The North Bank runs from Soberlie to the start of the climb up to the Kame for over three quarters of a mile at between 700 and 725 feet. Then it rises sharply up to the summit of the Kame at 1220 feet before descending in a series of dramatic curves and fearful overhangs, a further mile down to the western extremity of the island at Wester Hoevdi, which is a mere 500 ft. vertical drop. If you have never walked this cliff edge and felt for almost every step of two miles the strange seductive sensation that just one false step could be one's last, that one is walking a tightrope of death at the edge of suicide, then you have never lived. You have still to experience one of the most tingling and terrifying and inspiring situations that any reasonably fit mortal can experience in Scotland.

The Foula hills from Northveedal. L–R: Hamnafield, Brustins, the Sneug, the Kame

It is one of several 'mountain top' experiences which is truly numinous.

Jim and I ran out of time that day, for as his teacher I was already fighting a battle all Foula teachers have faced or will face; the struggle to get their pupils to go to bed in good time. One of my first shocks had been to find my pupils still up about the house at ten, eleven o'clock or even midnight before a normal school day; *"Oh I know, Mr Mylne, we ought to get them to bed earlier. Yes, of course they need their sleep. We really must try to persuade them to go up earlier."* But old habits die hard, the summer nights are never really dark and full daylight lasts till almost eleven o'clock for several months in mid-summer. And then the excuses run out in autumn and even more so in winter, but still they yawned their way through afternoon school and were often half asleep when they arrived in the morning. So as a newcomer to this particular problem of island life, I was determined that I myself should do nothing to further the habit. I would get Jim home at a reasonable hour and when we

reached my main goal for the day, the summit of the Kame, we set foot across the hills for home. We had a mile and a half to walk through Bonxie territories, down past the Flick Lochs, and through the great valley of Netherfandal to meet the road at Peter Gray's crofthouse, Burns. From there it was another half mile back to the Schoolhouse and the supper that was waiting for us. What with all the chat and my exchanges with Mima on half a dozen topics of birdy interest, it was getting late, almost dark, before I set off for home. I noticed yet again that the children, including my indefatigable guide, were still up, draped round the furniture or half sleeping in a chair, but beyond my jurisdiction. I stored up what I would say for another day. I had to admit to being well pleased with our exploration of the north half of my new island home. And I had achieved an ambition – I had seen at close quarters a fulmar nesting on a rock ledge 1200 ft above sea-level, while other members of his tribe were scarcely visible, circling like tiny white dots against the marbled sea far below.

Chapter 7: Writing Home

I had always been a good letter-writer from my schooldays onwards. When I first went to boarding school at the age of eight I was very distressed at this abrupt separation from my mother. Looking back now at her situation, suffering the bereavement when my infant brother Robin died just before I was born, so that I was the precious baby who replaced him, it is not surprising that she over protected me. Her separation from me was probably a worse trial for her than my homesickness was to me. At any rate from that first tearful letter written in my spidery childish hand-writing, my mother had a habit of keeping my letters, whatever their content. The ones I still have, like that very first one, are a far better aide memoir now than photographs, for they convey so much that is essentially personal and heartfelt. Some of them I wish I still had, like letters from my army days, when out of barrack-room boredom I often had plenty of spare time and the incentive to fill it, giving the family as graphic an account of service life as I could. On other occasions, like our expeditions to Norway studying bird migration in the 1950s, life was altogether too active and hectic to find the time to write letters. As a result I have forgotten much of the detail of those exciting times, though by then I was taking plenty of photographs, which I now have as a visual reminder. But fortunately for me my mother, who was undoubtedly more concerned than she need have been over my departure to Foula, religiously kept all my letters home from that period. I admit she had one particular reason to feel concerned for my safety. A short time after my departure, Michael Powell's film 'The Edge of the World' came to an Edinburgh cinema, and she went to see it to discover the nature of this place to which her son had exiled himself. There is a storm scene in the film in which the island mailboat is smashed to pieces on the rocks, which apparently convinced her that she would be lucky if I ever returned alive from such a violent place. My letters, therefore, might well be her best memoir of a foolhardy son, and so they were carefully preserved in her bottom drawer.

I wore out several typewriter ribbons battering out letters from Foula on my trusty old Oliver. I have never learnt touch-typing to this day, but from early days I could type far faster than I could write by hand,

and besides, typing allowed me to do a carbon copy for friends. So I now have a pile of typewritten sheets headed 'The Manse, Foula, by Lerwick, Shetland', which convey my first impressions and the actual feelings I had at the time far better than I could ever have described them from memory. They represent more truthfully the impact Foula made on me than any description I might now attempt in language moulded by my more considered attitude over fifty years later. And they reveal perhaps something of the sense of excitement at the newness of it all and the joy of working in such invigorating surroundings. It is not, alas, very polished writing; often rather hurried and badly phrased, but it has the merit of immediacy though inevitably also revealing my inexperience. Reading them now I am quite surprised at my emphasis on the pressures of my double job, and the sense of never having enough time, especially the pressure of that continuing deadline of the departure of the mails only once a week on 'Monday at 10.20' – the time on the notice in the Post Office window under the heading 'Collection'. I suppose it was one of the major changes in my life. Instead of an urban postbox with two or three times for 'Collection' every day, and in addition the accepted convenience of the telephone, I was now in a quite different world. Just how badly this upset my normal routines was evident from the frequent reference to the time of writing as after midnight. And with the marked difference in day-length so far north, this meant that it was often long after dawn when my letter-writing had to stop from sheer exhaustion at three or four in the morning in the broad light of the next day.

Considering how narrow the scope of my diary was, little more than a semi-professional ornithologist's log of his daily observations on the breeding birds and, in the appropriate seasons, the migrants, it is a good thing that fifty years on I still have the letters I had such a strong compulsion to fit into my crowded timetable. Certainly the very first ones in May 1954 give, I think, a good representation of my reaction to the newness of it all. Hopefully my frustration at the lack of time to fit in letter-writing as well as everything else can be kept in proportion, for I am sure now that my sense of adventure and anticipation of an exciting and worthwhile venture is the correct basis of all my memories of that period. Two points are worth emphasizing; the exceptional weather of that dry spring was a complete surprise to me and quite contrary to the dire predictions I had been given about Shetland weather; and my family knew only too well my addiction to ornithology and would not have expected me to do anything other than give it the priority that is evident right from the start.

The Manse, Foula, by Lerwick, Shetland
16th May '54

Dear All,

I had hoped this week to make up for the omissions of the past two by getting off a decent epistle to you all, but so long as this dry weather continues there is little chance for letter writing. Mail once a week is rather frightening when one gets about twenty-five letters all at once almost all calling for a reply. I have got 16 replies off today already, some of which simply couldn't wait and I'm afraid the family has had to wait till last. And now it's long past midnight. The reason for this shortage of time is not hard to seek. The weather has been wonderful, cold perhaps but unusually dry for the time of year and on some days quite warm too. Everyone here finds the same thing that when the weather is fine there is far too much to do. And they don't have the bulk of their day taken up in school and the birds to be recorded out of school.

But if it is a busy life, it is also a very pleasant one. In the first place the people are so warmhearted and friendly even though they are a bit shy of strangers and sometimes keep rather queer houses. Also the children are a delightful lot, with some real talent as well as some pretty thick heads. But they are willing and interested and like all children full of life and enthusiasm. And the birds are coming fully up to expectations. This last week saw some really good migration weather and of course when one is living in a place where almost anything might and does crop up at any time, it is criminal to be indoors when one could be out. And it is not difficult to find other excuses too for being out and about. First there is the old lady at the south end who has just lost her old sister to the hospital on the mainland and is feeling very lonely being without her company for the first time in her life. Then there is the old lady at the North end (about two miles away) who lives in a little one-roomed house all by herself and reads a great deal, but can't now get down for her own library books.

And of course there is a large garden outside here waiting to be dug and planted – it is half dug now but no seeds in yet – and stacks of peat on the peat banks a mile away waiting to be barrowed home. I usually take my barrow down to school with me and then return home with a load on my way back. There is peat to be dug too and the season for it coming up now so that the peats can get a chance to dry off before being stacked for the winter. I am hoping to get some of this work done for me this year, as it is a job which more or less has to be done during school term. But the great problem here is the shortage of man-power as all the able-bodied are fully employed in keeping the old folks supplied, and if one wants anything done one has to do it oneself. And they do too. They grow their own food, make many of their own clothes, make their own shoes, houses, gates, boats, barrows, and so on. And when someone like myself wants a plumbing repair, or a bird trap built, or his hair cut, or a tooth pulled out, you just have to do it yourself or go to your next-door neighbour for help. I'm lucky there as my neighbours are incomers like myself. They came in 7 years ago but they are still incomers and we talk about 'the islanders' and 'ourselves' as different people. But Mrs. Beagrie, who is real Aberdeen and no mistake, keeps cows so that I get good fresh milk every day, as much manure for my garden as I can take away, and after she has baked at the weekend a parcel of scones and oatcakes left on my kitchen table. I also get my spuds from her. I live in fact right in the middle of her croft with the little strip fields all round my garden fence which surrounds the house. The main road of the island runs through the middle of the croft and right past my house. The traffic of course is not very heavy – about ten wheel barrows a day and a pony cart belonging to the shop-keeper once a week. But even this tends to take up a lot of time for everyone that comes past has to stop for a chat if you are outside within reach. And a chat in Foula may only be one of three or four in the day for some folk, so they make it a good one while they are at it. Ploughing and digging are in full swing just now and so everyone is very busy. They all turn out into the fields especially when the communal (two-wheeled) tractor comes round their way. There's an old lady of 73 who wheels her own peats home from the hillside opposite every day, up the steep little hill which separates this little valley from the big crofting area at the south end. There is an old boy of 84 who comes past on shop nights (5 days a week from 6 to 9 in the digging season) wheeling his barrow back to his black house – the last on the island – a good mile from the shop.

Still I mustn't ramble on about the islanders, and I mustn't start on the birds either or I shall be here all night. I have seen 78 species since I arrived including three new ones for me and 30 new ones for Foula. The resident breeding birds are fascinating especially the skuas which wheel overhead all day long, but at this season the migrants provide fresh surprises every day as well. I have started trapping with a little box trap and have caught 4 birds so far, including a Black Redstart which I caught in my beret when I found it roosting in my front porch one night before I had even unpacked my nets.

(Following my birthday I sent thanks to the family for various presents recently received, which included, significantly, an alarm-clock from my mother, anxious, I presumed, that I should never be late for school in the mornings.)

The alarm clock wakes me every morning, Mum, and though I frequently curse it soundly I bless it in my better moments. I shall certainly need to set it for tomorrow as it is getting very late now and my typing is beginning to show signs of sleepiness. And then of course the birthday cake was the crowning achievement for which very many thanks to maker and icer. It did me goodness knows how many meals and late night snacks.

(Here followed the description of my birthday party I have already quoted in Chapter 6.)

Well I really must go to bed. Thanks for all your letters and I hope you all manage to see this one in due course. But don't expect me to be a good correspondent in a place like this until we get some wet weather. It's just been too good so far.

All my love
Chris

The theme continued in a much shorter letter written by hand on 30th May, showing that I was really taking a long time to get used to an apparently endless anti-cyclone:

The Manse, Foula, by Lerwick, Shetland
May 30th '54

Dear All,

If only we could get some wet weather! The mailboat didn't get out till Thursday last week with the S.E. wind, but I still didn't get any letters written except the essential ones about the school register, school meals, orders to the grocer etc. Now it seems likely it will go tomorrow – or rather today as it's now well past midnight. So I'm writing to say that whenever you hear 'thundery showers' or 'cloudy weather' over Scotland in the forecasts, we in Foula bask in glorious sunshine. Actually it's seldom very warm as there is always a sea-breeze, but yesterday was a scorcher and I dug at my peat-bank with my shirt off and still sweltered. Today a cold sea-fog came rolling in, in banks, and shut off the sun for half the day. But with two services to prepare and take (and good attendances at both) and a message that I had caught two birds in my little box trap in between the services – a Common Whitethroat and a Lesser Whitethroat, both at once! – and then a meal with the skipper's family at 3 o'clock, and then my own supper to cook tonight, the day has flown past and caught me with all my letters unanswered as usual at the end of another week. I seem to have done such a lot that I daren't now start writing about it or I'll never get to bed. The daily business of running a school, keeping track of the birds, fetching the peats, feeding the hens, and talking to everybody seems to fill all the time. And when one has the choice of sitting indoors or going up the hill to the Great Skuas breeding ground or out fishing off the cliffs in a boat, or hunting the Manx Shearwaters at the south end – well which would you do? Don't forget that no news is good news. And one day perhaps we'll get a wet day when I just have to stay in and write.

Love to all
Chris

P.S. It will soon be dawn so I must get to bed before it gets light or it won't seem right at all.

The next letter, dated 1st June, six weeks after my arrival, attempted to beat the problem of cramming everything into the night before the mailboat by turning the letter into a diary of events, written in stages. This not only appeared to offer more time and so spun out the contents but still failed to beat the unreliability of the boat crossings. I started it on Tuesday 1st, added to it on the 2nd and 3rd, tried to complete it on Sunday 6th ready for the Monday boat, but that didn't go because the wind was S.E. so I had to add a postscript on Wednesday 9th, "hopeful for a mailday" on the 10th. It clearly wasn't as the letter was not delivered in Edinburgh until the 16th, having taken over a fortnight to achieve a crossing to

Walls. But it does reveal how my daily life was working out and how I was dividing my time between school, church and visits to the crofts, with some leisure time for bird-watching and recording:

The Manse, Foula, by Lerwick, Shetland
1 June 1954

Dear Family,

As I have failed so badly in the last week or two to get my letters written in time for the mail boat, I am going to try this week starting early and writing a short bit each day. I have to sit down every night to make up my Migration Schedule anyway, to keep a record of the birds seen each day, so I will try to give you my news as I go along by simply an extra few minutes to my nightly book- work. Today should be fairly easy as I intend to go to bed early for a change and there is little to record ornithologically. It has in fact been a very typical day here both with the weather and also in the way I have spent my time. It has been bright but chilly with a fresh north wind. I don't know when one casts clouts in these parts but one always has to be prepared to put them on again. Last Saturday it was a perfect day with a sun temperature of 82 and the shade reading well in the 60s. And then comes a sea-breeze and although it is just as bright and sunny, the air is always cold. However it has been very dry lately, so much so that I had to water my seeds the other day and everyone is hoping for some rain. Things still seem to grow however, partly I suppose because of the long hours of daylight. It is now 10.40 p.m. and I am writing away in the study with no light and no need for one till after 11. The other night I went to bed just before one in the morning after being out fishing with my next-door neighbour's two boys, and could read – with a little difficulty – in bed!

To return to today's activities. I got off to a very virtuous start by leaving for school at 9.15 with all the jobs done before I went; hens fed, their food prepared for the next few days, breakfast (usually flakes, bread and marmalade with tea or coffee) cleared and washed up, boots oiled, bed made and in time to wheel my barrow down for a load of peats on the way home instead of taking the bike. One of my pupils who lives a mile from school at the south end of the island calls in every day on his way as he has to pass my house; and I go down, with him for company, the half-mile over the hill from here to the Schoolhouse.

From 9.30 till 3.30 are the official school hours. I give them a half-hour break before their cocoa at 11.15 when we take some sort of exercise as well, either skipping (which, incidentally, I had to teach them) or going down the burn to the harbour to look for any new birds in the gardens in the valley, and we have an hour for lunch. This is cooked by one of the good ladies of the family which rents the Schoolhouse from me, who is an excellent cook and most obliging. I decide the menu – or rather the children do, as we have one day of the week each – and look after all the food supplies. After school I often have to stay for a while to make up records, prepare work for the next day, etc. but I usually try to get away by 4.00 p.m. Although this seems very early in the day to be free, there are so many other things still to be done that I don't like to be any later if I can help it. Today I had tea with the school-house folk. The man of the house is the skipper of the mail-boat and I had to discuss with him the transport across from Walls in a fortnight's time of the annual school inspection party consisting of the Director of Education for Shetland, The County Architect, his Master of Works, the Nursing Superintendent, The Medical Officer, two members of the local education Committee and anyone else who can make it an excuse for a day trip to this seldom-visited island to share out the expenses. Panic stations on June 14th! As a result of this and having gossiped as long as one usually does when visiting anyone's house here, I got away at 5.00 with my barrow to the peat bank. This is just beyond the school so that it takes me about 20 minutes to go up, load up my barrow and return and then another 15 minutes or so to wheel the load home. I bring back about four loads a week usually, which at this time of year is far more than I burn so that I am now getting a fair-sized stack built at the back of the house in readiness for the winter. I want to get a complete stock laid in here for the winter months before the bad weather starts and this should not be hard at the present rate of progress. Being out most of the day I burn far less than most people and less than my predecessors who were a married couple with a child. Many houses here have a fire on the hearth every day of the year. The difficulty of dealing with my own peats has, I am glad to say, been greatly over emphasised by everybody. It is by the way excellent fuel with as good a heat as coal though of course it burns away much faster. Anyway my predecessor has left me a very good supply of peats cut and stacked on the peat-banks and it would not really matter if I didn't cut any more this year at all.

Anyway I got home about 6.30 p.m. eventually, after stopping to watch the Great Skuas bathing in the loch at the foot of the hill, and spent the rest of the evening stacking peat, building a protecting wall round the stack against the winter gales, unpacking my week's supplies and reading my week's mail (which came in by the boat yesterday), making and eating supper, consisting of fresh piltock, (alias coalfish or saithe,) steamed with fried potatoes and a fried skua's egg, brown bread and butter and treacle, and a slice of fruit cake from the island shop. Having done all that it was time to listen to the news, read the Shetland newspaper and finally make up my records and write to you. This last process was supposed to be only a few words but as you can see it has already kept me far too long, so I must stop and get to my bed.

Wednesday A perfect still evening, cloudy but quite windless which as you might imagine is not usual here. The Mill Loch, which lies about 500 yards from the house down in the valley under the steep slope of Hamnafield (1126 ft.), was like a sheet of glass tonight, the reflection only broken by a Great Skua landing beside a Fulmar Petrel. I was down with one of my pupils looking for Sundew flowers. We had a programme on the wireless the other day (Nature Study for Schools, which we listen to every week) and it was all about insect-eating plants. We have now found both sundew and butterwort out on the moors. But we don't do so well when they start talking about trees. There are currant bushes, brambles and one or two stunted sycamores but that is all. Needless to say these are growing in the one sheltered spot in the valley which runs down to the harbour, where I hope eventually to build my Heligoland trap ready for the autumn migration.

Weather-wise not a very exciting day. A very flat sea but misty and the Shetland coast hidden all day. I had an early breakfast and cycled down to the south end at 8.30 for a quick look round before going back to school. It's wonderful living in a place where one can go for a walk with as much chance of seeing interesting birds as on the Isle of May or other places where one usually thinks oneself lucky to be for a few days in the year. Today I saw a short-eared owl being mobbed by the lapwings and a white-throat on a fence, before picking up the boy who lives down there and escorting him back to school with me. Of course

one sees Arctic and Great Skuas everywhere one goes and there is an Arctic Skua's nest within 200 yards of my front door. After a bit one gets tired of them – well used to them should we say. One could never tire of the wonderful aerial chases of the skuas over their breeding grounds or the strange greeting calls of the Bonxies (alias Great Skuas) as they meet in flight, or especially at their bathing parties in the loch. At this stage with the birds all starting to sit on their eggs the unemployed gather there every day and there are often up to a hundred Bonxies on the loch when I come back from school. This wasn't till 5 p.m. today as I was making out my requisition of school materials for next year, so that by the time I had fetched my peat and got home it was 7 and suppertime. I meant to mention that one of the highlights of yesterday was the trapping of two Garden Warblers at mid-morning break. This evening I caught a starling on her nest when looking to see whether her young ones were ready to ring. There are three nests in the stone dyke of this croft within 20 yards of each other, such is the housing shortage for such species.

One of the best bits of news this week was a letter from Pat McLeod to say that she is coming to stay here with a friend later this month. She had planned this before she heard I was coming here and this has fitted in surprisingly well with her plans. She has just left her job at Springfield, I gather, and is taking a holiday between jobs. I don't know what the islanders will think but I could scarcely not offer her hospitality when they were so good to me at the Lodge when I stayed there, and anyway they will be much more comfortable here than at one of the crofts. In one way in particular I am pleased she is coming, and that is that she will be able to give you all a first-hand account of the place on her return which will save me feeling I have got to put it all down on paper. This as you can see is a more or less endless process when there is so much to tell you about so many things. However at this moment bed calls, so you will have to take your luck in competition with all the other letters that are to be written before next Monday's boat.

P.S. I see in this week's Shetland News that the Secretary of State has approved all the applications by Shetland Education Committee for extra payment for teachers in the remotest schools, so it looks as though I shall be getting all the normal remote school payments plus a bit extra for being out here. No complaints!

Thursday *I've got the Tilley lamp on tonight, partly because it's rather later than usual and also because it is a very misty night and not as light as usual. It's been a queer day with a light west breeze coming over the top of the hills and leaving them coated with a thin layer of cloud like icing sugar. At 4.00 when I left school this was so attractive that I tried to find a place from which to photograph it but found this more difficult than I had thought as the sun was shining directly through the mist. I went to the bottom of the hill but then found that the mist above me obscured the view. The trouble here is that one wants to photograph almost every scene one sees. I carry the camera about with me quite a lot and have taken one colour and one ordinary spool so far. When I get them processed they will tell you far more about the place than anything I can say in words.*

In my wanderings to take photos I found five broods of young starlings which were duly ringed. The nesting season is at its height and I could spend all my spare time simply going round hunting for nests, ringing young birds and taking note of the progress of the many nests I have found so far. When I went over to get my peat today the Arctic Skuas were all doing their injury-feigning tricks to lead me from the eggs, sprawling along the ground with their wings spread making a terrible noise like a child crying. I looked at an eider ducks nest and was shown another by one of the crofters, both birds sitting till one got within a few feet and then waddling off with a fuss of grunting and tail waggling like an old woman in distress. Peter also showed me the site of a Red-throated diver's nest which had had two eggs this morning but was mysteriously empty this afternoon. There were teal nesting on a small loch, and I added dunlin to the islands list and saw a pair of wigeon in the same place. I was dive-bombed by nesting Great Skuas and shouted at by the Arctics all the way across the moor and watched the crowds of kittiwakes bathing in a small loch. The children showed me a skylark's nest near the school this morning and Peter also showed me a most unusual inland nesting site of a fulmar on his croft. Such is the daily measure of interest for an ornithologist on Foula – and that was without going near the coast with the cliffs covered with thousands of nesting sea-birds or visiting the breeding ground of the Bonxies up on the hills. The next job is getting all the information which must be committed to paper onto paper – quite a formidable task when almost everything one sees is of interest and. worth recording.

By the time I got home tonight supper was a matter of some urgency. Then a spot more work on the peat stack and it was time to light the lamp and sit down to the typewriter.

Sunday *(or rather Monday morning early.) The system has rather broken down as you can see. As usual on mail-boat day the letters have piled up and now I am working late to get finished. It's 2 a.m. and nearly light again so I really must get to bed as I have to be up early tomorrow (sorry – today!) to get two boxes of library books down to the pier before school. That has been the real cause of my break in the story, because on Friday night I was up late checking the library books which have all to go back to Lerwick by this boat as we are getting a new lot in. So by the time that job had been done on Friday night I made a late start on Saturday morning. Being my first free Saturday since I arrived I was able to make up lost sleep for once and had my breakfast round about 12. I took sandwiches with me for the rest of the day and did a complete tour of the North end of the island taking two boxes down to the pier on the way out and bringing home a load of peats on my return. I found much of interest in the bird line and also had conversation with quite a number of folk I don't meet so often who live in the few remaining crofts at the North end of the island. I ringed a large number of nestlings on my way round, mostly starlings and blackbirds and found a large colony of Arctic Terns as well. I also got a good idea of the breeding sea-birds of the cliffs there which are all very low by Foula standards being mostly less than 100–200 feet. In fact this part of the coast even includes one place where you can get down to the sea over a beach of large boulders thrown up by the winter gales. There were a large number of Black Guillemots here which presumably nest among the rocks although I couldn't find them. Other species seen included: oystercatcher, whimbrel, curlew, ringed plover, dunlin, terns, eider duck, shags, puffins, razorbills, guillemots, fulmars everywhere, kittiwakes, mostly in very large numbers. It was a strange day with a sea-mist rolling in all the time in great belts, with periods of hot sun in between. I sat and had my supper in my shirtsleeves by a tern colony at 7 p.m. and basked in the sunshine thinking how criminal it was to have all this beauty to myself with so few to share it. I then walked for three hours steadily without seeing another human being as I made a circuit of the N.E. corner of the* *island; and finally came home down the central road where I couldn't make progress for meeting people still working at 11 p.m. on their peat etc. Today has again been fine and dry with a cool breeze as so often. With my first Sunday service at 3 p.m. I can afford to get up late and my Sunday programme of meals runs about two hours out of gear owing to their peculiar service times. Of course they pay no attention to summer time but peg along at sun- time, an hour behind. However there is no getting up late on Monday morning and so I really must get to bed now.*

Wednesday evening, 9th June *A postscript due to a typical Foula delay. Having once missed a post by reckoning, wrongly, that the wind one Sunday night was too high to allow them to cross the next morning, I now religiously write my letters in time for the boat – and the wretched thing never goes! There has been a fresh N.E. breeze all week so far with white tops on the sea all the time, and when you see them you can reckon it is 'no mail weather', as the saying goes over here. And certainly at this time of the year they might just as well wait for a good day as go on a bad one. I personally wouldn't like to cross in this boat in any weather rougher than when I came in eight weeks ago, which was a very smooth sea indeed. She is quite sea-worthy but very round-bottomed with a shallow keel for the Voe at this end, so that she rolls even on a slight swell. The crew don't mind it of course but they like to choose a good day rather than an uncertain one so that they can guarantee getting back on the same day. With so few to do the work here, it is a real nuisance if the crew get stuck out in Walls as sometimes happens when the weather changes suddenly after they have 'won out'. Today at last we woke up to rain, and it has gone on all day. We need it badly and it has transformed the crops and my garden overnight. The oats are coming up almost as fast as my weeds now. Tonight I have just returned from a birthday tea at the Schoolhouse for one of my pupils, whose father is the skipper of the mailboat and rents the house from me as teacher. They are*

very nice folk whose generosity knows no bounds, although they are a big family – parents, three sons, a married daughter, her husband and two bairns, and an aunt who is an excellent cook and does the school meals for us, as well as the cooking for the whole family. I really feel like a member of the family now and am under strict instructions to walk in and demand tea whenever I want – not that they ever give me a chance to as they always ask me in first. As a result I think I have had more meals in their house this week than I have in my own. I managed to take down some chocolate crispie cakes tonight which I put together in a hurry from a bar of chocolate and some cornflakes and raisins, and they went down very well. Mrs Gear is also extremely interested in birds and quite good at spotting them which is useful. But it tends to make our conversations in the house rather one-track. However the others bear with us very patiently. They are, like most of the folk, sympathetic though not very knowledgeable about birds. The wind really has dropped tonight and everyone is hopeful for a 'mailday' tomorrow. So you should get this by the weekend.

The carbon copy of this letter was sent to my former colleagues on the staff at John Watson's School in Edinburgh. I never heard whether they pitied me or whether they were secretly jealous? One noticeable feature of my file of the letters I sent home is the steady decline in the legibility of the text due to the wear on the typewriter ribbon. Getting a replacement ribbon on the correct size and type of reel for my old Oliver typewriter was difficult enough when living in Edinburgh. On Foula it was nigh on impossible. So I had recourse to the only spare I had taken with me, one of the type where the top half of the ribbon itself is black, and the bottom half red and one can change the colour of the type simply by setting the spool high or low. But of course half a ribbon only lasts half as long, so the black half was fairly soon almost too faint to be legible. It's scarcely surprising therefore that most of my later letters in the file for that year are in steadily fading red type.

Chapter 8: Post Office and Mailboat

After the first few weeks I seemed to be still struggling a bit with the irregular mails and keeping contact with my roots at home, but I was too busy to feel out of touch or in any way isolated. I had brought a good battery radio with dry batteries which lasted several months in spite of the amount of listening I did. Its special feature was good reception on long wave which I found the best quality. Some days were better than others but that is in the nature of long wave where reception depends to some extent on weather conditions and how well the waves are reflected back from the layers of the upper atmosphere. One feature I remember well was listening to the early days of 'The Archers – an everyday tale of country folk' which I found not only true to country life as I knew it, but a great escape for a bachelor living on his own in rather different surroundings from his norm. I got to know the characters so well that they seemed like a tangible link with my former life, second-hand but very real.

BBC Home Service News kept me well up to date in world news in the absence of any newspapers, though for a while I was sent the Weekly Scotsman as a way of keeping in touch with affairs at home. The fact that it was all at least a week late didn't seem to matter at all. And apart from the frustration of occasional fading on long wave, I was even able to listen to some excellent concerts to make up for not being able to go, as I always had done at home, to the Usher Hall in Edinburgh on a regular basis. Not having the Radio Times meant that such listening had an exciting element of chance in it, so that priorities would have to be hastily changed if the BBC Scottish Orchestra were suddenly announced as about to play one of my favourite classics, say Beethoven's Third Symphony. Not even the wild music of the Arctic Skuas outside could compete with that.

I seldom used the telephone as it was quite a complicated procedure. Around 6 p.m. one could ask Harry at the Post Office to connect one on his radio telephone, the transmitter of which was housed in a wooden hut on top of the hill to the south of the Post Office. The most impressive thing about this were the steel wires running over the roof and tied down to huge concrete blocks to prevent the hut from being blown away by winter gales. This was one of the first things one noticed on arrival, starting with the large shed above the pier at Ham Voe and applying to any boat pulled up for the winter or building lighter than a stone-built byre, that they were weighted down often with ropes and large stones against the wind. Harry was at pains to show me how even the radio telephone hut had moved on its foundation during one of the previous winter's fiercest storms, in spite of the weight of the equipment inside it.

To make a call one had to wait for at least half a minute. To save battery power, the equipment only connected every thirty seconds to the exchange in Lerwick who only needed to answer if someone had lifted the receiver on Foula. Once through, one was then connected to the national network, which meant waiting for an operator to make the connection as long-distance automatic dialing had not yet been introduced at that time. One snag was that as the distance decided the charge in those days, with local calls and trunk calls charged on markedly different rates, Foula had no local calls possible as the intervening sea-miles technically made every call a trunk call. So few were within the budget of the average Foula caller, and even the comparatively well-paid teacher had to think twice before making too many calls. As a former commissioned officer in the Royal Signals who had passed his training exams in Line Communications and Radio Technology, I was still able to carry on a meaningful discussion with Harry about the equipment the Post Office Engineers had installed and was amazed at his grasp of highly technical details quite beyond his call of duty as island Postmaster. Like most Foula boys he had been out to school at the Anderson Institute in Lerwick, where Foula boys along with others from islands such as Outskerries, Fetlar, Fair Isle, Whalsay etc. normally stayed in a residential hostel, some for a whole term at a time including weekends, unless exceptionally favourable weather allowed them to get home. For Foula boys and girls with a mailboat only once a week, this was not usually possible. The system had its problems, homesickness being one of the worst. But the education was good and bright boys like Harry learnt enough science to enable those with the interest and the initiative to build on this from books when they went home at 16. Harry thrived on anything mechanical or electrical. The simple answer was that he had a flair for such things and many of the islanders depended on it. For instance the hum of his generator was a frequent background noise at the school as he charged up the batteries for the telephone link, which was always reliable if little used. As I found later, in emergencies Harry was a godsend.

The Post Office must have been the smallest in Scotland. It was a little lean-to addition to the outside wall of the house at Mogle, but with no direct connection through to the building. So it was in fact seldom 'open' as the door was always locked. A notice however suggested that customers should knock on the front door of the house round the other side of the building where Harry always seemed to be available. Peter Gear and his wife Grace Anne, Harry's parents, were both well into their eighties and he was an only son, so that he had a full-time job looking after them and managing the house and croft. When summoned to his postal duties, Harry would come round to unlock the Post Office door, whereupon he would enter first, climb over the counter which occupied the whole six foot length of the building, and then ask the customer in so that he could serve them from behind it. I suppose two or perhaps even three people could have squeezed in together but normally he served the public one at a time. There was a letter-box in the end wall so that he could clear the letters from inside when it suited him and then on Monday mornings at 10.20 a.m. (presumably timed for a theoretical boat sailing at 11 a.m.) he would bag up the week's mail into canvas bags, seal them and convey them to the pier. One was often enough. All my memories of Harry Gear are of a kind and intelligent man who in one sense fitted his role on Foula perfectly and in another was completely out of place, his talent wasted. Though he never married he seemed to be a man fulfilled, and I cannot ever remember him, except perhaps on the day of his father's funeral, without a smile on his face.

One of the first things Harry told me on arrival was that he was expecting the island to get a telephone call-box that summer. I gathered that this was the result of years of requests and protests which had had to wait until the money could be found to justify enabling a community of only 70 people to make easier contact with the national telephone network. What Harry didn't know, and nobody was told in advance, was that this would be installed on a Sunday. I always felt that the Post Office would never have got away with that in the Hebrides. Fortunately Shetlanders do not have the same

strict Presbyterian traditions about the Sabbath as those from a Celtic culture. Foula folk were especially laid back about such things, much to my relief as otherwise I would have hardly been able to go bird-watching, let alone bird-trapping on a Sunday! But even I was surprised to be woken early one Sunday morning by a loud explosion from the direction of Mogle; and even more surprised on going down to investigate (after I was sure I was fully prepared for my Sunday service, please note) when I came over the brow of the hill to find a garish telephone kiosk in brightest Post Office red mounted on a newly laid concrete base outside the Post Office. The explosion had been the blasting necessary to make a level square platform for the base of the kiosk on the sloping slab of rock which formed the foundations of the house. This was bad enough and goodness knows what it had done to Grace Anne's nerves to be so rudely woken on a Sunday morning. But even worse, after all the talk of shortage of funds, was that they had chosen a day when overtime would have to be paid to all those involved, not to mention the specially chartered boat and its crew which had brought them across from Scalloway. The final insult was that the resulting eyesore wore the traditional coat of brilliant red paint designed to make a kiosk easily spotted in a busy street or along a line of village shops, in competition with signboards and advertising hoardings. In the context of our beautiful island this was frankly ridiculous. I had to laugh out loud at this idiotic demonstration of bureaucratic conformity to the rulebook. If I hadn't, I would have sat down on a stone and cried. From that moment on I had a secret longing to creep down one night with a large tin of green paint and tone the monstrosity into its gentle background of rigs of tatties and oats and the grey-green hills beyond. I am sad to confess that I never had the courage to fulfil this dream. Perhaps it would not, if detected, have been wise, in conflict with my position either as teacher or 'minister', to be seen even only in official eyes as a vandal. But I thought I knew who the real vandals were.

The telephone was a boon to those of us living in the centre of the island, though of doubtful value to such as Peter Manson at Blowburn in the north or the Isbisters at South Biggins who all lived more than a mile from the Post Office. But I could now go down in about fifteen minutes at any time of day, though after 6 p.m. was far cheaper, and after waiting not more than the 30 seconds for the radio transmitter to connect with Lerwick, could either dial a number in Shetland or 100 for an operator to connect me through for a trunk call. It was the standard type of public telephone of the day, with Button A which you pressed as soon as the number you had dialled answered, whereupon the money you had put in the box was swallowed up by the machine; or Button B if they did not answer and you wanted to get your money back. So far as I can remember you could always put in more money when a warning sounded that it was about to run out, and so you had a measure of how much the call was costing as the coins in your hand steadily disappeared. It seems antediluvian now but it worked well enough and was a big change for the Foula community.

The first sub Post Office dates back to July 1879 and the first mailboat service started soon after as part of a venture by Garriock & Co. of Reawick who ran the Foula shop at that time. Later the boat was run from Walls by one J. Jarmson; but the first Foula men to win the Post Office contract were Magnus Manson of Mornington and Laurence Gray of Loch in 1892. They were paid £2 per trip in their sixern, the *Advance*, which would use sail when it could but in calm weather might depend on six oarsmen to power the boat. The contract covered one trip a week in the summer, one a fortnight in the winter, and that was to serve a population of over 250 people in 40 occupied crofts. The advantages of the contract bringing the income into the island and having the boat on hand for emergencies must have become obvious as that first contract ran for 20 years. All that time the boat had to be hauled up onto the beach as the first pier wasn't built till 1913. It took two years to build out of mass concrete, was 75 feet long and cost £1000, incorporating a 5 ft high wall on the seaward side. It has stood up well to the weather now for ninety years. Soon after the pier was built, the *Advance* was converted to run with a diesel

engine but it was another 33 years before the pier was extended by 15 feet to cover the rocky outcrop at the end in 1946–49. This was the time when the slipway with its hand winch and the davits were installed to cater for the first fully decked boat, the *Island Lass*.

The Post Office funded the mail link with the outside world by contracting with the owners of the *Island Lass* that they would be paid for a weekly service to run to Walls every Monday. It always seemed to me a weakness of this contract – though I can see why the Foula men fought for it – that it was to be paid for a crossing on 'Monday or the first available day thereafter in the event of bad weather' – or some such wording. Perhaps the Post Office officials who drew up the contract never suspected that it would not be exceptional for the 'first available day thereafter' to be up to a month or even six weeks later in a stormy winter. The crew could therefore be paid for weeks in which no crossing was made simply because it was contracted as a weekly payment. Of course there were often strong reasons for making a crossing if supplies were short or there were lambs to go to market. But for purely financial reasons, to cross on a Saturday, or worse still on a Sunday when the shops in Walls were closed, must have seemed pointless if you were going to be paid to cross on the following Monday anyway. Of course it could rationally be argued that the upkeep costs of the boat and the readiness of the crew to be available whenever the weather did allow, were factors which deserved to be paid for and protected by the contract. One factor always struck me as significant. If you sent a humble letter to Foula even just from Shetland, your stamp was incredibly cheap for the value of the service

Ham Voe in 1954. The larger boat on the right was the mailboat which preceded the Island Lass, *the first sixern to be fitted with an engine*

provided by Her Majesty. There was not only the journey across Shetland to Walls, and then the long boat crossing over fifteen miles of open Atlantic, but on arrival the mail was sorted out by Harry and Peter Gray, as part-time postman, trudged up to two miles to your house on foot to deliver it to your door. For 2½ old pence that was some bargain.

The harbour was and still is the weakest point in the system. Admittedly it is on the sheltered east side but it is open and unprotected if the wind is easterly.

Between 1915 and 1949, the rock at the end of the pier limited the use of the harbour as bigger boats could not lie at the point of the pier and the mailboat had to make quite a wide berth to reach the deep water on the inner side. This was dangerous in bad weather. In 1954 when I arrived, the remains of two of Foula's former mail boats were lying hauled up above the beach of Ham Voe, a tiny stretch of sand at the head of the narrow inlet where the Ham Burn ran out into the sea. It was hard to imagine a time when the undecked sixern,

The Island Lass, *lifted on the davits and hand-winched up the slipway on her cradle, 1954*

The Ham Toun as viewed from Hamnafield. Following the road anti-clockwise from the Haa and the shop by Ham Voe: Ham, Gravins, the Schoolhouse, Mogle (the Post Office), Leraback, Groups, the nurse's house

which looked so shallow and frail, was the only link with the mainland, and that it had to be manhandled high up onto the beach out of reach of the winter storms by six men after an exhausting journey across from Walls. So far as I remember there was also a partially decked boat which preceded the *Island Lass*, alongside Alisdair Holbourn's boat which had come to grief in the Voe in a winter storm. There are many tales of ships in trouble off Foula but, apart from the wreck of the *Oceanic*, the largest liner in the world at the time, in 1914, surely the most dramatic tale of a whole series of disasters in the short time of 'a trial sail round Foula' simply to give his yacht its first run of the season, is the tale told by Marion Holbourn in her memoir of her husband at the end of his book 'The Isle of Foula' (pages 238–242). He and his son Hylas crammed more mistakes and accidents to boat, dinghy and themselves in the course of a few hours of terrifying episodes than were ever recorded by Foula's mailboats in one of the riskiest sea crossings in an area of strong tide-races and sudden storms. It is all credit to the wisdom and skill of the men of Foula that there has never been a life lost in running the mailboat or ferry to Foula since it started in 1880.

The *Island Lass* was a post-war boat, completely decked, with a broad hold big enough to house the mails, supplies for the shop, building materials, drums of paraffin or diesel, or, when occasion demanded, a new bull for the island's cows or a load of lambs for export. She was designed specifically for Foula's particular needs by David Howarth, a reputable Shetland boat-builder whose wider reputation was as the author of

'The Shetland Bus', an account of the wartime exploits of the fishing boats and their gallant crews who smuggled British agents into Norway and Norwegian patriots into Britain. I would describe her as serviceable but uncomfortable, for she rolled like a running cow in the sense that Homer meant when he called them 'the kine of the swinging gait', lurching from side to side as they progressed forward. If you've ever watched a pregnant cow running ahead of you, I think you'll find the simile apt, especially if you've also ever crossed from Foula on the *Island Lass* on a breezy day.

Sometimes one of the larger fishing boats from Scalloway, too long to swing safely round inside the pier, would tie up across the end of the pier while they sorted out a tangle in their nets or a fault in the engine. The mailboat had to come alongside the pier on the inside in order to be positioned under the two fixed davits by which she was lifted out of the water except in very settled summer weather. This was achieved by a slow but manageable system of endless chains working through geared pulleys to lift her heavy weight a height of 10–12 feet from the waterline until she cleared the pier and could be swung in and lowered onto the wheeled cradle. Before lifting there was a sort of rather primitive ritual of heaving out, one by one, by hand, a mass of rounded boulders, which were used as ballast to steady the boat in the water but added too much to her weight when being lifted on the davits. To complete this labour intensive process, the cradle had to be hand winched up the slipway with two men hauling on the long handles with a ratchet to hold the weight of the boat from slipping back. It was at least an hour's work to secure the boat before anyone could go home after arrival at the Voe. After a rough crossing it was demanding work. Later on I was to witness in dramatic fashion the vital need for such precautions. The alternative would have been for the mail to be delivered by a Shetland boat with a more secure harbour to leave and return to, from Walls or Sandness, or perhaps Aith where the local lifeboat was berthed. But this would have deprived Foula both of an emergency vessel which they could afford and was big enough to cope with risky conditions, and of the incomes for the crew from the mail runs which were such an essential source of much needed cash for at least four households. No wonder they always insisted that their mailboat should be based on the island. Many of the men crewed the boat during my stay but the stalwarts were Davie Gear, as skipper, and Peter Manson of Blowburn, Jock Ratter of North Biggins, Ken Gear of the Schoolhouse, Willie Umphray of Ham and John Henry when he was home from South Georgia.

If the boat did leave on Monday at the prescribed time, with usually a cheerful send-off from people bringing down their boxes with their weekly orders, or perhaps seeing off a visitor, there would always be the intention, especially in summer, that they would have a quick turn-round and be heading back by early afternoon. On these days weather forecasts were listened to and debated earnestly, and often it would not be settled until all the crew had arrived at the harbour whether they would risk going if there was a change in the wind due which might make a return crossing too risky. Boat weather meant good conditions for at least seven or eight hours to allow

for the two crossings and sufficient time for unloading, delivering the boxes to Reid's, collecting them again when the orders had been completed and loading up for the return journey. A weather change, a gale forecast, a rising wind against the tide which with its six or seven knot flow was such a vital factor in the calculations, any setback could cause a change of plan and the decision to stay overnight at Walls. Seldom did the crew depart from Foula without taking clothing and provisions for a possible stay over. They had a hut at Walls to give them shelter which was alright for a night but so often the decision to stay would mean several nights, perhaps a week or more, before the sea would settle enough to make a crossing possible. And all this time there would be two old women at Blowburn, or old Mrs Henry and the grandchildren at North Biggins, or Mary at Ham with her infant daughter, all coping with fetching water from the well, cooking and baking bread, washing clothes, fetching in the cattle at night, barrowing peat, going to the shop, and in summer perhaps trying to get in the hay in a dry spell or raising the peats before it rained again, and all without the strong arms and crofting skills of their menfolk. So naturally the women worried if the boat left in uncertain weather, and the crew were frustrated and bored if they were unwillingly stranded in Walls.

The other major factor in the decision whether to cross or not on a certain day was 'the cold'. If all was well we would see Peter Manson coming down the road past the school about ten o'clock in the morning and that would be a sure sign the boat was likely to go. From his house perched on top of the rise at the North end he could see the sea right across to Walls and nobody was

Halfway across from Walls. Standing (L–R): Davie Gear (skipper), Jock Ratter, Peter Manson. Sitting: John Henry, his wife and cousin Vida and Mrs Henry of North Biggins (grandmother of both)

more experienced at reading the sky and assessing the wind. He would know the tides and just make up his mind and either come or stay at home. If Peter did not turn up, the reason was usually obvious in the weather conditions or the forecast. But it could be that he or one of his household had been to the shop and picked up a germ, and now they had a cold at Blowburn. If so Peter would be the last to want to pass it on to the rest of the crew. So they would read the signs and if the weather was really good, a messenger would be sent up to Mornington to see whether young Alec would step in for the day as a spare crewman. But there weren't many alternatives if one of the regulars was sick, and they might go with a reduced number rather than miss a good weather window if it was set fair. Other hazards could occur so that sometimes even when everything else was perfect for a crossing, they would still be on the pier at mid-day with Harry bent over the engine, trying out a replacement battery good enough to get the engine started. Sadly one of the characteristics of many of the islanders was an inability to get jobs finished. With so many jobs always crying out to be done, it was often hard to be systematic.

But a boat demands systematic maintenance and upkeep. One of the first things I noticed about the mailboat was that when I first saw her she was only half painted, with the brush strokes of green paint stopping halfway down one side. I asked as discreetly as I could the reason for this and there was none except that time had run out one day on the repainting job, but nobody had – for several weeks, I gathered – taken the initiative to set aside the time to finish the task. In some families, putting off till tomorrow had become almost a way of life. The trouble was that so far as a boat's engine was concerned, this is a dangerous way of life, as indeed it later proved to be. I remember on a later visit to Fair Isle where the Foula folk had a bad reputation for being inefficient and slapdash, this episode of the half-painted boat was given to me as an example of something which simply could never have happened on Fair Isle. On Foula hardly anybody seemed to notice or to care enough to make a fuss. The best interpretation I could put on it was that it was noticed but nobody was prepared to raise the issue in case it aroused ill feeling between two families or caused a rift in an otherwise happy community. It could be said to be a good example of a form of insularity.

In the end although the *Island Lass* was repainted and did remain seaworthy, it was finally her engine, old and tired no doubt, which failed them on a stormy return crossing, on 1st March 1962. Davie Gear was the skipper

and had on board as crew his two sons Jim and Ken, then aged 19 and 21, and also John Holbourn, grandson of Ian, who had bought Foula at the turn of the century. A Foula man, Robert Gray, was the only passenger. As she had had a normal crossing only a week before, she had a light cargo when she left Walls at 5.30 p.m. in fine weather but with warnings of a gale to come. Sadly it struck when they were halfway across and the boat took in a lot of water which swamped the engine. She should have arrived about 8 p.m but the islanders saw her drifting past without power about 8.30. The crew did manage to get the engine started again but could make no headway as the weather had worsened. So bad a night was it that the Aith lifeboat, alerted at 8.50, could not even be manned to start with, such was the gale and blizzard, and did not get under way till 11 p.m. At 11.40 an Aberdeen trawler, having heard of the distress signals picked up the mailboat's flares six miles south of the South Ness and managed to get alongside. The crew of the *Island Lass* launched their liferaft intending to transfer to the trawler that way but such were the seas that it capsized before anyone could get onto it. So in a bold manoeuvre, the 98-ton *Star of Scotland* got alongside and all five men jumped aboard. They managed to secure a tow rope but after towing nicely for a short while, suddenly the boat wasn't there and they were forced to abandon her. The next day the lighthouse boat the *Pole Star* spotted her off North Ronaldsay in Orkney and again took the damaged boat in tow, heading for Westray. Eventually however she went down in 35 fathoms of water and was reckoned to be a total loss.

In 1984–85 discussions were started resulting in a parliamentary provisional order promoted by Shetland Islands Council to build a new harbour with an improved pier, a new crane hoist, deeper water and a new slipway with motorized winch. The total cost was over a million pounds. For reasons of cost it is not an all-weather harbour yet it is the key to bigger and better ferries and a far safer facility for the future. The *Island Lass* as I knew her served her purpose well enough though I personally dreaded crossing in her on a choppy sea because of her corkscrew action, which was the worst possible for bad sailors like me. Her design by David Howarth was a compromise between seaworthiness and the facilities she had to serve. She had to be small and light enough to be hoisted out of the water by unaided manpower for most of the year.

The day I remember most clearly when I had to admire the boat-builder's skill was one of the very few days when I had to close the school because of the

South-east gale (March 1955) in Ham Voe. The Island Lass *is secure at the top of the slipway (right)*

weather. It was blowing a full gale from the south-east so that the road up from the Hame Toun and Mornington was badly exposed, and neither the Beagrie children nor Eric from South Biggins were allowed to risk the walk to school. I had a struggle to get there myself and we made a pretence of doing a morning's work with the two Schoolhouse pupils. Davie was worried about the mailboat on its cradle at the top of the slipway when the time came for high tide, so I decided to go down with him and took my camera with me, loaded as was my wont in the winter, with black-and-white film to cope with the very low light levels in overcast conditions. I managed to get across the bridge over the Ham Burn but the seas were running right through the Voe and well up the beach below the wooden bridge. I struggled up past the nurse's house and on to a point where I could look down on the pier from the seaward side. Huge waves were rolling up over the rocks to the north and the blow-holes were jetting sea-spray high into the

air like volcanic geysers. The pier looked so inadequate with waves breaking right over it with green water and the white spray blowing inland up the harbour like driven snow. And there at the top of the slipway, snug on its wooden cradle just below the winch, sat this toy of a boat, dwarfed by the elements but secure enough from the storm, just waiting for a better day to return to duty. I had to wedge myself in to a cleft in the bank above the rocks in order to steady the camera enough from the buffeting of the gale to be able to take a picture. The thought crossed my mind as I watched successive waves surging past the pier and breaking almost up to the wall of the Ham Yard that it was not a day to develop appendicitis. In such weather Foula had no harbour and was completely cut off from any form of emergency service available to us at that time. But it was still a wonderful experience to give way to sheer wonder at the raw fury of it all and the adrenalin induced by the untamed forces of nature.

Chapter 9: Plentiful Peat

Many remote islands which once supported a thriving and then an ageing, dwindling population eventually became deserted. Yet Foula appeared to be a stable population in spite of all its problems. There was of course talk about 'the good old days' and dissatisfaction with some aspects of the present, but behind the usual sense of frustration at the lack of funds for the services which cost so much more for a remote island than a township on the mainland, there was no real sense of unease, except perhaps among a few of the most elderly about the long-term future. Foula folk came across as having a great pride in their way of life. Naturally I wondered where this confidence sprang from and it was not long before I began to be aware of one valuable asset

which set Foula apart as one of the richest islands in Scotland – its peat. A Shetland winter is long, very dark and usually cold and stormy. The long light summer does not absolve one from the basic need to keep warm in the winter. Ken Williamson, who knew Fair Isle so well, had told me how lucky I was to be going to a place where peat was so plentiful and so conveniently placed. On Fair Isle most of the good peat had been used up years ago and what was left was better described as burnable turf. St Kilda likewise had poor supplies of winter fuel of any quality, and most of that was a long – and steep – way from the Village. Foula, like much of the Shetland mainland, had enough peat for a thousand people for a thousand years.

Bobby and Aggie Isbister on the road past Hamnabreck to collect a cart-load of peats and
Eric with his model boat to sail on the Mill Loch

This was another way in which I had an easy landing, having inherited from the Chedburns a sound foundation for my peat supply, and the right tools for keeping it up. All I lacked at first were the skills. Every croft was allocated its own peat-banks, some near and some often quite distant from the croft itself. I had a small area just up the road from the house but my main banks were well beyond the school up on the Lioag where the road headed north towards Peter Ratter's croft at Loch. Peter was just the neighbour I needed near my peat supply. He had the job of maintaining the island's roads, which he did with pick and spade and a wheelbarrow to very good effect. Of course there was not much wear and tear from boots (however hob-nailed) and barrow wheels, but there was constant erosion from the weather, especially at certain points where heavy rain could cause deep ruts almost overnight. Peter's working material was gravel which he quarried at a few chosen spots where there was friable rock close under the turf. One such quarry was just at the side of the road where it approached the Mornington gate, a spot I passed twice every day going to

and from school. I soon discovered that a diversion from the lonely task of road mending was all too welcome for Peter and we had many a good yarn at the roadside setting the world's and the island's affairs to rights.

Peter's situation in the community was about as typical as you could find in a community of only seven clear cut families. His wife Bessie (neé Henry) was not only Mima Gear's youngest sister, but also the sister of Jessie, wife of his own brother John Thomas, who provided a home at North Biggins for their mother, old Mrs Henry. It would be hard to imagine a closer bond between two families than two brothers marrying two sisters. Even more unusual – except in close-knit communities like Foula – was the marriage between Mrs Henry's grandson John and Mima's daughter Vida Gear, who was Mrs Henry's grand-daughter, by marriage. At least that was how it appeared to us in 1954 when on his return from the whaling in South Georgia, young John Henry was first introduced to me as his wife's first cousin. Genetically there is always a risk of in-breeding in such situations, but they had splendid healthy children and

Peat banks on Hamnastours below the road to the Hame Toun. Recently worked curved banks show correct returfing to prevent soil erosion seen on older banks nearer the road

Peter Ratter cutting a two-moor bank. After laying out the top moor peats to dry, he builds the second moor into a ventilated dyke with spaces for the wind to blow through

young Vina was one of my star pupils. For years I used to quote their case as an example of how close-knit families like this can still avoid the genetic hazards provided the blood-lines follow the right rules. It was only quite recently that I discovered that in fact John's real father was not a Henry, so that, born out of wedlock, he was not of the Henry blood-line after all. The significant factor is that at the time of their marriage he was not aware of this himself but still happy to take the risk of such apparently close family ties. Such are the pressures of the limited choice of partner for young people in small communities. But I digress, Foula fashion.

If Peter was a good roadman he was an even better peat-cutter. I couldn't, in fact, have had a better teacher, for he was cutting a long bank that summer under ideal conditions. Peat banks for some strange reason are nearly always crescent shaped, as though in progressing slowly forward cutting down into several feet of soft, heavy ground, one is so fully occupied that one never notices that each thrust is slightly to one side of the previous one so that a gradual curve appears in the line. Sitting up on the slopes of Hamnafield one day later in that dry summer I could see the pattern of these crescents, far more pleasing to look at than precise straight lines across the folds and curves of Foula's moorland above the Mill Loch. These curved lines crept across the landscape at the rate of two feet per year. On the upper side was grassy turf growing in damp, mossy ground above peat often two spade lengths deep. The Shetland peat-cutting spade or tuskar is a long-handled weapon, with part of the round shaft flattened above the broader flat of the spade, on the end of which is the steel cutter. As this is pressed down into the 'mud' – for peat is almost as soft as mud but held together by the undecayed fibres of years of dead vegetation – the rectangular slice of peat slides up the handle until it is about 24 to 30 inches long. The skill comes in balancing this long, heavy, rather fragile slice of very wet peat on the tuskar while it is lifted and then thrown or placed in exactly the right spot at exactly the right angle.

Peter showed me how to 'flay' the bank first. Presuming the bank was cut last year, one starts at a vertical face topped with turf. In shallow peat this will be 30 to 40 inches deep. The turf is too tough to make a clean cut through from above, so it must first be removed, usually with a standard garden spade, preferably one with a good sharp edge. These square turfs or 'fells' are thrown down into the ditch at the bottom, the 'greff' where, if the laird is watching or likely to pass by, great care is taken to lay them systematically to form a new layer of turf which will provide good grazing for sheep in a few years' time. Failure to do this leads to erosion of the moor as the stones of the substratum are exposed and the hillside is lost as grazing ground. This was a great bone of contention for Alisdair Holbourn, who was always anxious to remind crofters of their obligation to set the turf correctly at the bottom of the peat-bank. Peter was a model in this respect. The bank he was cutting that summer's day was a two-moor bank, in other words five to six feet depth of peat below the turf. He stood on top of the newly flayed bank, with a strip two feet wide cleared ready for cutting, a long, dark, shiny ribbon waiting to be sliced into hundreds of uniform pieces, all heavy with water and as far from looking like fuel for a fire as can be imagined. Digging straight down into this from above, Peter would cut a dozen slices from the edge inwards, lifting each carefully and steadily and then

A fortnight later the cut peats have formed a dry 'skin'. Stacked peats from last year are protected from rain by 'fells', 'flayed' from the top grassy layer of the moor

throw it out onto the grass level with the top of the bank, so that they gradually covered the whole area, laid out flat to dry in the wind over the next few weeks – with luck. On a long bank this would mean lifting a ton or two of wet peat, several hundred long, flat slices which had to be laid out neatly on the grass in a pattern of rows, no peat touching another so that the wind could get at the edges to dry them thoroughly. But that was only the first moor. When it had been removed there was left a patterned strip of even darker, more solid peat three feet down the peat face, but still a full peat's length deep; and along the top of the cut bank, a strip of turf had been carefully left bare, its width exactly one peat's length. Peter would then work systematically along standing on this second 'moor' and repeating the whole procedure. But this time there was only this narrow strip of accessible turf left on the topside of the bank to lay out the second batch of slices. So clearly they could not be thrown out to lie flat on the grass beyond which was all fully occupied. So the peats from the second moor had to be built into a dyke, a perforated wall ten peats high, laid out along the top of the bank with an inch or so of space between each peat and the next down the whole of its length. This calls for precision of a high order. If the spacing is not consistent and correct, the wind will not blow through and the peats will never dry. One or two peats out of line or collapsing inwards will throw the whole wall and its pattern of uniform spaces out of kilter. A good cutter will leave a wall of peat perforated with square tunnels through its thickness, nine or ten peats high and perhaps a hundred yards long, all lifted to shoulder height from a position under your feet. What a wonderful way of keeping fit!

A well cut two-moor bank is both a work of art and damned hard work too, but few jobs well executed give greater satisfaction. The position at the roadside was the perfect incentive. The last thing I wanted was for the islanders who passed with their barrows to shake their heads, muttering about incomers who couldn't cast their peats properly and would surely be short of dry peats at the Manse this winter. My greatest reward for my first effort was Peter Ratter's praise for a commendable first attempt. Mind you, compared with his, it had to be admitted it was pretty rough. The most noticeable thing to an inexperienced eye like mine was how much darker and heavier the second layer of peat was. At the very top it was still quite fibrous, looking rather like compressed hay, but six or seven feet down it looked almost like coal. It was recognised that this was the best fuel, for it was smooth, dense and heavy, and when it dried out eventually it took

on a surface bloom which gave it its name of 'blue peats'. It burned like coal and lasted twice as long in the stove as the 'moory' peats from near the surface. I soon discovered that I couldn't load the wheelbarrow with as many blue peats as the lighter type without making the long haul up the brae from the Ham Burn impossible without rests on the way up. But I was glad to get it home as it was the ideal fuel for a stove like the Rayburn in my kitchen, and made oven baking a real pleasure. There's nothing worse than a loaf which collapses half way through baking because the stove goes cold on you. Opening the oven door to check progress and crust colour can also spoil a loaf, but a cold stove can ruin a whole batch.

Peter had an outside manual job. I had two self-imposed outdoor duties, to get round the crofts visiting the old folk and to get up the hills counting the nesting territories of the Great Skuas. For one of the tasks I had set myself was to get a reasonably accurate estimate of the size of what was almost certainly the largest Great Skua colony in the northern hemisphere. So we were both reasonably fit and able to enjoy such jobs as peat-cutting. There was however a real problem over crofts where there was nobody fit enough any longer to do the job. Ken Gear, Mima's second son, aged 16, was tall for his age and strong but in the unenviable position, having just left school in Lerwick and with no job for him in Foula, of being available for just such heavy work as ploughing with the two-wheeled tractor or peat-cutting.

Mima Gear at the Mogle byre with hay for the Schoolhouse cows; winter 1955

He seemed always to be working for other people and helping out elderly neighbours or relatives. I never enquired whether he was paid for this work but I always felt, knowing how little income the old-age pensioners had in those days, that if he was paid anything for his labours, it must have been a very small proportion of what he deserved or was worth. There was never any complaint from him; it seemed to be understood that as he was free the job would be done. After all, in one sense, there was nobody else to do it and one simply could not leave, for example old Robbie Isbister of Breckans in his black house or old Betty Gray of North Harrier, overweight and 76, without a supply of winter fuel for their open fire, which used far more peat than the closed stove if it was to heat the whole house as well as cook your food and boil your kettle.

Relatives would do what they could but some families simply had no members left amongst the young and fit age-group. Already I had watched old Meggie Ratter of Punds, a widow who now looked after her older sister Jeannie, wheeling a heavy barrow of peats over the hill from the peat banks on the Hametoun Wilse below the Manse, aged 75. Later in the summer I saw her wielding a scythe to cut some winter hay for her sheep. One day on my way home from the south end I passed Magnie Henry of Quinister, who was Meggie's nearest neighbour in the Hame Toun, putting the finishing touches to his peat-stack. Like Peter Ratter's peat wall this was a work of art, part of an old tradition learnt from many years of necessity. I asked if I could take a photo of it and he started to move out of the way. I insisted he stay in the picture so that the labourer could be credited with his

achievement, explaining I wanted to show my family at home what a wonderful work of art a good Foula peat-stack was. With such flattery and a bit more persuasion I won the day, but as he was clearly not used to being photographed, I suggested he look, not at the camera, but across the sea towards the distant mainland of Shetland. I have since been told that this was perhaps the only photograph ever taken of old Magnie Henry. What pleased me was that it showed to perfection the correct method of weatherproofing a peat-stack against the winter rains. It was a simple skill but an essential part of the whole process. When cutting with the tuskar down into the soft peat, the lifting action had to be done with a slight twist of the handle so that the end of the peat came away at an angle. So a square-sided peat finished up with a sloping end. Weeks later after the peats had been dried off and were ready to be built into a stack to await their transfer to the house, the long peats were all carefully turned the same way, heavy end out, so that the outer face of the stack consistently presented sloping ends of blue peat which ran the rain off to the outside and none of it was able to drain into the stack. By this means a simple roof of turves was sufficient to keep all the peat dry. To fill a barrow, all that was required was to remove a few turves from the top, load from the top of the stack, and replace the turf again.

While on the subject of Magnie Henry of Quinister, now long ago deceased, the story I never liked to tell publicly while he was still alive, can safely be told. It reflects rather poignantly the personal problems which can arise in such a small community, which would be quite incredible elsewhere but came to be accepted by

Magnie Henry with a newly built peat stack at Quinister ready to be covered with 'fells' to make it waterproof

Ken Gear, second son of the Schoolhouse family, in summer 1954

those who understood, from a closer viewpoint, just how it happened. In the early part of the 20th century there were two brothers in the Henry family at Quinister, Jimmy and Magnie who was three years younger. Jimmy had a tendency to asthma so that in later years he depended on Magnie as the active one who did most of the crofting work. A couple of miles away to the north was South Harrier, with another family of young folk, the Umphrays. Babbie was the eldest, with a sister called Betty and younger still her brother Scotty. Magnie and Babbie decided to get married. They might have been friends at school or had opportunities for meeting at the church where they were eventually to be married. But apparently although they must have taken it for granted that they would live together from their wedding day, they had never discussed where. It may have seemed obvious to Magnie that Babbie's home would now be at Quinister, but to Babbie her home was Harrier and when they came out of the church as husband and wife, Magnie turned south and Babbie turned north. Apparently it seemed to her quite unthinkable to leave her home just because she had got married to a Quinister boy, and she insisted that he pack his belongings and come north. After much

protest, Magnie packed his belongings in a large wooden chest and arrived at South Harrier where there happened to be already a number of similar wooden chests, which were a common feature of many crofts houses. Generally made of rescued driftwood they were an excellent way of storing clothes and materials away from the smoke and dust caused by the peat fire. Scotty who was by this time the man of the house, and a very hard-working and systematic character who liked to have everything well ordered, is said to have observed, when Magnie arrived to stay, that they had too many chests already and there really wasn't room for another large one. So Magnie went back home to care for his elder brother Jimmy, as he had always wanted to and Babbie stayed on at South Harrier, where Magnie would visit her occasionally. But they never lived together as husband and wife. Eventually Babbie died and was survived only by her sister Betty, who ended up living at Burns where she was looked after for several years.

By midsummer I had visited all the crofts and met in one way or another everybody who was living and working on Foula at the time. I found most people very ready to talk about island affairs and many knowledgeable

Harry Gear, Postmaster, with his traditional two-handled scythe

about the wider world. They were generally discreet about gossip or stories such as that of Magnie and his unusual marriage, but in some cases I was grateful to wise friends who would advise me on such matters so as to save me from the embarrassment of making awkward mistakes in conversation. I often felt it wiser, until I got to know families better, to ask questions on such subjects as peat or sheep where I was obviously learning from them about parts of their daily round that were new to me. I soon picked up plenty of useful tips, for instance about managing peat. Almost every house had, as its basic heat

source, a cast-iron stove with a chimney pipe running into the gable wall to carry away the smoke. The old tradition of the open central fire on a hearth slab in the middle of the house, with no chimney except a hole in the roof, had been replaced in every house except Breckans. Robbie Isbister lived there by himself, and every time I called he seemed to be out and about and not too willing to ask me in, so it wasn't until much later in the year that I got a chance to call on him at home and see for myself how most Foula families had lived a hundred years before. From outside there was always a wisp of smoke emerging from the centre of his thatched roof and when exchanging a greeting at his front door, with the hens picking about the yard and several cats running inside as I approached, it was obvious enough that his house was far from conventional and fairly crammed with what one could only call rubbish. From the state of his red-rimmed eyes he clearly lived in a very smoky atmosphere which one or two people, not least young Eric, had told me they found quite difficult to cope with for very long, though Robbie was completely acclimatized to it. What I was told several times was that his fire was always burning and moreover had almost certainly never been out in his lifetime of eighty years. I longed to know just how he managed but still by 1955 I had never gained access over his doorstep.

I got a better idea of how an open fire worked at North Harrier where Betty Gray gave me a warm welcome and asked me in without any hesitation. She lived in a tiny stone house with a felt roof just past the large well-tended croft in which Scotty Umphray worked so hard all through the summer on his six acres of cultivated land. It was more or less a single room where she slept, cooked, ate her meals and read her books. Her fire was also on an open hearth on the floor but up against the gable wall with a crude kind of chimney to lead the smoke away at the top. But though there was always a dusting of peat ash on most surfaces, it was not usually smoky. She seemed remarkably content with her lot though she had few possessions or comforts. Being well up in her 70s and not very able at walking, she lived a very isolated life so far from Ham and the shop or Post Office and with no communication except passers by and her radio. There had been a time, I think shortly before I arrived, when the old age pension on which people like Betty depended totally for their subsistence, had been increased by the Chancellor in his budget. Was it to a princely 10/- a week? I forget now the exact figure involved. Undoubtedly, as is the way with inflation, 50p, the decimal equivalent, would sound ridiculously inadequate now. The point was that the rise was, as so often, long overdue; and by the time it arrived was badly needed by most pensioners. But Betty would have none of it. What she got was quite adequate for her needs and as she felt she didn't need an increase why should she toil down to the Post Office to claim it. It took several months and a great deal of persuasion to convince her that she ought to accept what the government offered and if necessary save the extra for a rainy day. Yes, she agreed; she was likely to get plenty of those – but she meant the wet ones and not days when she would need more cash; bless her!

Because of its formation over many centuries from rotted but not completely decomposed vegetation, peat has a very fine ash, so that it is inevitable that in an open fire there is a great deal of dust. But this ash is an essential part of the correct management of a peat fire. A good bed of ash holds plenty of heat underneath burning peats and so only needs to be cleared when it gets several inches deep. At night when 'smoored' over the last embers of the dying fire, the ash will let through enough oxygen to keep the fire red and yet prevent it going completely out, so that in the morning a few selected lumps of new, dry peat placed on the uncovered red embers can soon be coaxed into flame as the basis of the new fire. The secret is in getting the dying fire into the right state before closing it down for the night. The final supply of fuel should be upright peats set up into a funnel in the centre of the fire to get them red at the bottom but unburnt at the top. This will usually do the trick. I used the same technique with the open fire I had in my study, which was in the normal grate used for a coal fire elsewhere, but without the iron basket for the coals. This would have created too much draught and burnt the fuel away. Instead I burnt my peat on the hearth and tried to get one or two larger peats to that half-burnt stage before closing it down with a covering of ash. The standard peat stove found in most houses had good draught control, but my Rayburn in the kitchen would still tend to go out from too much draught. So the trick there was always to have a bucket of peat dross or 'mould' (pronounced moold) of which there was always a plentiful supply at the bottom of my peat cupboard, to smother the red peat fire at night. It just had to be damped before application, rather like putting damp dross on a coal fire, to keep it in till morning. This covering killed the draught, dried slowly overnight and when stirred into life in the morning by opening the draught fully, had a roaring fire going in no time.

Learning to live with peat was one thing; exploring the material itself was of even greater interest. In the U-shaped valley called the Daal which separates the Noup at the south end of the island from the rest of the hills, is the largest bog of pure sphagnum moss I have ever seen. The valley is typical of those carved by ice and was clearly smoothed into its present shape by a massive glacier in the last ice-age, which ended at least 13,000 years ago. So all the peat on Foula must have been formed very recently in geological terms wherever there was more water than was able to drain away, which therefore prevented the decomposition of each year's growth of vegetation when it died in the winter. Full decomposing requires air, which is just not available in waterlogged ground. Such incomplete decomposition leads to partial decay which produces a slow accumulation of dead material year by year and forms peat. This is a very slow process. A rule of thumb measurement allows about 40 years for an inch of solid peat or roughly 500 years per foot as a convenient round figure. This would make the blue peats at the bottom of a two-moor bank six feet deep a minimum of 3000 years old, though the lowest peat, having been under considerable pressure for many centuries, could well represent 100 years per inch of the dense blue peat. No wonder it burns hotter! Perhaps 5000 years in the making of such a deep deposit would be nearer, with the rule of thumb applying more accurately to the shallower layers which cover so much of the island. But the weather conditions in Shetland are unusual, probably unique, and hence Shetland's reputation for having the slowest growth rate for peat in the world.

The essential condition for forming peat is high rainfall, 700 to 1000 mm per annum on an average of 150–175 rainy days. This is the norm for the formation of 'raised bog', the type where the peat holds its own moisture so that the level of the bog, undrained, is higher than the surrounding land. If the rainfall is even higher, then the peat bog is not just in areas of raised bog but spread over more of the land like a blanket – hence its name. With so many variables in the formation of this surface layer of locked-up carbon, making a very accessible fuel, it will always be difficult, if not impossible, to date accurately the age of any particular deposit. How much additional information we would have about Foula's past if only we knew, instead of having to guess. For example, we were told of a comparatively shallow deposit just below the road on Hamnabreck near the top of the slope down to the Mill Loch, where someone's tuskar had struck a hard object and revealed a birch branch, about two inches in diameter and perfectly preserved in the acid water below about four feet of peat. Further digging unearthed several branches splayed out from the root of what must have been a gnarled little tree but undoubtedly a birch, as was proved by one or two leaves stuck to the well preserved bark which looked as though they could have fallen the autumn before instead of perhaps 4000 years ago. What does this tell us about the climate in 2000 B.C.? It was a reasonably sheltered area well below the crest of the shoulder which the road climbs up south of the Manse en route for the Hame Toun. Above it the heights of Bodlifield and Hamnafield protected it from the west or north gales. But there is no way that a birch tree would survive there now, however dwarfed or stunted. So perhaps a milder and less turbulent period of weather prevailed for long enough then to allow trees to survive, with still sufficient rain to turn their foliage into the beginnings of a blanket of peat for us to dig and burn.

I have kept some of the sticks from that discovery now for over fifty years and they still look like any other birch sticks such as those we often used to burn in our wood-burning stove. I kept one or two hard black peats too so that when I was feeling nostalgic for the sights and sounds of the island, I could put one with its end in the fire until it smoked and as I carried it glowing through the house, I could at least have the real smell of Foula to bring it all back. One could call it the smell of survival; but now the new factor of the carbon footprint comes in to unbalance the equation. Burning peat releases all that stored carbon into the atmosphere in the form of CO_2 pollution, in just the same way as the thawing of the permafrost in the Arctic could release an almost infinite quantity of pollution in the form of the methane locked in by the low temperature. Methane has about twenty times the effect of CO_2 in preventing the escape of the heat from direct solar energy on planet Earth, and so increasing the 'greenhouse' effect on global warming. I was to discover much later just how the Foula community would attempt to reduce their dependence on peat, the 'fossil fuel' which has enabled them to beat all the other isolated island communities in the art of winter survival up to the 21st century, when there was no practicable alternative within their grasp. For the basic requirements of cooking and heating, peat will remain their cheapest resource, so long as there are able-bodied folk with the right skills to produce it. For electricity and other energy demands they will, like the rest of us, have to depend on new technology to save their own way of life.

This however is no longer a problem that involves only remote island communities, but the life itself of the whole human race. Small islands are however microcosms of that huge picture, on a more comprehensible scale. Could their story of survival perhaps help us to plan for and face the huge looming catastrophe of climate change, which threatens to be too big a disaster for mortal minds to grasp as the world's population continues to spiral upwards, already far beyond the carrying capacity of one small planet. As things are now, and unlike most other human communities, Foula needs more people and has available fuel to see many more through the winters to come. But climate change is a many-faceted problem and the increased turbulence it threatens to bring to the eastern seaboard of the Atlantic Ocean could negate that advantage in the long term. Meanwhile peat remains their greatest asset, free fuel as a bait for new settlers, provided that... Watch this space!

Chapter 10: Duties; Official and Unofficial

Professor Ian Holbourn, in his book 'The Isle of Foula', gives in his opening chapter a panegyric of Foula, starting with a geographical description in which he waxes lyrical about its most spectacular features. He praises the western cliff faces, the hills and lochans, the Sneck of the Smallie which he calls '*probably the finest rock-cleft in Britain*', and the Gaada Stack, '*perhaps the finest stack*'. He sees his beloved island in true romantic fashion through rose-tinted spectacles and writes, or should I say speculates, a romantic history for the island as the '*Thule of the ancient world*'. He gives it a religious status based largely on supposition and a few island traditions as '*the Iona of the North, and the source of Christianity*' in Shetland. He extols its recent history, this time based on remembered traditions passed down to and then passed on by islanders he knew and talked with in person, of udal tenure and '*its line of petty kings*'; and he calls it, almost as an afterthought, '*an ornithologist's paradise*'. But he reserves his highest praise for its people, '*Not least among the attractions of Foula is the charm of its inhabitants. The writer has travelled over a million miles in some thirty different countries, and except in the less frequented parts of Norway has never met a community to compare with it for courtesy, intelligence, genuine kindness and honesty*.'

As he was the Laird and loved nothing more than a good story, preferably with some mystical dimension to it, much of his remarkable book consists of strange accounts of supernatural events and tales of mysterious places and people. He recounts dreams and visions, all purporting to be derived from first-hand accounts by the islanders of past events in the history of Ultima Thule. This he firmly believed was the historical name given to sightings of Foula by the Romans when they sailed round Britain, conquered Orkney and saw distant peaks on the horizon even further north than they had dared to venture, as recorded by Tacitus in the Agricola. Such was Professor Holbourn's romantic desire to establish Foula as the Ultima Thule of history that he even tries to twist the derivation of the name Foula as being from the word 'Thule', which to the Romans simply meant 'The World's End'. He does so in spite of acknowledging that the local version of the name is often pronounced Fugley, as for instance in Bobbie Isbister's own composition called 'Farewell to Foula' of which I have a tape-recording where he sings '*Farewell Fugley island…*' pronouncing it with a hard 'g'. This traditional pronunciation merely serves to emphasise the obvious derivation of the name from the Norse words Fugl and Øy, meaning 'bird island'. To anyone approaching the island by sea in summer when thousands of seabirds home in on Foula ahead of you, making the position of the island clear even in thick mist, it is obviously the island of birds first, of man second.

Yet Foula has been inhabited certainly far longer than the arrival of the Vikings who almost certainly gave it its present name, so often mispronounced as 'Fowler,' where the meaning seems still intact, but the correct pronunciation as 'Fooler' gives away the Viking original. To assess the Viking influence one only has to have the smattering of Norwegian, which I picked up on three visits as a student, and a map of Foula with all the place names of cliffs, bays, geos, houses, hills or any other features, and one can see that the names are merely descriptions – 'the Wick of Mucklaberg' (the bay of the great cliff); 'the Hame Toun' (the township where we live); 'Strem Ness' (the point where the tide flows); 'Ruscar' (red rocks); 'Overfandal' and 'Nether fandal' (the upper and lower hanging valleys); and so on. When Roland Svensson, the Swedish artist, came to Foula to paint a series of evocative watercolours of 'Foula, The Isle of Shadows' (as he called it in his book 'Lonely Isles'), he was amazed how easy he found it to use a map in Britain in which the place names seemed merely to describe, in his own language, the features he set out to portray. Other names are more of a mystery to me but have a wonderful ring of the days when the Norsemen arrived, not just to conquer but to settle and make their home in what may well have been a more hospitable place with perhaps trees and scrub and less violent weather than we have now. Listen to the music of names like Surpeidles, Quirvidle, Shetlins, Murnaleugs, Skirnawilse, Swalbar, Sandstack, Roeski, Lamatuns, Ufshins – all parts of the dramatic cliff scenery between Helliberg's Wick and the Wester Hoevdi along the south west shore, dominated by the Noup and the great cliffs of the Wick of Mucklaberg (O.S. 6″ Map, Second Edition 1902).

Just read them through again, out aloud, and you will see what I mean. Likewise the recorded names of some of the old crofts undoubtedly tell the story of Foula, most of them now roofless, some little more than 'a rickle o' stanes', all with so much to tell that we shall now never learn. Close to the western boundary wall of the Hame Toun is the ruin of Guthren, possibly the original home of Guttorm who established himself as King of Foula when Shetland was ruled by the Scandinavian Jarls up to the 13th century, a time still celebrated in Shetland every January in the great fire festival of Up Helly Aa in Lerwick. The Guiser Jarls dress up in Viking helmets with corbies' wings, and a Viking Galley is set ablaze with a thousand torches from the procession of modern Vikings taking part in the pageant. Foula was probably never part of the Viking Earldom of Orkney but probably an isolated miniature kingdom all on its own. But Holbourn's claim of the island's role in establishing Christianity is based largely on a local tradition that Northerhouse, a ruined croft house by the Old Kirk, south of the Biggins, had connections with a monastery. There seems no evidence for this, merely a bit of wishful thinking along the lines

that Foula was surely just the sort of retreat that ancient hermits and saints were wont to make use of, like Ninian and Columba. Far stronger is the tradition that the Kings of Norway used Foula as an isolated school of the old Norn language for their princes, and there seem to be reliable records of the Lord's Prayer being known in Norn as recently as the 19th century. But there is no trace of Roman Catholicism in Foula and the recent history is first of a Congregational Church, followed by a strong Presbyterian tradition. The Old Kirk, beside which is the traditional burial ground, dates back to the Reformation but was already in decay in the 1930s. Michael Powell wanted to include a film sequence in 'The Edge of the World' of the church service where the islanders tie up their dogs outside the Kirk. So he reslated the roof and restored the weathered pews and pulpit for the purpose.

In 1954 the Old Kirk stood empty but with a sound, slate roof and more or less intact, even though it had never been used for worship for many years. The graveyard with its headstones engraved with family names like Gray, Isbister, Umphray, Ratter, Manson, was still used for burials, but the stones stood silent and neglected. It

The Wick of Mucklaberg from the west. The Daal, a classic glacial U-shaped valley, separates the Noup from the main line of hills, with the Sneck of the Smallie, a 200 ft deep fissure in the cliff at the Wastins, clear from this angle

The burial ground below South Biggins and the old Kirk in 1954, still with the slate roof restored by Michael Powell in 1936 for his film 'The Edge of the World'

was a rather sad place to visit, with few flowers though the grass was still cut every year and the weathered wall repaired as needed.

In the late 18th century, believe it or not, Foula was part of a triple parish with churches in Fair Isle, where the minister lived, and Out Skerries, 70 miles to the north and on the east side of Shetland. Not surprisingly Foula got only one visit a year for a week or two. In 1817 as part of J.A. Haldane's founding of the Congregational Church in Shetland, a small chapel was built on the shoulder of the hill to the north of the Hametoun. Congregationalism seemed to suit the islanders and with money left by his sister in memory of one William Baxter, a new larger church was built which is still marked on the maps as the Baxter Chapel. Finally when the Congregational following waned, it was transferred into the care of the

Church of Scotland, and this building is still in use today, supported, when a resident lay missionary can be found, jointly by the Church and the S.P.C.K. from Edinburgh.

My first impression of the building when I walked up the quarter mile of road between the Manse and my second place of work, was how spacious it was for such a small community. Apart from the slightly musty smell that all underused buildings have in a damp climate, it felt quite homely and welcoming and seemed to have been well looked after. There was a small vestry, in the cupboard of which I hung my black graduate gown which I had hardly worn since I left Cambridge, except for College formalities in Edinburgh. Here it seemed strangely out of place but I felt it necessary to make some distinction from the essentially informal clothes I wore in my daily life out and about in the Foula climate.

I plucked up my courage and went up into the pulpit and tried to imagine them looking up at me from the pews; faces, many of which at that stage I had not yet seen. I have always been critical of the organised church for being too organised when it comes to preaching. As a member of a congregation I had always admired the clergy who made me laugh, or gave a long pause for thought; who spoke without notes from the heart; or even – though this was very rare in any church in my experience – who asked a question and waited for a reply from the pews

The Kirk, originally the 'Baxter Chapel' on the Hametoun Wilse

The interior of the new Kirk, with the pulpit and pedal organ centre-stage

or invited an opinion or a comment. I hate the power of the pulpit, the captive audience, the pontification of views without any redress, the imposition of beliefs on others who may well not share your own convictions, or prejudices. So what was I going to do here? I was the incomer, the stranger, the alien even, from the busy, sinful, largely heathen outside world. What right had I to foist any ideas of mine onto these people who needed so much something solid and dependable and comforting to hang onto? Surely they had enough to contend with, so little enrichment in their lives, such a dreary round of inevitable chores simply to have a reasonable existence for themselves and their animals and all the people who would never make it to church and yet depended on them for their very survival? All my congregation would have less money, less freedom, less carefree joy in their lives than I had. Nearly all those I had met so far had some sort of problem in their family with the elderly or the infirm, or with their health. Besides they probably had a far simpler, uncluttered philosophy of life and faith in God than I had after four years of student debate and the turmoil of university Christianity. I was, quite frankly, still in a bit of a muddle over my Anglican upbringing in conflict with my newly found enthusiasm for Darwinism and the God of the mountaintop. The God of the Kirk, and worst of all, of the pulpit, was fairly rapidly becoming separated from the God of this wonderful world of nature and the sheer splendour of what I no longer called 'Creation' – but 'Evolution'. Surely the numinous quality of Foula would speak for itself? My favourite quotation to convey what I felt was from Elizabeth Barrett Browning:

> *Earth's crammed with Heaven, and every common*
> *bush afire with God;*
> *But only he who sees takes off his shoes, the rest sit*
> *round it and pluck blackberries.*

As I walked home to the Manse, listening to the sound of the Atlantic, the song of a skylark over the croftland, the wonderful plaintive cry of an Arctic Skua swooping at high speed over his moorland territory in a proud display of ownership, I vowed I would try to concentrate not on morality, not on the minutiae of the Christian creed, not on the standard subject matter of seasonal sermons on the great festivals of the church (Easter just past, thank goodness, as I began to wonder whether I really believed in the Resurrection any more) but on the common miracles of everyday life. In a place like Foula I could draw inspiration from the seasonal round of the natural world and point up the need we all had for

each other just like the birds in a colony or the animals who depended on us. I could surely find practical tips for close-knit family life to preserve human kindness and love and avoid the sort of feuding and bitterness which I had already learnt about or observed for myself as almost a tradition between certain sectors of our tiny community. Yet I mustn't preach at them. I must identify with their problems and their needs. I was very aware that I must appear to them to hold all the cards and have all the advantages which most of them simply could never aspire to. It wasn't going to be easy to get it right, but if I could just get their ear, their confidence that I had something to offer, I certainly would never run out of things to say, ideas to plant, lessons to be learned. My first lesson was clearly humility in the face of their superior experience.

But I was going to have to be very careful of one aspect of being an outsider. It was clear from what the Holbourns had told me that Foula folk were very independent, so that my position as representing authority in the outside world might bring me into conflict with my two major responsibilities to the school and the church. Unexpectedly this conflict soon appeared, not in my roles as teacher or preacher but in my dedication as an ornithologist. When I arrived in April, the Great Skuas had already arrived back from Africa and taken up their territories on the hills. I was well aware of the importance of this fact that my home was now in the middle of the largest colony in the whole of the Northern Hemisphere of this important predator species. I very soon found out that this was a privilege with problems, not just for other species of birds but also for me as an ornithologist and for the crofters as well. Almost my first thrill as a bird-watcher was the morning I almost tripped over a sitting Eider Duck on her nest in a tuft of grass not fifty yards from my own back-door. She sat tight till the last second, trusting to her soft brown camouflage to conceal her. In her panic as she flew she used an old trick eider-ducks have of covering her eggs with an evil-smelling faecal fluid, a potent deterrent to any ground predator like a fox. No foxes on Foula of course, so that instinct was little help to her against aerial predators like skuas who would have relished nothing more than a clutch of pale green eider eggs for breakfast. Luckily her other strong instinct to sit very tight and trust her cryptic colouring to hide her and her clutch of eggs was adequate and later I watched her with a brood of ducklings which she would eventually lead down to the sea. However several times I saw flying eider-ducks run the gauntlet of both Great and Arctic Skuas if they flew over their moorland territories. Puffins were even more at risk later in the season when flying home with a beakful of sand-eels for their chick in the nesting burrow. Puffins, everybody's favourite sea-bird, fly better underwater than they do in the air. So they are no match for the swift, aggressive skuas which will harry them till they drop the food in order to escape, or failing that will force them down onto the water and drown them. It's hard to like skuas when you have watched one rip a puffin's skin off and swallow it whole. They are also alarmingly aggressive against human intruders.

I had been aware of the problems skuas can cause to crofters from Kenneth Williamson's account of the Arctic Skuas on Fair Isle which were such a nuisance to the islanders going about their legitimate business of shepherding. Arctic skuas are even more determined and relentless in defence of their territories than their larger cousins the Bonxies. As a result the National Trust for Scotland, owners of Fair Isle, had been compelled to turn a blind eye to the occasional lapse of patience by the island's shepherds who went to the hill with a gun as well as a shepherd's crook. It just so happened that my arrival at Foula in 1954 was followed soon after by an entirely new legal situation with the passing by Parliament of the new Bird Protection Act, which protected nearly all British birds and especially scarce species like the skuas where the penalties were more severe. Imagine my alarm therefore when I discovered a completely new angle to the problem of whose side I was on. My barometer of such things was the conversation in the Schoolhouse kitchen when I soon realised in late April that they were trying to let me in on a secret they thought I ought to know about before I put my big foot in it. One Friday they were preparing baskets packed with grass and announced these were for the first collection that weekend of the skuas eggs, which were traditionally gathered at three week intervals, to allow the birds to relay a new batch for their larders. Bonxies' eggs especially are much larger than hens' eggs and just as tasty. Moreover I was assured this couldn't do much harm as the birds always laid again so all they were doing was delaying he breeding season by about a month. Over the next few weeks it became an embarrassment for me that in nearly every croft I visited I could, if I wanted to, see the evidence, seldom concealed as they saw no reason to be ashamed of it, of what was soon to become blatant law-breaking. It might be a bowl of beautifully marked skua eggs on a sideboard, or worse still in a small package, marked with my name, a contribution to my larder as I clearly didn't have the time or opportunity to go out egg-collecting

myself! What was I to do – cause offence by refusing a gesture which had cost them time and effort in a busy life, or incriminate myself by accepting their present with gratitude? Worst of all was being offered a boiled egg for my 'tea' and having to crack open the lovely mottled shell because it seemed so churlish to refuse. Then the trouble was that they were so delicious that the decision was really made for me for the future as I tucked in with uninhibited relish.

Before my first arrival in Foula in April 1954, I had thought long and hard about entering such a community, and especially how I would cope with the church part of my commitment. I knew some were strong traditional believers and others never darkened the door of the Kirk, but I had to try to get on with them all. There were many opportunities during my early days of going round the crofts, when my school timetable allowed, walking between the north-end crofts, the central Ham Toun, and the Hame Toun at the south end of the island, to think through my obligations and how to tackle them. They seemed to divide into three categories.

The first two were obvious, my duties to the school and the church. After that came a less definable role as the outsider with previous connections to other bodies like the Nature Conservancy, and with a typewriter and the mailboat to connect me with the 'authorities' in Lerwick and Edinburgh. Especially I was obviously an ornithologist, if only because I invariably arrived at their crofts carrying a pair of binoculars round my neck and ready to tell them about any interesting migrants I had seen or any aspect of the resident seabird population they might be prepared to discuss. I found most of them both knowledgable and interested and in agreement with my ideas on conservation. But now I had this problem over the skuas. To the islanders they were just part of the scene, from March when the first Great Skuas arrived back from their wintering grounds off the coast of West Africa, and then the later arrival of the Arctic Skuas in April. During the breeding season both species lived off our seabirds as parasites and predators, and then departed for the south again in autumn. The fact that this was such a vital colony of Great Skuas, described as of international significance, was of course a point of interest, even of pride; but it also meant that they laid a lot of eggs. In my first season of counting their nesting territories I had a rough estimate of 2000 pairs of Bonxies and 250 of Alans (to use the local dialect names) which meant that in the months of May and June there were at least 4500 beautiful fresh eggs free for the taking by anyone able-bodied enough to set off up the hill and gather the harvest. Compared with the cliff-fowling of the old days it was easy meat. It took time as the nests and eggs were well camouflaged; but what a prize! And for me what a problem! For families with agile children it was a fun-day as well as a challenge. The traditional collecting dates were in their mental calendar as one of those essential spring jobs to be done, to keep the food bills down and the protein in the diet up. My pupils were all involved so clearly I had to make up my mind which side of the fence to come down on. As their mentor and guardian could I deny them a rich source of food after the winter shortages which was sadly lacking in luxuries like eggs? The older residents also deserved a welcome change of diet and a boost in vitamins and calories, so that it was also traditional to collect for crofters no longer able to go to the hill. So it was both an excellent case for social welfare and even a good subject for a school project on the bounty of nature and the lives of the birds, with a healthy outdoor element into the bargain.

The Act didn't come into force until December 1954, so that my first spring season on Foula didn't technically produce a problem – except that it established me as one of the guilty if I continued to take the side of the islanders. They were after all aware of the need for the collecting to be controlled. They were also responsible enough to limit the collections to allow the birds to breed normally, but about four to six weeks late. So before the crunch came in spring 1955, I consulted by post with the Nature Conservancy in Edinburgh, and with the RSPB. Much to my relief they took the very reasonable attitude that it would do little harm if the islanders took a proportion of the first laying, provided the birds were then left to lay again with only the minimum delay to their season. They acknowledged that to make an official exception to the terms of the Act just for Foula, could be controversial and would certainly be expensive to administer, which could hardly be justified. They also seemed to accept my point that unless I tried to enforce the law myself (which I said I was unwilling to do) any measures they took to demand compliance would almost certainly be flouted anyway. So I was left with the unofficial but practical solution that the strict letter of the law could be ignored but my task was to try gently to introduce the idea that part of their traditional summer harvest ought to be curtailed.

I was also concerned that interfering with the birds' natural rhythm by postponing the feeding of the chicks for several weeks would put their breeding success at risk. For instance one of the main items of their diet was the crop of young puffins which came to the mouth of their burrows to exercise their wings before they left for the sea. Many would normally be picked off by the skuas at that stage, so delaying the peak feeding period of skua chicks might well give the young puffins a chance to escape. To study this as well as the breeding success of the skua chicks I selected a study area beyond the Ham Toun to the north-east where I could count the eggs of the second laying and measure their hatching rate. In addition I had selected one conveniently placed pair on the shoulder of the hill beyond the church for a more detailed study of one pair. It didn't seem much to ask out of possibly 2000 pairs all told, so I decided to chance my arm and put up a polite notice in the shop giving the facts about the new law, outlining the conciliatory attitude of the Nature Conservancy and their voluntary concession over egg-collecting, and asking for co-operation over my study area. I thought it only fair to ask permission from Bobby Isbister, the shopman first. As expected he argued strongly in favour of local custom and tradition but saw no harm in me displaying my point of view to his customers. I decided to risk stressing the condition of the concession that only the first laying of eggs should be collected so as to minimise the delay to the birds' normal breeding season. The notice had not been up more than a few days before it was made abundantly clear that it was not the detail that the islanders objected to but the principle involved. Outside interference with their daily lives produced a vigorous and outspoken reaction. I never knew who wrote across the top of my notice the quote from Rudyard Kipling though it was typical of Bobby's rather cynical style. I can hear him now answering with a rather wicked little chuckle, any of my ideas he thought would not be accepted, '*Well, of course, you wouldn't expect us to agree on that. It's not our custom, you see. We've always collected the eggs*'. And that would be that. Stalemate: nothing further to be said. So I always suspected that the quotation was written by Bobby and was very much to the point though of course Foula lies between 60'07″ and 60'10″ north. More outspoken and much less sophisticated was the word '*RUBBISH*' written across the bottom of my notice in pencil and rather childish handwriting. Might it even have been one of my pupils? Perish the thought! Clearly whoever it was didn't give much weight to my attempt to make a serious study of the problems their 'law-breaking' might arouse. I should have expected this reaction from an island which still ignored British Summer Time completely – '*What's wrong with the time the good Lord gave us anyway*? – and which has still not caught up with Pope Gregory's change to the old Julian calendar and celebrates Christmas 12 days late on 6th Jan.

THERE IS NEVer a law of God
or Man runs north
of 53

THE MANSE
FOULA
29th APRIL, 1955.
By LERWICK
SHETLAND

UNDER THE "WILD BIRD PROTECTION ACT" OF 1954 WHICH CAME INTO FORCE ON 2nd DECEMBER LAST, ALL WILD BIRDS TOGETHER WITH THEIR EGGS ARE PROTECTED BY LAW. IF THE LAW WERE TO BE ENFORCED THERE WOULD BE A $5 FINE FOR EVERY BIRD SHOT AND EVERY EGG TAKEN, EXCEPT FOR HARMFUL BIRDS SUCH AS THE GULLS, CROWS, ROCK-DOVES etc., AND THIS PROTECTION COVERS THE BONXIE AS WELL AS MOST OF THE SEA-BIRDS.

EXCEPTIONS HAVE BEEN MADE TO THE NEW ACT IN ONE OR TWO CASES WHERE THE BIRDS OR THEIR EGGS WERE BEING TAKEN FOR FOOD, WHEN SPECIAL PERMISSION WAS SOUGHT FOR THIS PURPOSE. NO SUCH PERMISSION HAS BEEN SOUGHT FOR ANY AREAS OF SHETLAND YET NOR FOR FOULA, BUT IT IS CLEAR THAT THE LAW IS NEVER LIKELY TO BE ENFORCED HERE. I HAVE CONSULTED WITH THE BIRD PROTECTION AUTHORITIES IN SCOTLAND AND THE NATURE CONSERVANCY WHO HAVE EXPRESSED THE OPINION THAT LITTLE HARM COULD BE DONE BY THE TAKING OF EGGS HERE AS BEFORE.

I AM ANXIOUS, HOWEVER TO MAKE A STUDY OF AT LEAST A FEW PAIRS OF BONXIES UNDER NATURAL CONDITIONS WITH AS LITTLE INTERFERENCE AS POSSIBLE. I WOULD THEREFORE BE MOST GRATEFUL IF THE BONXIES' NESTS ON THE LOW-LYING GROUND, AND ESPECIALLY ON CROUGAR AND SUKKIMIRES, COULD BE LEFT ALONE AND THE BIRDS ALLOWED TO INCUBATE THE FIRST LAYING OF EGGS. I ALSO HOPE TO MAKE AN INDIVIDUAL STUDY OF THE SINGLE PAIR WHICH NEST BETWEEN THE KIRK AND THE NORTH HOEVDI AND I WOULD BE PARTICULARLY GRATEFUL IF THEY COULD BE LEFT UN-MOLESTED. THE NEST WAS ROBBED IN 1954 JUST AT THE MOST INTERESTING STAGE OF MY OBSERVATIONS.

THANK YOU.

C. K. Mylne.

I suspect that my notice in the shop was the talking point of the island for a few days, and at least their written comments meant they had taken the trouble to read it. So I was lucky they didn't just tear it up and ignore it. I myself learnt several things from the whole episode – how to defend oneself from Bonxies' attacks by carrying a stick in ones' rucksack, protruding high enough to deflect the swooping dive-bomber above ones' head. Failure to take such steps could mean a sharp blow on the scalp which could sometimes draw blood from the skua's vicious hooked claws; also how to find their well camouflaged nests by locating the mound at the centre of each territory usually close to the nest, where the ground has been fertilised by the off-duty bird's droppings. I had so much to learn. The islanders knew it all already.

Apart from this fairly good-natured difference of opinion between us, I felt as time went on that I settled in to their community as well as could be expected. I was more apprehensive of my duties towards the congregation at the Kirk than anything else as this was a whole new world of experience for me. It was therefore an enormous relief to me to discover that there was none of the fanatical Sabbatarian strictness found so widely in the Celtic islands like the Hebrides but rather a decent respect for that most excellent ruke, the greatest legacy of the ancient Israelites to our world, the one day's rest in seven. For a hard-pressed teacher with 100 extraneous duties every Saturday as well, my Sundays were literally a Godsend, even though at first I still had two services and two sermons to prepare. As a result my Sunday lunch at Mrs Beagrie's was a blissful recreation, with homely conversation for the mind and healthy nourishment for the body. There's nothing like a good blether as an antidote to the responsibilities of ones' jobs. Once I had mastered her rich blend of Shetland and Aberdeen accents, she was a fount of good island gossip from which I also learnt a great deal.

With the help of steadfast friends like Mima Gear and Peter Gray's wife Muriel I was eased into the niceties of the vestry and the Kirk. It was easier to conform with what they were used to, and in any case I had few preconceptions about the right way to run a church and its' congregation. I was probably the least experienced lay missionary they had ever had. After the first strangeness and nervousness had worn off, and buoyed up by the attendances and the sometimes unexpected faces in the congregation, and the high standard and enthusiasm of the singing, I began to feel that perhaps I did have something to offer that was reasonably acceptable at least to some. Soon I began also to enjoy jotting down my half page of brief notes as my guide to what I wanted to say each week. Before long I began to question the tradition of two services each and every Sunday. Several people kindly asked me if I was coping alright when they saw how busy I was and how tired I was getting with my late nights trying to keep up with the inevitable paperwork. Finally the suggestion came from them that with many people choosing to come to one or other of the services, and attendances at both therefore being small enough to remove some of the atmosphere of shared worship and communion, it would surely be better for all of us to put our effort into one good service, rather than two not so good services, each Sunday. The elders agreed; and I thanked God.

I had three or four people prepared to play the organ and good enough to manage it without risk of breakdown. Peter Gray was reliable but very slow and the hymns became rather like dirges when he was on organ duty. Vida Henry from the Schoolhouse was reliable and made the whole service brighter. Very occasionally, usually because of illness, I had to step in myself and proved easily the least capable of playing all the notes correctly and not forgetting the G sharps or B flats. Often the singing, with so few voices to choose from, was remarkably tuneful and, most importantly, enthusiastic. One night of wind and rain we had a faithful congregation of five and managed four-part harmony for every hymn. All I had to do was to choose Tenor or Bass according to which part was not being filled. The ladies did the rest. One thing I had to get used to was their love of the rousing tunes and rhythms of the old, red Moodie and Sankey hymnbook of Choruses. They were cheerful enough and the tunes were easy and bright, but the sentiments expressed were not mine and often, I felt, unhelpful to the mind, though admittedly cheerful to the spirit. And after a few Sundays as the summer progressed and the weather stayed remarkably fine and dry, the numbers kept up and even increased; and from the long discussions I had with some people afterwards or round a peat stove late at night arising out of something I had said the previous Sunday, I began to feel that perhaps I wasn't altogether missing the boat or sending them all to sleep. There was one thing however which was slowly but steadily dawning on me as I managed to get round all the crofts for the first time, and on the second round began to get to know some of my parishioners a bit better as friends and not just watchers from the pews. It became clear that they all had far more to teach me of humility, and patience, and generosity of spirit towards me and their neighbours than I would ever have to offer them. They were indeed the sort of people that both Michael Powell and Ian Holbourn had told me they were, in the only two books I had so far found time to read on The Isle of Foula. The words that come back to me to describe them are '*sympathetic, intelligent and charming*'. They were good Christians!

One of the things I was most relieved about was their open-mindedness in matters of religion. They observed the Sabbath in a practical and sensible way, a day of rest but not a day wasted so far as croftwork or the routines of daily life were concerned. Mostly they were very private about their faith and quite frank if they had none. They divided quite openly into church-goers or not, some very committed and others who never came, even at the great annual festivals. They seemed free of such hypocrisies as late drinking on a Saturday till midnight, followed by strict abstinence on the Sabbath which had so upset me in the areas of Scotland with a Celtic heritage not a Norse one. Foula seemed to me a community with an inherited morality of caring for each other, of sobriety with one or two spasmodic exceptions, and with a markedly non-violent way of life. I never locked a door in my house the whole time I was there and never lost a thing that I was aware of. There were some petty feuds and some prejudices between families but I never remember hearing strong or foul language, even though I was often in amongst their daily routines such as rounding up the sheep or loading the mailboat. I know my presence as 'the minister' would have inhibited swearing, but surely I would have overheard some evidence if it was common parlance.

Punctuality was not a common virtue. But generosity of all sorts seemed to be endemic. I never lost my respect for them, nor my love for some of them, and especially the children. It grew as we got to know each other better. But one or two new words did start to creep in as my timetable became more hectic and some of their habits and little ways became more and more irksome with familiarity. Descriptions like slow, indecisive, dilatory, especially of certain families, led to words encompassing my own reactions – such as frustrating, or infuriating, or hopeless? Or IMPOSSIBLE! Of course it was part of my job to be understanding and patient, but – bless them – at last they were beginning to teach me, just ten years too late, exactly what is meant by that once dreaded word – INSULARITY.

Chapter 11: 'Spare' Time Activities

Weekends were a problem; not because of the Sabbath, thank goodness, but because my loyalties were seriously split between duty and leisure, especially on Saturdays. It was lucky that my teaching career had started in a boarding school where during term I seldom had a Saturday I could call my own. There had been official duties at John Watson's like sports fixtures or unofficial duties, organising recreational activities for the children, and every third weekend a full programme of responsibilities as the master on duty. So it was nothing new to me to have to 'work' my weekends. At the start I had two services to prepare each Sunday, which occupied both my mind and my time for the first few weekends, until I got into the swing of it. I also had to plan next week's school programme, so although I did not need to turn up at the school on a Saturday, it was often my best opportunity to get the school records up to date or to prepare for the following week's lessons or projects. But Saturday was my only chance to visit those members of my 'parish' who couldn't come to church and whom I never saw if I didn't visit them in their own homes. Added to these obligations was a yearning to explore the island and to find out what I could about its teeming wildlife.

The weather of the spring and summer of 1954 was exceptionally dry and sunny, which was a big factor in exacerbating the conflict between recreation and duty, but made both much more enjoyable. I took binoculars and a pocket notebook everywhere I went, even when I took my rubbish over to our little private tip over the cliffs at the back of the Beagrie's house. When you can combine doing such mundane chores with watching puffins, those comic and self-important little clowns with their colourful beaks and bright orange feet, it is hard not to be diverted. In May they had settled in and I used to watch them strutting on the grassy cliff top outside their nesting burrows, making exaggerated threat gestures against their neighbours, heads nodding and beaks held open. Occasionally they came to blows with fights, where two birds locked together by their bills would roll over and over down precipitous slopes, biting and wing-flapping until they had to break off in mid-air as they tumbled into space. How petty and yet how urgent their social squabbles seemed to be, but they seemed to thrive in spite of it and between fights looked happy enough. I sometimes wondered what would happen if our community settled their grievances with the occasional outburst as the puffins did. Their sheer numbers on the island indicated a well organised and successful system for survival against the same odds that we faced – with one major exception. When the autumn storms came they had wings and could escape the harshness of winter by leaving the land and finding their food out at sea. Meanwhile we all enjoyed Foula in summer weather, birds and people alike. Looking across that stretch of water at the grey shapes of the Shetland mainland gave me a smug sense of happiness in my own private paradise.

While following up a couple of pairs of razorbills during such a diversion on Saturday the 15th of May, I was aware of an aggressive raven driving other smaller birds out of its territory. Eventually I was able, by patiently watching the pair of ravens, to spot their nest on another visit after church on the evening of Sunday 23rd May with at least one chick visible in a well hidden and inaccessible cleft in the rocks. I suspected there would be others, with so much suitable habitat round the cliffs and so much food available to large scavengers like ravens; but my hopes of studying the raven population of Foula by gradually accumulating records of this sort were dashed the very next day when I heard that John Henry, who had sheep in that area of the island, had shot four birds – one adult and three young from this nest. I could hardly blame him as ravens were generally agreed to be quite the worst menace to the ewes at lambing time, and known even to attack a ewe in the act of giving birth when she was helpless. Crofters like many other people who witness such acts take a very anthropomorphic view of the predator, calling them cruel and justifying their persecution of the villain of the piece on that ground. I had many quite philosophical discussions with Foula crofters on this topic, that birds are not capable of cruelty, which is essentially a human attribute. The raven is doing what it must for the sake of its own kind; but it has no capacity for pity or restraint, having no consciousness of its actions. But John Henry's

An adult puffin in full breeding plumage

sympathies were with his ewe and her lamb, who needed protection from the 'cruel' ravens. I concurred in that he had a right to protect his own livelihood and so we agreed he was justified in shooting the ravens but for quite different reasons. If only all human destroyers of wildlife would acknowledge that they do it for self interest, including those who kill for entertainment or so-called sport, then both the conservation and the blood-sports debates would become more honest. The argument against human licence to kill would get stronger as we recognise the gross disproportion of our numbers against those of any other vertebrate species on earth. It was humbling to think that on Foula we were outnumbered by birds by several thousand to one and yet still claimed dominance over nature. I was just beginning to see how much easier it was to think

straight about such issues on a remote island. We had so many more natural restraints, than in the city.

I remember when my younger sister started her first job in an Edinburgh primary school, how horrified she was to discover during a lesson on farming that many of the children in her class thought that milk came from a bottle and beef or mutton from a butcher's shop. In that context my five pupils were so lucky to have the sea, the sky and the wildlife as their teachers and not just me. But sometimes the lessons they would learn from nature were in conflict with what they learned from adults, especially if they went to church and learned that God is the fount of all goodness and man the source of all evil. In which case who created spiders?

The weekend of 15/16 May produced a good example of this when Mima Gear arrived about midnight with a gull in a box, which was clearly in a very sorry state. I had seen a sickly Glaucous gull during the week when out looking at the progress of the Bonxies in their breeding area up at Overfandal with Jim and Vina after school. It was unusual to see this species in May as they are winter visitors which return to the far north to nest; and it had seemed very weak and flew only slowly over the moor towards the road. Now it looked near to death, so I kept it overnight till the Sunday morning and tried to feed it with strips of fish, which was not easy as in spite of its weakness it was aggressive and quite vicious. It couldn't swallow any food down however and died shortly after. When my Sunday duties were over, I dissected the bird to discover the cause of death and found that it had a large sea-urchin stuck spines-downward in its gullet. The bird must have attempted to swallow the sea-urchin and suffered both pain and starvation for weeks, being unable to regurgitate or swallow such a rigid, spiny object. It was desperately thin and its gut was empty though it still had a crab's claw in its stomach which it

would normally have ejected as a pellet. It was in full breeding plumage which was in good condition in spite of its starvation. So I skinned and preserved it as a museum specimen, one of my first attempts at taxidermy, using an excellent instruction manual lent to me by the Natural History Dept. of the Royal Scottish Museum for just this purpose. It took me longer than I expected but I was pleased with my first bird 'skin'.

I was later to see many Glaucous gulls in Shetland waters in winter when they are not uncommon. The wing measurement was 57 inches from tip to tip which makes it a big bird, and their very white appearance makes them easy to spot and identify in the field. It was a new species for my island list. I love the name Glaucous gull. It sounds so exotic. Yet this is the only context in which I have ever seen the adjective 'glaucous' used, except perhaps to describe the colour of the blue-grey bloom on ripe grapes. But the gull is not grey except as an immature bird, rather a gleaming white, and gleaming is the sense in which Homer used the word 'glaucopis' to describe

The Glaucous Gull which tried to swallow a sea-urchin and starved to death

'*the grey-eyed Athene*'. In my teenage vision of the goddess of beauty when I was first reading Homer, her eyes were blue, but if the translator chose 'grey', I reckoned it was to give her a specially seductive look. Perhaps the epithet in this mysteriously beautiful bird's name means that type of white like washing powders tinged with blue for effect, to create that whiter-than-white appearance. My old friend Professor Maurie Meiklejohn of Glasgow University, who loved to poke fun at fellow bird-watchers, also loved the name but always referred to it with a wry smile as 'the Glucose gull'. Sadly there was no sweetness in this bird's sticky end. How sad that its natural instinct, instead of enhancing its chances of survival as it was supposed to, had ended in this painful death. Was this part of the beautiful Creation? It most certainly was nothing to do with sin.

I was struck by Mima's diligent care for the disabled bird and her distress at its innocent end. Mima was like that, as I had discovered early on by her attitude towards all animals in her care. The language she used seemed to me almost to belong to a vanished era. When I told her about the gull's affliction and miserable end, she exclaimed '*Alas! Alas! The poor pirie bird!*' It was like a phrase out of an old nursery rhyme or fairy-tale book, only it sounded like '*Less! Less!*' But her concern was genuine and she really meant '*Alas*' to show how upset she was. And in such matters she often used the phrase '*poor pirie tings*' using the very expressive Shetland diminutive derived from the French '*petit*' when you say it out softly. It was such a lovely sentiment, acknowledging their helpless innocence.

It led us to discuss the so-called cruelty of nature and I even wondered whether there might not be a sermon in the fate of our Glucose gull. But I decided that this congregation was not the right audience for my view that this is the way God's Creation is. The predators flourish; the strong prevail; diseases or viruses respect only the resistance put up by those who have suffered in the past – a lesson all Foula people would understand from their own known vulnerability to infection. God put the sea-urchin in the path of the gull which in all innocence swallowed it as a God-given breakfast. So what sort of a loving Creator is he? Or should it be 'she'? Or have we just invented him as a good God because it suits us to cling to that dream? That was in all honesty what I was beginning to think from my studies of the competitive natural world, but I didn't dare preach such dangerous ideas to the islanders, though I would discuss such topics with some who were remarkably wise philosophers. The furthest I remember going in

directing their thoughts about God as Creator was to quote to them, when basing a sermon on the weather and the storms of life, the lovely comic rhyme on the biblical idea that the rain falls on the just and the unjust in equal measure:

> *The rain it raineth every day*
> *Upon the just and unjust fella';*
> *But more upon the just because*
> *The unjust stole the just's umbrella!*

At least there was an obvious moral plea for making human behaviour more reasonable, and I could leave it to them to ruminate, if they chose to, on God's part in that little drama.

Some visits to the elderly included an ornithological slant, like that on 20th May when, at last, I managed to arrange a dusk visit to the Manx Shearwater colony at the back of the Noup in company with old Robbie Isbister, Eric's grandfather. Robbie 'owned' the shearwaters; at least they were always referred to as 'my' shearwaters, and it seemed a very private affair as he led the way along the rocky cliff path in his carpet slippers, past the Hametoun dyke and out onto the steep slopes, covered with huge boulders amongst which the birds nested in holes and rabbit burrows underground. The hollows and cavities between the rocks are numerous and the ground very broken, even dangerous, dropping away alarmingly in places to the sea far below. It's best moreover to go quite late when it is nearly dark so one needs to tread carefully. It is impossible to estimate how many shearwaters there might be in such a habitat, and how many nest-holes might be accessible. Robbie took us to his special nests, their concealed entrances covered with slabs of stone, which he carefully removed to reveal the burrow underneath. Then, stooping down and putting his mouth close to the open hole, he 'sang' to them – '*cock-a-leeko, cock-a-leeko*', his 85-year-old voice well suited to make the croaky, squeaky type of sound which was soon echoed back by the sitting bird from far under our feet answering with a muffled '*cock-a-leeko*' in reply. The match between Robbie's imitation and the bird's answer was perfect, and once he had ascertained they were at home, he reached into the hole and drew out the protesting and snapping adult, being careful to avoid the rather wicked looking hook on the end of its bill. Both the birds he retrieved were found to be ringed already. Some have been ringed for many years and come back faithfully to the same burrow in successive seasons. Occasionally one could see small rafts of birds gathering at dusk out on the waters off the Noup or round in Mucklaberg; tiny numbers compared with the Isle of Rum where countless thousands nest high up on the mountains.

But still there might be hundreds on Foula, and probably Storm Petrels nesting with them as often happens. One visit can give no idea of the size of such a colony. Robbie elicited replies from perhaps half a dozen sitting shearwaters, some hidden away behind huge boulders. On that occasion we heard none of the crooning or chittering flight calls of petrels which are usually all you have to go by in ascertaining their presence. All these underground nesters are night birds, which for survival have evolved a pattern of coming and going under cover of darkness. They are more or less helpless on land, being surface feeders on water, with their legs and feet designed for swimming, not walking or running. They are therefore notoriously vulnerable to the big robber gulls, which wait for them outside the burrows at first light when they try to escape back to the sea; and in the 'simmer dim' of a Shetland night there's

precious little darkness to protect them. On St Kilda the casualties among Leach's Petrels from dawn predation by gulls is reckoned to run into thousands. Survival of the fittest is a harsh law.

I always enjoyed my visits to the Isbister family at South Biggins, but this one was special, and it was obvious that Robbie really enjoyed an audience for his shearwater demonstration. It was a wonderful experience to meet up with such an enthusiast, so involved with his local environment. I found most of the islanders sympathetic to my interest in their wildlife of which they were enormously proud, though few as knowledgeable as Robbie. I found him a little difficult to understand, as his speech was full of dialect words I hardly knew yet and his teeth did not help. But to his shearwaters he was like a Dr Dolittle and spoke a language they understood well. I left him with the problem we all wanted to solve; whether there were any Leach's Fork-tailed Petrels on Foula. They are the ultimate case of sea-birds only coming to land on a handful of small, remote islands at

Robbie Isbister of South Biggins and his grandson Eric at the back of the Noup with a well grown Manx Shearwater chick, taken from its underground nest still in juvenile down

night, on places as difficult of access as North Rona and St Kilda. Their numbers were then completely unknown and the species had only been known to science since the 19th century. Their call is mysterious and distinctive and had been heard on Foula, but few ornithologists know it well enough to be sure of their identity by call alone. At that time I had never seen or heard one in my life. Eric's mother told me tantalizing stories of birds which the cat at North Biggins, the neighbouring croft to theirs, had brought in. One of these had been examined in the hand before being released and was said to have had a forked tail. Another account was of a bird found sitting on an egg in a burrow, which was thought to have had the right diagnostic features. But they are very like Storm Petrels, small dark birds with a similar white rump and strange musty smell, which were thought to nest in small numbers near the Sneck of the Smallie, on the other side of the Noup. So in 1954 the first breeding record of Leach's petrel on Foula was still to be proved.

My visits to other houses in the Hametoun at the south end, and especially to the northern crofts, emphasised just how cut off from their beautiful surroundings some of the old people had become. I found that for the house-bound, or the bed-ridden as with 90-year-old Jane Gray at Burns, anything I could tell them about the birds and the flowers of their island took them back to their youth and happier days which they remembered with such clarity. If I had the chance I would take something from the natural world in my hand, perhaps some cotton grass in late summer or some vernal squills in spring, or

things the children had been learning about in school from one of the excellent BBC Schools programmes on natural history. This gave the old folk a link with the outside world and the next generation from whom they were in some cases completely cut off. Jane was our oldest inhabitant and was well cared for by Peter and Muriel at Burns, a good two-storey house built by Peter's father in 1912. They gave up their best room on the ground floor and a great deal of their time and energy to caring for her with her old-age pension as their only reward. This small but vital cash input was a major factor in the simple economy of many families, so much so that a death, especially an unexpected one, could cause real problems if the old-age pension had been relied on for many years.

Muriel was the sister of Harry Gear, the Postmaster at Mogle. She always welcomed me with a pot of tea and perhaps some Black's biscuits served on a tray in Jane's room, with cups which I found it best not to examine too closely. Most houses had very primitive facilities and I realised that whereas I had a hot water system from my Rayburn stove, their water for all washing and cleaning probably had to be fetched from the well and then heated on a peat stove. One had to accept the fact that they had got used to a lower standard of hygiene and cleanliness than I was accustomed to and were doing wonderfully well – even if the cups were not spotless. I noticed how Jane, who was no relation to the Grays, always made a point of telling me how well she was looked after and how kind they were to her. She loved her books from the

Tiger lilies and elder bushes in the shelter of the garden wall at Burns

library and appeared always to have read the last batch I had brought. As she could hardly walk she had very little else to occupy her time, yet I don't ever remember hearing her complain of her lot. Peter and Muriel kept an interesting garden with some showy Tiger lilies by the gate which grew to the height of the wall, an apple tree that never grew any apples so far as I remember, honeysuckle on the gable end of the house, and an elder tree also protected from the gales by the sheltering stone wall. Nothing in Foula ever grew higher than its shelter, but even the modest growth in the Burns garden seemed so lush by contrast with the windswept, barren moorland that was its setting. The situation could have been described in a house agent's prospectus in idyllic terms: '*Beside the traffic-free, well maintained road to the North end of the island, a good footpath leads down to a wooden footbridge over a stream of crystal clear water. A rustic gate opens into an attractive garden with a path, bordered by flowers, leading to the front door over which a plaque on the lintel carries the date of construction, 1912. Set in hand tilled and sown agricultural land, the house commands wide views of the dramatic skyline of the hills. Plentiful peat close at hand*.' In summer all this would ring true and paint a wonderful picture, but in a winter gale…

On the opposite side of the road from Burns to the south was the site of a drained loch, a flat marshy area with a path across it to Loch, a small isolated house where Peter Ratter and his wife Bessie lived. This was possibly one of the houses I visited least, as they were both young (in their thirties) and busy, and having no family, seldom at home. Beyond Loch and just opposite Burns the metalled road stopped and a footpath was the only access to the North end crofts. Without any off-road vehicles in those days, transport of heavy goods or even a week's shopping to the four houses beyond Burns was hard going with only a wheelbarrow. South Harrier filled six acres of the lower ground on the left of the path with the best kept agricultural holding on the island. It had neat rigs of oats or potatoes or kale, green in summer, golden in autumn with the oats cut and stooked or the hay cut and raised into coles; the drains well maintained dividing many of the small fields of crops; and all the work of one man, Scotty Umphray. The house, with several byres alongside, was well roofed and maintained and everything inside was clean and tidy. Scott lived with his two sisters and they all worked hard to maintain as high a standard as they could for themselves and their animals. I can't now remember whether books for South Harrier were on my list. I doubt it as they certainly wouldn't have had time for reading

in summer when they worked their land and their crops late into the evenings. This was one part of the island where I could see for myself as a present reality how Foula had carried a population of 240 souls not so very long before. It is always tempting to think of the winter as the testing time, and the community's ability to survive as depending on their hardiness in coping with the rigours of winter weather. But this is perhaps to look at the problems of a remote community from the wrong end, so to speak. When I walked up the road, after loading my barrow with peat at my peat banks on the Lioag ready for the road home later in the evening, and, after a call at Burns, resumed my way north on the footpath, I would see Scotty Umphray busy scything his hay, with his sisters turning the cut swathes to take advantage of a drying breeze, almost certainly not for the first time, or even the second or third in some summers. Then several hours later as I was on my way home again after calling at North Harrier or Blowburn, the furthest north of all the occupied houses, there he would be, still labouring, making a slow but steady progress with a hundred and one jobs to be done on his 12 hectares in the crucial months of summer. Without such labour and plenty of fodder for the cows, without the careful maintenance of his buildings after the ravages of last winter before the equinoctial gales started the onslaught once again, without the crop of potatoes which, with occasional fish or '*reestit*' mutton, formed the staple diet for the long, dark months, there would be no surviving the winter for either man or animals. There was no shortage of daylight. Twenty hours a day were possible for outdoor work. The critical factor was stamina physically or determination psychologically, for months on end. Fortunately Scotty had both, but with no children and only one man in the family, the challenge for a man of 57 was considerable. The Umphray family had been on Foula for many generations, probably since the smallpox epidemic or even before, so they had experience. Scotty was also abreast of change and was the first crofter to acquire a tractor. It was a two-wheeled tractor, very slow but strong, called '*The Iron Horse*'. It must have made the world of a difference to Scotty's workload, and certainly was a vital factor in his ability to keep such a large arable area under cultivation single-handed. It's still on the island, a well rusted memorial to a remarkable man who upheld so deliberately the old virtues of hard work and loyalty to the family. He had little time for those who fell short of his ideas of what was right. To me he was a hero, and I was glad to have known him and his kind-hearted sisters.

In the winter I would call and be welcomed with a clean tablecloth and fresh scones or bread for tea. There'd be time for a chat and a bit of criticism of some of the other crofts where things weren't quite as efficient and well organised. There was electric light on a 12-volt system, if the Netherfandal burn was running full enough to power Scott's homemade waterwheel and dynamo. He had built a small stone 'mill' beside the burn and a sluice to guide the water onto the paddles of the wheel, using as materials for the purpose some of the rescued aluminium from a crashed plane that came down on the hill high above the house at the end of the war. I remember how impressed I was, not just with his electrical expertise, but with the device he had rigged to light the table in the middle of the room. There was a lamp hanging from the ceiling, or perhaps a rafter, which could be raised or lowered by winding a handle at the wall, which pulled a long chain, like a motorcycle chain, over a sprocket wheel with a ratchet till the height was exactly right to light the table. I was told that it was all made out of parts of the aileron control system from the plane's wing. Scottie had designed and engineered this simple but effecive mechanism in his own workshop, as he had with his private hydro-electricity. His ingenuity made a real difference to their quality of life.

Betty Gray of North Harrier lived in one of the smallest houses on the island, but at least she had a tarred felt roof like South Harrier, even though it was almost a black house with its fire on a hearth up against the gable wall, and a hole for a chimney half way up. I cannot now remember the detail of her domestic facilities but they must have been very primitive and did not include running water. She must have lived and fed simply, because she had minimal cooking facilities. She cooked, ate and slept all in just the one room into which I was welcomed as though it were my own home. I never had any impression that she was discontented with her lot or felt hard done by, and she always seemed to appreciate the books that I brought as she had very little else to entertain herself with or pass the time of day. She had a peat stack which I guessed was just another of Scotty's responsibilities, as she was in her mid-seventies

View from Blowburn of their hay coles in 1955, and the croft lands of North and South Harrier,
showing extensive crops of oats and hay, the fruits of an exceptionally dry summer

Scottie Umphray's horizontal water wheel generating hydro-electricity for South Harrier with the original, now disused, vertical corn mill on the same stream above, in summer 1955

and not really able to cope with much outside work at all. I always regretted that I never took any photographs of her living conditions but it seemed quite inappropriate to invade her privacy in this way, as her invitation to come in was one of genuine friendship and trust. I wish too that I had made a note of some of her views about Foula as it was then and as it had been in the past, because I remember having some long and fruitful conversations, after which I felt it a privilege to have shared her simple interests and views on life. There would have been few people in the whole of Scotland at that time so content

with so little, and so grateful for the humble place she occupied in our community.

The age range at Blowburn at the end of the north path was even older than at South Harrier. Peter Manson, a member of the regular crew of the *Island Lass* was in his mid-sixties but still seemed to be strong and able. His wife Katie was the sister of the late Walter Ratter, whose widow Meggie still lived at Punds in the Hametoun, but Katie was eight years older than Peter, and his sister Kittie three years older. It was a good house, though very exposed at the top of the ridge, with a wonderful view down the length of the valley between Crougar and the main body of the hills. In the evening light Scotty's trim fields gave the whole area a well cared for appearance, almost of a kind of prosperity. I couldn't help thinking as I walked home down the path to collect my barrowload of peats, how fragile the whole set-up was. Each croft seemed to have a key personality on whom its whole future depended. Where the main prop had already gone, there were left houses with a smoking lum and a peat-stack at the door but little other cause for hope for the future. I enjoyed the talks we had at Blowburn for instance, often about the old days or previous crises in their affairs, or about more hopeful topics like the children and the plans of some of the younger folk. But always lurking in the background were the unspoken worries about the future. Nobody was getting any younger and yet nobody was talking about leaving. Their future, whatever it might bring, was always taken to be understood as a future in Foula. It was their home and they were staying.

Apart from offering the opportunity for talking about problems or worries and for assessing any immediate needs of the inmates, my visits had one very practical commitment which was to take library books to these elderly or house-bound folk, some of whom were avid readers. I tried always to give them as wide a choice as I could within what I had noted down as their chief area of interest or favourite author. Requests could be submitted to the library in Lerwick who made up the boxes that came in on the mailboat. I barrowed these to the Manse and set out a display of books on shelves in the Manse porch, where the outer door was always open so that passers-by could call and help themselves and enter the details in the book provided. We got through a lot of books. I tried to plan my visits in such a way that I could dovetail in one or two bird-watching ploys to each journey, simply to make the most effective use of limited time. Treading the North end path would allow me to assess how the Arctic Skuas were doing on the lower ground where they dominated the scene. At the end of May there seemed to be about seven pairs of Great Skuas holding their own on the east side of the path, scattered through the whole area among the territories held by the more aggressive Arctics and having a fairly rough time of it as a result. Some of the Great Skuas were sitting by this time whereas I still hadn't found any of the smaller skuas' eggs. The balance between the two species was competitive but they seemed to achieve some kind of working relationship. There are several small lochans scattered across the low ground north of the Ham Toun between the road and the shoreline, and I was beginning to collect sightings of Red-throated Divers on most of them, none of them big enough to hold more than one pair.

I planned to leave study of these till later in the summer as they always nest close to the waters' edge, being awkward on land where they can do little more than shuffle on the flats of their tarsi. Divers are generally shy so it was best early in the season to leave them alone while they still had eggs. The islanders called them 'Rain Geese' because their movements were supposed to predict the weather. One only saw them flying occasionally, long-necked torpedo-shaped birds with a distinctive flight silhouette and wing action and often a haunting, wailing cry like a paeon of possession of their tiny aquatic kingdom. But I could never make out any connection between rain and observed flights from lochan to sea or back again, though the crofters seemed convinced that they were a reliable form of forecast.

Obviously my weekends with visits to be made kept me mostly to the crofting areas, but I was still able to combine visiting with some interesting bird sightings, as these areas had the best cover where migrants might find food and shelter. Occasionally I had red-letter days like 25th May, when I found a handsome male Redbacked Shrike perched on cables at Leraback, near enough for me to see his striking head colours and chestnut back. In the evening at the south end I found a Wood Sandpiper, one of my favourite wading birds. They are normally very shy but this one seemed hungry and may have flown a long way to reach Foula. It was feeding at a small pool near the byre at Dykes and allowed me a very close approach so that before it flew I had noted all the details of its delicate plumage markings –a pale eye-stripe, speckled brown back, striking white rump and barred tail which with its paler flight pattern separated it from its nearest look-alike, the Green Sandpiper. It was a species I had seldom seen before and never at such close range. Even after being disturbed it circled and returned to continue its feeding, a sure indication of a tired traveller. With such birds still on their migration journeys it was a surprise to find a family of Ringed Plover chicks down on the South Ness so early in the season, with the frantic parents trying to lure us away as we caught and ringed the chicks. It is essential to ring such agile young as early as possible. Once they become scattered they are almost impossible to find, for they have the instinct to crouch dead still when they take on the appearance of the clumps of moss which cover the whole area and so render the chicks invisible. The adults still try to work the trick of trailing a 'broken' wing to lure you away, with anxious calls to draw your attention. It's worth following them for a while if only to witness their sudden recovery and quick easy flight back to the family at the spot where the deception started. And if that isn't a form of intelligence, I'm a Dutchman.

Two days later, on 27th May, the Red-backed Shrike was still to be seen down by the Ham burn. I had asked the children to keep an eye out for it, so when it appeared they were keen to help me in an attempt to trap and ring such a prize. I set Norman and Jim to searching for black beetles, favourite shrike food, while I fetched the little box trap I had made with a drop door on top, released by a delicately set perch just below the door. If a bird landed on the perch inside, the door banged shut on top of the quarry. At least that was the theory. So we tied the bait of beetles and worms with thread to a piece of white card, and placed this tempting prize on the floor of the trap. The trap was then placed on the ground below the shrike's favourite perch among the patch of shrubs at the corner of the burn below Leraback. We retired to the opposite bank to watch with binoculars. There was an agonizing wait while he slept or preened until we thought he had finished feeding for the night. Then suddenly he looked straight at the trap and flew down to the ground beside it, struggling to reach the bait through the netting which formed the sides of the trap, ignoring the open door on top. Excitement was at fever pitch when the bird flew up to settle on the door itself, thereby springing the trap without catching the quarry. The shrike fled. So near and yet so far; but at least the boys knew what a shrike was, what its favourite food was and that it was a prized rarity; and that their teacher wasn't Superman and could sometimes be defeated by a mere bird. But I wasn't unduly upset. If I had failed to catch the shrike, perhaps I had achieved two budding bird-watchers instead. And that was a far more satisfying prize.

Chapter 12: The School

The Schoolhouse was a solid stone-built two-storey house designed to provide a large schoolroom occupying more than half the ground floor, with accommodation for the teacher's family in the rest of the house. This was originally four rooms but a kitchen had been added as an extension in 1939. Two bedrooms were attic rooms with skylights with access up an extra stair because of the ten-foot high ceiling of the schoolroom below. This family house was rented out to the Gear family because of the construction of a new Manse in 1938. This had provided a more modern house as their home for the teachers whose husbands performed the duties of lay missionary, which had then freed the building which originally went with the job, to be let to an island family at an annual rent of under £5. The rent for the Manse was £10 a year and this seemed to me so cheap that I felt there was no question of me expecting any payment from the Gears for occupying the Schoolhouse. Right from the start I was acutely aware that I was the only person on the island with a professional salary for doing my job. There were a few jobs financed by the Post Office or the Shetland Islands Council (such as Harry Gear, the Postmaster or Peter Ratter, the roadman) but it was quite a new experience for me to be the plutocrat of the community I lived in.

On the front of the house was a small porch and a door which led directly into the school from an enclosed playground area surrounded by a wall. In the top corner of this grassed playground was a small toilet block for the pupils. The schoolroom had three windows and was light and airy – in a gale often a bit too airy. It was heated by a traditional cast-iron peat stove for which a supply of peat was provided, one of those small part-time jobs on which many island families depended for what little cash they could earn. I was given to understand that in former times every pupil had to bring a peat to school in the morning as his or her contribution to keeping warm, which would have been fine when there were twenty or more pupils, but five peats from my pupils would scarcely have lasted an hour. There was no direct access to the rest of the house through the school's porch, the Gears having their own front-door; but there was a connecting door through to their kitchen from the schoolroom.

Though it seems hard to believe, this doorway was cut through in 1939 as a precautionary measure in case of an air attack, so that the schoolchildren had access to the cupboard space under the stairs which was considered the only space suitable as the obligatory air-raid shelter in case of emergency. Although it was never used for this purpose, it is sobering to realise that after Norway was over-run by the Nazis in 1940, for a while a regular reconnaissance plane of the Luftwaffe flew West over Foula at noon every day, apparently using the hill of Hamnafield as a guideline. The opportunity was taken in building the kitchen extension in 1939 to install piped water for the first time with cold water to a sink. By 1954 a Rayburn cooker had been added which provided ample hot water to what was effectively the school kitchen.

However, by far the most important item in the Schoolhouse kitchen was Mary Henry, Mima Gear's unmarried sister, who cooked for the whole family and also for the school dinners. Both she and the Rayburn stove worked overtime when the three male members of the Gear family were all at home and expecting fish and tatties for their lunch, at the same time as five hungry children and a teacher were requiring theirs. Mary was always punctual and her meals were wonderful. I soon learnt to leave the organising of the menus to her as she had far more experience in that field than I had. One surprise that I was introduced to in my first week at school, and a great favourite with the children, was apple muesli for pudding. Apples were a rational choice for fresh fruit, in that a case would travel well and keep for weeks, and the rolled oats and raisins that formed the basis of the mixture were also easily stored. But health diets were not then fashionable as they are now and I gathered the recipe had been introduced by my predecessor, Vera Chedburn, to children who were deeply suspicious of an uncooked pudding that merely had to soak overnight before serving. As so often, when constrained to eat the new-fangled food they found it delicious and I was expected to fall in line. I was more than happy to do so. We depended largely on tins especially in the winter so I laid in a good stock of nourishing foods that are also what children usually like, such as Heinz Baked Beans and Corned Beef. These

*My five pupils – L–R: Jim Gear,
Joyce Beagrie, Vina Henry,
Eric Isbister, Norman Beagrie*

were obligatory, topped by mashed potatoes, as the main ingredients of Mary's 'Mogle Pie', a great favourite. And the teacher liked it too!

Teaching was more or less a case of individual tuition according to their needs but to a rough timetable of subjects, so that they felt a sense of order and routine in what they were expected to do. There was a fairly wide divergence of ability, the two Beagrie children requiring a good deal more stimulation with the subjects they found the most difficult like arithmetic. Normally in a class of 25–30 I had been a great believer in making games and competitions out of things like mental arithmetic, going

round the class with quick fire sums or problems to be solved in their heads until somebody made a mistake and so let down the side, to be greeted with groans all round. If I tried this technique of trying to make lessons fun with the Foula five, it didn't work, as Jim and Eric were bright and seldom made mistakes, and Vina the youngest by a couple of years always got the right answer first. So it was always one of the Beagrie siblings who got it wrong which was discouraging for them and boring for the rest. So I found that much of the classroom experience I had gained at John Watson's was of limited practical use to me on Foula. To compensate for this was the joy of

*Home made toy boats on the
Ham Burn at lunch break*

teaching children who were receptive and eager to learn, without any stress from discipline problems at all.

Some of the best learning experience for them, and the best sense of progress for me, was achieved through the BBC Schools Programmes, which were a godsend for my situation. The documentary type of programmes about people's jobs, with drama used to make the story more interesting and real, were helpful not only because we could all prepare and then listen together at the same time, but because quite often the subject matter – about railways for instance, or city workers, or industry, or perhaps airports, or even woodland – was quite outwith their daily experience. A large component of this type of radio programme was the sound effects, which of course were often meaningless to Foula bairns. So much of the follow up was telling them about simple things like urban life or travel or transport and what made the noises they were hearing without comprehension. There were a few books in the schoolroom I could use to reinforce this with images from encyclopedias, but I often found the blackboard at the end of the afternoon covered with quick sketches or diagrams of such mundane things as railway signals or double decker buses, street lamps or traffic lights, a policeman or a bus-conductor, a taxi or even a four-wheeled farm tractor. Some of them had been to Lerwick or even to Aberdeen, but one at least had never been out of Foula in his life and didn't look as though he would ever get the chance – Eric Isbister. There were of course many positive things for Foula kids about living on an island which did not even have a village street anywhere, just scattered crofts spaced out over the landscape. I had two adages often in mind – 'Familiarity breeds contempt' and 'Distance lends enchantment'. I felt that a major part of my job was to teach them about the outside world, so that they would better understand its faster pace, while deliberately playing down its glamour and glitz; and to the same end helping them to appreciate their own familiar environment and to see the wonder and complexity and beauty of what they took for granted. For instance they had a whole island with its fields and streams, harbour and coastline, lochans and wildlife, as their own recreation area, and I encouraged them in their play down on the Ham burn with home-made boats and harbours. We made a model in the schoolroom on a big board of the harbour at Ham Voe, with a pier and a mailboat as models made from plasticine and scrap materials where children in the urban environment might have modelled a modern farm or a garage or a railway station. In some ways this seemed to be emphasizing the restricted view of the world which Foula offered, but it didn't stop them using just the same imagination an urban child would have done when they nailed two blocks of wood and an old cork onto a driftwood plank, and Hey Presto! a trawler or even a Russian factory ship for the fishing industry.

Perhaps the most successful school radio programmes were the ones which brought history to life, or the musical programmes, especially 'Singing Together'. This often had children in the studio performing, which encouraged my five to join in and sing with them. Sometimes there were recordings of the children in other schools. An enthusiastic presenter like Barry Appleby was a genius at getting reluctant children to take part and get thoroughly involved, and by the end of a series I would overhear my pupils humming the tunes or even singing the words as they played outside or walked to the shop. One song sticks in my memory because it was very English in style and content – 'The Flowers of the Valley' – and had one of those catchy tunes one cannot get out of one's head. I used to find myself singing it as I walked up the road to the North end or across the moor looking for skuas' nests, and thinking how appropriate it was in one way, extolling the beauty of the countryside and naming the flowers as well as the instruments in the orchestra which helped us to celebrate them. As a follow up we went looking for our own selection of typical Foula flowers and naming them. We could have done the same with the instruments as the islanders were good music-makers. Harry the Postmaster played a lively fiddle, though he held it on his knee and seldom tucked it under his chin in the conventional way. Bobby Isbister was accomplished on the keyboard and composed his own songs and ballads. One could tell from their singing that music was part of the islanders' tradition, both the

children when we started each day with a hymn, and the adults in church or at the Thursday evening gathering in the school when we sang the evangelical hymns from the Sankey book of hymns and choruses. Most of these were new to me but the tunes were so catchy that I soon picked up the favourites. The Salvationist sentiment in the verses wasn't much to do with my kind of faith either; but I felt I had a duty to enjoy what they enjoyed and found important in their lives. They had so much to teach me that I felt more like following their example than setting one of my own. I have also always found that singing together with other people, almost regardless of what one is singing, is a wonderful way of establishing rapport. And 'Rock of Ages' was surely apposite?

One thing nobody had warned me about, in taking on a teaching job in Shetland, was that my pupils would be bi-lingual. In Edinburgh I often had difficulty with children who came from homes with a strong local dialect, even though I was used to the broad Lothian accent of the mining community who were our nearest neighbours during my first twenty one years, when I lived near Bonnyrigg in Midlothian. At school in

'Arts and Crafts' – Jim and Eric with their cardboard harbour and plasticine boats and skerries

Edinburgh I was often accused of not being a Scot, having been educated almost entirely in England, and having an English mother and a father who regarded the way one spoke as a major part of one's education. But on Foula I was up against something on a different scale. The native Shetlanders, Jim, Vina and Eric spoke a colourful dialect, not only with the pleasant sing-song lilt of most districts of Shetland but with their own grammar rules as well. My speech was so far from their native dialect that they just accepted that that was the way 'teacher' spoke, partly because it was just like most of the BBC presenters on the school radio. The bi-lingual characteristic of all the children became most obvious when we sat down to lunch and as part of the incessant chatter of five youngsters eating at the same table, they would speak to each other in one language and then turn to ask me a question or make a comment in a completely different language and intonation. It was tempting to correct them over such Shetland habits as ignoring the plural of 'this' or 'that' – '*did du see a' dat selkies I' da Voe last night?*'; or '*I couldna' do half o' dis sums du giv us for homework*'. But as all their adults spoke like this anyway, there seemed no answer but to teach them to write one grammar and let them continue speaking another. They seemed to manage it with ease, and I loved listening to them at lunchtime: '*Quars du gyaan efter skil? Oot tae da banks to look for maalie's eggs?*' which, being interpreted should read: '*Where are you going after school? Out to the cliffs to look for Fulmars' eggs?*' For a long time I took the New Shetlander in an attempt to learn from their frequent articles or stories in Shetland dialect how to write down what I heard. But it clearly takes longer than the few years I gave it to learn this language, so my Shetland readers will have to forgive my feeble efforts to convey their lovely rich dialect in print. Incidentally I chose that snatch of schoolboy conversation because it encapsulates one of those dares that children love of suggesting doing the forbidden thing just to show off. I don't think there was one of my children who would have dared risk their parents wrath by '*gyaan tae da banks*' for the cliffs were absolutely verboten, especially for a dangerous ploy like collecting birds' eggs where there is always that temptation to reach out a little further than is safe to reach a tempting prize. As a sideways comment from fifty years later, perhaps one of my happiest memories of Foula is having associated closely with the younger generation there for so long without ever hearing foul language or the sort of swearwords that are now so commonplace and, to me, distasteful and demeaning of

them and their parents. But then I never heard it from their parents either which of course tells its own story.

I did not need to include much nature study in the school curriculum, simply because I included the children into some of my work with birds, and other things arose naturally and often out of school hours from that. The subject matter did tend to be skewed towards such subjects as migration, but if the understanding they all had about why and how so many interesting birds came to their island was gained at the expense of other aspects of nature study, there was considerable benefit in having an in-depth experience at first-hand of one of the most mysterious aspects of wildlife study. Some of them developed real skills in, for instance, bird identification and because they were interested and their parents had the right books in the house, they learnt also how to find things out for themselves. One incident will demonstrate what a thrill this could be for me. I had been paying a social visit to the Haa and called at the Schoolhouse on my way home where Mima told me that Jim had a bird for me in a box. He had been passing the kale-yard at Ham when he noticed a strange bird under my Heligoland trap. Knowing how to work it, he had carefully closed the catching box first (left open to avoid birds being trapped while I was absent) and then driven the bird into the trap and caught it. Jim had looked it up in their bird book and thought it was a Lesser Grey Shrike. I was extremely sceptical. I had no doubt he had caught an interesting bird, and it was possibly a Great Grey Shrike which is a regular autumn migrant and winter visitor to Scotland with frequent records up and down the country every year. I myself had never seen a Lesser Grey Shrike in Scotland and had only ever seen one in my life in Britain. The two species are closely related and very similar and are notoriously difficult to identify in the field. They come from Eastern Europe and would be rather unlikely to reach Foula so far out to the west in the 'shadow' of Shetland. While I was expressing my doubts about the bird, a smiling twelve-year-old bird-trapper with a shoebox in his hands emerged from the house. We opened it carefully and I took out an undoubted Lesser Grey Shrike, which was duly ringed. I don't know which pleased me most – that we had identified and ringed a new species for the island or that I had a budding ornithologist to my credit. It is interesting that most Scottish records have come from Fair Isle where it was first recorded in 1913, with only 14 further records over the next 80 years, so Jim's bird was probably within the first ten records for Scotland – quite a rarity. There was a rather sad follow-up to the capture.

The date was the 9th of August and as it was dark by the time we had examined and ringed the bird, it was kept in the house overnight and released the next morning. It was an adult female and very strong and lively. It flew strongly and perched on fence posts and peat banks and the tops of walls looking for food. It was seen to catch and eat a beetle so we had high hopes for its survival when an Arctic Skua appeared and the shrike was last seen being hotly pursued by the skua towards the Mill Loch. Two days later it was found dead on the beach at Ham below the cliffs there. The hazards of migration are legion and surviving the long flight across the sea to a remote landing place does not guarantee survival when it turns out to be a haven full of agile predators. It's a harsh unforgiving world for wildlife, and what a lot there is for a budding ornithologist to learn!

The visit of the School Inspector is supposed to be an event that strikes terror into the heart of any teacher, especially a lone Head Teacher who has no hope of blaming anyone else if the Inspector finds anything amiss. I confess that I felt quite confident that I could manage the annual visit of the Inspector to the Foula Primary School because it seemed inconceivable that he would ever reach the school unexpected. Such was the vigilance of Foula folk in spotting boats heading our way long before they reached the Voe, and so effective was the bush telegraph system of early warning that I felt sure I would have adequate time to prepare for his inspection and have my five children washed behind the ears and ready for the test. I did occasionally take risks, which could be awkward if any official visit coincided with some of my bird projects straying into school hours. We had developed a habit, especially in the spring migration season when there were interesting birds about in the Ham area, of nipping down to the Voe in the lunch break just to see if there was anything of note asking to be trapped. The kids were invited to come down if they wanted to. The boys especially were quite interested in birds but even more in the fun of driving the trap and the treasure-hunt incentive of seeing how many we might catch at once.

One day it was fine weather and they came down with me on the off chance. We had to be quick as time was limited and it wouldn't do for the teacher to be seen encroaching on school hours for such frivolous goings on. Down past Gravins, hoping neither Tom nor Jeannie was around to waylay us with their questions and non-stop prattle; on to Ham, past the byre, turn right and down the path by the house, wondering what we would find in the walled garden below. Steady; binoculars out;

check carefully through the cover to see what's there. Yes! There happened to be a bevy of starlings, mostly young birds fresh out of the nest and not too strong on the wing. A skilful approach worked for once and the sight of three agile young lads leaping over the garden wall at Ham, followed by a bearded teacher, was too much for them and the whole flock panicked into the bushes, round the corner of the wire funnel and into the catching box. We got a record haul of 24 birds in one drive. This was a brilliant success, as I was trying to ring as many young starlings as possible this first summer to see whether the Foula breeding birds were the Shetland subspecies of *Sturnus vulgaris*, which is distinguished not in the normal way by the plumage of the adults, but by the distinctive colouration of the juveniles. Most starlings have pale brown young. Shetland starlings in their first summer are almost black. So first I wanted to find out whether our breeding birds were resident all year round or whether they moved out in the winter. Ringing might tell me but I needed a big sample. So in some haste, and determined not to lose this opportunity, we extricated 24 birds one by one from the box and put them into the little cotton bags which I always carried with me for safe transport of captured birds back to the school. Luck was on my side because the process we put the birds through, weighing, measuring and if possible removing their ecto-parasites (feather lice, flat flies etc.) took some time, especially for such a large number. And I never liked to keep the birds in the bags longer than necessary. But this was the day when the BBC History programme for schools was on at 2 p.m., so while the radio taught the lesson, I was frantically processing my starlings on the schoolroom windowsill and letting them out one by one. It was all completed – well, nearly – by the end of the programme and as I resumed my normal stance in front of the class for the rest of the afternoon's periods, the thought did occur to me that it was good to think I would get ample advance warning if the Inspector was coming as his arrival about lunchtime today could have been extremely awkward. In fact I made some remark to the Schoolhouse folk like '*Good job the Schools Inspector didn't come today!*' when they commented on the unusual numbers of starlings in their garden this afternoon. They knew me by now, and only smiled.

It happened the very next day. There was a bug in the Schoolhouse family and I only had two pupils in school. Towards the end of morning school there was a knock on the door – which was most unusual and indicated trouble – and the Schools Inspector for Shetland walked in, totally unexpected and without warning, and we shook hands. I wonder whether he heard my silent sigh of relief in my '*Welcome to the Foula school. What a lovely day for your visit!*' I almost cast a wary glance at the window sill in case it was still covered in feathers and bird droppings. But all was spotless, my two pupils were brilliant, the Inspector was in holiday mood and, I expect, only too thankful to be off the boat he had hired from Scalloway, and we all got on like a house on fire. I almost thought of confessing and saying something like '*Good job you didn't come yesterday or you'd have found a school full of starlings at this time of day*' – but discretion was the better part and I kept my mouth shut. It would have been interesting to know what he would have said had he come the day before.

Apart from that one visit my work on Foula was completely unsupervised. I took it seriously and often thought about the curriculum I was giving these children in such unusual separated circumstances, with so little contact with other schools or other children. I concentrated on the basics, literacy and numeracy, but wondered about my responsibility over such equally basic subjects as sex education, at least for the older ones. It was an area of education on which I had strong views that the right grounding and understanding at an early age, presented in a matter of fact and open fashion, is essential for youngsters approaching puberty so that they can understand and not be afraid of the changes they are beginning to feel in their bodies and in their minds. I wondered whether to ask the parents first. Perhaps in a crofting environment with so many animals going through their breeding cycles before their very eyes, it wasn't nearly as necessary as in an urban environment totally divorced from such realities. I got a valuable demonstration of this one day when young Eric, aged eleven, arrived at my house from the Hametoun ready to walk with me the half mile to school. Five minutes before he came over the hill, one of the old Henry sisters from Niggards arrived with her cow on a tether. I knew something was up because the Beagrie's bull in the next door field to the Manse started roaring. Sweetie Henry's cow was in season and she had brought her to be served by the only bull on the island. Sweetie put the cow in with the young bull and went up to Mornington to negotiate the service fee with Mrs Beagrie. Eric arrived asking what was up with the bull and why was he making all that noise. I suspected he knew the answer really but was, in a roundabout way, asking me to explain things a bit for him. I was almost ready for school so I told him to come in and watch from my window. I explained that Sweetie's cow was ready for mating, and that being in

season meant she gave off a smell which the bull could detect and which told him that now was the time for him to make his contribution towards her having a calf. I have seldom seen a pupil more eager to learn as Eric stood with his face glued to the window watching while, only a few yards away, the young bull got on with his contribution, mounting the cow without hesitation and with conspicuous energy and eagerness, and Eric had all his questions about the physiology of copulation answered in a couple of minutes. I really felt there was nothing more for me to say, but I noticed it was a rather quiet and contemplative boy who walked to school with me that day.

Few Head Teachers would be able to say, as I could on Foula, that they knew all the parents of all their pupils personally. Some I got to know really well like Davie and Mima Gear at the Schoolhouse, Jim's parents, both of them strong personalities with whom I could discuss problems or seek advice and know I would get a considered reply. Davie's health was not very good as he had been a gas victim in the First World War, though it was a subject he never mentioned. He was a gentle very deliberate man, not given to making quick decisions but as skipper of the mailboat a good foil to some of his more fiery crew members, like the Ratter brothers. Mima was one of the most rounded characters in the whole community, and a forceful personality who became a very good friend. Her daughter Vida was also very friendly and intelligent, married to John Henry, many years her junior in age, whom I also liked very much. There was no work for him on Foula so he seized the opportunity made available by the whaling industry to set himself up financially so that he could provide a home for his family. Vina was their firstborn, conceived when John was still a teenager, and David, their second child, was part of the school's future. John came back from South Georgia with almost two years savings from a job where he earned good money and had little opportunity to spend it. They took over a tiny croft house called Groups, just up the hill from the nurse's house at Ham and John set about restoring it the first summer after his return. Like so many Foula men he was a jack of all trades and built himself a sound house that stood up well to the winter gales. All the while he was away Vida managed the croft and the children single-handed with never a word of complaint. Vina was the product of a sound and caring home background. So indeed were the Beagrie children, though they too had an absent father earning his living elsewhere as a stockman. It was a sign of the increased expectations of what was needed for family life that fathers had to leave home and their families simply to earn a reasonable living. I found it hard to imagine how Foula ever supported a population of 250, except that this meant they all had to keep enough animals and grow enough produce to be entirely self-supporting within a subsistence economy. The great advantage of that system was not being so dependent on imported goods and the mailboat.

Once we had got over the initial problem of Eric's long absences from school due to an almost hysterical phobia about infections, he settled in well with the others and showed talent in almost everything he undertook – except ball-games where he was surprisingly lacking in coordination. But his chief talent was for drawing and painting, for which he had a real flair, though his writing and arithmetic were also well above average. His mother Aggie Jean was an ally as one of the best bird-watchers in the community and kept on sending messages about interesting birds seen at the south end. She had obviously looked after Eric's education at home during the long spells when he hadn't attended school as he was

well up to scratch on all the basic skills. But she was a Gray from a long-established Foula family and as well adapted to life on a remote island as one could imagine. Nevertheless the South Biggins family kept themselves to themselves rather more than most families, largely due to the independent temperament of Bobbie, Eric's father. As shopkeeper he was about the only 'business man' on the island, and never very happy about it. Running a retail business in a small community with very little spending money and a tiny turn-over was indeed more of a service to the community than a profit-making enterprise. We all depended on Bobby in times of crisis, and yet by force of circumstances sent for most of our orders to Reid's of Walls if only because Bobby simply did not stock much of what we wanted. He had a great sense of humour and always had a quick reply to any complaints about the service he offered, and I always enjoyed a visit to the shop when Bobby was behind the counter. But one had to admit that as the proprietor of 'R. & J. Isbister General Merchants' he was at the centre of a vicious circle, running a business venture with

John Henry's restored cottage at Groups as a two roomed family home, summer 1955

too little money, chasing too few goods for far too few customers and consequently earning very little reward for a great deal of hard work.

One fascinating side-effect of this isolated business venture on a remote island only cropped up years later, long after Bobby had closed the shop, when the falling population figures made it no longer viable. In fact I didn't hear about it until after his death and Eric was left to run the croft and look after his ageing mother towards the end of her life. Much of their inheritance from the business was in the form of a large collection of bank-notes, some of them no longer valid currency, some even notes of banks which had long disappeared from the financial scene. For years they had never left the island, having been paid in to the Post Office by Bobby as cash deposits in his Savings Account, been paid out by Harry to other depositors withdrawing cash for their shopping, and then been paid over to Bobby again for poultry food or paraffin or Black's biscuits. Nobody of course on Foula bothered their heads as to whether they were any longer legal tender on the mainland so long as the shopman would exchange them

for goods. Luckily a friend was able to advise Eric at a time when his funds as an unemployed crofter were running particularly low, that he was sitting on a goldmine in one of the drawers where he kept what had been the cash float for 'R. & J. Isbister, General Merchants'. It was before the days of the internet, but a little research of the records of the auction rooms which dealt with rare bank-notes revealed that some of the notes, such as those of the defunct Union Bank of Scotland, were worth to collectors even hundreds of times their original face value. The revelation tided him over just when he needed it most. Such benefits of extreme insularity are few and far between. Normally what counts on a place like Foula is the experience that gives wisdom rather than windfalls, courage rather than cash.

Eric Isbister's story is unique, due to his dangerous susceptibility to infection through a lifetime of isolation. It affected him while I was his teacher and prevented him from having the secondary education he deserved. I have kept in closer touch with him than any other of the five pupils and many a long phone conversation has not only kept me informed about the island for over

Magdalla: Jim Gear's new storm proof house in 1993, next to the old cottage, Groups, now the Post Office

fifty years since I left, but has left me with a picture of a unique and valued friend. He has a wide knowledge of world affairs. He has a cultured mind and is a talented artist. He is a competent photographer and an expert pony-breeder; has an almost professional expertise in North Atlantic shipping; has contributed to Jane's famous books on ships used by mariners the world over; is a man with whom I can talk shop (his fund of knowledge about Foula's history and genealogy is endless and encyclopaedic) or discuss almost any topic I would discuss with any other well-read, educated man in Glasgow or Edinburgh. Yet he has no electricity, and I know of no other person in Scotland who has had a more insular and restricted and isolated life than he has, now living alone in the southernmost house of only half a dozen left occupied in the whole of the Hametoun on Britain's most isolated island.

I have sadly lost touch with the three pupils who left Foula to complete their education. But Jim Gear, who married Iain Holbourn's grand-daughter Sheila, built himself a splendid new house at Magdalla, designed – oh, so wisely! – to withstand winds of up to 200 mph. His family now forms a substantial part of the Foula population and he has for many years now spent much of his time fulfilling his role as the local councillor for the east side of the mainland including Walls. Likewise I can have a conversation with Jim – who as a lad of eleven introduced me so expertly to his island in 1954 – on current problems like climate change or the merits of various computerized methods of sustainable energy production for small islands, which reveals a similarly cultured mind and a sophisticated understanding of such scientific topics of global significance. I am immensely proud of them both.

Chapter 13: The Fat of the Land

There's no doubt that I took on too much in that first summer on Foula. It was all so new and exciting and the attraction of working on the study of the Skua colony, which then turned out to be a much bigger project than I had anticipated, meant that I didn't allow enough time for all sorts of chores around the Manse. The school holidays from the end of June to the beginning of August gave me a false impression of scope to tackle too many jobs. Apart from keeping the house clean and doing my own cooking, I had trouble with a water pipe which needed soldering, which James Andrew Gray of Dykes helped me with, though neither of us were plumbers. We eventually turned a leak into a drip, which was manageable. The chimney needed pointing to keep the rain out. My hen house door had to be refitted as my five hens were laying me five eggs a day, which were going into store for the winter in Oteg. I was running out of time to fit in my visiting as well as the unavoidable paperwork, so I asked Mary Umphray of Ham to help with cleaning and laundry, on a very part-time basis, which suited both of us well enough. I was putting in my weekly order to A. & K. Reid's when the mailboat was regular but Mary agreed to bake an extra loaf for me if there were serious delays. Every Sunday I went for my lunch to Mornington, and as often as not Mrs Beagrie would give me some of her latest batch of scones to help out my bread supply.

I was all the time discovering new opportunities to get involved, which were too tempting to miss. One was '*going to da eela*', which meant going fishing towards dusk in a small boat off the coast just south of the Voe. I went first with the Beagrie boys, who were not as experienced as the Foula men but who seemed to know the ropes. I was to bring small white feathers from my hens as my contribution, and we tied these to the hooks, with several up the length of each line and a weight at the end. I remember one night we set off quite late, though of course it was still light enough with the western sky glowing with red, then orange, then yellows, where lines of thin cloud on the horizon hid the setting sun; and the sky above paled into that exquisite soft green, shading gradually to duck-egg blue, which then lights up the dappled surface of the sea with a kaleidoscope of colours. It had been a quiet day and the sea was as smooth as it ever was off Foula, but the swell still broke at the foot of the cliffs, sending concentric patterns of ripples back out to the boat so that there was every shape of broken surface like a million mirrors reflecting back a million different shades from purple through to the palest green. It was quite hard to concentrate on the constant tugging

James Andrew Gray of Dykes,
jack of all trades, with
his sheep-dog Bob

The Stremness 'crue', gathering in most of the sheep at the North end for rooing

of the fish at the lines as we ran into shoals of saithe and then a few mackerel and then more saithe, coming up sometimes with several fish all hooked at once on the same line. There was scarcely time to take in the sheer beauty of the oily surface, glistening with colours from mauve to turquoise, before it was almost dark and we had to head back for the Voe with the bottom of the boat ankle deep in fish. It wasn't always like that; but Jock Ratter, coming back in his boat behind us, seemed to have done even better, and it was a case of wheelbarrows to the pier to unload and transport the hundreds of fish to the shed at the head of the pier to await the long job next day of cleaning and salting. Most of the fish would end up dried and tied by the tail in pairs to hang over a pole or a string as a winter supply. Some would go to Old Robbie at Breckans for example, who would hang them in the smoke above his centre-fire to cure that way and taste all the better for it. We took a bucketful home and had fresh fish for several days. One of the first jobs was to find any female fish carrying the 'hard' roes (i.e.,

the eggs) to be cooked separately. Next we removed the livers from the piltocks to make 'crudie mudie', a rich dish of which a few spoonfuls made a meal in itself. In late summer the livers could be the major part of the fish, and the secret was to fry them first to extract the oil, which was mixed with oatmeal and onions before cooking. Piltocks were rather lacking in flavour just cooked on their own. Some said they tasted of damp blotting-paper. Try frying them gently in the liver oil; they are transformed into a treat.

Another ploy which took up a lot of time, but also sometimes ended in a good dinner, was helping with a crue (pronounced croo-ie). Foula sheep were, as they say, 'something else'. But when a decision had been made to have a crue, it was all hands to the pumps. As an able-bodied man, the 'Meenister' was another valued pair of legs to pursue the devils wherever the crue was being held. I was a learner and did what I was told, because the sheep always know best and can only be herded according to their daily routines and habits. We would set off from

Mansie Henry and his wife Betty rooing, i.e., plucking the wool by hand, from one of their sheep,
on one of the rare occasions they ever met

one of the crofts to cover one particular area of the island that was a recognised gathering area, with a specific route which it was known, or should I say expected, the sheep would follow. The women would come armed with a tea-towel or an old jumper so that when the sheep decided to go the wrong way or to double back to the hills they loved, we could line up waving our flapping garments to deflect them back into the chosen line. Hand-clapping, shouting, even throwing small clods of peat were all used as devices to do what proper sheep-dogs would have done, had there been any. But Foula dogs, though they mostly looked like sheep-dogs, were as useless as the sheep were clever and often merely got excited and created even more chaos by rushing at the sheep in the wrong direction and scattering them to the four winds.

A month after my letter home at the end of June I wrote again on 26th July, by hand this time as my typewriter ribbon had finally given up the ghostly pink writing of the past few weeks.

On Thursday last week, which was the only decent day since my return from Lerwick on the twelfth of July, we went out rooing sheep, that is driving them across the whole North end of the island into a pen (or 'crue') for rooing, that is plucking rather than clipping the wool, as they do here. We had quite a successful drive in lovely weather and got about 80 sheep without any of them breaking back into the hills, which was considered quite good going.

This had been my first experience of rooing. With the unpredictable weather always leaving a possibility of rain and a chilling wind after clipping the sheep, nobody on Foula shears the wool off their sheep down to the skin as one could do further south. Instead the outer fleece, which was often quite loose on the underwool anyway, and later in the summer could drop off completely if a sheep hadn't been rooed, was pulled and plucked off, or held in one hand while the other, holding a sharp kitchen knife, cut away the tough bits to loosen the long fibres from the close, warm underwool which it was so important to leave on the sheep against the weather. It probably took longer than shearing but the sheep succunbed to it fairly readily and, though they looked 'shorn', they didn't look exposed after the event. After all the hard work and when most of the sheep that had been gathered into the crue had been released again, the saucepans of water came out and a Primus stove, and loads of sandwiches, scones or other goodies were unpacked and a picnic followed. There were usually a number of children helping and this was the moment they had been waiting for. Tea and a mountain of baking would disappear like magic. In my next letter dated 15th August I wrote:

> *We have had four drives so far and each one has gathered 50–100 sheep but there are many more still to do. They usually kill one sheep from each drive and share out the meat among all the helpers so that there is a more or less continuous supply of meat all summer.*

Normally Foula sheep are extremely wild and hard to drive by conventional methods and will even make for the cliffs if allowed to get too far ahead. There they will creep down to those places where they so often go to get that tasty bite from a patch of green on a precipice, when the green grass at the top of the cliff seems to us just as tasty and a lot safer. This can be a menace when the young lambs are still unsteady on their feet and many are lost to this craving the ewes have for their cliff pastures. The lambs go where their mothers lead and then lose their footing on the unaccustomed steep slopes. If the sheep head that way during a drive, they are best left alone for fear of driving them over to their death.

> *Among the sheep was a young ram, hence the leg of lamb now nearing its time in my pressure cooker. This I suppose was a kind of reward for my helping in the driving of the sheep, although goodness knows I did*

well enough for food at the picnic which they always lay on as a break from the wool cutting. However this seems to be a tradition that they should look after the nurse and the missionary in this way, so far be it from me to stop them.

The sheep were all colours, some grey, which is I believe the true colour of 'Shetland sheep', others white or coffee-brown, some as dark as Soay sheep, yielding the almost black wool much used in the knitting patterns made entirely with natural wool colours. Many were mixtures, some black-faced and some with white on their noses or lambs with a small white 'star' on the top of their head, called 'starry lambs'. Shetland sheep are famous for the quality both of their tender meat and their warm, soft wool and both, when the markets are good, can fetch premium prices. But first they have to be exported, which calls for a special run of a larger boat so that there is freight to pay; and second they have to be sold to buyers who know that they cannot be held back if the price is not right, as it would never make sense to go through all that hassle again. So the bidders or the auctioneers contrive a price, often half what similar or even inferior sheep will fetch on the same day in the same market. On 14th October I wrote home about my preparations for winter and gave an account of the annual cattle boat:

> *Last week the cattle boat came in, an annual event which always causes a lot of feeling. The boat was long expected and anxiously awaited. When it did come on 7th October it arrived early in the day and quite without warning. After it had gone there was little*

Vari-coloured sheep feeding at the Daal at the Wastins

*Mary Umphray taking a cow to
the byre at Ham, winter 1954*

*enthusiasm from those who had been lucky enough
to get rid of their cows. This is their only chance in
the year of finding a market for their cattle and one
would expect them to be very pleased when it came
along. But it is for that very same reason that they
are not; for the people who take the cattle are well
aware of this and the result is that it is 'my price or
nothing'. They all got a flat rate of £20 a cow this
year as the purchaser was a butcher from Burra Isle
near Scalloway and he only wanted the cattle for
slaughtering and sale in his own shop. But the market
price for similar cows on the mainland of Shetland this
year is between £40 and £50; and in Aberdeen they
would fetch even more. This is apparently an old story
and I suppose more or less inevitable where there is no
alternative. Of course one answer would be to refuse
to part with the animals at their price and to send
the purchaser back empty-handed, and with £40 hire
charge on the boat to pay. But that would mean far
too many cattle on Foula for the available fodder in
winter or the available labour to look after them, and
probably no cattle boat at all next year.*

Many of the crofts had cattle, which in the summer fed
out on the hill but were fetched in every evening. There
was a great deal of hard work attached to keeping cattle,
but most people had ready access to fresh milk. Turning
this into butter was another labour intensive operation.
The milk would be left to turn sour and then the whole
milk, not just the cream, churned in traditional style.
I used to watch Mary after school in the Schoolhouse
kitchen making butter in one of the tall wooden churns,
which James Andrew Gray of Dykes had made himself
out of driftwood. It stood about three feet high, about a
foot in diameter at the top, tapering down to a narrow
base, and the churning was done with a long wooden
pole with a 'kirn carsus' on the bottom, a flat wooden
blade with holes in it, which really pressurised the milk
as it was vigorously lifted up and then pushed down into
the churn so that the milk fairly bubbled up the sides
and through the holes. Mary would work at this – and
I mean work! – for as long as 25 minutes before the
butter would start to come to the top and be scooped
off in a saucer, still with some buttermilk making its
texture rather soft. Often they would ask me if I would
like some to take home and by the time I got there more
of the whey had settled out. A spell of stirring the butter
with a knife would separate out some more until the end
product was almost the sort of firm butter one could
buy from the Walls shop. I admit that I seldom did buy
shop butter as I was so generously supplied, at least in
the summer when the cows were feeding well. I can still
remember that fresh slightly sharp flavour which made
a piece of bread and butter a luxury item of my diet. It
used to set my mind running through all those flowers
which brightened up the Foula scene so wonderfully in
summer. *'Fair are the flowers of the valley'*, as the children
used to sing in the school.

The climax of Mary's butter-making was producing
'kirn' after the butter had all been removed. Now the
reason for using the whole milk became apparent. A
large pot of water, at least a gallon so far as I can recall,
was brought to the boil. This was poured into the churn
on top of the whey together with four pints of fresh milk,

and it was this which caused the remaining solids to coagulate, coming to the surface and forming a white cheesy layer on top. This was then scooped out, put in a bowl or on a deep plate where it solidified into a soft cheese one could cut into slices with a knife. The children would be given a slice to eat in their fingers or it would be served on bread. It was an acquired taste but the texture was itself delicious and I learnt to like the sharp flavour as a welcome change in my diet. I remember watching Jim spreading a large slice of kirn with jam, in the same spirit as the more daring boys at Dalhousie who used to put marmalade or black treacle on their porridge as the ultimate indulgence of a sweet tooth. A much more difficult taste to acquire was the liquid which was left behind after both butter and kirn had been removed – which was called 'blaan' and regarded by the likes of Davie Gear as better than beer. Mima's brother up from London said that if he had plenty of blaan he would never want beer. On Foula with no pub that could be a useful alternative.

In my letter home on 15th August I was very much on the subject of food:

The garden at the moment is keeping me and one or two other households in good supplies of lettuce, young carrots (still eating the thinnings), early turnips, sprouts, and Foula cabbage; and I think a few cauliflower are slowly on the way but not making very good progress. But the things I do have are good and I can have fresh salad every day if I want it. As I have also had either fresh fish or fresh mutton every day as well, I have been eating really well and haven't

needed to fall back on eggs for weeks (I should hope not!!). So I am storing them up for the winter and eating a few now as well. I already have about 100 in Oteg and another lot ready for the preserving jar. All the cows have been calving recently and the island is overflowing with dairy produce. I get about a pound of fresh butter every week and two pints of milk a day and occasional parcels of 'kirn', their peculiar but rather nice variety of cheese made from the buttermilk. As you can see I am not starving and in fact will have to be careful that I don't get too fat here living as I do off the fat of the land. My larder always seems to be well stocked – even so well that my hens get what I can't eat. What is more I scarcely pay for any of these things except in kind.

My small vegetable plot on the north side of the house did exceptionally well. I manured it with good cow-dung from the Beagrie's byre but the soil was good anyway. I certainly grew record size root crops and far more lettuce than I could eat. Potatoes had long been a staple crop for the islanders but were also labour-intensive because there was only a limited amount of mechanised cultivation. On Fair Isle they had used bullocks in years past but I never saw animals being used to provide power on Foula. One day walking up from Ham to the school I came across the Ham trio, Mary and her husband Willie Umphray (who was in residence at that time on holiday from his job elsewhere) and Elisabeth Wiseman who lived with them, planting potatoes in one of the rigs opposite Gravins. They were using the traditional Shetland spade, a metal blade at the end of a wooden handle with a step

Elizabeth Wiseman, adopted daughter at Ham, takes her cow for a drink at dusk

on it. With three diggers in line all putting their spades in at the same time, a very long clod was turned over in one heave; but to turn over a whole rig was a long job. There were three two-wheeled 'tractors' primarily designed as motorized ploughs, one of which Ken Gear used on several crofts which was a big improvement on hand 'delling'; but the season was too short for him to be available for all the digging that needed to be done. (Incidentally although I remember 'dig and delve' as a phrase from a nursery rhyme book, I never came across the use of the word delve, in the context of digging the soil, until I got to Foula where it was the preferred word for spade cultivation.) Most crofts still grew potatoes as their staple food crop.

On the question of tractors I had made an application to the Highland Fund, on behalf of the Beagries, for one of the new 'Croftmaster' tractors, supposedly developed especially for low budget agricultural set-ups as a small-scale work horse. We heard in July that their application had been approved and in their case they were to be supplied with one without having to wait till they could pay the deposit. I wrote about it in my July letter:

It is supposed to be on its way and should arrive within the next week or two. Young Alec Beagrie who is looking after the croft while his father is out on the Mainland working, will have to drive it and Mrs B. has commissioned me to teach him. It will have a trailer and, though small, is a four-wheeled tractor so that we can use it for cartage as well as ploughing.

There are three other tractors here already but they are all 2-wheelers and very difficult to use for haulage and anyway none of them have trailers. So we should be able to save a great deal of labour and help out some of the old folk when it arrives.

Not surprising perhaps that my August letter three weeks later says:

The telephone kiosk is up and the tractor is definitely on its way, so we are progressing. Both should be in action within in the fairly near future but the phone may not be working for a few weeks.

Looks as though I was learning – slowly.

With all this wealth of natural produce from Foula's fertile soil, provided one was prepared to work for it,

Fresh vegetables from my own small vegetable patch at the back of the Manse, summer 1954

The Ham folk, Willie and Mary Umphray and Elizabeth Wiseman, planting their 'tattie rig' with the Shetland spade after spreading the manure from the byre, spring 1955

I began to think rather differently about the situation in the 19th century when the population was so much higher and one had wondered how so many could survive on Foula on subsistence crofting. One answer in those days had been the bird-fowling tradition on the cliffs, where there was a limitless supply of meat, provided the men were daring and skilful enough to acquire it. With literally hundreds of sheep on Foula's 4000 acres, seabirds were never such a necessity for survival as they were on St Kilda, but James Andrew Ratter of Broadfoot had many tales to tell of the bird-fowling days. There were some favourite places for catching birds that were not too high or dangerous but with plenty of quarry; Ruskie at the back of the Noup and the Stacks; but others like the Wester Hoevdi and the Little Kame must be amongst the most precipitous places in Britain. Puffins, Fulmars, Guillemots and Razorbills were the prime targets either for eggs or for eating. He himself had gone fowling at the age of 18, i.e. in the late 1920s but admitted that the purpose by then was merely to keep up a tradition and to test out their skills, rather than as a mainstay for survival as it must have been when Foula had a population of 240.

He still had in his workshop both old ropes and 'budies' which were the baskets made of rushes for bringing back birds and eggs. The ropes were never more than lengths of 20 fathom but sometimes joined into 60 or even 80 fathoms. They used permanent stakes at the cliff-tops as anchors with occasional calamities if they weren't inspected properly. They liked the Little Kame, a turf area on a steep slope half way down the Kame precipice whose turf was peppered with puffin burrows. But this was a long way down from the top, so there was a recognised way of getting in there by coming across horizontally from the North Bank, roped up in a team of four or five together. Sadly there were tales of casualties on the cliffs. Presumably the ones James Andrew told us were the more recent tragedies. One concerned two men working at the back of the Noup where the rock always seemed to me to be looser and more broken-up than the main wall of cliff in the west. They had two ropes, one for climbing down from the top and one for working across horizontally. When they had gathered a number of birds they would tie them in a bundle to the rope half way between them, and then follow the normal procedure of

Mima Gear and Vida Henry 'delling tatties' on the Mogle croft below the Post Office with grandson David John 'helping'

moving on one at a time while the other acted as a belay. The birds would be heavy and cumbersome so they were tied out of their way. The joke was that if anything happened to the men, at least the harvest of birds would be saved. And tragically that was what happened. One man slipped and pulled the second down with him and both were killed, but when they found them the bundle of birds was still intact on the rope between them.

The value of their ropes was made clear in the story of two neighbours who used to go to Soberlie for guillemot's eggs, but only one of them had a good rope. When he was out at the fishing his friend decided to risk his luck by tying five strong fishing lines of the sort used at the haaf fishing, each line doubled and then the whole ten tied together by knots, to reach a place he knew that was good for a guillemot nesting ledge. But it was steep and he had to hang by the rope at one point to reach the eggs. So he really had to trust his improvised rope but succeeded, reached the ledge, hung off the cliff while he collected the eggs, and managed to pull himself up complete with his harvest. The next year the man with the good rope decided that if his friend could make it with such a poor rope, he ought to try too but he wasn't

such a good cragsman. He reached the spot, tied himself on and lowered himself over a ledge of rather loose rock to hang opposite the eggs. When he tried to climb up his rope he couldn't get over the ledge because the loose rock kept breaking away, and so had to go down again right to the bottom. His only chance then was to secure his good rope firmly to a belay at the bottom and climb up the tight rope hand over hand. So when he reached the top, instead of relief he only felt that he had now lost his good rope, secured to the foot of the cliff. So he had to ask an older man to come back with him and, using the usual technique of one fixed rope (his) tied to the peg, and one tied to him but controlled by his companion, he had to be lowered all the way to the bottom solely for the purpose of recovering his precious rope.

On Foula there was no tradition of preserving the seabird harvest and no cleits for storing salted birds for the winter. The birds they caught in the summer were eaten fresh and presumably saved time and effort for such ploys as smoking and drying both fish and mutton – known as 'reestit' mutton – which lasted them through any bad weather spells when fresh fish or mutton were not available. Amongst the birds available in summer the favourites, according to James Andrew Ratter, were the fat young 'Leeries', the Manx Shearwaters now so jealously guarded by Robbie Isbister. No ropework or serious risks necessary there; but he was also anxious to assure us that that was long before his time. He had seen young Leeries but never taken one. Nor had he ever taken or eaten a Fulmar which had never, so far as he knew, been on the Foula menu. Fulmars' eggs were a different story, regarded as excellent eating. I tried them once or twice and though they tasted good, the consistency took a bit of getting used to, the white especially being almost rubbery and still transparent after cooking. The arrival of the Fulmars – or Maalies – on Foula was a well-known and much rehearsed story, how they had followed a dead whale to feed on the carcass for many weeks when it was washed up in the early 1850s. Then a couple of pairs stayed on to nest in an inaccessible part of the cliff. Once breeding had started the numbers soon began to multiply and, largely because they were never molested, the colony soon became very large. This fact alone seems to me to testify that life on Foula for the human population must always have been less of a struggle, less precarious, than life on St Kilda. Even there where fowling was always – except in the last few years – an essential part of their way of life, the St Kildans probably had a better protein diet than all the rest of the Hebrides simply because of the guaranteed seabird harvest. But that guarantee was of course entirely dependent on a viable population with both the physique and the spirit to tackle the challenge of the cliffs.

Chapter 14: Autumn Letters

I had an unexpected request in the summer of 1954 from Fair Isle. They had a supporter of the Bird Observatory whose son was anxious to get field experience studying migration as part of his scientific education. He was at Oundle School and had wanted to go to Fair Isle with a friend to do some original research. His father was already there, doing some research on the blood groups of birds in co-operation with the Observatory, using the trapped migrants which they handled for ringing. Ken Williamson hadn't room for them, nor the scope to let them loose on the observatory birds, and had suggested they come to Foula where they would have greater freedom and be able to do a parallel study on blood structures of any birds we trapped and handled. As a bait to me to take them and give them accommodation, which would otherwise have been a bit of a problem, the father had agreed that he would supply me with the equipment for the scientific work, and suggested the boys would be willing to help me with the building of my proposed Heligoland trap. As I knew I couldn't do this on my own and as spare labour on Foula in autumn was non-existent, this was an offer too good to refuse. Moreover, some company in the house might not be a bad thing for a couple of weeks, and I did have a spare room and all the facilities. So I agreed to the request. I was expecting Mr Mackintosh, the Walls minister for a week in late August on his annual visit to his Foula parishioners, so I arranged for the two boys to come after that. Their visit was not the success I had hoped it might be, as my letter home dated 26th September will show, written just after they had left. But it did highlight the problems of living in an ageing population and also just how different was our scale of values with that of the sophisticated world from which my visitors had come.

The Manse, Foula, By Lerwick, Shetland
26th September 1954

Dear All,

Mail has been very uncertain with this shocking weather. The last boat was delayed a week and my two schoolboy visitors were delayed here long enough to eat me out of house and home. Unfortunately they were not very much help while they were here and I don't think I shall repeat the experiment of having unknown visitors again. The one thing I cannot afford is extra time to look after visitors, and the understanding I reached with the boy's father who arranged the visit was that they would get their lodging and their local supplies (e.g. milk etc.) in return for their help on the traps, and provided they looked after themselves. All very well on paper but it didn't work out in practice. The trouble was that the father gave his son a generous cheque to give me when they left to cover their holiday. I hadn't asked for nor expected this, but of course the boys knew I was going to be paid for keeping them. At least I presume that was at the back of their minds when they left the washing up in the sink and expected me to do all the cooking etc. In spite of all my hints and efforts to get them to help, in the end I think they regarded this as a kind of hotel. So I was really quite glad to see the back of them and get some time to myself. The only value I got out of them was some help with the new trap which is now well forward but still not finished yet. But even there I had to undo half the work they did and do it again properly to withstand the wind. I suppose the answer is that it is very hard for visitors to adjust themselves to a place where money as such has little value and where labour is the only really valuable commodity. Certainly their cheque was acceptable but I would far rather have had their active help.

In so many ways the numbers here are now reaching a point where one or two extra pairs of hands make all the difference. Nowhere is this more true than with the hill-sheep which cannot be driven with dogs into flocks and where a certain minimum number of people is essential to do the job. I was talking to Mima Gear of the Schoolhouse, who dropped in here for supper tonight after church, and she reckons that three quarters of their sheep are still carrying their wool on their backs. With wool at 5/- a pound and 2–3 lbs to a fleece and 70–80 of their sheep on the hill, they are suffering a big loss simply because of their inability to find enough folk to do the job of 'caaing', i.e., rounding them up. It is such factors that make the people here wonder just how long the island can continue, at any rate in its present capacity as a crofting community. Our news is very day to day with few major excitements. The biggest single item of news is the weather, which could scarcely have been worse for hay or corn. Most of the corn is still standing though they have been cutting this week, but much of it is still green. Tonight we walked back from the Kirk while the snow whitened our coats as we passed a field of standing corn. Some of the hay has been cut and is up in 'coles', little haycocks all tied down to the ground with stakes and ropes to stop them blowing away in the wind. Much of the hay has been turned a dozen times on fine days only to be soaked again the next day. Today's rain was torrential for about six hours and the whole island was running with water by mid-day. The wind has seldom been below 'fresh' for three weeks and some days has been really strong. Only once have we had a real gale and that wasn't a severe one by Foula standards, I understand. I mean you could still stand upright in it. But there have been several days when I certainly couldn't cycle home from school. We are expecting the Post Office Engineers and they have been waiting an opportunity to cross for some time now. The most serious news is that our new nurse has called off. We have been without one for a month now and there seems little prospect of one in the meantime.

The autumn migrants have certainly been coming through but I have not seen as much of them as I should have liked. There have undoubtedly been some rarities which I have missed but I have seen my share. Last week I added two new birds to my life list and quite a few to the island's list. And of course nearly all the birds were at one time or another sitting right in the area covered by the half-built trap. They included a Barred Warbler, a Scarlet Grosbeak, two Redpolls, Blackcaps, Garden and Willow Warblers, and Chiffchaffs; there was a Lesser Whitethroat in my hen-run one morning and a Robin the next; Turtle Doves, a variety of common waders, Yellow and White Wagtails and an influx of Kestrels and Merlins. This week has seen the arrival of Snow Buntings and sure enough with them the cold weather they are supposed to herald – delightful little birds and quite tame. The strawberry plants arrived safely and are now all planted and doing as well as can be expected in this wind.

30th Sept. *Nothing but gales and rain just now, but the sea has settled today at last and they are thinking of going; so a boat day – just!*

September is in one sense the start of winter in Shetland, when the summer weather breaks and the equinoctial gales set in and the problems begin. One's first autumn therefore is a test of one's foresight before one has had the necessary experience to be able to anticipate the difficulties of depending on a single 5-ton 36 ft boat for all supplies. My letter of 14th October shows as well as any description I could record from memory how this period of my stay kept me very fully occupied preparing for the really testing times ahead:

> *The Manse, Foula, by Lerwick, Shetland*
> *14th October 1954*

Dear All,

Three mailboat runs within a weekend at the beginning of the month seem to have been too much of a strain, and things have been very irregular since then. As we date our lives by mail runs here I rather lose count when they become so erratic. Life seems to be a day to day business anyway and the time simply flies past with so much to do. The week-days at school go the quickest and the long-awaited weekend is always upon me before I have had time to think of preparing a sermon for Sunday, or to decide which of the many outside jobs I am going to catch up on. So the usual situation has arisen tonight when there is the prospect of a mail run tomorrow; namely all the letters still unanswered and only one evening left. Last night was one of the worst since I arrived, with a strong wind which had been a real gale during the afternoon, only moderating when the rain started. I spent most of the evening at South Biggins having gone primarily to take some schoolbooks to young Eric who had been absent for two days because of the gales. But of course I stayed to gossip and to play their organ and see the pet starling and so on, until it was too late on my return home to be worth sitting down at the typewriter. And now tonight I finally got home about 8 p.m. having spent the time since school (or since my tea at the Schoolhouse) helping to get the nurse's house clean ready for her possible arrival, if the boat does go and return with her tomorrow. This is our big item of news this week, a message having come in over the radio telephone from the doctor earlier in the week to say that a new nurse has arrived in Lerwick on her way to Foula.

As the nurse's house has been empty for two months we have had to light fires and try to get rid of the traces of the mice which are always bad at this time of year. So I got two of the bairns to help me and we made her larder and kitchen ship-shape tonight and got the house aired. There is always an effort to get things as good as possible for an incomer on their first arrival, as there was for me when I first arrived, so that they will get a good first impression and not be tempted to back out. Of course there is always a good deal of speculation going on about what the newcomer is going to be like. People here are well enough aware of the limitations of this place to realise that anyone taking a job here must be peculiar in some way or other. When they discover, as in my case, that the peculiarity is nothing worse than ornithology, then I think they are rather relieved.

Tom Umphray of Gravins scything what's left of a windblown crop of oats

The weather is a topic I hardly dare start on for fear of using language unworthy of a Missionary! We now have to be prepared for periods of 4–5 weeks isolation and have to look ahead accordingly so far as expendable supplies are concerned. I have already been caught out with several things and am learning from my mistakes. My wireless is working at the moment from three bicycle lamp batteries but working very well and I am expecting the new ones in by the next mail. My larder is well stocked as is also the school canteen. This is as important to me as it is for the children, as it provides me with my main meal of the day, so that except at weekends I don't eat a great deal at my own house except cereals etc. for breakfast and an egg to my tea when I get home after school. The shop seems to be well stocked with all the staple foods such as flour and oatmeal, sugar and fats and I have a good supply of tinned meat, and eggs, as well as a variety of other tinned foods. The things that may well run out this year are potatoes and root crops and fodder for the cows. The potato crop is poor and some of them are rotten in the ground from damp, although it is still early for lifting them in a normal year. The corn is pathetic to see even though the corn here does seem wonderful at withstanding the wind and the rain. But these last few weeks have been altogether too much for standing crops. About half the crop is still standing – and by that I don't mean it is standing upright but just not cut yet. But there is virtually no grain left in the ear as the wind has thrashed it all out where it stood and laid down the straw in a tangled mess which can only be cut like hay and then raked up into piles. Some of the hay is not cut yet, and much that was cut is still lying on the ground because the corn had to get priority. All things considered the islanders have done remarkably well to get up as much as they have done, working between showers and often having to put wet corn up into coles simply for one night to avoid it being blown away.

This year the cattle boat day coincided with a special run of the mailboat with a stretcher case – old Magnus Henry of Quinister – and also the departure of the Post Office Engineers who had been in fitting up our new radio telephone. The doctor had been in on a special run earlier in the week the day after the engineers arrived, but the old boy had not improved as a result of the prescribed treatment so he had to go out to hospital. Luckily the weather was good and the boat was able to make the trip and return

on the next day. The telephone lads wisely decided to go while the going was good with this unsettled weather making prospects of a crossing scarce, and so they went out on the same boat in rather a hurry. They left behind them an improved telegram service but I regret not yet a telephone service considered good enough to be opened to the public. Before they went I got them to explain the equipment to me in case of any emergency when an engineer could not get in. Although this is considered strictly irregular from the official point of view of the Post Office, the Engineer in charge of the installation was most co-operative and willing to enlist my services. He even ran over all the circuits with me and showed me the complete series of tests to be made on the equipment in case of breakdown. With memories of my Royal Signals Training I was able to understand most of it and we worked out a set of instructions for replacing valves etc. in case of trouble. Harry Gear who runs the Post Office here was also shown what was what, so between us we should be able to keep the system working. The trouble at the moment is that the equipment being installed was designed for rather shorter links and the reception is just not quite good enough to be fit to connect to the public telephone system. I spoke across to the Mainland and it was fair but noisy, but apparently trunk calls to anywhere further than Shetland were inaudible at this end. So they have had to leave it meantime in the hope that by modifying the equipment on the receiving end over there, they will be able to get a satisfactory link established without doing any more to the works at this end. They were a nice set of fellows and it was good to see a change of faces when they were staying at the Beagries' just across from my house. But it was just another job for yours truly, which meant a little less time for all the other jobs while they were here. They were most helpful over the hospital case and their establishment of a telephone link with Walls was just in time to be very handy over contacting the doctor and making the arrangements for Magnus to go out to hospital in Lerwick. All of which emphasises our need for the link – and for the new nurse. I have no further news since they left in a hurry on 7th Oct. of our prospects of getting a satisfactory telephone service, but it may well be soon if the tests at the other end are as anticipated. Meanwhile Harry can now make contact with Sandness at any time of the day by lifting the receiver, and does not have to catch them at certain fixed times of the day as he used to do. This gives Sandness far less chance to be inefficient as I am afraid they often were before, and means we can send a telegram at any time of day and be fairly sure of getting it sent off straight away.

The new tractor arrived at a very convenient time – by the boat before the P.O. engineers. It was used to cart all their heavy equipment up to the wireless hut on top of the brae. It has been in constant use since then carrying peats. It is small and slow but a great improvement on the wheelbarrow and should prove a great asset to the island. It is of course a frequent topic of conversation and it is as amusing to listen to the criticisms of the islanders as it is to hear the enthusiasm of the Beagries. The owners quite naturally can see no fault in it at all whereas the rest find every fault that could possibly be picked in it. Nevertheless they seem quite willing to pay for it to fetch their peats home, and admit, if rather unwillingly, that it is an improvement to drive one load home than to wheel ten. I hope to make use of it myself this weekend as my supply of peats at the house is beginning to dwindle with this colder weather coming in. I have a lovely fire on tonight made entirely from peat which I cut, raised, stacked and barrowed home myself. Like the food one cooks for oneself it seems to be far better than bought fuel and to glow in the hearth there with something like the inner satisfaction that I feel in my own labours. It is perhaps a comment on the island temperament (and also on the shortage of labour) when I say that the peat I am paying to have cut for me this year is still wet and unstacked, whereas that which I undertook to handle myself is already home and dry and keeping my house warm.

When I last wrote my Heligoland trap was half built. It was finally christened on 4th October and has since caught a number of birds, although as you might have expected from MacPherson's Law the migrants stopped coming the day it was completed. The best drive so far got 24 birds in one go so that the catching box was bulging. The children are enthusiastic trappers already and the question at every break at school is "Are you gyaan' to caa the trap?" Of course this weather is hopeless for seeing much of the autumn migration which I suppose is going on as usual elsewhere. There are a few unfortunate stragglers which turn up like the robin we caught the other morning, or the Goldcrest which greeted me when I went to feed my hens yesterday morning. But generally speaking there had been very little evidence of migration here except one

very marked movement of thrushes which started on 8th October. That day there were redwings everywhere and a few fieldfares, blackbirds and two song thrushes to represent other members of the thrush family. The redwings seemed to drop out of the sky as I walked to school and goodness knows how many passed through during the day.

The Ham yard where I built the Heligoland trap was a walled enclosure about twenty-five yards by ten, down beside the path from the crofthouse to the bridge over the Ham Burn. They usually planted out their cabbage seedlings at the east end but in the shelter of the stone walls was a good thick belt of green growth, and amongst the weeds the remains of a few currant bushes and a couple of stunted sycamores. This cover must have looked very inviting to any woodland or hedgerow species fresh from an exhausting flight over the trackless sea.

There was a resident Wren which treated the trap as an additional attraction, harbouring spiders and other delicacies. House Sparrows and Starlings often sat on the metal hoops or the wire, joined occasionally by Twite. Although fairly low it was still a walk-in trap, and being built into the corner of the yard, the walk went round the corner inside giving the intended appearance of offering an escape route. However it very soon narrowed inside to a box, standing on legs, with a sloping glass front which again gave an illusion of an escape route. The birds hit it at an angle of 45° and so were gently brushed down into the box itself which had a hinged roof on a central swivel which let the birds in and then closed over the top of them. One or two birds could then be safely left in the catching box with no escape route left if one wanted to do a second drive to catch any birds that had doubled back. The only danger then was catching a large predator in the same box as an innocent passerine, who might end up as breakfast for the former. On the Isle of May we once had a Long-eared Owl in with some small birds and had to effect a quick rescue operation by removing the predator first. It was possible to drive the trap with only one person but three or four was best, forming a line past which the birds were reluctant to try to escape. Ideally a drive was a quiet act of persuasion, easing the birds in the right direction without panic. However if the children were in enthusiastic mood and the quarry was unusual – or numerous, like a whole flock of starlings – the scene probably more resembled a mob of dervishes shrieking as they closed in for the kill. I don't remember any casualties and eventually the trap trained a number of expert bird handlers able to hold a bird in the palm with the wings firmly restrained and the head between the first and second fingers, firm but with no pressure. The smallest birds are the most difficult to hold and Goldcrests require special skill and care. But I think we had a good record for handling our birds well and getting them safely into the linen bags in which they were carried up to the school for ringing. Some of the birds we caught were a revelation of form and colour to the children who never ceased to marvel at the perfection of their plumage and their spirit of independence.

My next letter after that of 14th October wasn't started till Guy Fawkes Night – but no fireworks on Foula. On top of the typescript is written in pen: '*Nov. 14th Boat-day at last after some dreadful weather.*' So we were well into the winter season of constant delays and uncertainty. However after weeks of waiting after the news that the lovely collie bitch at the Schoolhouse was expecting a litter soon, and then that there was a spare dog pup for me if I wanted it, I had something to write home about at last. I selected him for his beautiful

'Flossie', the Schoolhouse collie bitch with Norie, the pup from her litter selected to be mine

markings and his affectionate temperament. Finding a name wasn't difficult. All districts in Shetland tend to have a nickname for the local inhabitants, often a bird species. In Foula they were 'Nories', their name for the Puffin which is everybody's favourite bird anyway. So far a pup who was black and white and always pantin' and puffin', what could be more suitable than Norie? (The full name is 'Tammy Norie'. I left the Tammy out as too difficult to use when calling the dog to heel, in spite of the Foula tradition of double first names.)

The Manse, Foula, By Lerwick, Shetland
5th November 1954

Dear All,

I never did like hot-water bottles but I have one tonight keeping my lap warm for a change. He is black, about 14 inches long, extremely wicked, with four white paws, a white waistcoat, white spots on his head and neck, and a white tip to a ridiculously short black tail. He eats everything and leaves a trail of trademarks all round the house, is a nuisance at school and at home, and of course is the perfect time-waster. But as I have completely lost my heart to him (no, I had better not say completely as he woke me at 6.30 this morning) I don't really see what I can do about it. His mother is a delightful Foula collie at the Schoolhouse where there is also an equally delightful older brother now fully grown. His father is, I regret to say, unknown but the truth may out when he grows more recognizable as a dog and looks less like a furry sausage. The possible alternatives for his father are a spaniel, who is a lovable creature, but also a prize fighter, and another collie who is an excellent dog but an awful barker. So far Norie's ability to fight with my socks and to bark at my trousers when I am dressing in the mornings is not much help in establishing his parentage; added to which he is also lovable and an excellent eater and sleeper on present evidence.

Apart from my acquisition of a dog, which is a fairly major event in anyone's life I suppose and especially in a place like this where one has to look after it entirely single-handed, the chief item of news is, as ever, the weather. I know it is a fortnight since my last letter and that there has been one boat since then. It took out only seven letters from me compared with the twenty on the previous mail, and it brought back only about 25 instead of the previous 35. I have been checking up on my correspondence register and I seem to have written about 236 letters since I arrived

here just over six months ago. That is an average of well over one per day and yet I still can't keep up with what comes in. Mail is both the greatest pleasure and the greatest dread of the week. It really is wonderful hearing from so many friends in the south and getting regular news from home so that I don't really feel out of touch at all. But it really doesn't pay to have a well developed conscience when it comes to replying, when there simply isn't time to fulfil all ones obligations to this fascinating community.

I am awaiting anxiously news of whether my article to the Edinburgh Evening News has been published It was far from easy to write, I may say, when one has to be so careful not to use one's position of confidence in the community to say things about the people here that they don't want you to say about them. And they are all very reticent about publicity.

I suppose quite a lot has happened in our small way since I last wrote. The new nurse is now well established and will, I think, be a great success. She comes from Peebles, knows Edinburgh well and is comparatively young and active and though completely new to this way of life seems to have the right psychology for dealing with these folk. Her arrival was much more eventful than my own. The boat had crossed in freshening weather on the morning of October 23rd. She should never have returned that night at all as the tide was high and the wind high from the south east which blows straight into the harbour mouth. However it wasn't too bad when they left Walls so they came on and we got word over the telephone as usual that they were on their way. By the time they were due it was a night of heavy rain and the waves were washing over the low part of the breakwater occasionally. I had spent most of the day, being Saturday, in the nurse's house hanging her new curtains and repairing her lavatory – some of those many jobs that one cannot get a tradesman in to do here and which one has to do oneself. I went down to the pier in the pouring rain when the boat was about due in and found only one other man there – the postmaster, Harry Gear with his storm lantern, doing his best to give them some kind of light as it was pitch dark. We all blinked with our torches as she approached blinking in reply, and after what seemed an age she approached the pier. By this time one other hand had appeared on the scene. Harry went out to take the line from the boat and nearly got washed off the pier by a wave which swept him clean off his feet. We rushed back for a lifeline and then John went out hanging on to the other end of it and took the rope from the boat. She had by this time passed the end of the pier, and in reversing in the swell she nearly stove in her stern on the point of the breakwater. However one of the crew jumped off and kept her clear, and we finally pulled her in alongside.

Soon after she was in one or two men appeared, but it always seems to me that it is a matter of pure chance with perhaps a slight degree of natural telepathy that anyone gets down to meet the boat at all. After all there is no way of communicating with those at the south end of the island that she is even on the way. After she was in I got the nurse, who was soaked and frozen, escorted up to her house where I am pleased to say there was a fire on, hot water in the tap, and tea ready in the pot for her. All this again was achieved more by good luck than by any organization. All the jobs in her house were left to the last minute, because there are always other more urgent jobs to be done by the same last minute. And nobody ever gives the orders or tells anyone to get a job done like preparing the nurse's house. It either just happens or it doesn't. But if it is anything to do with looking after other people's welfare, then it usually does get done. The only snag with the system is that the willing horses get the brunt of the work.

To resume – after the nurse herself had been catered for, there was still the routine work of unloading perhaps two tons of cargo, carrying it up the steep little hill to the shed, lifting the boat up onto the davits by chain pulleys (all five tons of her), swinging her onto the cradle and then pulling her with the hand-winch up the slipway out of reach of the water should a gale get up overnight. While this latter part of the operation was in progress I was barrowing the nurse's luggage up to her house, still in the pouring rain. I thus fulfilled an ambition that I formed on my first night on the island that some day I would do the same for somebody else that they did for me, when I wondered so much how on earth Peter could see his way on the bumpy road and wheel such an enormous barrow-load of luggage in the dark. Like so many other things it's all a matter of practice; but I really felt quite an old hand when I reached the door of the nurse's house that night!

Well, such is life here though the weather is not always so unkind I'm glad to say. All that was fully a fortnight ago now, and the time has simply fled past since. This week has been typical of many.

Monday saw a lovely calm day and the boat made her scheduled crossing to Walls, returning soon after dark but with enough light in the Northern sky to light her into the Voe without any need for lamps at all. We have only had one really good display of Northern Lights so far, which is apparently much less than usual at this season. But it is seldom really dark. At the moment there is a good moon of course, which makes a tremendous difference as it is dark now by 5.30 p.m. or soon after. Even with the moon there is often more light with the aurora. However torches are still an essential part of our equipment – 'blinkies' as they are called – and with the ground so waterlogged, we have only to leave the road to get our feet wet if we can't see where we are going.

We had our harvest thanksgiving last Sunday evening with a congregation of 27 and the church filled with enormous cabbages, carrots, turnips etc. and the windows decorated with barley and oats. There were model hay 'coles', of the kind they make here roped down to prevent the wind carrying them away, eggs, fruit, flowers and a large skein of wool slung between two windows and decorated with marigold flowers. The work of decorating the church is a communal effort which was done by the women on Saturday night. On Monday night I divided all the produce up into boxes for the older folk who don't grow their own now, with the help of two of my boys when they weren't too busy eating the centres of the cabbage stalks which I had cut off before packing them up. (This is a practice we encourage as it is such a good source of Vitamin C. Better than a stick of rock!) I then had to rush down to the pier to rescue my goods off the boat, and just in time as it came on to rain on my way down. By the time I had barrowed the school supplies up to the Schoolhouse and taken my own box home, and read my mail (collected from the Post Office on my way home at 10.30 p.m.) it was well past bed-time.

Tuesday night was Women's Guild night. We started a fortnight ago and they come up to the Manse one night a week and knit away for the church funds while we talk and while I read to them from 'Three Men in a Boat', which they love. It makes a good break for them and they are a very cheery crowd. We have tea at half-time and finish up with a reading and a prayer. This week was Mima Gear's birthday (wife of the Skipper, and mother of one of my pupils, Jim) so we all shared the currant cake which you sent, Mum, decorated with one large candle and

Norie as a pup, autumn 1954

48 matches for her age. This kind of thing is very much appreciated and any excuse for the party spirit is seized upon with great gusto.

On Wednesday they decided to have a round-up of the sheep to gather in some more of the lambs for sale. It's far too late in the season but the weather has held up everything so it was a case of better late than never. So I let the school out early and took the children up with me to help in the drive, which brought the sheep down from the whole North end of the island to the crue by the Shop, down at Ham Voe

in the centre of the East side. It was a good drive and we got a good haul of lambs, but the rain came on half way and we all got soaked. It came a dark night with low cloud and after I had sent the bairns home to get dry, I spent the rest of the evening wheeling the lambs in barrowloads to the nearest croft to put them in the byre overnight. That may seem strange but these sheep are wild and will not drive in the usual way, so that once caught they are shackled and have to be carted about from one place to another in wheelbarrows. This is a lot of work and as there was a big lot of sheep, it was a case of all hands to the – barrows. It was well after dark before we got them all sorted and shifted, so that by the time I had had tea at the croft in question, made my way home lit the fire, and put my things out to dry, there was another busy day gone.

Yesterday, Thursday, was very showery so after school I unpacked two crates of glass for the school windows, then had my tea at the Schoolhouse before coming home to pick up some books for the old boy at one of the south end crofts who recently came back from hospital. (Magnie of Quinister.) I also brought Norie home for the first time so that by the time I had fixed him up with a box and some food, and had fed the hens and shut them up for the night, it was eight o'clock before I got on my way. So as you can imagine, two visits after that took up the rest of the evening and it was after eleven before I got home, having spent most of the time with the returned invalid who lives with his older brother (ages about 75 and 85). I got nothing to eat there and so had to make myself supper on my return so that it was once again past midnight before I finally got to bed.

Friday And so the days pass – and the letters don't get written. Tonight I promised myself a night at this but since I started I have had John Henry from the Schoolhouse and Mrs Beagrie my next-door neighbour in for coffee and a chat. So now it is an hour past midnight and a recumbent black sausage on my lap has at last given up trying to bite the typewriter keys or to kill the bits of paper in the wastepaper basket, and is reminding me that it is high time I was in bed. So I'll make up the fires and read another chapter of 'The Shetland Bus' by David Howarth, with the glorious prospect of a lie-in tomorrow morning and a weather forecast of at least no worse than showers so I might be able to get some of the many jobs left over for Saturday actually done this week – for a change. But that depends on what time I get up, which in turn depends on what time I get to bed which in turn depends on not writing any more to you now. So Goodnight!

Sunday night It has been a windy day and towards evening rather wet too. But now at 11.15 p.m. there is a lovely moon and it is a glorious still night. So there

A meeting of the Women's Guild at the Manse, winter 1954. L–R: Mary Umphray, Nurse Mitchell,
a visiting evangelist, Mima Gear, Mary Henry

is a good chance of a mail day tomorrow. I did have a busy day on Saturday fixing up a new hen-house for my hens as the old one was on the point of collapse. That together with cooking my dinner took up most of the daylight hours. Then in the evening I was kept busy by Alec from next door, writing away about his tractor and roofing materials for its shed and so on. I hope that the present generation of Foula bairns will be well enough educated to write their own business letters without having to go to the schoolmaster to get it done for them. You will know who to blame if they're not, of course.

Reading these letters which I wrote to my family in Edinburgh, over 50 years after they were written, is an interesting lesson in introspection, seeing how I really felt at the time of writing. By November 1954 I had been there over six months and was beginning, first of all to understand the dialect and secondly to weigh up the nature of the people who made up this community. I was too close to them and too much involved in their very obvious problems to be able to stand back and write about them dispassionately. Although our origins and experience were mostly at opposite ends of a spectrum, I was thoroughly enjoying their company and finding how much we had in common rather than how different we were. Like me they all had differing views on all sorts of subjects, but with a few exceptions I felt easy about discussing almost any topic, learning from them so much about their expertise in sheep, cattle, crofting, the sea and the weather, sharing views on religion, politics, the natural world especially birds, and, with a few, philosophical topics like evolution and morality, There were some very thoughtful and intelligent folk on Foula, whose company I was coming to enjoy perhaps much more than I had expected. But the pace of life was slow and their insularity often showed through in a reluctance to be hurried, to reach decisions, to organise their lives too much for the future. And these letters show the beginnings of an appraisal of all this side of island life, and a quite difficult irritation that it appeared to lower standards I was used to in efficiency

L–R: Mansie Henry, Eric Isbister, Jimmie Henry at Quinister, winter 1954

Meggie Ratter and her elder sister Jeannie Isbister at Punds, winter 1954/55. Note the drawing of a fishing boat above the mantelpiece, a present from Eric, one of my pupils

or punctuality or the persistence called for to see a job through against such odds as harsh weather, pressure of time, or sheer physical weariness. As possibly the best paid and the best housed individual on the island I had of course no cause to criticize others, but at the same time my irritation was real and inevitable considering my background. I seem to remember being aware of the need to control it and never to allow it to show in my dealings with the islanders. I do remember finding it a real cure for any feelings of frustration at jobs which didn't get done or promises which were made over-optimistically and never fulfilled, to go down to a croft like Punds and spend an hour listening to old Meggie Ratter talking about the old days or reminiscing about her husband Walter's life as the island's skipper of the mailboat. Then crossings to Walls really were hazardous and very hard work, but there were good times in summer when she and her even older sister Jeannie had been young and when Foula had seemed to them like a little paradise. I think they warmed to my accounts of how exciting and enjoyable I found my work with the Skuas and the miracle of migration. But though I shared their view of the little paradise in summer, winter was coming fast.

Chapter 15: Foula Funerals

On 15th September, a month into my second school term on Foula, James Ratter's wife Lily died at Broadfoot. This was my second funeral but I remember very little about it because it went quite smoothly and by this time I knew the drill fairly well. I suppose when one is in a position of responsibility, the first time is always going to be the most memorable, simply because everything is strange and one has to make a very conscious effort to learn as one goes. Taking normal services was not an entirely new experience as at Cambridge, where I was for a time College Secretary of the Student Christian Movement, we would take it in turns to conduct, in a very informal and personal style, weekly prayers in the College Chapel. At St John's this was an imposing building as large as some cathedrals in English cities, with a superb organ and a choir with a world-wide reputation. In spite of all this, taking a funeral on Foula was much more nerve-wracking, especially the first time. There was another reason for this. It was the first funeral I had ever been to in my life, in any capacity. I was 27.

I frequently knocked on the door at Mogle, the house just below the Schoolhouse where Harry Gear lived with his aged parents, Peter and Grace Anne. If one ever needed postage stamps, there was seldom any chance that Harry would be at the Post Office, so it was customary to go round the back of the house and knock. He was always available, if not in the house, in his workshop or attending to the Post Office generator or batteries. He came promptly, and then I went on my way. Harry never came to church and was not a believer, and they were a very private family. So I think I had only been inside the house of Mogle once before the evening I called when I heard Peter was seriously ill, and probably near death. I had been warned by the Holbourns that Harry's old father was melancholic and had more or less given up on life at the age of 80. It was no surprise therefore when I was told that he had died.

I went to school the next day as usual, where not unnaturally the talk in the Gear family was much about Peter and his long life on Foula. I was informed that there was a slight problem over wood for the coffin which Peter Gray would be making, and that an approach had been made to the Holbourns for some boarding from a store

they held at the Haa'. I later heard that this was a normal procedure, as there was never time to send for wood, never any spare wood on the crofts sufficient to make a coffin and the job clearly couldn't wait. To me it sounded rather like communal blackmail of the laird's goodwill, with a sort of understanding that it would always find a generous response. What did surprise me, having heard that if the coffin was ready in time the funeral would be on Thursday, was when Andrew Umphray knocked at the school door one morning. When I answered his knock and found him standing there in his Sunday best, he made a typically courteous but formal announcement that the funeral would be at mid-day on Thursday, and would I please therefore come to Mogle on Wednesday evening for the 'kisting'. I had been warned about this part of the ceremonial of funerals and agreed at once that of course I would be there. But surely there must be a mistake about the time of the funeral itself, as I would normally be in school until 4 p.m. So perhaps if I closed the school a bit early I could arrange to be free to take the funeral, say, at 3.30 p.m. to allow plenty of time before dark?

I cannot now remember the detail of the reply that this evoked, except that it was only slightly apologetic, that this could simply not be considered as Foula funerals were always at mid-day; it was customary and everyone would expect it and turn up at Mogle at 12 noon to collect the coffin and carry it to the Kirk. It was not that they were unaware that, for the first time in their history, the job of teacher and that of lay missionary were combined in only one person. But surely it must be obvious to me that as this was a funeral, my responsibility to the Kirk came first and the school would have to look after itself. I wasn't asked if this could be arranged. I was told. So of course I agreed. A couple of days later I was at the door of Mogle again, dressed as I would be for a Sunday service and wearing my black gown and hood. There was a fair gathering of the able-bodied menfolk, but no women, and so far as I can now remember dressed in normal, not Sunday, clothes. The furniture had been rearranged, and we sat on either side of tables set down the middle of the room in a rather hesitant atmosphere where it seemed nobody quite knew who should speak first. Before very long, after the usual comments about the weather had been exchanged, I was asked if I would accompany Harry and one or two others including Peter Gray, upstairs to the bedroom for the kisting. There the coffin was set on a couple of chairs with the lid removed and the body properly shrouded but with the face uncovered, laid out ready for the coffin to be finally closed and sealed in my presence, as the official witness from the Church that all was in order. There was nothing in the Church of Scotland funeral service in the Prayer Book to cover this situation so I had prepared a reading and one or two short prayers that seemed appropriate, while we stood round the open coffin. The old man looked frail and shrunken, his skin waxen but the expression on his face peaceful, and I made some informal comment to the effect that he looked happier now than I had ever seen him in life. It was Harry who covered his face with the sheet, and then Peter, as the senior Elder present and the coffin maker, picked up the lid, beautifully finished in plain pine with little wooden stops nailed on the underside, and placed it on top of the box so that these stops fitted very precisely against the sides. I had expected that the lid would be nailed down but no, nothing so undignified or disrespectful to the deceased as even a light hammer blow was allowed. There were holes already drilled at intervals round the sides covering other holes drilled exactly in the centre of the upper edge of each side. Peter produced a handful of galvanized three-inch nails, and gently but firmly pressed a nail into each hole. I noticed that each time the head of the nail was only just slightly proud of the lid until by the pressure of his thumb alone it was pressed home until it gripped the wood. And so with quiet precision, but without so much as one intrusive hammer-blow, the beautifully crafted coffin was sealed and we repaired downstairs.

In the room downstairs there was only a moment's lull in the conversation when we returned. We were offered cups of tea and Black's biscuits, and a special baking of scones and cakes with Mary's beautiful home-churned butter, and the talk flowed. The occasion, and mostly dark clothing, gave a solemn atmosphere of respect for the bereaved family, but there was more to it than that. We were there not just to close a chapter on Foula's history, for Peter was well over 80 and had been a prominent figure in the community for many years; but this was an opportunity, not often available, to discuss the future, to air views, to listen to opinions, to share ideas. There was almost a lightness of mood as though perhaps a relief that the old man's melancholy was over. It was clear too that everyone was glad of the opportunity to exchange news and discuss island affairs, released for an hour or so from the pressures of croft work, animals, old folks and children. As soon as we were all present after the kisting, the pattern of the conversation changed and only one person spoke at a time, as we covered all sorts of topics to do with our daily lives. I had hoped I could get Harry to tell us a bit about his father and his life, as I really needed at some point to pick up a few facts about Peter for my address at the funeral service the next day, and had hoped that some of the others present might also like to hear what I hoped he would say. But the opportunity never arose as it became clear, when various people present raised new topics and the conversation flowed, that everything could be discussed and almost any opinion expressed so long as the dead man was never mentioned. So there was much exchange of news and views with some quite forcible views on the problems people were having with peat or harvest or fishing or current topics like the number of rabbits or the tirricks at the North Ness or the midges. I was even asked to explain what it was I was planning to build in the kale yard at Ham with all that wire netting? Mourning was clearly being reserved for tomorrow.

The next day I gave the children work to do and a radio programme to listen to after lunch and explained how sometimes the dead come before the living, just for this one day. I was happy to leave them to Mary's loving care for the rest of the day. I knew that none of the womenfolk would be seen in public on a funeral day, except the two from the family who would take the necessary crockery and food supplies up to the vestry, where they would prepare refreshments for the funeral cortege when it arrived.

They would then lay out plates and cups on alternate pews, and in between each two 'places' set a plate of biscuits and another with butter and a knife. Water would be boiled on a Primus stove and tea prepared at the expected time of arrival but the women would be effectively incarcerated in the Vestry until it was all over, when after the men had departed for the burial ground, they could clear up and depart for home. I knew it was considered very bad form for a woman to be seen by the men taking part in the funeral. There was a story of one of the old sisters at Niggards having tried to put her cow out to the hill before the funeral procession appeared and when its arrival caught her still outside the house, she had to hide behind the peat stack, with her cow, for several hours until it was finally out of sight.

Meanwhile I presented myself at Mogle at the prescribed time and watched while the coffin was brought downstairs and out of the front door and laid on three oars on the ground. When the coffin had been lashed very expertly to the oars, six men were allocated for the first carry, each man picking up the end of an oar and lifting to order.

I wasn't at all clear what my role was supposed to be at this stage but somehow I felt that they had the carry so well organised, with a change to a second six half way up the long hill from the bridge over the Ham Burn, and another at the Mornington gate before the last stretch along to the church, that my role was to lead the cortege walking at their pace out in front. The rest of the men walked behind the coffin which was placed, still on its oars, on the ground outside the church while I led the way in and the rest followed. I went into the vestry to check that all was well with the domestic preparations and found Mima in charge and everything in order. I kept the service short and simple and as soon as it was over, two or three of the men of the family went out to fetch in the teapots which they used to fill the cups on alternate pews to which they had access from the central aisle. The mourners then were able to lean over and help themselves to milk and sugar and biscuits as they needed, so that apart from a few whispered comments there was only the tinkle of teaspoons and the exaggerated sounds of sipping of tea and munching of biscuits to disturb the silence of the church. Both during the silent procession of the cortege carrying the coffin and again during the time for refreshments in the church, there was plenty of opportunity for those taking part to share in silent thought their sadness at the loss of an old friend and their sympathy for the family expressed by their presence at this committal.

There was obviously an entirely practical basis for this strict tradition of food and drink at the funeral service itself. Sometimes when the deceased had lived close to the burial ground down at the old Kirk on the South Ness, there was little real need for it as the mourners would assemble at the church first for the funeral service, and not collect the coffin till afterwards. If the funeral had to start from a North end croft with a two-mile carry to the church, much of it over wet, rough ground with only a narrow path down to the road, the mourners would be much in need of refreshment by the time they reached the church, with the prospect of a further carry of nearly a mile down to the burial ground afterwards. We are all human however; and the mixing of such a solemn occasion with something

as social and domestic as eating biscuits and drinking tea is a risky mixture where human emotions are concerned. At one of the four funerals I conducted on Foula, I think that of old Lily Ratter in mid-September of 1954 which left poor James, her crippled husband, very bereft at Broadfoot, the decorum of the church service was shattered by one of those unfortunate lapses in self-control which is particularly embarrassing to those not affected by the breakdown of emotions. I am not, as you may be expecting, referring to a breakdown due to uncontrollable grief which could be understood. Rather the opposite, which left me fairly helpless to know how to deal with the situation, in that at first a few and then perhaps even the majority of those present were overwhelmed with a fit of the giggles. It started, I expect, with some innocent accident, perhaps the spilling of a cup of tea, or a biscuit dropped butter side down, which in the silent and very solemn atmosphere of the church suddenly seemed such a ridiculous contrast with the funeral as to be overwhelmingly funny. Somebody trying to suppress a giggle suddenly let it out so that everyone was aware and turned to see the cause. This spread the sense of breaking the tension and almost everyone burst out laughing at the giggler, so that suddenly the funeral became a moment of great relief and almost joy – that we could be so relieved by the ridiculous that we could unload a whole mood of sadness to the realization that we were all just humans after all. Several people commented on it afterwards along the lines of '*Wasn't that awful; all that giggling at a funeral*', while agreeing that it really had helped break the tension of the occasion and thank goodness for our ability to see the funny side of it – with no disrespect to anyone. My memory of the event is that the most helpless of those caught up in the merriment were the three tough, hard-working, outgoing sons of the family. To them church and the subduing of natural human emotions was another world from their robust and energetic daily lives. In their loss of control like children, they presented a new face to those present, which was perhaps an eye-opener to us all. Personally I loved them for it, and hoped their mother was also laughing on cloud nine.

There was another funeral I shall never forget, which was much more serious in that it involved the living in a crisis with the dead, but was also much more funny, probably the most humorous memory I have of my whole time on Foula. The croft involved was Dykes down at the south end of the Hametoun, not more than a few hundred yards from the burial ground. The Grays were on old Foula family, who get a whole long chapter to themselves in Professor Holbourn's book. Tom, or Tammie, Gray was a widower and had long passed his three score years and ten. His three children all still lived with him; Louis the eldest daughter (45); James Andrew (40), a talented and educated man, a skilled carpenter and watchmaker well known and appreciated for both types of skill; with his wife Anna (36), who came from Leith in Edinburgh and had adapted well to life on Foula, where she was bringing up her three-year-old daughter Marion Jane; and Edith, the youngest (34), a spinster and expert knitter. Anna was over eight months pregnant with her second child when old Tom Gray died on Saturday, 4th December 1954. I think his death was a little unexpected as I remember taking a photograph of him not long before, scything hay on the croft. It was the last film on the roll and an upright picture so that when the film came back, the last frame was clipped a little and poor Tom had lost his head. I was always anxious to show people my colour transparencies, which to Foula folk were a new thing and attracted much interest. So I took some slides round when I called at Dykes to see Anna who had been having a few maternity problems and was not as active as she usually was. I seem to remember we had a good laugh at my apology for the slide of her father-in-law because I had '*chopped his head off*'. A few days later that little joke seemed in rather poor taste when Tom was dead. There was at the same time some concern about Anna and the nurse was anxious to arrange for her to go out to Lerwick to have the baby as she had apparently had some problems over the birth of her firstborn. Her time was approaching fast and we discussed dates and possible mailboats for her journey. No panic but we wanted to be ready in case of trouble.

Meanwhile the funeral was arranged for Wednesday 8th, and on the evening of Tuesday 7th I turned up at Dykes for the kisting. Under the influence of James Andrew the Grays were a more modern family, where I always felt more at home than in the more traditional crofts like Mogle. Anna also was very up to date, having until comparatively recently lived, as I had, in the capital city, Edinburgh. The kisting ceremony was still done correctly but the tea afterwards was more like a family gathering with everybody included and a lot of interesting chat about everyday matters. Amongst other things I was able to ask openly about the kisting tradition and learnt a great deal from James Andrew, who was very well informed about Shetland culture and Foula's traditions in particular. In my next letter home in which I recounted the events of this week I explained to my family as follows:

> *The kisting ceremony dates back to the old days when the tax on Irish linen led to some of the dead being buried without a shroud, and so it was always arranged for a representative of the church to be present as a witness when the body was consigned to the coffin (i.e. 'chested' or 'cisted') to ensure that the proceedings were carried out correctly. The custom has remained long after the need has disappeared, and it has outgrown its original purpose in that it has now become a general gathering of friends and relations for which a special baking is done and where the conversation covers every possible subject except the bereavement in question or the deceased. It has become an accepted part of the funeral procedure largely because all those attending have never known anything else so that in their minds it is just an essential ingredient of a 'proper' funeral. Foula is perhaps the only place left in Britain where the custom is still upheld.*

The funeral was due at 12 noon on the Wednesday as usual. Everyone was to assemble at the church on the hill just above the Hametoun gate. We would then hold the funeral service, but this time without the coffin, and we would then process down to Dykes where the coffin would be collected and carried across the short distance to the burial ground for the interment. Everything was in order, Bobby Isbister was to dig the grave in the Grays' family plot, and as the mailboat was not due to sail till next Monday, all the crew were in Foula so there was no shortage of able-bodied men for the funeral. There had been a slight snag over the coffin, which James Andrew had made in the house at Dykes, but found on completion could not be manoeuvred out of the house through their front door due to the configuration of the porch and the door. So, as it was too late to alter the coffin, he had taken out the living room window and the coffin would be passed out through the window when the cortege arrived at Dykes. So no real problems – until we were all actually gathering at the church door, just before noon on Wednesday for the funeral service, and the nurse was seen panting up the hill from Mornington to say that she had received a telegram from the doctor on the mainland in response to hers describing the condition of her patient at Dykes and her pregnancy. Anna and the baby were both considered to be at risk and the doctor had ordered the patient be sent out to hospital without delay. Poor James Andrew was now in a cleft stick. As the chief mourner at his father's funeral he had a clear duty to see the old man properly buried, a duty which could be all over in two or three hours. As a husband and father he also had a clear duty to give priority, if it was needed, to the safety, perhaps even the life, of his wife and unborn child. The nurse was adamant that the doctor was serious and regarded the boat-run as essential for her patient. So we asked the mail crew, who were all present at the church, whether they would agree to go. I said, and James Andrew agreed, that we could still hold the funeral on Thursday and could just scrape together enough able-bodied people to carry the coffin if they couldn't get back in time.

The crew looked doubtful and Davie asked if they could discuss the pros and cons of a crossing to Walls in view of the easterly swell at the harbour and a forecast of freshening winds. So while they started to talk together, I took James Andrew and the nurse on one side and reassured him that I would take full responsibility for his father's funeral if he felt, as indeed I strongly felt, that he should accompany his wife out to Walls. The nurse was new to Shetland and not a good sailor and I would be happier if he was there to take over at the other side getting Anna safely to hospital. I think the nurse was relieved at his agreement with this plan. However the crew came over and Davie, as skipper, said they were not happy with the feasibility of a mail run today in view of the weather, and they would suggest calling out the Aith lifeboat which could be here in 3–4 hours and was a better boat in adverse conditions, both for the Voe and for the crossing. The nurse repeated that the doctor had emphasised that there should be no delay, and she was not happy at the suggestion of at least 6–7 hours before reaching Walls, with another hour into Lerwick, when the mailboat could get her there within three hours if we fetched Anna down to the pier straight away. This was an impasse calling for further contact with the doctor, either to authorize such a delay or to give us an ultimatum for the mail crew. None of us could otherwise make a 'right' decision. So I agreed to go down and ask Harry to get me a phone link if possible with the doctor and to be ready to call out the Aith lifeboat if necessary. I spoke to the doctor who had in the interim consulted the surgeon at the hospital. When I asked if he would call out the Aith lifeboat to come and fetch the patient as she would then have a safer and more comfortable journey, he more or less said, '*To hell with comfort; time is of the essence and the surgeon wants her here without delay if at all possible.*' Even the much shorter time the mailboat would take was a serious risk for Anna. Besides, nobody had yet alerted the lifeboat, which in the remoter districts sometimes took a considerable time to launch. So would I please plead with the Foula mailcrew to come if they possibly could to save time and possibly the patient's life.

I felt sorry for James Andrew as we hurried back up the hill to the church to present the case to the crew. He knew as well as I did that they were the best judges of the safety factors for their own boat – which were of course also the safety factors for him and his wife, not to mention the baby – and of course the nurse, who had made it clear she wanted to go with Anna in case of an emergency on the way. As we returned to the church she said she would go straight down to Dykes to prepare her patient for the journey to save time whatever was decided about the means of getting her there.

James and I went back to the church where the mail crew was waiting to hear our verdict. I put the case for taking the stretcher case on the mailboat if at all possible as cogently as I could, quoting the doctor's exact words about the absolute need for the quickest option. When I told them that the doctor had in fact refused to call out the Aith lifeboat because of the delay, there was a voluble amount of complaint along these lines, '*If it had been anywhere else but Foula…*', or '*the doctor knows nothing about the weather conditions on this side…*', etc. I knew that there was always a general feeling of victimization on the part of Foula men that they were discriminated against by mainland authorities, which is I think probably justified by the facts. But in this case the doctor was clearly thinking only of the facts of the medical case and I emphasised that only he could judge on those. I asked them also to consider the position of the nurse who was morally obliged to do the best for her patient and medically obliged to abide by the doctor's decision. I felt bad about asking the crew to go against their gut feelings about the risk, which after all they and not I were being asked to take. However, bless them, they decided they had no alternative but to give it a go and get Anna out as soon as they could. I sensed Davie Gear's wisdom and influence behind such a difficult decision.

The stretcher was already at Dykes; the nurse would soon have her patient ready. As soon as I had announced the decision to hold the funeral at noon tomorrow, in the absence of James Andrew, who would go with his wife to the hospital, all that was required of us was to go to Dykes. Would the first two carrying teams of six please organise themselves to carry the stretcher to the pier – instead of the coffin to the burial ground, and would the crew members necessary for preparing the boat for the journey please go straight to the pier to get her on the water. What a godsend in the circumstances that we were all ready to go without delay! Well, that was the theory. The trouble was that though they had agreed, if a little reluctantly, to abandon the funeral for a rescue mission of some urgency, they were in funeral clothes and funeral mood. So when they reached the crofthouse at Dykes and had managed to get the stretcher on which Anna was lying trussed up like a mummy, out of the window, leaving the coffin behind for tomorrow, the first six took up the stretcher and started off up the road on the mile long carry to the pier. Sadly Andrew Umphray, who I have described elsewhere as the slowest man I have ever met, was at the front of the stretcher and in funeral mode. Carrying a coffin is done at a measured pace, dignified to suit the occasion, and it was this pace which dominated the journey of a very sick patient to the boat. The nurse and I tried to exert pressure from behind but it was impossible to make any impression on men who had come to a funeral but were now assisting with an emergency. It was a funeral procession which wended its funereal way up past the church and down the hill towards Ham Voe. It would have been funny if it hadn't been so unreal and so bizarre. As it was we fretted and encouraged and very gradually managed to induce a better pace into the stretcher's progress. At the Voe, Foula added the final touch to the pantomime. The crew had arrived at the pier to discover that the heavy seas of the past few days, with an east wind, had swept all the ballast rocks off the pier into the Voe, and it had taken a long time to recover them from deep water. They had successfully winched the boat down the slipway and lowered her into the water, and while they were loading the ballast discovered that the engine would not start. Harry was summoned and eventually the engine sputtered into life, and all was ready with the stretcher in the hold and the patient, husband and little girl aged three all safely esconced beside her – and the nurse. Funnily enough she was the one I was most sorry for at the end of an extraordinary day. When she had first arrived on Foula after a horrendous crossing in the dark, she had vowed she would never go on 'that boat' again till the day she left. And now here she was, faithful to her job and her patient, ready to go on a bad sea with a rather reluctant crew and a patient who might need her help in case of emergency en route. We saw them off with a wave and a prayer just before dark. The habitual smile on James Andrew's face was no longer there. I wished him God speed, and wondered just how long it would be before they won back.

It occurred to me that taking two days off school for funerals might make my schedule of obligatory hours for the pupils difficult to maintain. Moreover here were all the men we would require for the funeral already assembled and correctly dressed, so I suggested to them that perhaps, as it was a full moon, we could still go ahead with the funeral and bury Tom Gray that night if they were willing. They were not. It had never been done before – which of course is a Foula way of saying 'quite impossible'.

So they all went home and I went down to Dykes to sit as long as I could with the two spinster sisters who faced an unusual, and for them rather uncomfortable experience of spending the night alone in their house with no male company except their dead father in his coffin. I did not offer to stay the night with them though I think they might have preferred me to, but I was exhausted and had tomorrow to think about. My funeral sermon would have to be drastically altered for one thing. The day it should have been held, Wednesday, was calm and fine, though the swell was still from the east. I had planned a few words using metaphors from calm, peaceful weather to offer a thought of comfort for the bereaved in the image of a peaceful end. I had hoped I could look out of the church window and they would see in the day's beauty what I was getting at. Thursday was a foul day, with driving rain and a cold easterly wind with the waves once again breaking over the pier. It was interesting, even humbling to think that we had lowered Anna on her stretcher into the hold while the boat hardly moved on a light swell at the pierside. The next day that would have been a very tricky operation, if not impossible, and as someone pointed out not even the Aith lifeboat would have chanced trying to get into the pier at Ham Voe under those conditions. In fact the state of the sea, coupled with a full moon for the crossing in the dark, made the day the mailboat did its mercy run for Anna the only one in about six weeks when such an operation would have been possible. Not surprising then that my funeral address on the Thursday was of Tom Gray achieving, at last, rest from the storms of life, and of his final act of love to his daughter-in-law in giving way to her safety yesterday, so to speak, before going to his rest today. It really did seem that our decisions had God's blessings yesterday, for the message was that they had arrived safely, Anna was fine in hospital and all looked to be well now for mother and baby. Wouldn't a posthumous grandchild for Tom be a wonderful, God-given compensation to the family for their grief at his passing? We owed thanks to God and the mail crew.

After the service, at which the refreshments for the mourners from the North end were really appreciated on such a miserable day, we proceeded to Dykes, removed the window and lifted Tom's coffin out into the storm. We carried it with just 12 able-bodied men left in the whole community who could be said to be up to the task, and that included me this time. At the burial ground I had to shout the words of committal against a gale and driving rain and I don't suppose many of those at the graveside heard a word. But old Tom was at peace at last, even if we were all soaked to the skin. It was a day, or rather a couple of days, I wouldn't forget in a hurry.

At the end of January 1955 the nurse called on me one night on her way to Broadfoot where old James Ratter was terminally ill and asked if I would come down with her. He had lost his wife Lily in September, and her death seemed to have dragged him down too. He was propped up in his bed when we got there, his breathing very laboured and there wasn't very much any of us could do. He was 77 and very crippled from an injury sustained when he was on a sailing ship and fell into the hold and hurt his back. Latterly he was so bent that when he wheeled his barrow, as he insisted on doing till the last, his face was nearly in the barrow. That night the nurse was very good with him as he couldn't keep any food down and was in great distress. She indicated to me that the signs of approaching death were clear to her, so, as he couldn't speak, all I felt able to do was to hold his hands to indicate that we were there and he was cherished.

He had been a remarkable man, a saint in every sense of the word, kind and considerate to all, a much respected father of three sons, an elder of the Kirk and our Treasurer, a duty he performed meticulously. He worked till the day he died and I think it is true to say that both he and his wife Lily died of overwork, never letting up just because they were old or he seriously crippled. They both seemed happier to be up and doing than sitting about being cared for. So the outcome of that night in which he died was far better than if he had become increasingly helpless. On the day of his funeral we carried his coffin over boggy ground in the pouring rain the half mile or so to the burial ground, mustering our full strength of 16 men. If the mail crew of five is out at Walls for any future funeral, we shall for the first time in Foula's history have less than two shifts of six to carry the coffin for burial. Let's hope it is not from one of the North end crofts over two miles away. It is perhaps no wonder that the remark is often heard on such occasions – '*Yes, it's going down fast now.*'

As a footnote we received notice the day after Tammie Gray's funeral that a grandson was born to his daughter-in-law in Lerwick on the day after she arrived in hospital, the same day as his funeral. Everyone remarked how sad it was that that was just too late to gladden the old man's heart before he went. Such is life – and the harsh reality of death.

Chapter 16: Christmas New and Old

Foula is famous for its Christmas tradition, which is no different from any other except that it is celebrated on a different date. The history of this is quite straightforward. The noticeable thing is the independent spirit which produced the difference 250 years ago and still preserves it today. For sixteen centuries the Julian Calendar, a remarkable achievement in its time, to organise our annual timetable to fit the movement of the planet Earth round the sun, worked well enough, with the Roman months making a total of 365 days, on one of which, the 25th December, the Christian world celebrated the birth of the founder of its religion. However by the middle of the 16th century it was becoming obvious that a year was 365 and a quarter days, plus a bit more, and that the accumulation of these extra bits over such a long time had produced a discrepancy of about twelve days. When the Julian calendar was first started, the 25th December was very close to the winter solstice, making the festival of the Nativity an excellent blend with old pagan mid-winter festivals, when mankind liked to celebrate the turn of the year and the promise of light after darkness. It was of course Pope Gregory whose scholars had worked out the real length of a year and the correction needed to make the man-made calendar fit the God-given passage of time. He decreed that twelve days must be lost and the new calendar could then keep the old months and days, which with the judicious use of Leap Years, adding one whole day every four years, would keep mankind right with God for the foreseeable future.

Of course there were objections at the very idea of 'losing' twelve whole days. Many felt that part of their lives was being usurped by meddling priests. So much so that it took until 1752 before the British Parliament got round to facing public wrath and conservative resistance and decreed that the change should be made in September of that year. Those who lived in the world where such enactments were known and debated soon fell in line and forgot about the stolen days, as it became obvious that the new calendar was simply the old calendar adjusted to fit what man can never change, the movement of the Earth round the sun and the resulting seasons of the year. But for those who lived far away, out of touch with London or even Edinburgh, and who probably never heard about the change until well after September 1752, there seemed no reason to change what their fathers had always done. If the rest of the world now called the day they celebrated Christmas the 6th of January, to them it was still the good old Norse festival of Yule which they had always celebrated on 25th December by the old calendar. So they would stick to their date, twelve days after everybody else, even if they had to call it by another name. Besides who were these politicians and authorities who sought to impose this new-fangled system upon them? The same as those who introduced all those ridiculous taxes on poor hard-working, exploited crofters and most unforgiveable of all, a tax on tobacco. In the 1950s they were applying the same reasoning to British Summer Time. On Foula sunrise and sunset and the weather in between determined how they would organise the summer work so as to have enough to survive the winter dearth, and not Big Ben as adjusted by Westminster. (The BBC was my yardstick for school hours.)

So it was that Christmas on Foula came to be celebrated on 6th January and New Year on 13th, as the rest of the world called them, and though they were forced to observe the Gregorian calendar in many other respects, it soon became a matter of pride to the Foula folk that they still resisted the change and could make their protest clear in this simple way. As my first Christmas approached since I arrived in Foula, I was more concerned about where I should celebrate it than when. Who knows if I played my cards right? I now had a unique opportunity to have two Christmases, one with my own family as I had always done on 25th December, and one with my new community of non-conformists on 6th January. So I started planning how to achieve this, recognizing of course that everything, as usual, depended on the mailboat. First I consulted the parents and they agreed that I could fiddle the school dates a bit provided the children had the correct number of days at school to satisfy the authorities. So it was agreed that from 10th December onwards I would be allowed to seize the first mailboat opportunity to go south, returning as soon after Christmas as was necessary to restart school early to make up the days if necessary. I think the way the three families involved allowed me to integrate into their family circles as much as they did, showed that they realised that family was an important concept to me. And it was not difficult, with a little embellishment of how we used to celebrate Christmas at home, for me to convince them that in our family Christmas had always been an important event in our winter programme.

In fact if I had known about Foula as a child in the 1930s, their Norse Yule, celebrated as the Norwegians always did, would have seemed quite a strange thing for Scots to be doing. In the mining area of Midlothian where we lived, nobody seemed to bother. The Church of Scotland hardly celebrated Christmas and special services were the exception. Local shops stayed open on Christmas Day and there was none of the card-mania and commercial promotion of Christmas which now prevails. At Dalhousie Castle where my father ran his boys school, we had an empty school for our Christmas holidays; the perfect setting for a Christmas party for all our friends. Imagine hide-and-seek in a real Scottish baronial castle with dungeons as our air-raid shelters in the war and secret passages in the thickness of massive stone walls. We always had a full size fir tree reaching up to a fifteen foot ceiling, decorated with a hundred real flickering candles, mounted in little tin holders, clipped to the ends of branches to avoid the flames setting fire to the branch above. My mother, following the dictates of her mother, always made sure she had handy a wet sponge tied to a garden bamboo, ready to extinguish any candle which looked like causing a major conflagration. Somehow the old-fashioned glass bobbles and baubles which decorated our tree always looked more sparkling and fantastic in the light of real candles. Another detail in which the Foula folk saw eye to eye with me over Christmas was the little gaggle of geese which Mima kept on the Mogle croft, and my story about Richard, our tame goose, which my mother kept one year with Christmas in mind. The trouble was that Richard was a favourite with the pupils and used to accompany them to the rugby field half a mile from the castle. I can see him now, waddling proudly up the drive, head held high, to the field gate where a nice bite of grass kept him busy till the games were over, when he would waddle back again with his young friends like a fussy child-minder. In this way he took so much daily exercise that by Christmas his sinews were so tough that he was virtually inedible. This was perhaps the dawn of my lifelong interest in and support for animal welfare. I was convinced that it was a judgement on us for even thinking of eating the

beloved Richard that he ruined our dinner for that year. My mother was never allowed to forget it. Otherwise Christmas dinner was a big event in our family as it clearly also was to the Gears. So Mima always made sure that her family's Christmas goose was not only edible but did not depend on the mailboat to fulfil its role on the day.

I wrote home on 5th December with Christmas very much in mind. That was the day we nearly got an extra outgoing mail via the Aith lifeboat, which had been called out by the doctor at Walls, who felt that Tom Gray's illness was serious enough to warrant a visit in person. However he died in the morning while the lifeboat was on its way; and as they received a radio message when they were only half an hour out, they turned back. I tried to explain some of the vagaries of our weather and what factors affected the boat so that my folks at home would understand my elaborate preparations for a possible exit in time for Christmas. In fact they had had much the same dreadful weather as we had, so I wrote:

The weather has in fact been nothing like as bad as it might have been here had it been from the west instead of the south. It was, for two days last week, and we fairly felt the difference with the gusts coming down from the hill. A steady gale can at least be gauged and battled against, even though it does blow the rain down the chimney and spread sooty water all over the kitchen floor. But the west wind is treacherous, calm one moment and the next fit to blow you off the road, but at least bringing a mild spell. We are beginning to feel the cold tonight with the wind round in the north. But it is a change to see a relatively flat sea and not pounding up on the East side here. All the bad week it was coming straight into the harbour and washing right over the pier. So it's a good job we can hoist our boat up onto the slipway. I watched the sea one day breaking right over a cliff marked on the map as 67 ft high.

I summed up my chance of getting home for Christmas somewhat pessimistically as follows:

If this weather keeps up, my decisions will be made for me as there is no question of crossing in these seas. If it improves it is still very unlikely that I shall risk coming because of the risk of getting held up on my return. In any case I wouldn't get nearly so long a break as I would if I stayed here till April when I could take a full month. Altogether Foula in winter is a place for staying in and not travelling to and from! I will let you know my decision when I can but don't get too hopeful. I have got ready for this mail the draft of a circular letter which I am sending to George Waterston's firm in Edinburgh, asking them to duplicate it and send it out for me to a list of addresses.

George Waterston was an old friend, and the founder and Secretary of the Scottish Ornithologists' Club, to which I had belonged since school. So it seemed sensible to ask his professional help in solving my Christmas card problem for me. This he was able to do thanks only to the emergency boat which took Anna out to the maternity hospital, crossing on 8th December, our first mailboat for weeks. I wrote the letter on December 2nd to a long list of family and friends, many of whom didn't even realise where I had landed up:

I don't know when you will receive this letter. I am writing it in the schoolroom on the Shetland island of Foula in the interval between the end of afternoon school and the mid-week service which we hold every Thursday at 8 p.m. to lighten at least one of the long winter evenings with some hearty singing.

I then described the island's geography and weather and referred my addressees to an article I had written for the Edinburgh Evening News in November which I had hoped might catch the eye of many of my friends to whom I simply didn't have the time to write individually. I explained:

You see it is all a matter of time and labour. Both cost money and are commodities which can normally be bought. And most school teachers and those working for the church reckon to be provided with enough salary, as indeed I am, to be able to buy a plumber's time, for instance, or the results of the coalminer's labour, or the baker's or greengrocer's or bus-driver's time and perhaps even a gardener's skills and labour. Of course if you have a wife's time and labour to call on as well, then everything in the garden is probably lovely enough to do without the gardener. But when one lives alone in a six-roomed house in a community with neither tradesmen, nor coalman, nor shops, nor pub, nor transport of any kind, a community of crofters whose time is already all taken up with animals and crops, and peat and fishing, and running their mailboat, who are mostly ageing and some disabled, who are usually busy and often overworked, who are always willing but seldom free, then it becomes a full-time job to run

one's own house and garden, fuel and food, hens and dog, the island's school with its five pupils, with the church work in addition and the attempt to establish an ornithological observation station as a mere after thought – then full time becomes overtime. But this is not written in any spirit of complaint. I chose life on Foula and I do not regret it. It is as refreshing as it is exhausting, as full of interest as it is lacking in variety – except the endless variety of sea and sky.

In these days when 'normal' life is a complex round of engagements and social activity, when the necessities of life are technical and superficial, a place like Foula is news. Here 'normal' is natural and life is free and untroubled in a way that is rare today. Here the clock is the servant not the master and British Summer Time is an irrelevance. Here cows and sheep, the wind and the rain, the fishing and the harvest are the daily round. The necessities are really necessary for survival, the luxuries remain beyond our grasp, except perhaps white flour to replace the traditional oat and barley meal; the paraffin which burns in our Tilley lamps rather than fish-oil or candle-wax; the tinned food which brings variety to our diet; and the tobacco which gives contentment to the young and old. Here on 'the edge of the world' it is easier to see life as it really is – real.

'Teacher-Missionary-Bird-watcher' was what one newspaper called me when I left John Watson's School in Edinburgh to come here last April. I am responsible for the education of the youth of the island up to the age of twelve, and for the moral and spiritual welfare of the community of 65 souls up to the age of ninety. My job with the bairns is easily assessed and a pleasure to perform. Running what is probably the smallest Primary School in Scotland can hardly be described as arduous. It is in fact often a tonic, when the weather is depressing, to enter the school in the morning with its cheerful and boisterous atmosphere. My job as Lay Missionary might be described as that of keeping a declining population cheerful by visiting their homes and conducting their public worship – a worthwhile task but not always easy in face of dwindling numbers and crofts going to ruins on all sides. My attempt to record the avifauna of the island, breeding birds and migrants alike, has been squeezed in somehow. The results are a list of 119 species so far in seven months, a total of 546 birds ringed and a small Heligoland Trap built, ready for the spring migration of 1955.

But these three aspects are not all that make up the daily round. It is rather an assortment of jobs to be done which can only be categorized under the heading of 'life'. All the shopping has to be done by post, all the transport by wheel-barrow, especially peat; all the work by Joe Soap; there are boots to be oiled – a sermon prepared – a dog to be fed – a lavatory cistern to be cleaned this weekend – a brood of young wheatears to be ringed – 'Peter, will you play the organ at tonight's service, please?' – must mend that window before the next gale – 'What's that bird on the peatstack, please teacher?' – 5 eggs a day from 5 hens (and 6 one day last week! How's that for productivity?) – those arithmetic books to be corrected – must visit old Betty this evening – 24 birds in one drive of the trap, mostly starlings – 'another two dozen 2½d stamps, please Harry' – a row of carrots to be dug – 'The Women's Guild will meet at the Manse 8 p.m. Tuesday' – Will it be a mail day tomorrow? – 'There are gale warnings for sea areas Faroes, Fair Isle …' – must mend these socks before Sunday – now who might help me sweep my kitchen chimney? – a dead merlin to be skinned – the bread should be about ready by now – 'Dear Sir, With reference to your letter about the new Croftmaster tractor for the Isle of Foula…' – just enough apples for the children's Hallowe'en Party – a neighbour's wireless to be repaired – note: paraffin and meths from the shop before the weekend – better get down to the pier with my box for Walls – definitely too big for a Garden Warbler; has to be a Barred – 'Coming out fishing tonight? Could try for some mackerel' – a leg of mutton to be cooked ; should make good broth too – Time to order a new batch of Library books – the wrens of Foula appear to belong to the Shetland subspecies Zetlandicus – what on earth can I give the children for Handwork tomorrow? – 'The funeral will be at 12 noon on Tuesday, Mr Mylne' – several Blackcaps in with that S.E. wind – must get the school record of work up to date this week – This East wind always floods the kitchen floor – You must see my new batch of colour slides; some good ones of the young Bonxie chicks – A lovely display of the 'Pretty Dancers' tonight – Hymn Number 165 in the Sankey Hymn Book : 'Let us with a gladsome mind Praise the Lord for he is kind.'

Yes, not a bad idea; it's a good life after all and Christmas comes but once a year.

Happy Christmas!

Christopher Mylne,
The Manse, Foula, by Lerwick, Shetland.

As part of the run up to Christmas my family had asked me for suggestions for Christmas presents – a normal procedure in our family. We hated giving useless things nobody wanted. My answers make interesting reading now – a map of Shetland (to help me sort out all those shapes on the eastern horizon) – batteries for my radio (my sole source of power for my daily dose of culture and news) – '*Anything edible, especially sweets unobtainable in the shop – A haversack to carry on my back; must be big enough for half a dozen Library books – Half a dozen single cell torch batteries; we get through them like wildfire here – a calendar to help decorate my walls.*' All I could think of to send as presents was Foula knitwear. At the same time I couldn't think of anything nicer as it was all hand knitted, with traditional Fair Isle patterns, some of them peculiar to Foula, nearly always a tasteful selection of bright colours, or even more stylish using only the natural colours of the wool, white, black, grey, brown and moorit. Edith Gray was my chief source of supply and for the hours she put in and the sheer quality of her knitting, her prices were ridiculously low. The jumpers she knitted for my two nieces in London were exquisite, and eventually served three generations of three- and four-year-olds in the family.

The letter carrying these requests was the last I got out in December. It brought my family up to date with various aspects of my winter life:

The new Nurse is doing wonders and pleases everybody. The only thing she can't do is to prevent people dying of old age. The tractor is still out of action and I am having to barrow more peats home every day that the weather allows. There are many people far worse off than I am with all the peats still wet and the weather seldom fit for getting them home. We have had a cold on the island which has caused havoc with all social activities and has upset the school considerably. You simply cannot understand what a cold means on Foula till you have experienced it on the spot. It is like the plague to them, and is often fatal to the old folk so that nobody will come near you if you have it, and woe betide you if you go near anyone else who hasn't had it yet. Luckily the version I got was a very light cold and scarcely worried me at all. The days are getting very short now. It is dark by 4 p.m. and the sun actually sets over the hill to the west of the school at 1.30 p.m.! At the North end crofts now, in the shadow of the hills, they don't see the sun all day long. Here it both rises and sets over the sea to the south but in any case we have hardly seen the sun for the last few weeks. Some days in November were really dreadful with howling gales and driving rain all day, for which the only descriptive adjective is 'horizontal'. Must finish now just in case there is any hope for tomorrow but I can hear the wind rising again in the chimney which doesn't sound too good. So goodnight and bless you all.

Of course the boat did not go that Monday, the 6th, but did on the emergency trip on the 8th. The mail crew managed to 'win home' on the 11th and were lucky to do so, as the wind then went round into the west. But it moderated on 13th and was very calm and everyone expected a boat day on the 14th. This seemed like my big chance so I stayed up till 4.30 a.m. packing and preparing for a long absence. Norie had to go back to

Nurse Mitchell near her house at Ham Voe, winter 1955

the Schoolhouse while I was away, and I even had my travel plans ready – the 5 o'clock boat from Lerwick to Aberdeen, or failing that the plane from Sumburgh the next day. At 8 a.m. the next morning, after less than four hours sleep, I had breakfast, aware of a slight breeze getting up. But I went to school prepared to send the children home if they decided the day was suitable for a mail run when all I had to do was pick up my luggage from the Manse and make for the pier. However the breeze freshened all morning so that by 11 o'clock it was already clearly hopeless. The tantalizing thing about that day was that as I walked down to school looking across the sixteen miles of sea to Vaila sound and the cliffs of Sandness, it was as flat calm as I have ever seen it and not even any sign of a swell. But there it was, and we just carried on with our school day as normal – except that I could hardly keep awake.

December was a wild month until Christmas with no hope of a mailboat crossing. So I had no excuse for not catching up with some of the more tedious correspondence which always seems to go with responsibilities, like the church accounts and the annual cheque to the General Treasurer and the end of term school records. But as I was clearly now going to be on Foula for Christmas we started planning an event I had never dreamed of organising until the Women's Guild informed it me was an old established custom on Foula which had lapsed in recent years and they were keen to revive – a soireé in the church. I described it in my letter home dated 1st January 1955 in the following terms:

On 24th December we had a Soireé in the church. It was more or less a concert held in the church and consisted mostly of hymns, carols, songs, etc. with a few spoken items by yours truly and of course the inevitable refreshments at half-time. The kick-off was an hour late as usual; one simply says a time an hour before you want the event to start and then it is more or less 'on time'. The odd thing about Foula is that this conspiracy of unpunctuality is not universal, and there are always a few gallant souls who turn up on time, and then sit complaining bitterly about the lateness of the rest. If only they would learn from experience what to expect, then I could turn up late too and all would be well. But as it is I daren't be thought to be contributing towards this bad habit of unpunctuality and so I too have to wait and complain like the rest. However when 'they' did come, they came, as they do to all these events, laden to the scuppers with food of all sorts. The Vestry was

turned into a sort of kitchen once more and we were off. Almost as good as a funeral!! I dare to suggest that it was rather a successful evening although by the normal standards quite unrehearsed. I gather that they usually practise for weeks for this, but this time I only gave them a week's warning and it still went alright.

Well, as you can imagine after all that and the clearing up afterwards to be done, with the whole of my first day after closing the school spent preparing for my part in it, the departure of the mailboat on Christmas Day was not very welcome. To start with it didn't take much mail of mine as even though I stayed up till all hours writing off some essential letters, non-essential people like one's own family just got neglected and the same was true of my proposed Christmas presents, which are now on their way; so don't despair.

The reason for a boat run on Christmas Day was sheer necessity. There was a load of sheep, gathered in with some difficulty as usual and they simply had to take whatever opportunity the weather allowed to get them out to the mainland. But it made for a disruption to social life especially at the Schoolhouse where Davie, John Henry and Ken Gear were all members of the mail crew. I had an invitation to have my Christmas dinner with them as they kindly appreciated that 25th December was my normal day for celebrating the event. Their day was turned completely upside down by the business of loading the boat with shackled sheep and then victualling and seeing off their three menfolk on the journey without any idea how soon they might win back. So after the boat had departed we had a cup of tea to recover, and I went home with a barrow of peats – a daily chore when the weather allowed – and listened to the Queen's Christmas Message as I changed into my party clothes after doing all those little jobs about the house which are so easily neglected on holiday. I returned to the Schoolhouse at 4.30 for dinner which those gallant women had prepared with great care, largely in my honour. I had some little presents for the bairns, though they don't exchange gifts normally until January 6th and we then sat down to goose and all the trimmings in style. I think the rest of that day is best described in the words of my letter home in which I told my family how I celebrated the evening of our Christmas Day after my wonderful Christmas dinner with the Gears.

After our dinner we spent the early evening at the Schoolhouse till 8.30 and then we all battled our way against a cold wind and pouring rain down the road to Ham where the real Christmas celebration was taking place. Mary, the woman who 'does' for me, lives at Ham and as she originally comes from Glasgow she celebrates the normal Christmas. The Nurse was there (her house is quite close by) and with her two 'Faith Mission' pilgrims who are staying with her for several weeks. They are quite reasonable people but rather helpless in this weather and situation, and at the party were, I am afraid, rather more like ornamental puddings than anything else I could think of. It was good fun and we sang and danced and ate as one does at all parties. But there was something rather pathetic about it at the same time. Twelve people was all we could muster and with very little space it was not exactly easy to do an eightsome! But it is amazing what one can do if one tries – and we all tried very hard. Astonishing quantities of food appeared from 'butt' (we were celebrating 'ben' i.e. in the living area), and by constant winding of the gramophone it was persuaded to play a very wavering version of several reels and two-steps. We ended up by singing carols to the Ham harmonium which were sung, as most things are on Foula, in four-part harmony.

On Sunday 26th I held a Nine Lessons and Carols Service in the Church in the evening which took quite a lot of preparing and to which, considering the night, we got a fair congregation. Since then I have had my 'holiday'. After the keen frost we had at Christmas we have had the remarkably mild spell which I gather you too have been having according to the weather reports. We prefer the frost here because it is a sign of no wind. All things considered the wind has been very moderate lately and the weather much better than it usually is when I am 'free'. On Monday 27th I got round to visiting one or two crofts at the south end and also got on with some jobs at the house. On Tuesday we spent the evening preparing for the children's party on the next day, decorating the school and the miniature Christmas tree which is apparently always a feature of the party in treeless Foula. The toys are normally collected by the Women's Guild though we have had so few meetings recently with bad weather and bereavements that I had had to get them myself. Most of them were sent by charitable organisations like the Ladies' Highland Association and we managed three for each child this year. I had also ordered a generous supply of balloons and the like so our preparations went on well into the Tuesday night.

However it all had to be postponed when the day came, as we heard that the mailboat was returning in the pouring rain. (Wed. 29th) So we spent the evening barrowing and getting wet and opening the Christmas mail. I had a whole bag to myself and I spent till 2 a.m. and half the next day unpacking it – 83 letters and cards; 16 parcels and 8 magazines. I was quite delighted and overwhelmed by your presents and can't start to thank you all for them. I am at this moment wearing my new jersey and slippers and in spite of the weather going distinctly colder this evening I have still got warm feet after several hours typing. My old pair are only fit for Norie to chew on now. Of course he agrees but has also staked a claim on the new ones which is not so good. He thought that undoing parcels was quite the best event of his year and adds his thanks to mine. He is really a splendid little fellow and does much to lighten my evenings at home – which are very few. He is growing fast and is now almost too big to sit on my lap although of course he doesn't think so. He is very content and plays outside by himself for hours. He brings all sorts of horrors into the house and takes particular delight in carrying the contents of the wastepaper basket all over the house. Except for occasional lapses he is now completely house-trained and knows to sit and to lie down when he is told, which is essential when I am visiting other folks houses.

The childrens' party was eventually held on the 30th and we were blessed with a fine night so that they all turned up and the adults with them to make up a total of 25 or so. They had an enormous tea after the games for the five under-fives. And later they had trifle and orange jellies before going home. As many of these children live, as their parents do, on bread and tea, the annual party is something of an occasion for them as you can imagine. Their chief delight was the balloons which they played with all evening until they burst. After tea John Henry, one of the younger married men, gave out the presents off the tree and there was much blowing of squeakers and eating of chocolate Santas before the games for the older children which went on till 9.30. At the end of it all we had a sing-song and then refreshments for the weary adults who had survived the ordeal.

The next day I spent doing some outdoor jobs, the most important being the cementing up of my chimney which has been letting water into the kitchen for some time whenever a south east wind blows. It's not quite finished yet but I've covered over the worst cracks. I also had to replace some plaster over the study window where the rain had come in. What with peat having to be fetched as ever and cement and sand for the chimney and all the other jobs on the house, I got precious little else done at the end of my short week's holiday. On Friday 31st we had a watch-night service at 11.30 p.m. after which it is always customary for the congregation to bring in the New Year at the Manse. I had 14 guests for whom I had spent most of the evening preparing, and who stayed till 2 a.m. We drank a toast to the new year in sherry and orange juice out of the cups, which we then used for our coffee. I served them date sandwiches, sardine fingers, Norwegian Gaffelbiter on Ryvita, Norwegian cheese on biscuits, Christmas cake out of a tin, raisins and chocolates. So don't you believe any of those newspaper reports about starving, isolated Foula! We finally sang 'Auld Lang Syne' and nearly lifted the roof off and frightened poor Norie nearly out of his little wits. As you may imagine I spent New Year's Day relaxing, had my dinner at Beagrie's (goose again), replaced two fallen roof tiles (nothing to do with Auld Lang Syne the night before!), cleared up the house and started to write this letter. Today Sunday 2nd January has been a lovely day, very mild and still. The sun was out for quite a time for a change, and though very low in the sky, really brightened up my day. Fair Isle was very clear across the water when I went to empty my rubbish over the cliffs at lunch time. And this evening when I went up to light the heaters in the church there was a glorious red sky in the north over the misty outline of the Shetland coast reflected from the golden sun sinking in an almost cloudless pale blue sky. When we do see the sun, such is the variety of colours which it produces here. Tonight the moon is up and it is certain to be a boat day tomorrow with the sea really remarkably flat for the time of year. I feel this could be one of the warmest places in Britain tonight under the influence of the Gulf Stream.

Talking of warmth I am really well stocked with socks after Christmas as three of the islanders gave me home knitted ones. I have finally thrown away my old army socks – or rather given them to Norie to play with. As for warmth, I really am now mastering the art of keeping myself warm in these winds with a windproof top and layers of jerseys down to thermal vests underneath, I reckon I could reach the North Pole now.

Norie is yelping in his sleep, my peat fire is lovely, my feet are so warm, my sweet drawer, thanks to you, is full and my larder well stocked, school starts again tomorrow but I get a long weekend next week as I am giving the children time off for their Old Yule celebrations. So I am as busy and happy as ever,

Your loving son, brother, uncle or whatever

Chris

These old letters from Christmas 1954 are barely legible now. My faithful old Oliver typewriter must have tapped out thousands of words while I was on Foula, anxious to communicate to my family back in Edinburgh what life was really like and without a telephone to enable me to tell it in person. The ribbons were used and used and I even had to go onto the red side of a two colour ribbon when my black ones were all so worn as to be scarcely legible. No wonder they are almost invisible now. But after New Year things got so bad weatherwise that replacing things like typewriter ribbons became impossible, with no mails for weeks and weeks. So there is no letter describing the way I celebrated their Christmas, Old Yule on 6th January. And that was a truly memorable evening about which I wrote a magazine article in 1968 which has helped me to remember almost every detail of the event. The article was titled 'A Taste of the Forbidden' and covered many of the tasty dishes I learnt to cook on Foula and the 'forbidden' foods like the eggs of protected birds. My attitude when on Foula was 'when in Rome do as the Romans do'. Besides, life was hard and nature bountiful, so who was I to deny anybody the natural resources of the island as a source for survival of just another type of inhabitant, a hungry human.

After eight months I had formed a very close relationship with the Gear gamily at the Schoolhouse. They, more than anyone else, provided me with a home from home. I saw them every day I was at school and often stayed for a cup of tea after school before going up to the Lioag to fetch my barrow of peats. Even so I was honoured and delighted when they invited me to join them for their big event of the winter, their family Christmas dinner at Old Yule on 6th January. When I arrived at the suggested time, there was as usual no sign of anything being ready or prepared. I should not have been surprised at this as they were as unpunctual and casual over time as they were generous and warm in their welcome. Mima was one of the most punctilious at attending church, but more often than not she would arrive panting slightly, probably from running, about five minutes after the service had started. It was part of her personality. As I waited, the warmth of the peat stove in the kitchen where I was almost invariably entertained and before too long the smell of something delicious cooking in the oven, helped me to relax and be patient. It was going to be a long wait as someone was still out looking for the cows, which tended to wander off across the moor and take their own time coming home for the night. They still had to be milked before we were eventually all assembled and sat down at the table. There were pans bubbling away on the Rayburn and steam everywhere, and Aunty Mary was obviously very much in charge of the cooking as usual. Mary was the kindest of women, but shy and rather self-effacing. But cooking was her forte and she took such an obvious delight in it as a means of pleasing others. She seemed just a little conspiratorial however, fussing over whatever was in the oven. Mima kept a number of geese round the croft and I had no doubt we would be getting the biggest and best of them for such an important occasion as feeding ten people at Christmas. But the bird that Mary eventually lifted out of the oven and onto the table in a steamy haze of delicious aromas was the biggest and most sumptuous bird I had ever seen cooked. It was a monster. It looked and smelt delicious and was promptly carved up into enormous helpings and distributed to all present – Davie, skipper of the mailboat; Mima his wife and ten years his junior; Mary her unmarried sister; Vida, her daughter with her husband John Henry and their daughter Vina, one of my pupils; the Gears' three sons, Andy (19), Ken (16) and Jim (11); and myself making ten. Jim was big for his age and had a hearty appetite but the drumstick Mary put on his plate was enough to feed a grown man; it was the largest bird's leg I had ever seen served onto a plate. While Jim set to on his meal of brown meat, we all feasted on large slices of tender white meat with slices from the other leg thrown in. And still the other half of the bird was as yet untouched on the dish.

While conversation flowed I began to get more and more suspicious as I was asked rather pointedly for about the tenth time whether I was enjoying my dinner. Wasn't this a splendid feast, a truly magnificent bird? Mima was proud of her geese but this was indulgent self-satisfaction; and why was I the only one to be asked to reassure them that I thought it a wonderful feast. The conversation turned to birds, as it so often did when I was there. They all knew a great deal about them. It was part of their way of life to know about the natural world around them, but Mima set a lead in her knowledge and interest in birds in particular. Had I seen anything interesting in recent days? Had I been up to the Mill Loch recently? Finally Ken got up from the table and went into the next room, returning with something wrapped up in newspaper which he laid on the table. First he asked from me an assurance that I had thoroughly enjoyed my meal. It was so obvious to all that I had that I scarcely felt the need to answer but he insisted and I declared my satisfaction and my admiration of Aunty Mary's skills. Then he opened the paper and there lay the beautiful white head and long beak with yellow side patches of an adult Whooper Swan, a protected bird under the newly passed Bird Protection Act 1954, a subject of frequent conversation between me and the family since it became law in early December.

Of course I was well and truly snared and there was nothing I could say except thank you for a wonderful Christmas dinner. I had to admit that it was one of the tastiest tricks that had ever been played on an unsuspecting ornithologist. Ken was commendably frank. Faced with his mother's dilemma of how to feed ten people from one measly goose (or should she be extravagant and kill and pluck two?), nature presented him with an answer in the form of a wild swan, perhaps lost and certainly lonely. Perhaps more reprehensible than having shot a protected bird was the fact that, in common with most of the Foula men, he had a shot-gun without a licence. What a farce being expected to pay good money for procuring an honest dinner for your family! Mima was perhaps the most genuinely concerned at what he had done and though she too had enjoyed her dinner, she confessed to have been genuinely sad at having to pluck such a *bonny white bird*. The stripped leg bone on an empty plate told me exactly what Jim thought about his big brother's escapade. But what he had enjoyed most was the discomfiture of his teacher, who was now as guilty as the rest of them in the great whooper swan scandal. I noticed that Davie, the J.P. for the community, was very quiet. Like me he was also obviously seriously compromised by his lawless son and that unlicensed shotgun, not to mention the large helping he had been served. Moreover, he had known the truth when he ate it. He was by nature a strong, silent man, but responsible and law-abiding. So his silence after dinner clearly indicated, without a word of admonition being spoken, that silence might be the best policy for us all. And so it was.

Chapter 17: Stormy Weather

My first experience of really strong winds on Foula was shortly after that extraordinary day on 8th December when Anna Gray was taken out to the maternity hospital in Lerwick and we had to postpone her father-in-law's funeral. It had been poor weather before then with no mailboats, but the wind mostly from an easterly direction. This is bad for communications because Ham Voe faces east and has virtually no protection, so that putting a boat on the water or loading and unloading at the pier is almost impossible. On the plus side, an east wind reaches most of the crofting areas over low ground so that even a strong gale is less gusty and reasonably predictable. So even if the boat cannot get out, people can go about their business without too much difficulty and after all a good breeze dries the washing and the peats ready for winter. Apart from the brief lull which allowed the emergency boat, almost miraculously, to get out and back, we entered a three week spell when the west wind was never less than strong. We got used to it but I found it wearing, a constant battle whenever I was out of doors. Pushing a barrow of peats home became a struggle and I learnt not to try on the really bad days. During that spell I had my first real experience of what they call 'flans'.

These are a special feature of Foula because of its unique geography. It stands with its grass and heather covered hills, whose slopes face east towards the mainland, as though a giant had come with a great knife and made a clean slice right down its western seaboard, making a severely abrupt barrier to a wind which has met no obstacle for two thousand miles. There are higher sea-cliffs in the British Isles, in Ireland and on the north face of Hirta on St Kilda, where Conachair presents a jagged, almost vertical cliff 100 ft higher than the Kame. But the way the great outcrop of Foula's sedimentary rock rears up from the sea as a perpendicular wall of rock, showing only the edges of layer upon layer of Old Red Sandstone sloping back downwards at a giddy angle under those hills, creates a unique feature in the whole British coastline, a solid wall two miles long facing north west from the Wester Hoevdi at 500 ft, rising up steadily to the Kame at 1220 ft, and then never less than 700 ft all the way north to Soberlie. Weathered by wind and

wave for millions of years, the edges of the strata still offer many jagged ledges beloved of tens of thousands of seabirds as safe nesting places in summer, but in places like Nebbifield the weathering is so smooth that nothing can gain a foothold; and at the astonishing curve of the Scrodhordins the whole 600 ft wall is undercut by the sea, leaving millions of tons of rock overhanging. I don't know which is more impressive to us puny humans: to look up at this natural wonder from below, where the whole massive edifice seems to blot out the sky and be about to fall on our tiny boat; or to look down from above where the marbled sea disappears into a massive cavity under the overhang. In autumn the scale of the scene from above is heightened by the sight of rows of grey seals lying on the boulder beach far below, looking for all the world like rows of shiny sausages drying out in the evening sun. Sometimes the faint sound of their singing adds to the mystical atmosphere, a sad wailing, like mothers in labour, for this is the time they give birth to their sleek, white-coated pups.

In summer that boulder beach is deserted, but the narrow rock ledges, rising layer after layer above it, are tenanted by countless nesting auks, whose thousands of grunting and crooning calls merge into a background babble that floats up on the inevitable updraught of air, bringing with it that indefinable smell of the guano which paints the cliffs white every year. Above the Kame, half a mile further north, a new sound has been added to the summer cacophony: the guttural croaking of hundreds of pairs of gannets, jostling for places to establish their territorial rights to a corner of rock at the foot of the precipice in the new breeding colony, which started in the 1980s with half a dozen bold pioneers. To stand on the cliff edge on that N.W. rock wall of Foula on a still, hot summer day, to listen to the chorus from so many thousands of cackling fulmars, grunting guillemots, rasping razorbills, growling gannets and kittiwakes shouting their own name, is an unforgettable experience. The real impact on the human spirit however, comes in a North West gale, as I saw it once from the East Hoevdi just north of Soberlie: a huge Atlantic swell with a quarter of a mile between wave crests, driven by a rain-laden storm-force gale bringing black thundery clouds in at a screaming pace. I watched waves breaking right through the massive Gaada Stack, and the swell surging at the foot of the North Bank in curling walls of water which ran along the foot of Bloberg, heaving thousands of tons of water up the rock wall in what looked like a slow-motion film, so massive was the scale of the whole spectacle. It is this which makes Foula unique, and which creates havoc on the so-called sheltered side in the shadow of the hills where we lived. This is the giant's cauldron in which the flans are created.

Naturally what has, up to that point, been a steady wind in two dimensions across the face of the Atlantic suddenly assumes a third dimension, being flung vertically upwards for a thousand feet. This creates a turbulence which involves a tremendous updraught at the cliff top, with a highly dangerous back-draught to fill the vacuum. This then sets off strong eddies drawn up vertically and setting in motion a circular pattern horizontally. Not surprisingly there is a compensatory downdraught to fill the space which tends to form miniature whirlwinds which travel down the hills to the east of the cliffs and descend on the crofting area as 'flans'. Because the air is so unstable, these are irregular and vary a great deal in strength, and if the gale increases, as it can do, almost to hurricane force, with gusts caused by cloud formations and temperature variations, then what the islanders call the 'whirlwinds' are formed, which are even more damaging and dangerous than flans. It is reckoned that in a Force 10 gale, the induced speed in the twisting action of a whirlwind can produce wind speeds of over 100 mph and even gusts up to 150 mph.

This is real 'weather' and not a time to be outside, where the chief danger is from flying debris. Sheila Gear, in a more recent episode of her 'Foula Diary', described seeing a heavy lawn-mower flying through the air past her window on a night which took the roofs off most of the buildings at Ham. And there is the famous event of Mrs Traill's house, the foundations of which can still be seen on the green opposite Gravins, where the house used to stand. She was a benevolent lady from Edinburgh who visited Foula and fell in love with the island because it was so peaceful and quiet. Eventually she decided to build a small wooden house there "*to get away from the noise of the trams.*" Luckily she was a 'good-weather' visitor and was not in residence on that winter's night when a wee whirlwind picked up her house, in spite of the fact that it was bolted down to its concrete foundations, and the folk in Leraback across the other side of the valley saw daylight under it as it flew across the green and then down to the rocks where the flan finally deposited it in the sea, leaving behind a trail of broken plates and teacups and shattered furniture to mark its passage. Mrs Traill was wise enough never to replace it.

One night in December 1954 I remember walking home from the Schoolhouse with Ken Gear who was going on to the Hametoun. The Gears had just acquired a new Rayburn cooker and I had loaned them my large heavy frying pan to test it out on the new stove. I was carrying this home under my arm as we trudged up the hill from the Ham Burn towards the wireless huts on top of the ridge. This was a very exposed part of the moor and very liable to flans, which often picked up water off the Mill Loch so that one could get soaked as well as battered. The wind was whining in the stays of the radio transmitter hut as we passed and we could hear the flans passing below us in the valley at the foot of Hamnafield. We had to walk down the length of

Harry Gear wheeling home a barrow of peats in the snow

the road from the huts to the Manse, listening to flans passing us or coming up from behind, sometimes to within a few yards, though we seemed to be in almost still air where we walked. We seemed to have escaped the worst of them when suddenly as we reached the point where the wind starts to come round the south end of the hills rather than north round Hamnafield, a flan, stronger than expected, hit us from in front. It was a strange feeling. One had no choice but to give way and I found myself staggering over the ditch and onto the moor, trying to remember the dictat – never run before the flan or you'll never be able to stop! So as this 'natural' hazard passed us by, poor Ken nearly caught it from a very unnatural hazard in the form of a large heavy cast-iron frying pan over which I had absolutely no control but which fortunately did not crown him as the missile was flung past him. I could see the headline – "*Missionary fells Foula strong-man with frying pan!*" We had to laugh, until we reached Mornington, where the hill gate was down, as was my garden gate at the bottom of the hill. As Ken battled on south I found my tea box of peat mould at the back door had disintegrated and the new felt off my hen-house roof was half way across the green. It was a comfort to arrive home safely but difficult to get to sleep with the gale howling in the chimneys all night.

One reminder of the treacherous weather which can strike in the seas round Foula is the Hoevdi Grund, a notorious reef of rocks two miles east of the south end of the island. On a calm day from the cliffs near Mornington there was nothing to be seen but flat water to the horizon, and on many days that first summer I was more intrigued by watching the mirage effects over the water from the Shetland coastline. This only occurred in fine weather when the sea was calm and there was a temperature inversion causing the light rays to be deflected. Land features appeared to be reflected or duplicated in reverse so that hills looked like islands or reefs in the sea, and rocks became magic castles along the shore. Often there would be a shimmer over the sea so that everything was unclear through binoculars and identifying flying birds became impossible. But on such golden days there was no menace in the sea and absolutely no evidence of the hidden threat two miles off. Life on Foula could seem so idyllic under such conditions and the mainland of Shetland, terminating in Fitful Head to the south, seemed so much closer that the sense of isolation was pleasant not fearful, and one was glad to be free of all the noise and traffic and pollution problems of civilization.

How different in a southerly gale, especially when the tide was running south against it and the shallow water over the Hoevdi Grund caused a huge swell and such turbulence in the limited depth over the rocks that the waves actually broke and giant overfalls stood up many feet high like columns of solid water. Watching with binoculars one such wild day, I clearly saw, several times, the black rocks of the Foula Shaalds showing in the troughs of the swell before the next giant wave crashed over them, obliterating my view in clouds of blowing spray. In Simon Martin's book, 'The Other Titanic' is the story of the Foula fisherman looking for piltocks on a calm day who, seeing the rocks just below, lowered himself from his boat and tried to stand on them and just keep his head above water, and reckoned he would have done so if the tide hadn't been too strong and swept him past. The *Oceanic* drew 32 ft and supposedly went onto the rocks sideways, trying too late to effect a manoeuvre to escape. That was on 27th September 1914, the day after she pulled out of Lerwick to do an Atlantic patrol to the Faroes. She was hopelessly stuck as a result and though this meant that everybody was able to get off alive and a few things like her guns were salvaged as priorities, it only took one westerly gale on 29th to break the whole 30,000 ton ship into pieces. The size of this disaster and its awful finality are simple evidence of the power of nature, a power which many of the inhabitants of Foula feel for themselves every winter. Incidentally it is puzzling how many recent reviews of the *Oceanic* story reduce the size of the ship to a 17,000 ton armed merchant ship, when in truth she had been second only to the 50,000 ton *Titanic* and even more luxurious in her fittings. But for all her 17,000 metal plates held by 1,700,000 rivets and a total length just over 700 ft, she was no match for the Foula Shaalds in rough weather.

Bobby Isbister, aged 15, saw it all and remembered it well. It's not every day that you witness what had been the greatest trans-Atlantic liner of her day, wrecked on the rocks two miles from your house one day, and a few days later gone, broken to pieces by a single storm. If you want to get the seaman's perspective on the fury of a Foula storm on a more believable scale, read the account in 'The Other Titanic' of the loss of their salvage boat *Trygg* in Ham Voe in an unexpected gale. Foula has never had an adequate harbour and so has always had to make do with boats too small for the needs of the crofters and their animals. The *Island Lass* was as big, at 35 ft, as could be managed with the harbour facilities available, in that she could be lifted right out of the water. As the loss of the 50 ft *Trygg* proved yet again, Foula is really an island without a safe harbour for the size of boat required to make its economy viable. And yet in the 1950s with a diesel engined boat, a covered -in deck, and an experienced crew, they were able to supply us with our basic needs and at least an intermittent mail service. Compare that with the old days of a sixern with a sail and you have almost a revolution in transport. The difference is, of course, that in those more primitive times a far larger population could survive, or even thrive, on Foula because they ran a sustainable subsistence economy of self-help. In the 1950s we were long past that stage, with the preponderance of elderly and disabled islanders making dependence on the mailboat a vital factor in our economy. That disadvantage was soon to be put to the test when the winter of 1954/55 proved to be the wildest and coldest in Shetland for many years.

Over the period of the two Christmases we had a mail run on Christmas Day, 25th December, where the boat retuned late on the 29th with that part of our Christmas mail which had reached Walls by Christmas Eve. The next boat was on 3rd January when to everyone's surprise the boat left on the scheduled mail day, Monday, almost at the scheduled time of 11am designated by the Collection time in the window of the Post Office which was given as 'Monday 10.20'. And, better still, she returned on the same day, as she was meant to but seldom did in the winter. This was partly because there was 'flu in Walls and the crew had a strong disinclination to stay overnight when the chances were much increased that one of them would pick up an infection over there. This was a constant battle. The need to collect supplies and all the orders for bread and foodstuffs from A & K Reid, the grocer in Walls, was balanced against the need to avoid infection. A cold was bad enough and could play havoc with school or church attendance or any social events, especially for people with someone elderly at home for whom a cold might be much more serious. But the 'flu was dreaded like the plague, with memories of past epidemics where there were barely enough fit people to carry out the essential tasks, and where on some crofts ill people were tempted to go out for the sake of the animals and thereby develop pneumonia. Being careless over picking up an infection could easily cause a death in the family. So the weather window which allowed a trouble free mail run and a prompt return was an unexpected blessing, the result of a surprisingly good spell of winter weather. I described it in a long letter I wrote home at the end of the month as a prelude to my description of the blizzard that was to follow:

The Manse, Foula, By Lerwick, Shetland.
30th January 1955

Dear Family,

I'd better start at the beginning, i.e. after our last mail on 3rd January which returned the same day. My news is of course just weather, weather, weather. It controls our lives but never so much as with snow. The week of Christmas was cold and changeable but largely dry. "It's the frost that holds down the wind" they would say on some of the crisp mornings we had then, with a breeze from the North. The week of New Year and Old Yule, when I gave the bairns two days special holiday for their Christmas celebrations, was mild, calm and dry. This is an astonishing combination for Foula in winter. No explanations were offered. The old weather rules just seemed to break down and we had a wonderful week. For instance I finished cementing my chimney with ease, completing the job by moonlight. On that same night after visiting one of the crofts nearest here, I was walking along the road with a magazine they had given me to look at and found that I was able to read it with ease by the light of the moon, and even to see the colours of the of the coloured photographs in it easily. For about three days there was virtually no wind. That is the pleasantest change of all here; to see the Mill Loch like a mirror, and to carry out your bucket of powdery, peat ash in the morning without having most of it blown all over the kitchen as soon as you open the door a couple of inches. The fact that the good week coincided with two days of my Christmas holiday from school made it all the more surprising, as it is almost a legend here now that my free days, normally Saturdays, are notoriously bad.

And then we paid for it. Snow. I had already taken several photos of the snow at the beginning of the week but I might as well have saved my film. I certainly took plenty at the end of the week as it was really worth taking by then, not just a white covering with the hills looking ridiculously close and the Shetland coast glistening white to the tideline on the horizon, but the mail-boat snowed in up to deck level on the slipway; my back-door buried to the handle every morning; the boats on the beach at Ham peeping out from under drifts; Tom's smithy at Gravins levelled off from the roof; peat being sledged home or barrows sinking in over the axles; the Mill Loch buried under snow on a coating of ice; black showers under black clouds sweeping across the water and blotting out everything

The Manse after the blizzard

in a few moments; and the dreaded flans outlined in blowing snow and visible for a change as tiny whirlwinds, catching up the lying snow and whisking it over the fields and out to sea.

The blizzard struck on the afternoon of Wednesday 12th January during school. There was no question of sending the children home while it was on. One couldn't see one's way at all, and one was likely to choke in the fine powdery snow blowing before a full gale. So I kept them till nearly five and gave them their tea at school. Eric who has the farthest to go was fetched by his father, who said that his journey north to the school was the worst battle against the elements he could ever remember on Foula, and that he had been walking blind most of the way. So I escorted my two neighbour children home, and it was all we could do to hang on to each other and keep our feet along the top part of the road. The folk here call the dry, powdery type of snow that blows in the wind 'mealie moorit' which means that it is like flour with the same choking effect. We had to make a little hollow behind a hand or a scarf to make it easier to breathe as we walked. It is quite justifiably feared and was in fact quite dangerous to go out in for fear of losing one's way when the road was completely covered, especially at night. I can still remember the welcome of genuine relief we got from Mrs Beagrie when we arrived home safely. We had no means of keeping her informed but she needed no explanation as to why they were two hours late. The white-out surrounding her house and mine, now invisible only two hundred yards away was evidence enough.

We spent most of the week dodging showers, digging out doorways, taking peat, oil, and flour to the old folk on sledges which we often pulled over the top of walls and fences which were completely buried. The worst feature was that the strong winds persisted for several days so that the road was blown quite bare in parts and yet was perhaps ten feet deep in a drift a little further on. Both barrows and sledges were therefore extremely heavy work. I received a phone message on Monday 17th in the afternoon telling me to close the school, in common with all others in Shetland till Monday 24th. The extra time gained was very welcome. It was altogether too cold to do much writing in the house with the possibility of peats being worth their weight in gold very shortly; but I was also glad of the time and opportunity to be of service to the old folk who simply were not able to get to the shop for supplies. Even so I did get some time to myself for a change on those days when it was positively dangerous to go out, and caught up with some letters and some sleep. I also indulged in a little bird trapping with a net in the garden, and caught about 30 starlings with bait, several of which were ones I had ringed elsewhere on the island in the autumn. It was interesting to note that none of the 100 nestlings which I ringed in the summer were among them. So it looks as though our breeding starlings all leave Foula for the winter, and our winter population is composed mostly of autumn arrivals.

I suppose that all things considered we were better off than most folk in Shetland. In Foula we are always prepared for bad weather and keep good stocks of the essentials. *The only thing that has now completely run out is margarine (no butter since Christmas). Sugar and tobacco are very low, tinned goods virtually sold out, but otherwise the shop still has most of the things it normally sells. Admittedly this is not very much. For instance it does not include potatoes which are very scarce as many of the crops are very poor this year. Vegetables generally are low though I have still a good supply of my own carrots from my garden. I also have two dozen eggs left that I preserved, and today my hens produced the first egg of the new season. Our shortages on the island are in fact nothing to do with the snow crisis but just the seasonal normal here aggravated by few mails before Christmas and a bad harvest. The worst hit by the snow were the sheep, many of which were buried in drifts, often sheltering behind walls, and died before the weather was fit for us to go and look for them. Not long after the wind dropped, the thaw came anyway and the survivors were freed by a very rapid disappearance of the snow. Since then the weather has again surprised us by being unusually mild though we have had steady fresh winds with no hope of a boat.*

I have just missed the ten to twelve weather report and so can't even guess whether the boat will go tomorrow or not. But I can hear the wind in the chimney which is a bad sign at this time of night. Sadly if the boat goes the nurse goes with it, so let's hope the new nurse comes in soon.

1st February *Nothing doing on 30th Jan. so now still hoping for tomorrow, and just in case I am getting my letters all ready again. The poor nurse who has got herself ready to go out about four times now, received word yesterday that the new nurse is unwell, and could she please stay in here a bit longer. She had to agree though she is getting fed up with the uncertainty of this existence which I must admit is hard for her to get over. It must be getting her down. We are all hoping that the new nurse who is apparently in her late fifties is not getting cold feet. A glorious day today but the usual fresh wind and a choppy looking sea from the worst possible direction, south east, which comes straight into the entrance of the Voe. A very clear night tonight with a lovely moon again and a wonderful sky at sunset with no clouds but a glow merging from orange through all the colours of the spectrum to duck-egg blue, with the Kirk a black silhouette against the skyline to the south. It's still very mild but today's sunshine was a welcome change, as usually the sun is too low at this time of the year to shine through the cloud. The nights are so much lighter already with light in the sky till 5 p.m. instead of being dark at 3.30 as it was in mid-winter only just over a month ago.*

Well, the boat did not go on 2nd February, nor any other day with fresh winds day after day, until our stores really did start to run out and there was little left in the shop except Ovaltine and some hen pellets. School lunches began to be a problem as I was down to my last tins of corned beef and the Schoolhouse family had very little protein food for their many mouths.

Deep snowdrifts along the shore of Ham Voe

We were not the only people in trouble as most of Shetland was affected and it didn't help us that Walls has several times been cut off too. Shetland seldom gets prolonged snow like this, which is probably why it all got onto the morning BBC news, so that one felt the whole country must know that we still hadn't got in our main delivery of Christmas mail. At least I had no need to write letters home about our plight when all they had to do was to tune in to the radio to get an update. And then, after seven long weeks without a mailboat crossing, and the shelves of the shop virtually empty and no sign of the wind easing, and after many phone calls about our plight, we were relieved by the government in the form of a visit by the Fishery Cruiser *Minna* on 20th February 1955 – early on a Sunday morning!

Chapter 18: Rescue

Snow is comparatively rare in Shetland, as very few places are more than a mile or two from the sea. So the blizzard of mid-January took us rather by surprise. We soon gathered from the radio reports that the same problems of drifting and buried sheep and closed roads applied all over the islands, so another problem was added to our own, that our chief source of supply at Walls had also dried up. Added to that was the news of a bad 'flu outbreak over there so that the mail crew were opposed to going even if the weather had allowed. But all these factors were secondary to the wind, which stayed impossible either at the Voe or out on the open sea for weeks on end after the first calm spell. However it was soon clear that supplies would run dangerously low unless an attempt was made soon, when at the end of January it was four weeks since the last mail day. Then, as a final coup de grace to all plans and intentions, a

second blizzard in February once more snowed the mailboat in on the slipway, which itself formed a sort of deep gully which trapped blowing snow and formed a drift about ten feet deep. One night with a good forecast, it was decided to dig the boat free ready for an attempt at a crossing the next day, for which it was important to get away punctually so that the crew could return without having to stay over, which would greatly increase their risk of bringing back a 'flu infection. The plan was desperate but sound in principle except that a very fresh wind blew up overnight and with fresh snow showers and blowing surface snow, we were back to square one in the morning with the boat buried deeper than ever.

The Government declared an official rescue plan for the whole of Shetland called 'Operation Snowdrop', with aerial drops of supplies to beleaguered villages and houses, organised from Lerwick. We followed its

The mailboat snowbound on the slipway, with the Minna *anchored off Ham Voe*

progress on the Scottish news bulletins from BBC and wondered when our turn would come. Harry Gear, on the end of the phone line, was the key contact with the authorities and soon we were quite used to hearing his weel-kent voice over the airwaves.

Harry was the classic example of the unflappable spokesman, and we seemed to be always 'managing' and anxious not to make a fuss. But about 18th February Harry finally admitted to a journalist that things were really very short on Foula and gave a few details of what people were surviving on – "*bread without either margarine or jam for a couple of weeks now*" or "*porridge but no milk*"; and then "*no flour or oatmeal left except in a few crofts, and the Schoolhouse family of ten have lived on bread and tea for a week now with rice soup, which they all loathe, as the only filling thing left!*" The Gears were Harry's next door neighbours and I guessed that they had suggested he stop the heroics and plead for help. I myself, by strict rationing, had managed not to run out of anything completely till about the middle of the month, though admittedly I got a gift of half a pound of butter when I was just running out of my last fats. But I was onto my last two days' supply of sugar, coffee, tinned milk (no fresh for some time then) and tinned meat or fish, largely because I had supplied such items both to my immediate neighbours the Beagrie family and to the Gears in the previous weeks when they ran out completely. But a larder for one can't stand supplying fourteen for very long.

To add to our troubles the phone was out of order for several days. However we heard on Saturday 19th February that the Fishery Cruiser, the *Minna*, was standing by in Walls with stores already loaded and ready to cross at the first available opportunity. We knew she was doing a series of rescue operations since the return of the blizzard conditions and would not want to hang around, but Harry had told them that it was "*quite useless*" coming over on the Saturday as the wind was fresh in the east and the swell was hitting the pier fair and square. However on the Saturday an R.A.F. reconnaissance plane came over for the second time since the emergency was declared, and as we were later told had announced that the sea was "*quite alright*" and the *Minna* should come as soon as possible. This of course is an old story to Foula folk, who feel that nobody acknowledges that they should know best about what is and is not possible for our boats and crews on our island. So the decision was made between the aircraft and the captain of the *Minna* to come early on the Sunday morning, with the six tons of supplies they had loaded in Walls. When Harry phoned

early on Sunday to say that conditions were no better than he had reported on the Saturday and to ask them to wait to see how the day developed, he was told they were half way across. We none of us expected her to come from what Harry had told us. Being Sunday I wasn't up till about 9 a.m. and I went up to the ridge at 10.15 to see if anything was happening and there, about five miles off, with the spray bouncing off her bows, was a lovely white vessel heading straight for the Voe. So after snatching some food I dashed down to join the rest at the pier.

The first small boat was already battling out to where she was lying about 500–600 yards off, a ship about the size of a small minesweeper, and lifting a lot on the swell in spite of her size. I was told that they had decided not to send out the mailboat, partly because of the time it would take to free her and get her on the water, and partly because she would be too heavy to fend off by hand from the cruiser and nobody wanted to risk damaging our only future link with the mainland. There was only one other boat with an engine which could be used as a flit boat, and she was having a rough passage going out with her screw coming right out of the water several times. The consequent racing of the motor soon loosened the propellor shaft, just the sort of obvious risk Harry had had in mind when asking the *Minna* to wait till the swell had died down. But they cut the engine and rowed the rest of the way. There was only one other small boat big enough to get safely alongside and load under those conditions, so it was a slow and arduous job. I described the landing of our supplies in my letter home on the 3rd of March as follows:

The two small boats managed wonderfully well, bringing back several bags of meal or flour, or packages of sugar and margarine, often a bit the worse for wear and rather wet. It took us all our time to clear the pier of goods as they were landed before the next flit-boat came back; and as usual the men were desperately slow at getting organised or working out any system. It is no use anyone like me making suggestions or giving orders, so one just has to get on with what one thinks is the best method on the spot, and hope that others will follow suit. Admittedly we were all taken rather by surprise, but the island temperament which absolutely refuses to be hurried, or even to take things at all seriously, can be very exasperating on such occasions. Later, just when things had got going, the snow came on again which didn't exactly make things easier.

I managed to slip away and get all my own mail ready up at the school and handed in to Harry who was busy making up his mail bags. At the same time I snatched a cup of tea in the Schoolhouse kitchen to make do instead of dinner. I then took down some of the mail bags which were ready, and arrived at the pier in time to see the last boatload of goods come in and the last lot of passengers go out. Then the First Mate from the Minna came ashore to telephone to Walls, and at about 3 o'clock the ship headed back to the mainland, and we were left with the job of shifting all the stuff up to the shop and the store. The shop was in a glorious state with boxes everywhere and several people took packets of margarine away with them then and there for their evening meal, the first they had tasted for over three weeks.

I remember Bobby Isbister, the shopman, was in jubilant mood and broached a whole case of oranges on the pier and invited everyone to help themselves to some well-earned exotic refreshment. There was something significant, even symbolic, in peeling a hot-climate fruit in a snowstorm on Foula at the end of February, luxury in the face of need. They tasted fabulous. I couldn't help thinking that the old *Advance* probably never brought in a case of oranges in all its days of serving the island as its mailboat. Now we had a far bigger and safer boat, a better pier and slipway, and yet still had to depend on a government ship to rescue us with many staple foods, but also much that was outside the normal experience of the earlier subsistence economy.

Of course, the law of natural perversity, known to many of us at that time as McPherson's Law, dictated that the day after our dramatic rescue was sunny and flat calm but there was nothing to fetch, as we knew Walls was still cut off by snow and so isolated from further supplies of mail. In any case some of us were not interested in any more as I personally had three whole bags of mail to myself which it took me about three days to get through and read. However we heard on Wednesday that the *Minna* had taken another load, including mail from Scalloway to Walls by sea, so the *Island Lass* went out on Wednesday and returned the next day. That day was however one of those deceptive ones where the weather on Foula was lovely all day with a light S.W. breeze, from which Ham Voe was well protected, and a very flat sea. By contrast, only 18 miles away at Walls, where Vaila Sound faces into a westerly breeze,

Flit boat at the pier unloading stores from the Minna *on relief day, 23rd February 1955*

there was quite a swell and a stiff wind in their faces, so they had decided to wait. They eventually left at 5 p.m. rather against their better judgement, but they were very anxious to get home that night, because back home on Foula they knew that in the winter, especially with snow, the work is very demanding on their womenfolk who are left behind to cope. I was down at the Schoolhouse when the word came through that they had left so late and were expecting a rough passage at least on the first half of the trip, before they reached some shelter from Foula itself. At the Schoolhouse, the women of the Gear family were extremely anxious, especially at the thought that the men had put themselves at risk for their sake. They always emphasised to Davie that the safety of the crew was all they cared about, however much extra work they had to do when the men were away. But their wishes usually fell on deaf ears. I just wished the men could have sensed as I did the palpable atmosphere of concern in that kitchen, voiced largely by Mima who after all had a husband, a son and a son-in-law on that boat out there in the dark. We decided to go down to the pier with torches, though it was a clear night but pretty dark with no moon. I think we all felt the need to do something rather than sit with the unbearable tension created by Mima's anxiety. She had brought down a big bell she kept for the occasion – originally the school bell though I never used it – and she relieved her feelings somewhat by ringing it heartily from the wall of the pier. At about 8 p.m., a little after the usual two hours and forty-five minutes for the crossing were up, I too began to feel anxious and we lit a Tilley Hurricane lamp, which is a lot brighter than any torch. Soon after we spotted the flashing of a tiny point of light from a torch and I heard several quiet prayers of thanks offered for such a joyful relief. There was a lot of ice on the pier and extra care had to be taken when she came round the end of the pier and pulled up to the steps without incident. When the tension is over it all seems such a wonderful thing to be doing when it is really just the same old routine of first removing all the cargo by hand onto the slippery pier; then the ballast stones to lighten the weight; then fixing the chains from the davits onto the boat; pulling the endless chains through the pulleys, which was for fully 20 minutes because on this occasion it was low tide which meant another five feet extra to lift her five tons from the water to the pier; then swinging the bow through between the two davits first, followed by the stern; lining her up with the cradle; lowering the boat down and then hand-winching her slowly up to the top of the slipway, another 20 minutes hard labour.

On this trip the cargo had included four 50-gallon drums of paraffin weighing six cwt. each, so the whole operation took two hours before we could turn our thoughts to carrying up our own supplies and our shop order, and eventually reaching the Post Office to see whether Harry had unpacked and sorted the mail yet. Being a Thursday night I should have been taking the usual mid-week service in the school but a night time arrival means fewer hands on the pier. That night there was only one other man there, apart from the five crew, so I tried to help in whatever way I could. Of course often the boat would return and one knew nothing about it; so for once in a while I was on the spot anyway, having been on the way home from school when I heard the word of her departure from Walls. So when I had put round word that the service would be postponed for tonight, I felt it part of my job, especially to help relieve the tense atmosphere at the Schoolhouse. Having therefore been able to experience in full what is involved in a mailboat return, I was full of admiration for the crew who take it all in their stride, so often in far worse weather than that quiet, dry night. They certainly deserved their Post Office pay for a good day's work. But often I felt that it was the women who deserved a gold medal for their patience and fortitude when their menfolk were on the sea and for their hard work holding the fort, whatever the conditions, when the crew were detained by the weather at Walls.

After our few brief days of fame, I expect nearly everybody in Scotland knew where Foula was, even if only somewhere remote off Shetland, though I have usually found that due to the economies made by printers in making maps of Scotland, most people think Shetland is in a little square somewhere just east of Aberdeen. It was useful to me to know that my family and friends in Edinburgh had probably alerted each other to the news stories on radio and so all knew about our isolation and rescue. Nevertheless I wrote home on 3rd March after I had, eventually, opened and read all my three bags of mail – which included a big batch of further Christmas cards – to give them the details of the exciting days which brought us back to more normal diets and the routine of a school term. Having missed my chance to go south for Christmas, I was now thinking of my planned return home for a break at Easter. Also, after all the trauma of so much unexpected snow, I was revelling in the experience of the first signs of spring on Foula:

The Manse, Foula, by Lerwick, Shetland
3rd March 1955

There has been that strange sensation of impending spring these last two days with the browns and greens of our rather bare landscape once again visible, and I have started noticing birds again, having almost forgotten about them in these past birdless weeks of snow and frost. After the snow we had some really cold weather with the wind-chill effect of constant wind to offset the slight rise in temperature. Today the wind was only fresh; it rained only half the afternoon; there was an occasional splash of blue in the sky. And the sea on the sheltered side of the island was not actually breaking over the pier. So it was labeled 'a lovely day', really springlike. Such is the relativity of weather standards and such one's appreciation of small mercies here. There are daffodil shoots at the foot of the wall on the warm south side of the house; the burn is back to a reasonable size at last after doing a real spot of overtime with melting snow these last few days; there are only a few small patches of white left on the north side of the hills and dykes and peat-banks; and today I saw 15 Oystercatchers, wonderful harbingers of spring, back feeding on the fields, as well as several handsome Black Guillemots on the sea in their black-and-white summer plumage. It is now light at 6 p.m., when the weather forecast comes on, and getting lighter each night at a remarkable rate. Moreover I am now putting the same month at the head of my letters as I hope to see on the calendar when I come south for my long-awaited holiday. It might be tempting providence to say more at the moment, but look out for a telegram any date from the 21st of March. At present it looks as though that may well be the first boat as the winds are really strong again now, which would be sad as the exam papers for my pupils sitting the Secondary Entrance Exam haven't come in yet, and the first papers were scheduled to be taken yesterday. So there are still plenty of snags in my programme.

Snags, yes; but what faith I seemed to have in our transport, so soon after seven weeks of isolation ended by rescue!

Chapter 19: A Dog, 'The Cold', and a genuine 'Black House'

I firmly believe that one of the greatest privileges we can have in this life is to own a non-human animal as a companion, and to share a relationship with it for long enough to be able to understand at least some of the intricate workings of its mind. Nobody who has ever done this to the point where a true bond of friendship is achieved can ever condone the cruelty and exploitation of our fellow passengers on this planet which is so widespread today. Because they lived so close to their animals, nearly everybody I got to know on Foula had achieved this bond and had a genuine respect for the animals they looked after and depended on for their livelihood and survival. It was true of their cattle and sheep, but especially of their dogs.

Except when I was away from home in the army or at University I never remember living without a dog. In fact I tend to think of the stages in my life as the periods coinciding with the particular dog our family had at the time. My first memory is of Bobbie, the black spaniel of my childhood. He always knew when we were going on holiday and kept as close to us as he could for fear of being left behind. On one occasion when we were packing our suitcases in an upstairs bedroom on the fourth floor at Dalhousie Castle, he appeared at the window from which an external fire-escape led down to the ground in several stages of wooden steps fixed to the outside wall, including the crossing of a flat roof. He had never been on that fire-escape before, nor had he been shown where it reached the ground, nor had he ever been upstairs inside the house. He lived in an outside kennel on the opposite side of a very large and complex building. Yet he appeared outside one of a hundred windows, the right one. So I have always concluded that dogs have some uncanny senses which work in a way that we mere mortals cannot possibly explain, and I attribute this to our discovery of language which has dulled our access to these senses through disuse.

My father loved riding to hounds and went out every Tuesday with the Linlithgow and Stirlingshire hunt, more for the ride than the pursuit of the fox. He used to 'walk' fox-hound pups, as many hunt followers did, taking responsibility for their training and exercise at an early age till they were well grown. I remember vividly how fond we children were of these pups and how sad to see them go back after only a few months to the hunt kennels. At Keble College at Oxford he had a dog all through his student days, which lived in a foster home in the town (no dogs were allowed in college) but was fed and exercised by him every day. I seem to have inherited his love of dogs, but not of hunting, to which I have always been implacably opposed. My sticking point is that the huntsmen seem to regard as legitimate sport the great cruelty inflicted by hunting on the most intelligent and attractive mammal we still enjoy as part of our heritage of wildlife. Cruelty and torture never should be fun.

I still have the 1936 school group photograph of my first school, with over a hundred boys lined up in four long rows for the camera. The bottom row consisted of the youngest boys seated on the ground; the second row was mostly the staff, with the Headmaster and his wife occupying the centre two chairs, with Mrs Bruce-Lockhart holding their Cairn terrier in her arms and their huge deerhound lying at their feet. One small boy aged nine has managed to get himself into the one position in the whole group of 150 people where he could sit with his arm round the deerhound's neck – and that was me in the bottom row. It would soon be obvious to anyone in a family with a dog or children that I relate easily to both and that I could often be found talking to the children, or the dog, rather than the adults. Most of the teachers in Foula before me had been married women. So I suppose the Gears reckoned I was lonely living all by myself in the Manse. And as most other houses in Foula had a dog of some kind, it was natural for them to offer me one of their collie bitch's pups to keep me company. I expect they also noticed that Flossie was a favourite of mine, a very pretty collie bitch of the three-coloured type, black, white and tan, an intelligent animal and unlike most Foula collies, useful about the croft with the sheep and cattle. So, after six months on my own in 1954, from the end of October I was the proud owner of the first dog I could really call my own. Norie transformed my life, both in the house and everywhere I went on the island. From then on it always seemed the most natural thing in the world to have my dog with me, and to take him whenever I went visiting. A dog is a wonderful bridge between people who perhaps have little else in common, and I found Norie a valuable asset in my contacts with the more confined and sometimes lonely crofters I visited. He would often be the central subject of conversation with some of the older folk, who loved fetching a biscuit from the cupboard to give to the *"poor pirie dog"*; and would then tell you their favourite story about their own dog or perhaps one long dead, which had similarly fulfilled their lives many years before.

Feeding dogs on Foula was often a haphazard business, and many times I saw a plate of porridge oats put down as the dog's main meal of the day. I never forgot my shock and surprise at the method used in the Schoolhouse by the Gears to feed their dogs much of the time. They would sit down to a meal of their staple diet, fish and tatties. There would be scraps left on the plates, potato peel, fish skin and bones. Someone, clearing the table, would pile all these leftovers onto one plate and then scrape the whole lot straight onto the floor just where they sat. At first this seemed rather bizarre behaviour, but on reflection it was entirely rational. Of course as it was all part of the routine of any meal, their dogs were just awaiting the moment. So contrary to my expectation there was never a revolting mess on the floor, for the food barely reached the linoleum before it all disappeared in a few seconds of the survival of the quickest. It was the fastest disappearing trick I had ever observed and really very clean and hygienic.

On the crofts the dogs were very territorial and barked furiously as a stranger approached. Sometimes this was intimidating for Norie, and occasionally he was attacked, but the other dogs soon learnt to expect him when they saw me and serious fights were really quite rare. However it was a hazard I never quite got accustomed to, though it did not deter me from taking him. The other hazard was of course the attacks by skuas on the nesting grounds in summer when they were defending their territories. Dogs were often struck by diving Bonxies and some were terrified by these aggressive tactics. Arctic Skuas could be very fierce and insistent and I several times saw Norie completely bowled over as he tried to avoid them. He soon learnt to give the more aggressive ones a wide berth.

I knew my family would take a great interest in any dog I took on and trained. So in my letter of 1st March 1955 I brought them up to date with our progress:

Norie is growing into the most splendid fellow, a real collie with a very wise face and gentle eyes. He is sleeping in front of the stove at the moment (I am writing in the kitchen by the Rayburn as the warmest place) or rather he is pretending to, but looking up with a watery eye every now and again as if to suggest that it was time for some more fodder. One finger of mine moving towards his dish or the biscuit tin and he will be transformed from a black lump of inertia to an alert pair of ears – slightly outsize due to his paternal spaniel connections, but rather endearing for that very reason – with a quizzical pair of brown eyes between and a seemingly insatiable stomach somewhere below. Two things fill his life at the moment –no, I should say three – eating, fetching, and keeping me in sight. His greatest love is a rubber ball, but he will fetch anything that one can throw for him from a tuft of grass to a lump of peat, and bring it back religiously to one's feet. He expects this game to go on all day and doesn't seem to appreciate the difficulty of wheeling a heavy barrow of peat and throwing things for him at the same time. So my path is littered with objects which he vainly hopes I shall pick up and throw for him, and when I pass them by he fetches them from behind me, carries them on ahead and lays them once more in my path until my heart is melted by his urgent need.

He has been very trainable, is quite infallible in the house now, keeps to heel on command, lies down, sits or goes to his bed as required, 'dies' on his back with all four feet in the air (for food of course), counts to ten before taking a biscuit, says 'Please' (one bark), 'thank you' (two barks) and 'Yes' (one bark) when I ask him if he wants any more – never yet been known to refuse! He knows the meaning of so many words now, such as 'biscuits', 'bones', 'cocoa' (at mid-morning school break) as an interesting variation on that theme, and such comments as "What on earth is that filthy object on the carpet, you little horror!" So he is altogether a most intelligent dog and, as a companion, both interested and interesting. Of course I always take him to school with me, which is normally trouble-free. His worst crime so far, and it was as unexpected as it was horrific, was the sudden appearance in the middle of the schoolroom floor, after a rather longer than usual absence during the dinner hour, of the semi-digested remains of one and a half complete rabbits, innards and all, in the middle of a BBC History broadcast. Not the best recipe for pupil control or concentration. Normally he just sleeps on the floor in front of the schoolroom stove and the children are so used to him that they pay no attention at all. Another notable exception to this model behaviour was when he tried to join in the singing of our morning hymn in his own inimitable head-back style of wolf howl, matching the high pitch of the children's voices, but less in tune, a performance which is apt to cause a breakdown into giggles in the middle of the verse.

The mailboat which I had hoped would take that letter out never materialized and I added another page to it on 7th March after I had recovered from a cold, which recorded two other aspects of Norie's usefulness as a house dog, but also gives a good indication of how different the whole business of catching a cold was in such an isolated community as Foula:

7th March. *Well, time marches on and since I last sat at the typewriter my cold has taken its course, and life is now getting back to normal again. In fact I think it was a mild dose of 'flu and for that reason it was all the more urgent to keep it away from other folk, not that one gets much choice in the matter as everyone shuns you like the plague anyway. One really has to adjust one's whole way of thinking about infection in a community like this, which must be one of the few places left where it is still possible to keep clear of those infections which people in the south (like you!) seem to take so much for granted. I spent Friday and most of Saturday in bed. Being confined to bed is, to say the least, a bit inconvenient when one is on one's own, but I managed to look after myself without aggravating the trouble and got over it by dint of simply keeping warm. Norie was of course chief hot water bottle. He also acted his part as guardian of the house in his own loud and inimitable style, whenever anyone passed by. The road which runs right past the house is just outside my bedroom window so that I was able from my bed to observe the traffic. On Friday this consisted of two dogs, a cow, three men with wheelbarrows, the Shopman without a barrow, and three or four shoppers from the Hametoun in the south going to the afternoon opening of the shop down by the Voe. Saturday was more exciting as some people had to go twice for peat, being the day before the Sabbath; and also the island tractor, back on the road again I'm thankful to say, went past twice. As the tractor stuck once at the gate about 100 yards up the road, and then two of the passing men met just outside my window for a long natter, and finally one of the Beagrie's cows broke into my garden and put the finishing touches to the remains of all my cabbages in the back garden, I had altogether a most*

exciting and eventful day. What was even better was that I was by then feeling a little less like an aching void under an inflated pumpkin and was actually able to enjoy some reading for a change. Since then I have also got down to some writing – yes, even poetry, for which my conscience is quite easy when I know there is nothing else I ought to be doing instead.

I was back at school today and found that most of the Schoolhouse family have also had the cold. So far we have managed to keep it to only three houses, no sorry, four as Harry the Postmaster also got it yesterday. Almost all the menfolk seem to have suffered it as 'flu, leaving us feeling rather washed out, whereas the womenfolk have only had a slight head cold. I really dare not think what would happen if it got into the Hametoun at the south end. There are four houses in which if only one person got it and had to stay in bed, someone from outside would have to come in to look after the household; and two of these have cattle to be looked after. Apparently what has happened so often before is that people have had to go out in the cold and look after their animals when they should really have been in their beds, and so they contract pneumonia or something far worse than the original infection. And usually if one person contracts it, the infection goes straight through the whole household. Nor does this improve their resistance, so that an infection of any kind here is a nightmare, and 'flu has been known to go round the island three times, and each time worse than the time before. Everyone agrees that this winter we have been very lucky, and that this is largely due to the infrequent mail runs. It's no wonder that the mail crew are so unwilling to cross over to the mainland, unless they are sure of being able to get back without having to stay over in Walls, where they almost invariably pick up some kind of germ.

During this 'flu crisis I witnessed, and managed to secure a photograph of, a rather bizarre incident at the Schoolhouse. I was talking to Mima in their kitchen after school when one of the children came in from outside and said that Aunty Jessie wanted to talk to her by the byre. Jessie Ratter, Mima's sister, was lame and only rarely came north as far as the Schoolhouse. I was puzzled why she couldn't come in to talk in the kitchen, as it was a cold, blustery day to stand outside and talk. Mima explained *"It'll be because of the 'flu."* Intrigued, I grabbed my camera, which luckily I had with me that day. When I arrived at the byre down by the Post Office, there was Jessie, happed up against the weather, at one end of the sheltered side of the building, and clustered at the other end of the long stone wall were Mima and one or two of the children engaged in a rather loud conversation about the welfare of various members of their families, shouting to each other the intimacies of private family life against the wind and the rain. I stepped back some distance before I could encompass both parties to this private conversation Foula-style in the same picture. What I was really photographing was the twenty yards of God's good fresh air between them which in their view guaranteed that neither party would either transmit or receive the infection which Schoolhouse people were always suspected of having and the good folk of North and South Biggins were determined not to catch. After all Jessie at that time cared for old Mrs Henry who was well up in her eighties and mother of them both, and of Mary our school cook. So I was the last person to complain about the Schoolhouse Henry taking every precaution to avoid the cold. After all our vital school dinners, not to mention old Granny Henry's life, could

have depended on such elementary precautions. Even so the title of my photograph, 'Family conversation on Foula in winter' must need a bit of explanation to anyone except a Foula 'Norie'.

My letter of 7th March continued on a more domestic, culinary topic:

Footnote before I go to bed. I had rather a good supper tonight. 'Hash, a la Manse.' Want the recipe? Take half an onion (these quantities for one person), a carrot and a large potato. Slice thinly into the frying pan. Fry until the carrots and potato are soft, in the minimum of fat. Then stir in a mixture of boiled rice and sardines (half a tin, to taste?) with a sprinkling of raisins. Turn frequently to avoid burning. When it is beginning to brown and crisp slightly on the bottom, turn onto the plate, sprinkle with a little salt and eat piping hot.

Or (if you are in a hurry and have no time for the niceties), take the remains of the weekend's left-overs of cooked vegetables, rice pudding and that half-used,

Family conversation by the Mogle byre in winter, when Jessie (left) visiting from the Hame Toun has a cold which the Schoolhouse family (right) don't want to catch

rather old tin of sardines, stick it all in the frying pan and mix. When you have had to scrape it off the bottom four or five times to stop it burning, turn onto the plate and eat quickly before the dog smells it and persuades you to let him have half. Either method is calculated to keep you company all evening and make you thankful you have nobody else to hear your audible symptoms of appreciation.

I enjoyed cooking, on a very simple level during the week, and at weekends, when I did not have Mary's excellent school lunches to help in saving my time spent in the kitchen. However over that first winter, when the weather and her commitments made it more difficult for me to depend on Mary Umphray of Ham for domestic help, I decided I had better learn to bake my own bread. Everybody had their own ideas about leavening, and many used baking soda rather than yeast to save time. But from what I sampled, bread properly leavened with yeast seemed to me far preferable and I was strongly advised to try the newly available dried yeast in the form of fine pellets. With warm water and a little sugar for

the yeast to feed on, and a minimum of salt for fear of killing it prematurely, this could be mixed up in a saucer and left to prove. Kept in the right warm temperature in a bowl beside the Rayburn covered with a cloth, this soon began to froth and blow bubbles, and could then be mixed into the flour to make a large lump of dough. When this had risen, been thoroughly kneaded and reduced in size, and then left to grow again to twice the size twice more, it was ready to be broken into chunks, weighed and fitted into warmed baking tins and cooked in the oven. Good preparations, especially of the stove to get adequate heat in the oven when you needed it, and time for the proving and kneading processes, were the essential ingredients of good bread. I know of few domestic chores which yield greater satisfaction than taking three brown, well-risen, loaves with that heady aroma of fresh baking, out of the oven, yielding the enviable prospect of scrunchy toast or a crust dipped in your soup or perhaps delicious egg sandwiches out on the hill for the days that followed. My best baking was three one-pound loaves which I could just fit in the oven.

A batch of three crusty loaves, baked in my Rayburn oven fuelled by peat. A weekly task

I was so proud of it that I took a still-life photograph of them on the kitchen table – just to impress the housewives on the island and at home.

One person to whom I showed my bread portrait was Pat McLeod, the friend from Fife who had followed me to Foula within a couple of months of my arrival and, with a friend of hers, had stayed a week at the Manse in my first summer. Correspondence had followed over many weeks during which it became clear that we were both rather smitten with the romantic situation of both having a love affair with Foula which gradually seemed to be changing into a rather distant love affair between us – a match, or so it seemed, of identical views on islands and remote places and the quiet life. She seemed quite unperturbed by my letters (often just the carbon copies of my letters home to Edinburgh) detailing the snags and problems of winter. Instead she seemed sufficiently fired up by my accounts of rough weather and challenging conditions to be willing to contemplate the idea of joining in and sampling island life herself. In correspondence which became steadily more exciting in its possibilities, things had got no further than this rather vague statement of shared interest and enthusiasm by April 1955 when I was planning my first proper break from island life for a full year. Both our thoughts, from totally different viewpoints, were focused on the idea that two lives with such similar ideas and ideals would be happier shared than conducted hundreds of miles apart. But of course from my angle, alone in the Manse on many a long winter night, however busy I might be, I could not help feeling how much more meaningful and congenial a life it would be with company, and best of all with a wife to share its joys and its frustrations. These thoughts soon translated into definite plans to spend at least part of my April holiday, not in Edinburgh with my own family but in Fife with Pat's. She lived with her parents in the Lodge at the entrance to a vast Scottish Renaissance mansion called Melville House. Formerly home of the Earls of Leven and Melville, the building had been much upgraded but was no longer used by the family, and so happened to come on the market just when my father was planning to move his school from its original home at Dalhousie Castle in Midlothian. To save costs I had spent much of one University vacation in 1950 helping to move the school and all its accoutrements, with frequent trips driving an ex-army three-ton truck across the Forth via the ferry, the old paddle steamer which at that time was the only road link between South and North Queensferry. After the move I spent short periods helping out when my father

was ill, taking his classes for him as good practice for my future career. It was during this period that Pat and I first met, and where later in 1953 she first learned of my plans to take up the post in Foula. So she hatched the plot to come up and see for herself what it was that had attracted me to such an unusual teaching post. It was all beginning to look as though this course of events had been almost planned for us, as though our paths had crossed for a purpose neither of us had previously dreamt of. We both badly needed closer acquaintance and time together to assess our future more adequately than the very intermittent postal exchanges that winter allowed. And we both expressed frequent frustration that the telephone link never materialized into a reliable and usable service. So April looked like being a crucial month for us both, while in the meantime distance continued to lend enchantment.

My memories of that bitterly cold and eventful winter include two which are etched more deeply than most, partly because I have photographs of both which fill in those details the memory loses after fifty years. One was when, on rare occasions admittedly, I found time to sit by own fireside in my study at the Manse and work on a new skill I was learning – taxidermy. I had made contact with the Royal Scottish Museum, as it was then known, which had expressed interest in any specimens I could send them provided they were properly prepared as 'skins'. I borrowed an excellent museum booklet giving the bare bones of elementary taxidermy, more the simple preserving of skins rather than any fancy making up of lifelike specimens for display. The museum was particularly interested in the island sub-species of the Foula fieldmice, if I could catch any without harming the skins or skeletons. As in the case of some small birds like wrens, less likely to cross the water between islands and so almost certainly geographically isolated, the mice on islands like Foula or St Kilda, which may have been isolated for thousands of generations, have had ample opportunity to demonstrate the mechanics of evolution by gradually developing different physical characteristics from their mainland cousins. They have therefore a unique importance to the student of evolution in assessing how long and by what means the formation of identifiable sub-species, and eventually species, occurs. It takes many years of collecting many specimens before a statistically significant mean could be achieved; but in the meantime any specimens I could collect would be at least a starting point in the study. Apart from such defined areas of research, there were always chance opportunities to enhance a record

Taxidermy by Tilley lamp. Writing data labels for a Foula field mouse and a Merlin found dead and made into a skin for the Royal Scottish Museum in Edinburgh

with a good scientific specimen, as for instance the freshly dead Merlin I found. It's not every day that such trophies occur, which all add their tiny fund of data to the national total in our understanding of wildlife. I found the work difficult, painstaking but privileged. A bird specimen in perfect condition is such a masterpiece of design and the fulfillment of millions of generations of slow and subtle change, as to take one's breath away. In the careful handling of all the feather tracts, one discovers perfection of cryptic colours offering perfect camouflage, or extravagantly sematic colours offering stunning display patterns, all of them formed by a process still little understood of gradual improvement and change, to fit the creature to its environment and the last degree of perfection needed to survive in the fiercely competitive world into which they were all born.

I worked at my study table by the light of a Tilley lamp, which uses pressurised paraffin heated to a gas to light a fragile incandescent mantle to white heat as it surrounded the tiny jet of vapour. This makes the ideal light of a high colour temperature to reveal all the details

of the skin I was working on, with the true colours as in daylight. The lamp also provided a welcome and comforting glow of warmth where I worked, which however did little to warm one's toes on those cold windy nights when the gale howled in the chimney and the draught blew under the door. No wonder Norie quickly learned that the warmest place in the room was on the soft hearthrug immediately in front of the peat fire's cheerful glow. In spite of many attempts I singularly failed to teach him to sit on my feet instead. With a little persuasion he could be cajoled however to lie on my bed for a while before his late night toilet walk, creating that nice warm patch which was so comforting when putting one's cold feet in between cold sheets. His role as a warming-pan was one of my many joys in having another warm-blooded creature to share my house. But the gradual revelation of his complex personality was a far deeper source of fascination and pleasure.

The other winter memory was of visiting old Robbie Isbister of the Breckans in his hovel of a home in the last inhabited black house in Shetland. The contrast with my own home could hardly have been greater and yet he seemed content, even happy with his inheritance. I had been reminded of his presence only about half a mile from my door beyond the Kirk, during the freeze-up of 'Operation Snowdrop' when I had to help him one evening with his wheel-barrow of groceries from the shop where the snow had drifted several feet deep at both of the croft's stone walls. In truth he would have been struggling had the road been quite clear, and his breath was laboured with the exertion of pushing his load up the hill towards the Kirk. He never asked for help nor complained at his lot. All he needed was a bit of encouragement to get him 'over the hump'. On those occasions he had little breath left for chat, only for his effusive gratitude for a helping hand. I was conscious that he was a past pillar of the Foula community but now very isolated. So a week or two later, returning from a visit to South Biggins, I decided to call at Breckans, with, I admit, a certain apprehension as to what I would find. As with Tom and Jane Umphray at the Gravins, on the road to the pier, I was never invited to the house or asked

in when I met them outside. The entrance to Robbie's thatched 'but-and-ben' was in fact quite forbidding, in that the approach through the yard around the house was muddy and fouled by sheep and poultry, and the debris of rough living and a lack of either time or energy for any form of tidiness or order. Such things have no priority in a Shetland winter if one is old and infirm and fighting for survival.

The contrast with my own life-style made me apprehensive of appearing to be intrusive or even nosey, if I expected a welcome into his very different world. I had also been wisely warned by Mima at the Schoolhouse that I might find his standard of cleanliness a bit of a shock. But my visits to Betty Gray at her tiny cottage at North Harrier had been such a pleasure, in spite of her open hearth peat fire and the inevitable dust that came from it, that I felt I could surely venture into the only real black house without causing offence. So I turned left off the road to the Kirk and knocked on the outer door of Breckans. There was no obvious reply or "*Come in*" but yet there was clearly somebody at home

Robbie Isbister of Breckans sits on his 'resting chair' by his open peat fire with his kitten on his knee, in the last genuine black house in Shetland, surrounded by the boxes used to bring his supplies from the shop

as I could hear a voice. I paused to listen. Perhaps he had a visitor already, in which case I had better come back another day. The talking went on so I knocked louder and still got no reply. So I opened the door and in the next few moments both entered another world I had never experienced before and stepped back in time at least a hundred years, perhaps longer. It was dim but there was a Tilley lamp burning, though much of its light was lost in the smoke which hung about at eye level. Stooping a little I could see a figure sitting on a wooden bench, still talking, but to himself. So I spoke a bit louder and introduced myself. When he looked at me I was perturbed at how red-rimmed his eyes looked, a feature I had noticed before when I had met him on the road but now looking much worse, presumably due to the constant irritation of the peat smoke. I don't think he realised who I was at first, but as soon as he knew he invited me to sit down on a chair beside the hearth, a wide bed of peat ash with a few peats glowing red in the middle under a huge chain hanging from the ceiling. He remained seated on a wooden bench as we talked but I could see no other furniture, partly because the room was rather dim, and partly because it was almost completely full of junk, mostly old boxes of every shape and size, presumably brought back from the pier or the shop and never put away or disposed of, and all covered with a thick layer of peat ash and dust.

It was of course dark outside when I called but I could just make out one small window in the slope of the roof, so it was hard to make out how much light there would be in the house in daylight. I enquired about his supply of peat and he assured me he was being well looked after and had a good peat stack out in the yard. Indeed he emphasised to me how grateful he was to his neighbours and friends as he was no longer able to manage his own peat supply. I knew he was at least 80 years old so this was scarcely surprising. But once he started talking and realised he had an interested audience when I asked a few questions about his welfare, there was no stopping him. He seemed proud of the fact that he represented the old way, the style of living his family had always known and cherished, and he apologised for nothing. His fire was his lifeline, it kept him warm and he cooked on it and made his tea; and so far as he knew it had been alight for all of his life. For at least the 75 years or more that he could remember, the fire I was sitting beside had never gone cold, day or night, summer or winter.

He told me of his daily routine. Soon, before he went to sleep, he would make sure he had a good red fire burning with enough fresh peats on it to last till morning, and then he would 'smoor' the fire with the grey peat ash till there was no air could get at it at all, but not too much to smother it. Then in the morning all he had to do was uncover the smouldering peats and stand two or three on their ends until they caught alight, and then keep feeding it with new peats all day according to the weather and his needs. Peat did indeed seem to be the perfect fuel for this way of life, and he insisted that every type of peat had its special role. 'Blue' peats burnt far hotter and were ideal for cooking on, especially for baking scones on the grid iron lying there in the ash. Light, fibrous peats from the top of a peat-bank burnt more easily and at a lower heat and were needed just to keep the fire in during the day or to kindle it into flame in the morning. Peat mould, the equivalent of sawdust from wood, was ideal to dampen down too hot a fire or to help preserve it overnight.

He seemed interested in my experience with my peat-fired Rayburn stove but scornful of its capacity to devour more peat than he felt it was worth. His system was undoubtedly much more economical, but possibly less efficient and infinitely dirtier. He confessed that the smoky atmosphere was beginning to be a problem for him over the winter, with little let-up when he was confined indoors all day. Like nearly all the elderly folk I visited he admitted to being overweight and to having a great deal of discomfort from indigestion. I gleaned that his diet was largely oatmeal porridge, or bread and tea, supported by such tinned protein food as he could afford. I suspected he had smoked fish in the rafters but it was too dim for me to see any. But strange to say after my enquiries about food and fuel because I was seeking re-assurance that his basic needs were satisfied, his talk was partly about the future of the island and the problems like the mailboat and communications – no wonder after the crisis we had just come through over Christmas. I sat enthralled by his reminiscences about other places and his wide travels in the Merchant Navy in his young days, with stories and tales about South America and the great ports and harbours he had visited as a sailor. Like John Henry's stories of the whaling in the Antarctic, it was all a revelation to me and in Robbie's case quite unexpected, so that we spent an hour or two in nostalgia for a far more exciting and eventful world out there. And yet there was no hint of complaint or dissatisfaction to have ended up his days back in Foula where he seemed to feel he was really at home in a quite different way. So I left him towards midnight with a sigh of longing for the days long gone but also a genuine pride in his place in his home community. Nearly all the time we had been talking he had cradled a kitten on his knee and I felt glad for him that he too had a companion to comfort him in his rather bleak and lonely old age.

Before I said goodnight, I plucked up my courage and asked him if he minded if I took a flash photograph to remind me of my visit, using the kitten as a kind of excuse as the subject, whereas in truth of course I was aware of the value of preserving an intimate record of something possibly now unique in Shetland, possibly in the whole of Britain, a bit of history soon to disappear for ever – except in museums. I think the flash startled him a little, but he did not complain and we parted friends.

As I got into bed that night between clean sheets, after banking up the Rayburn with damp peat mould to keep it in till morning, I marvelled at the thought that generations of Isbisters and Umphrays and Ratters and Grays had lived in the smoke and the dust like old Robbie, so that I could now be paid a far higher wage than they had ever dreamt of to come and teach their children, amongst other things, about health and hygiene in their daily lives. I couldn't help wondering whether Robbie slept in his rubber boots which he had worn throughout the evening's conversation, and whether he just slept on his 'resting chair' with a blanket over him and whether he even had a bed to get into. How little I knew about the real meaning of living in a house like Breckans or Gravins. I found some slight relief in the thought that at least he too had the comfort of a Tilley lamp which I found so essential for my own well-being, one of man's best ever inventions before the advent of electricity. I turned mine off and went to sleep a wiser and a humbler man.

Chapter 20: Long, Dark Winter; Houses, People and Mice

Emerging from my first winter on Foula I remember how much I appreciated the increasing day-length and the speed with which it progressed towards the equinox in March. I have never lived in the tropics, nor anywhere without the marked changes which come with the seasons. So, born and bred in Scotland, I have always just accepted that seasonal variations are part of the trials but also the joys of life. When I was a child winters were colder, often very much colder, but also more exciting, when our world was transformed by snow. Summers brought holidays and sunbathing, and in fashion with the times I was a sun-worshipper at heart. Midsummer had always been my favourite time of year, especially the long warm evenings in our northern latitude. In Shetland they were even longer, but seldom warm. Likewise, even at mid-day it was seldom really hot and I only remember one sunny spell when I was tempted to take my shirt off when working on the peat. And then the midges soon put my shirt back on again. Normally I have found that for some strange reason midges cannot tolerate direct sunshine; but on Foula the midges were, as they say, 'something else'.

Throughout the year Shetland weather was like being on the sea in a boat – always cooler than one expected. In a boat one is always moving, creating a breeze, a factor which one tends to forget when deciding whether to take that extra jersey for the trip. In Shetland the air itself is seldom still, and right from the start I had learnt to wear an extra layer of clothing at all times of the year. In winter the chill factor of the constant wind was something for which I was constitutionally unsuited and negatively biased. Perhaps the most significant difference one notices in winter, even in such a comparatively minor shift in latitude from Edinburgh to Shetland, is the amount of time in each day one has to operate under artificial lighting. In the school, on overcast mid-winter days, we often had to light the Tilley lamp quite soon after lunch, and the sun would be setting when the children left for home. For at least four mid-winter months I spent virtually no time at my own house in daylight during the working week, so that my Tilley lamp became my friend and companion for almost all the work I did except school-work. Hence peat

was essential for my comfort but paraffin was the key to any achievements in most of my endeavours. Before the invention of vaporizing paraffin by pressure and the magic of the incandescent mantle with its brilliant white light, I would have had to work with far less speed and far greater difficulty, and possible damage to my eyes, by the light of a simple lamp, either a candle flame or the old-fashioned collie-lamp where a wick lay in a shallow channel at one end of a dish of oil. As on St Kilda, fulmar oil would have been the cheapest oil available, being a by-product of the harvest of birds by the fowlers from the sea-cliffs for their feathers and meat.

In the 1950s only two houses on Foula had that magic harbinger of instant light, the electric switch. James Andrew Gray had a simple 12-volt system powered by a small wind propeller on a pole outside Dykes, his house in the Hametoun. At South Harrier Scottie Umphray had constructed a small waterwheel in the burn that ran through his croft, made mostly from metal parts salvaged from a crashed aircraft up on the moor not far from his house. Beside the dam across the stream to provide the modest head of water required, he built a small power-house from concrete to house the dynamo, and ran a cable to his croft only a hundred yards away. By such skills he provided the means for the two ladies of his household to achieve far more than they ever could have done by Tilley or lamp-light alone. All this from a hill burn only a couple of feet across.

Long darkness was not the only thing I had to get used to in my first winter. Really dark darkness was such a change from the bright lights of Edinburgh – or Oxford or Cambridge or any other urban area I had lived in. Not since the days before the war, when I lived on the Dalhousie estate in Midlothian in the wooded valley of the river South Esk, had I enjoyed a living environment without street lights and the glow of the city night sky. I remember even on my very first night on Foula noticing how bright the stars were, a myriad of patterns of light in which the better known constellations my mother had taught me to recognize seemed lost amongst so many thousands of fainter stars. From the start, the moon exerted a real influence on my life. For one thing it made a world of difference if one had to leave the house and go anywhere in the dark. A full moon in clear weather solved most problems unless the weather changed while one was out. I had been warned by the Holbourns to take a good torch and, just as important, a good supply of batteries. But with the cloudy skies of so much Shetland weather, the darkness of the middle fortnight on either side of a new moon made a torch essential. One tried the tricks of walking in the dark such as I had learnt walking home from a late bus at Dalhousie. The path, bordered by rhododendrons, took us down to the river through dense, mature woodland. It was a good path and by watching the sky and recognizing the silhouettes of the trees as one passed them, outlined against what little light there was, one could usually manage. But on Foula there was virtually nothing above the horizon except a few low fences or walls, and they were black on black. It would have been easy to get hopelessly lost when there was no moon or starlight to guide one.

Many times I would set off in daylight to visit a croft, stay too long talking and be overtaken by darkness without a torch. They would always insist on my borrowing 'a blinkie' to see me home, and many was the time when, on my next visit, I would take it back to its owners only to repeat the performance yet again, having forgotten to bring my own torch as well. At times I would have at home two or three torches I didn't own until I made a concerted effort to get them back to their owners. I soon discovered too the value of a reliable torch whose switch mechanism didn't let you down just when you needed it most. (I shall never understand why so many designers of simple electric torches fail to provide what you most need, a switch that always works.) It was typical of my scatter-brained approach to planning my days that I found myself more than once deliberately going to Blowburn, the furthest croft from the Manse, to return their borrowed torch, forgetting to take either theirs or my own, and having to borrow their only other torch to get home. Which of course meant another visit the next day, so as not to leave them torchless for a second night, carrying three torches in my haversack on the way up the hill. It was the penalty I paid for the pleasure I found in their company and the wide-ranging topics of conversation we had in common, which kept us yarning long past my intended departure for home in daylight. Besides winter evenings at home on my own, however busy I might be, were still lonely.

There were compensations for the long winter darkness. A still night with a full moon was breathtaking, with the golden orb rising over the mainland thirty miles away down by Fitful Head, always exaggerated in size by the psychological effect of it being related to familiar features at ground level. High in the vastness of the night sky the moon's disc looks a tenth of the size sailing alone against the stars or among scudding clouds. On the road south to the Hametoun, if it was very clear, I could just see twinkling lights, often very faint, along the mainland coast, masked by the brightness of the silver ribbon of a full moon's track across the sea, moving with the swell or broken by wavelets close in shore. Croft house windows lit up were a sure guide; but even plantie crubs close to the road or the line of a familiar ditch or peatbank were clearcut, with my own moon shadow alongside me for company on the road. And overhead more stars than one ever thought possible until I took my binoculars out of my haversack and, focusing to infinity, let the wonders of the universe completely overwhelm my credulity as the thousands became literally millions, stretching to the end of time. My usual reaction was to feel that if there is a God, that is where the Holy Spirit dwells, far beyond my comprehension or the scope of my imagination. The scale of the Universe and those millions of galaxies, most of them far larger than the one where our own solar system occupies but a tiny corner, is not for me to try to get my mind round, but rather to wonder at and worship. But increasingly I found that all these wonderful things I was seeing and comprehending slowly more and more thoroughly day by day, were in just the same category of marvels which inspired in me that sense of the 'numinous' that I had first learnt about from C.S. Lewis' book 'Miracles' when I was a teenager getting my first experiences of worship through nature on the Yorkshire fells at Sedbergh. Now, living far closer to nature than I had ever done before, I was in the strange position of finding wonderful material for my unconventional sermons in the Foula Kirk from the night sky; but only at the cost of preaching a gospel somewhat far removed from the Bible that was supposed to be my Presbyterian guide. I often planned my sermons walking home in the dark. Perhaps I had better make my text for next Sunday Luke 12, 6 substituting 'Twite' for 'Sparrows'. That would tickle Mima Gear's sense of humour. And I could certainly put across my belief that every Bonxie that dived at my head in daylight, every fulmar that cackled to its mate on a cliff ledge, every gaudy puffin strutting on green cushions of thrift adorned with pink flowers, was as full of mystery and wonder as those myriads of stars over my head.

I often wondered whether my congregation, who had always had starlit skies on clear nights, noticed them or were appreciative of their humbling effect on the soul,

Foula has so many such effects – the looming darkness of the hills so close and steep that they obscured the whole of my western horizon; the long low outline of the Shetland mainland to the east with the reminder of the scattered human settlements in the few twinkling lights visible across the water; or on wild nights the relentless tearing of the wind; or on rare still nights, if one stopped to listen, the distant sound of the sea, sometimes in summer little more than a quiet hush under a luminous sky. All these were huge new experiences for me, the most significant being the mid-winter sense those myriads of stars gave me of the sheer wonder of being alive as I arrived back home at the Manse on a moonlit night. At least here on earth we had the comfort of the miracle of life. Was the human mind which enabled me to contemplate, to worship, to wonder, a one-off as a result of a mind-boggling series of chance encounters and formations of atoms, molecules, elements, and then cells of protoplasm, mutating a million, million, million times to produce a brain which could create and then harbour a soul? But were there any other souls, or even brains to create them, out there in the infinite emptiness of space which twinkled and glowed over the hills of Foula and left me bewildered by the scale of a universe which I was really experiencing for the first time in my life. I longed to share this new sense of wonder with all my friends in the south who had never walked home in the dark on a winter's night in such a magic place. Foula both inspired and humbled me as no other place ever had before, and now that I am old and humbled by disability ever will again.

I had coined a phrase I found myself using over and over in the more serious talks I had with some of the islanders – "*the miracle of the commonplace*". If we couldn't see God in the natural world all around us, in the huge visions of the night and the tiny details of the day, we could easily lose our sense of the numinous, caught up in the harsh world of survival in a Foula winter. And yet I knew only too well that it was far easier for me than for most of them to think past the difficulties of everyday life with all its discomforts and hardships, especially in old age. So perhaps there was a chance that the inspiration I found in the night sky might help them too? I could but try. I wasn't ever likely to find an easier way of getting close to God than this and perhaps I could take some of my new friends among the Foula folk with me? And if the vastness of space was too difficult to comprehend, the Shetland wren and the Foula field mouse, the marsh marigolds on the Ham burn or the vernal squills at the roadside by Gravins might do the trick in a more intimate way instead. All were "*crammed with heaven*" as Elizabeth Browning had put it; but strangely there were no blackberries to pluck on Foula, though in the Kirk we could all "*take off our shoes*".

Once or twice I enjoyed a fine display of the Aurora borealis, which can be spectacular in Shetland if conditions are right – great billowing curtains of yellow and green and pale red, forming and reforming right across the sky behind the outline of Hamnafield. They would ask me at the Schoolhouse the next morning if I had seen the "*pretty dancers*", and then compare them with other, quite different, displays they had seen on previous occasions.

A Shetland wren with a beakful of food for its young, on a tuft of thrift at the Sneck

And often there followed the supplementary question *"Did you hear them fanning?"* – but I never had. Whether it was that they knew it is a form of electrical discharge which, in thunder, always makes itself heard; and so heard what they thought they ought to hear, I never could make out. But for me that kind of lightning is silent and all the more mysterious for being so. They described it to me as a kind of distant singing noise, very eerie. 'Choirs of angels' perhaps? I only remembered seeing the Aurora once before at Dalhousie when we watched a spectacular display over Edinburgh when I was a schoolboy. That was the year of the 'blue moon', caused, we were told in the press, by a huge forest fire in Canada which had drifted wood-smoke high into the stratosphere causing unusual atmospheric conditions. In Foula there was nothing unusual or unexpected about the display, just an added bonus as some sort of compensation for the long winter. I remember how the islanders gave the impression of having great personal satisfaction that here was something they could offer me as part of their special world, as though it was a sort of proud possession they were pleased to share.

The worst experiences of the dark mid-winter days were when stormy weather coincided with any need to venture into the darkness. Even opening the outside door against a gale could be hazardous. On such occasions which usually involved visiting a croft with perhaps only two, or even worse only one, elderly inhabitant, the presence of just another human being was all that was required to quell fears and anxieties. But when I had to leave them with only the yellow light of an oil lamp to keep them company, surrounded by the hostile blackness of a long winter night, I would struggle home clutching my blinkie and praying it wouldn't let me down this time. As I probed the night I could not help but marvel at the generations of Foula folk who had weathered countless winters, depending solely on their own resources of courage and inherited knowledge for their survival against odds I had never known or suffered. No wonder they developed a deep attachment to their own safe haven, even if, in the old days, it had been a black house with little comfort or joy in a long winter. In the Foula of my experience all but two of the islanders had a far more comfortable house with at least a wooden floor, decent windows and a cast-iron stove, the fire hardly ever out and great for cooking a simple diet. Their houses however still lacked most of the physical comforts and mental stimulation of even the poorest city dweller's home in the 1950s; features like electricity, piped hot water, cushions or carpets or easy chairs, for instance.

Just how tied Foula folk could become to the home where they were born was made clear by the case of one of the two Henry sisters who lived at the Hametoun croft called Niggards. I am sure I was told by more than one islander that, though as a child she had gone to the school at Mogle like all the other children, she had never in fact been north of the Ham Toun, and so at the age of sixty had never visited the northern half of the island she lived on. It started only a mile from her house, but it was like a foreign land. Her home was in the south and that is where she was content to live. Perhaps it was not surprising that she had never married. She and her sister, of all the islanders I met, were perhaps the most difficult to visit and talk to. They were by nature very shy of strangers and I felt that we had very little in common and so very little to talk about. So our conversation proceeded in a few observations about the weather and perhaps their health and then just petered out. Sometimes, though in one way I felt sorry for their patent insularity, in another way I envied them the simplicity and contentment of their lives. It was impossible moreover to find fault with the cleanliness of their house or the peaceable yet industrious character of their crofting way of life. An image springs to mind, strengthened by being recorded on film one summer's afternoon, of the two sisters bringing a couple of their black cows back to the byre from the grazing down by the Mill Loch, while old Meggie Ratter of Punds walked bravely past on the rough footpath across the moor, wheeling a fully laden barrow of peats at the age of 85. She had little choice of course as her sister Jeannie was 95 and unable any longer to leave the house. Meggie's rosy cheeks and smiling face are one of my happiest memories of Foula.

This strong attachment to home gave most of the islanders a tremendous sense of pride and of belonging. In the early part of last century, perhaps encouraged by a benevolent, if over-romantic landlord in Professor Holbourn, several families found the inspiration to build new houses to a new standard of shelter and living space. In 1912, for instance, Peter Gray's father built Burns, a conventional Scottish two-storey house with dormer windows. Several single-storey houses in the Hametoun were improved with felt roofs replacing thatch, but several like Walter Ratter, as skipper of the mailboat, found the resources to build Punds, a solid two-storey house, far better than anything on St Kilda except those houses financed and built by the laird – like the Factor's House and the Manse. In many cases on Foula the house name became, in everyday use, the surname of the owner –*"Tam o' the Gravins"*, *"auld Robbie Breckans"*;

"*Andrew Leraback*"; "*Peter Mogle*"; or "*Peter Burns*" – when their real names were Isbister, Umphray, Gear and Gray. Later I was to find this sense of place in the form of the family home, standing separate from other houses in its own land, quite lacking on St Kilda, though both islands had comparable populations in the 18th and 19th centuries. I once interviewed old Neil Gillies in the ruins of his former home at No. 1 Main Street which he had left as a teenager at the evacuation of the remaining population in August 1930. His family had all benefited from the 'modernisation' of the Village by McLeod of Skye, their benevolent landlord. But was it really to their benefit to be told how they should live?

In 1860 the old black houses on St Kilda, each standing at the head of their long narrow rigs running down to Village Bay, were reorganized into a single village street of butt-and-ben type cottages, all exactly the same in style and lay-out. One wonders whether this wasn't fatal to the individual morale of the islanders, however popular it was as an upgrade in their standard of living at the time. Moreover, most of the former black houses

had stood with their gable end facing the prevailing SW wind, whereas the 1860 plan – surely never endorsed by any St Kilda native – had the long front of the house, with a door and two windows, facing into the gale. As on St Kilda the Foula roofs were tied down by ropes weighted with stones or metal bands nailed securely onto the stonework and any overhang was limited to just enough, often only an inch or two, to run the rain out beyond the edge of the wall head. It only took one serious gale to prove that overhanging eaves were a recipe for disaster.

I remember discussing some of these factors in house design with Peter Manson at Blowburn on one of my visits there with library books. As a regular member of the mailboat crew, Peter was one of that first group of Foula men I met on the old pier at Walls on the day of my first arrival in April 1954. He had a soft Shetland accent and always wore a flat cap, and was surprisingly active for his 64 years. The Holbourns had described him to me as 'reliable', a description I fully endorsed after several journeys on the *Island Lass*. He was always there, just quietly getting on with his duties as a

Ruins of the deserted croft at Da Logat, with the old drainage ditches, picked out by the low light of the setting sun, disused for more than half a century

Boats pulled up on the beach at Ham Voe, with winter 'noosts' and the stone sawpit still in use, with timber ready for cutting, in 1954

member of the crew. I also found him easier to engage in conversation than most, and always ready to satisfy my curiosity about island families and their history of which he had a wealth of knowledge. It was several months after my arrival, and many visits to the North end crofts, before I first met him inside his house without his cap on. At first I hardly recognized him, and I can remember quite clearly the discovery that day, with something of a shock, that he was quite bald. But then so was I!

Rather like his neighbour Scottie Umphray at South Harrier, Peter was always busy outside in the summer months when his active lifestyle and his faithful cloth cap made him look younger than his years. His wife Katie, who was eight years older than Peter, was the twin sister of the late Walter Ratter, who for so many years had been the trusted skipper of the mailboat. Walter, having married Meggie Isbister of South Biggins, had settled in the Hametoun where he had built the two-storey house called Punds, which had also become the home for Meggie's elder sister Jeannie. Likewise, and in typical Foula fashion, when Peter married Katie Ratter, their house Blowburn (or on some of the older maps Blowbersburn) became the home for Peter's elder sister Kittie. There did not appear to be any children of either family, but in both cases these crofting men, both with a full commitment to the mailboat as a part-time job for at least one full day a week, not only managed a croft with its strenuous and traditional routine of crops and vegetables and hay and peat, not to mention cattle and sheep, poultry and dogs, all demanding of time and energy, but also undertook the daunting task of building a new house for the family.

This indicates very clearly that at that period in the island's history, the future must have seemed secure. One major factor in this atmosphere of confidence must have been the Post Office contract of 1892 guaranteeing about 40 mailboat crossings a year for a sixern with a sail and a paid crew, to serve the 40 crofts, amongst other things, with the sort of supplies that housebuilders would need to tackle the job. That contract was first granted to Peter's father Magnus Manson of Mornington, when Peter was two years old. It was 21 years later that the first pier at Ham was opened and the new contract guaranteed payment for a weekly crossing, and as a result they were able to invest in the first diesel engine to replace six oars and a sail. Peter then had to wait another 36 years before the extension to the pier, and the means of lifting the mailboat out of the water onto a cradle at the foot of the slipway, enabled the investment of the first decked, fully motorized mailboat, the *Island Lass*, to provide the much reduced population, down from 250 to less than 100, to feel that their greater dependence on imported supplies was no longer a threat to survival.

However it was Peter's wife's family, the Ratters, who provided what was to me the most interesting part of his story about the housebuilding techniques employed by Foula families at the period when the Northern crofts finally became untenable due to changes in the climate. In these days when climate change has become a global issue with truly frightening proportions that threaten the

Aerial view of Wurr Wick, Stremness, and the north-east coastline

future of the whole human race, it is hard to imagine how a tiny community at the North end of a remote island, which had always had to battle against the forces of nature for their survival, must have felt when their whole way of life was suddenly threatened, on a purely local level, because they were too close to the sea. In the north west corner of Foula, East of Logat Head and the Ness, and close to the famous Gaada stack, is a tiny bay offering just enough shelter to have made it possible to establish a place where boats could be hauled up out of the water and beached. Two crofts, Freyars and Springs, had been established on the low ground inland of the huge boulder beach at Wurr Wick where crops could be grown, though it involved a big investment in drainage ditches across marshy ground. At that period fishing was the more important means of earning a living and the North end of Foula gave good access to the haaf fishing, worked mainly by sixerns, boats manned by six oarsmen who often penetrated fishing grounds many miles offshore but where prolific hauls of fish could be obtained, though not without both considerable risk and effort.

Walter and Katie's father Magnus Ratter had built a house at Logat, south of Logat Head, after a period of disastrous storms and major losses of haaf fishermen at sea in the 19th century had spelt the end of fishing as the mainstay of the North end community. For some time the Foula crofters had to depend on their crops and cattle for their livelihood, but this was soon threatened by a change in the climate which meant increasing losses to their crops from salt spray. I took one photograph of Wurr Wick in the sort of northerly wind fresh enough

to blow a continuous rain of salt water inland from the boulder beach, which showed me only too clearly why Magnus had had to abandon his croft and move to Bankwell at the south end of the island. As a precursor to this family move, Katie herself moved to the Hametoun at the age of four, presumably partly because this would enable her to attend the school at the Ham Toun more easily. Eventually all the North end crofts on the low gound near the sea were deserted, with the last inhabitants being old Jimmy Umphray of Risti and Katie's brother Peter who stayed on until the inland croft of Loch became vacant. At that point Blowburn, just on the south-facing side of the Heights of Skiordar, then became the most northerly inhabited croft on Foula, just out of reach of the damaging salt spray.

The ruins of those old crofthouses at the North end, the relics of the original fishing community and the failed crofts that followed, are a fascinating record of a revolution in house-building techniques which was to affect the whole community. As late as the 19th century there were no proper masonry tools such as hammers and cold chisels to fashion the native stone, so that houses had to be built out of what was available. As a result walls tended to be very thick with all the most awkward shapes used in the middle, and manageable stones with flat faces kept for the outside. Timber was very scarce, most of it driftwood, about which there was a deep-seated tradition that floating timber belonged to the first man who spotted and thus claimed it. There were tales of men watching over a specially valuable floating prize day and night to be the accepted claimant when it finally came ashore. Cheating on this agreed tradition was taboo. Several times I asked about what looked to me like very valuable baulks of timber, some very large indeed, lying apparently rotting near the shoreline or somewhere on the rocks, only to be told that it was so-and-so's timber but he had not yet managed, sometimes years later, to organize getting it to the saw-pit. Although it was often held against the claimant that the value of the timber had thus been eroded and its use to the community therefore lost, the right of the claimant was never disputed – merely regretted. It was true that such inefficiency seemed endemic to some families, unthinkable in others, but it could be said in general to be a peculiarity of Foula's social etiquette.

The first result of the chronic shortage of timber, especially long lengths of good quality wood, was that the narrow roof span meant a narrow house; and doorways were often low, even as low as four feet i.e., cattle height rather than human height. Roofs had traditionally been thatched with oat or barley straw, the pitch of the slope shallow and virtually no overhang at the eaves. Later overlapping strips of roofing felt were used when this became available, as quicker and easier both to make and maintain. The strips were nailed down at all edges and also in lines down the centre of the roof, the nails being applied through tarred twine which prevented them from tearing the felt. This system had prevailed up to the present day, as also the method of securing the whole roof from the lifting force of severe gales. Close to where the roof timbers were supported by the raised inner edge of the wall-head, a loop of galvanized wire was attached to the wood at the top and at the bottom to a wooden peg inserted deep between the stones further down the wall. A twist was made in this loop so that it could be tightened by further twisting to shorten its length and take up any slack. The whole roof was thereby held tightly bound down to the solid house wall. The main consideration therefore when planning to build a new house, which normally meant downgrading the old house to become a byre for the animals, was whether to make one of the long walls common to both house and byre. When labour was scarce and the desire strong to improve the living standards for the family, the temptation to avoid building one complete stone wall containing many tons of stonework usually prevailed, especially when the new house could benefit from the wind protection offered to it by the old house on the windward side. So a new wall only one stone's width, usually about one foot in all, would be built alongside the old outer wall of what was

to become the byre. This of course meant two parallel roofs sloping downwards to a common wall, creating a gently sloping channel to carry away the run-off of rain from both slopes. This seldom worked well for long and most houses built alongside the byre were troubled with 'wall water', a problem of damp along the common wall. Some attempts were made to avoid this by concreting the wall head to make a waterproof drainage channel but this seldom worked in practice. Peter quoted the example of the 'auld hoos' at Broadfoot where Lisa Robertson lived, where he remembered the wallpaper along the wall next to the byre hanging down with an air-space between the paper and the stone wall and yet still being constantly damp. Another problem was if the new house was lower down a slope than the byre, in order to take advantage of the shelter offered, then the drains from the byre had to run under the floor of the new house, which was often 'not sanitary'. He quoted the ruins of Steol as demonstrating this problem, with the old drains still visible under what was left of the old floor of the house. On some crofts the need to save both labour and materials in house-building had resulted in three parallel structures, a barn for storage, a byre for the animals, especially cattle, and, furthest from the prevailing wind, the family home. One result of this was a completely windowless byre in the middle, lit and ventilated only by the small doors in the gable ends, which was not ideal for the health of the cattle in a long, dark winter.

When the time came to decide on a new house at Blowburn, Peter and his brother at first thought to build the new house onto the end of the 'auld hoos'; but then because of the problem of damp, decided to break with tradition and build a completely separate house with all walls new. They recruited James Andrew Gray of Dykes to help ("*if there's one thing James Andrew can do, it's build a roof*") first to build a new roof on the 'auld hoos', which was to become the barn, and then to be responsible for the roof of the new house. The decision in favour of a separate building was enabled by two factors. There was enough timber available for the wider roof, much of it from driftwood. There is no doubt that world wars with many cargo ships lost at sea, when timber was increasingly being traded, benefitted islands with shorelines at the receiving end of the prevalent transatlantic south west winds. Even when I was in Foula the old saw-pit, close by the beach at Ham Voe, was in working order and occasionally used, especially when a death suddenly precipitated the need for some wood for making a coffin. One man stood astride the narrow walls above while his workmate guided the long, heavy cross-cut saw from below. The work looked arduous but the skill was for the upper man simply to lift the saw so that the next cut could be made using the weight of the saw itself to do most of the work. The work called for fitness and reasonable stamina rather than any unusual strength. It must however have been a long slow job making the floorboards for a whole house.

The other factor which influenced their decision was the skill of John Ratter, originally of Friars, the croft nearest the old boat harbour at Whiora Wick. His father, Andrew Ratter, was the brother of Magnus Ratter, who built the crofthouse at Logat and fathered six children, amongst whom were some of the islanders of the older generation I had the privilege of knowing in the 1950s, like Jimmy of Broadfoot, my senior elder of the Kirk, and of course Peter Manson's wife Katie. Two of the North end ruins, Logat and Springs, show evidence to this day of the highly skilled masons' work of the Ratter family, with beautifully shaped stone-work at the gables and round windows and doors. So the Mansons recruited John Ratter to fashion the corner stones for the gable ends of their new house at Blowburn, as well as lintels and sills for the windows. All the stone had to be carried

The finely crafted stonework of the gable end of the abandoned croft of Springs at Wurrwick

or barrowed to the site and the job took a full two years to complete. Round the windows their technique was to cut alternate courses of stone down the side of each window, the full thickness of the wall, with the intervening courses forming part of the facing pattern for the long outside wall. The lintel, cut to the full width of the window, rested at each end on one of the larger stones forming part of the long wall of the house. All this, fashioned to an exact size for the wooden frame surrounding the window, called for far more precise stone-work, chiselled out with the new steel tools by hand, than had ever been possible in the older style of 'black house' of previous generations. Incidentally, but emphasizing the close interconnections by marriage between the few island families, John the stonemason's sister Annie married into the Isbister family and was the mother of Bob Isbister, the shopman during my stay on Foula. As evidence of the new era of house-building to these higher standards at the turn of the 20th century, Annie's husband Robert Isbister built the croft at South Biggins which is still the home of Eric Isbister, my former pupil at the school. Meanwhile Magnus Ratter of Logat, her uncle, moved when his croft became unmanageable because of climate change, to Bankwell, also in the Hametoun at the extreme south end of the island, and his eldest son Walter then married Meggie Isbister of South Biggins, cementing the close bonds between these two families. Walter then built the new house at Punds, which as I have described above lasted Meggie's elder sister Jeannie until her 100th birthday, and is now the home of Frances, one of Iain Holbourn's grand-daughters.

Living in the house your father or grandfather built with his own hands must be the strongest incentive to keep it in good order, to pass on to your own children and grand-children. Likewise crofts well spaced out, with enough room and tillage to keep cattle and poultry, is not just a better basis for continuing with the sort of subsistence crofting a few of our community on Foula were still able to manage, but also does a lot more to create a sense of belonging and of ownership. Holbourn makes great play in his book 'The Isle of Foula' of his fascination with the policy of 'udal' tenure and the benevolent status it gave him as laird, still technically owning the land but giving the crofter who paid him rent more freedom to manage his croft as he liked. The law and the Crofters' Commission have taken over since then and given the crofter much greater security, and rights upheld by the Land Court. In the 1950s the old system, which at one time had enabled a self-supporting

population of over 200 people to survive, was running down, faced by the reduction in numbers and the increase in average age. The ability of the islanders to build themselves better houses enabled the old system of sustainable living, largely dependent on their own produce for food and fuel, to keep up with rapidly changing standards in the outside world. At the same time the sudden increase in communications, which was only just starting in 1954 with the advent of the telephone, a more regular postal service, and battery powered radios in nearly every house, all this meant that many of the conversations we had during my first long, dark winter were with people surprisingly up to date with current affairs in a world that seemed so far removed from their simple life-style. And though most of them had very little, if any, experience of city life, they could hold a city-dweller like me entranced with their knowledge of the seasons and the weather, the management and problems of keeping sheep, working peat, growing food on a gale-swept island, and the genealogy of all the island families sometimes back several generations. One subject tended to crop up more often than most. Was there a future for a dwindling population on Foula and how could the decline be halted?

Undoubtedly the greatest single factor in the decline had been education. The industrial and then the technological revolutions may have brought better communications and mechanical aids, both in the house and on the land, but these were slow to reach the outer fringe of human living and were more and more dependent on education as the means of taking advantage of what society offered. So the children had to go out to Lerwick from the age of twelve to continue past the three 'R's, if they were to succeed in life. This entailed staying in the Lerwick Hostel, run by the Education authority entirely for children from the remoter parts of the mainland or the islands. This was home for all of them during the week, but the island children were often constrained either by the cost or the weather to stay for weeks or even months on end as boarders. All that time they grew quickly accustomed to a new standard of living, with electricity and modern conveniences which made the Foula winter seem a poor alternative life-style. Some Foula children from the traditional families were quite capable of progressing to University education as Andy, the eldest son of the Gear family, proved; but that meant going south to Aberdeen. Of my five on the school roll, only the two Beagries were recent incomers. It is always a hard decision for parents, without a very strong attachment to an island home, having to face the disruption of their children as young as twelve spending long periods living in a hostel. Most island children could at least reach home some weekends, but this was seldom practicable for Foula bairns who often went back to school in late August and never 'won home' again till Christmas. This topic was often discussed on winter evenings as part of the never-ending debate on the future of the island, and there was much genuine sympathy for both parents and children at the dilemma they faced. As the older folk often stressed, in their young days the island school had been adequate for the demands of crofting as a way of life, but now Secondary education was only the essential beginning of the blossoming of young minds to cope with a totally different world out there. Eric Isbister was the only one of my pupils who, for his own particular reasons of his vulnerability to infection, never went out to Lerwick but completed his education entirely at Foula Primary School. It is a great credit to his parents, to his various teachers and to Eric himself that he turned out at the end as articulate and self-contained as he did, with as many musical, artistic, literary and intellectual interests and skills as other more privileged pupils on the Shetland mainland.

My first winter in 1954/55 had been unusual for me in so many ways. It had given me a chance to visit all the crofts when the inmates would be certain to be at home and often quite glad to take a break and talk the evening through. Though I was supposed to be the teacher, I was certainly the one with the steep learning curve. In spite of the long hours of darkness I still found it hard to find any time for my own indoor pursuits or paperwork, apart from those that applied to preparation for my immediate jobs in school or church. Also I felt that it was an important part of my job to get out and meet people who became more and more interesting and rewarding as I got to know them better. Once a week through the winter months it was traditional to hold a meeting in the schoolroom to sing hymns, making a nice blend of my two jobs. Most of the women who normally came to church usually made the effort unless the weather was too difficult. They liked best the rather boisterous and rousing hymns in the Moody & Sankey book of Hymns and Choruses, which they sang with gusto and real enjoyment. Mary Henry, our school cook, would always make it an excuse to bake and others would often bring a contribution. So there would be a break for tea and a chance to catch up with all the island gossip, surely as good a tonic for the winter blues as the hearty singing.

One interlude which often took place in the tea-break could surely only have happened in a place like Foula. There were field mice everywhere in Foula and in autumn they would tend to invade houses as food outside became scarcer and daylight shorter. There was a crack in the schoolroom skirting well known to the children – and the cook. Sooner or later the nose of a mouse would appear and someone would fetch a plate, put some crumbs on it and tempt the hungry intruder out. It was so incredibly tame that they demonstrated to me the first time it happened by picking up the plate, complete with mouse, and bringing it across the room to show me. Naturally the next time I brought my camera and was even able to catch on film a shot of this little bit of Foula's winter entertainment. There was no end to the surprises of Foula's night-life. Where else would you find a 'wee timorous beastie', normally scared out of its wits by the mere sound of a human being, interpreting 'Rock of ages, cleft for me' sung with gusto at the top of a dozen strident voices, as an invitation to crumbs for the taking?

I couldn't better it as an example of 'the survival of the fittest' and 'natural selection' that this complex descendant of the species *Apodemus sylvaticus* had adapted to its environment so thoroughly as to join in our tea party without a sign of trepidation. This wasn't nature producing another 'miracle of the commonplace'. A miracle being by definition something that makes us marvel, this was a double miracle. The 'wee moose' with the long tail was a marvel in itself, but it was its un-natural behaviour that really amazed, and flattered, us.

In fact the scientific credentials of the Foula field mouse are fascinating in themselves. David Wilson, Foula historian extraordinary, has unearthed for me an article in 'The Scotsman' dated 21st January 1929, by Professor J. Arthur Thomson in which he puts forward the apparently conclusive theory, based on incontrovertible taxonomic evidence, that the Foula variety matches most closely not the mainland type, which is probably the commonest small mammal in Europe, but the field mouse found on Fair Isle. He, mistakenly in my view, gave this the binomial nomenclature of a full species, as *Apodemus fridariensis*. Nowadays this would be given the trinomial (genus, species and sub-species) as *Apodemus sylvaticus fridariensis*, namely the race or variety of the European field mouse found only on Fair Isle. According to his method however the Professor gave the Foula mouse the label *Apodemus fridariensis thuleo* as its scientific trinomial – in other words he calls it the Foula variety of the Fair Isle mouse! The much more likely explanation is that both are island races of the mainland species, which have evolved, by parallel subjection to very similar natural pressures, to reach a stage where both can be given separate sub-specific status as island races. To qualify each must display features that are recognizably distinctive, based on a statistically significant number of specimens, which may take a long time to establish. He based his identification on the size of the hind feet with a white dorsal surface and small pads, apparently common to all the distinctive Fair Isle variety.

How it all started still has to be explained however. Professor Thomson's theory for the Fair Isle mice is that somehow, possibly as stowaways on a 'fishing smack', at least one pair of common mainland field mice reached Fair Isle where, in isolation from all others, they bred for many generations and gradually developed their own specific characteristics. Thus, strictly in accordance with Darwinian theory, he believed a new species was formed. In his view the same thing is now happening on Foula, namely that a new species is in the process of formation, field mice having arrived there either by chance on some vessel or perhaps by deliberate introduction. This certainly seems the most likely series of events, the original progenitor, the mainland species, being so commonly found throughout Europe. Where

he went wrong however, was his conclusion, based on the coincidence of their distinctive subspecific features, that the Foula race was derived from the Fair Isle race. This now seems almost impossible to believe, namely that somehow at least one pair of mice somehow travelled from Fair Isle to Foula. The most fascinating part of his theory is the speed (in terms of evolutionary development) with which the new species he claimed might be born. And yet if we consider the Galapagos Islands, where Darwin first found such conclusive evidence of the formation of new species in the conditions of isolation provided by small islands, there is no reason why Foula should not also provide just those same conditions, with no rivals and no competition for their chosen ecological niche, for a new subspecies at least, *Apodemus sylvaticus thuleo*, to be steadily stabilizing its unique characteristics before our very eyes. The difference between 1929 and now is that no taxonomists would now accord full specific status to an island 'race', the result of contemporaneous parallel evolution on an isolated island. But to me, our own special sub-species was quite enough to be worth skinning a few for the Royal Scottish Museum, who were only too pleased to increase their very limited collection.

Apodemus sylvaticus thulensis, *a species in the making, enjoys our tea-break in the school*

Here was yet another example of an activity I could, with a bit of juggling, just fit into my winter timetable but which would have been impossible to find time for in summer. As a beginner I found taxidermy very time-consuming, and I have no doubt the skins I sent in were about the worst they had ever received from a field naturalist. But it was fascinating work. I felt privileged to have my finger on the pulse of evolution. The specialised richness and rarity of Foula's fauna was a reward for the naturalist almost as exciting and memorable as the couthy but cheeky character of our schoolroom 'moosie'. *A.s. thuleo* – take a bow.

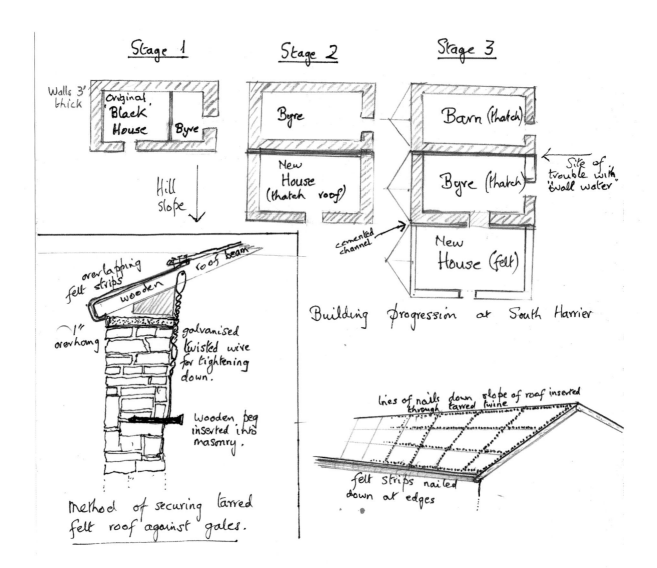

Plan of buildings with cross section of roof

Chapter 21: From Spring to Summer; Water-mills

For crofters winter was the time to fill the long dark hours with as much meaningful activity as possible. Midsummer was the time when the demands of outdoor work on a croft were never ending, with animals to care for and so many jobs to be done without the aid of machines. I could for instance be walking home from Blowburn at the North end at ten or eleven o'clock at night, and see Scottie Umphray still working on his coles of hay or sheaves of barley. I knew what he would be thinking. An extra hour then might ensure they were protected from an expectation of rain which might set back the job of drying the crop by another two or three days – or perhaps even weeks. So in summer the active crofter might be working sixteen or more hours a day, and sleeping perhaps only five or six of the twenty-four, simply to ensure a food supply for his family and his animals. A wet summer could threaten their survival when the peat cycle competed with the demands of agriculture, however long the daylight. Good drying time could completely dominate life with the pressure of so many jobs that could only be done at all under those conditions. However long the daylight, it was often not enough. And even crofters had to sleep some of the time.

No wonder that a system of special days with special names had evolved and become an almost obligatory time-table in order to advance through the season of growth to harvest, without missing out on any of the vital processes of subsistence crofting. For instance April 26th was reckoned by some to be the first day of summer, or Simmermill, the time when the puffins ('Nories') started nesting, disappearing underground into their burrows, and the Arctic skuas ('Alans') were first heard setting up their territories with much caterwauling over the lower moorland areas. Some folk would start on the outdoor jobs before that, in the Bogel Days, when a major change would take place by driving the sheep outside the Toun dyke and shutting the 'grind'. This gate had kept the sheep inside all winter so that they were within reach of help in severe weather like the deep snow we had had in January/February 1955. Before Simmermill some jobs could be started like planting up the first cabbage seedlings in the stone circles called Planticrubs, which were found clustered round all crofting areas. Soon after, the back-breaking tasks of sowing either corn or potatoes by hand had to be tackled, for which there was much preparatory work to be done with the Shetland spade. This was an efficient weapon for the job, with a wooden step low on the long straight handle, so that the foot could bear the brunt of the 'delling'. Leg power was essential to dig into ground hardened by a year's rain and sun since it was last turned over. There was seldom a shortage of good manure for spreading out first, by

Planticrubs beside the Ham Burn

Hand-sown oats ripening at the croft of Burns

'muckin oot da midden' and the byre where the cows had spent so much of the last few months. From the 'first week of simmer' at the start of May, the weeks were all either numbered or remembered by natural events like the nest-building activities of the Kittiwakes or the Bonxies starting laying (which of course meant a glut of fresh eggs for a while) or the weather became settled enough to risk getting the boats down on the water for the first time – with the promise of some fresh fish for the larder. There's nothing like a fresh mackerel after a winter of dried or smoked ones.

Winter had been so utterly different. Such short days and still so much to be done. After all winter weather is the testing time for storm damage, for the maintenance of house and croft against rain and wind, for keeping up the supply of peat, bringing in sheep off the hill, repairing boats and wheelbarrows. In the old days there were so many essential jobs, like making clothes; spinning, weaving and knitting; preserving food, like fish or mutton, by smoking or salting – anything in fact which had been put off in the summer by the sheer pressure of

time, especially fine-weather time. All the summer work was laborious and time-consuming; sowing by hand, (or foot when delling with the Shetland spade), reaping with the scythe, digging peat with the tuskar, a heavy demanding routine which subsistence crofting imposed if one was to survive the next winter. Early in that first spring I watched Peter Gray one day in the small rigs round his house at Burns, sowing a field of oats, a staple crop for both human and animal consumption. It was just like the romantic coloured picture in my children's illustrated Bible of the parable of the sower. He walked in marked lines up and down the length of the rig, with a sling round his neck containing the seed from last year's crop. As he progressed with a measured pace, first his right hand and then his left would pick up a handful of grain and with the skill of long, long practice, throw it evenly over the ground in front of him, which over a period of weeks he had slowly but steadily tilled from last year's stubble to this year's seed-bed. To reduce the newly turned clods of earth to a finer tilth, I had, a week or so before, seen him hauling his home-made harrow over the dug ground by a rope over his shoulder. It consisted of a heavy wooden frame, inevitably made from rescued driftwood, nailed into a square, from the underside of which rows of wooden pegs bristled as his only means of breaking up the clods. It had to be solid enough to survive the rough treatment it was getting, but also light enough for one man to be able to pull it without getting utterly exhausted. It was no easy task and Peter was, to put it politely, a portly man, and no youngster. A couple of months later there was an evenly prolific crop of oats growing there, which any man would be proud to have produced solely by his own hard labour.

At the time I arrived on Foula there was one motorised two-wheeled tractor, which the ploughman walked behind, holding two long handles for control. This was owned by Harry of Mogle and operated mostly by Kenneth Gear, who was the strongest young man on the island and constantly in demand at seed-time. Of course one man could not be expected to plough up all the croft-land, though Ken seemed to take a pride in how many

rigs he tackled. But weather, or sometimes 'the cold', took their toll of the available time so that inevitably some crofters like Peter Gray had to rely on their own strength and not the tractor's horse-power to achieve their annual harvest. Of course old-age pensioners, who at that time were paid only ten shillings a week, might just be able to afford a bag of oatmeal from Bobby Isbister's shop. Yet many of them either had no croft land or no animals, and were not fit to do such heavy work anyway. If they only had themselves to feed they could perhaps manage, but there is no doubt it was a struggle; and the worst shortage was not money but labour.

For the first time in my life I was learning real lessons about true values, simply from such observations of my neighbours. Look for instance at the huge intrinsic value, in terms of time and labour, that was invested in such items as a single sack of oatmeal. Porridge was probably a highly significant proportion of many a crofter's basic diet all the year round, especially in winter. In our recent winter it was a real crisis when oatmeal ran out at the

Peter and Muriel Gray in the garden at Burns

The croft of Burns, the house built in 1912, by the road to the North end crofts

shop when the mailboat failed to achieve a crossing for so long after Christmas. But when at last I was able to buy a bag of oatmeal, costing in my case such a tiny proportion of my daily wage as a teacher, and put it in my wheel barrow to walk home up the hill past the nurse's house to the Manse, I remember pondering for those fifteen minutes the investment of so many man-hours of hard labour that the crofters on Foula used to have to make to achieve a bag of meal, when there was no shop. There was then no viable means of supplying such goods when a sixern with a sail was the only contact with the mainland. I had arrived on Foula at a stage when the shop was viable, but only just. With a population of only seventy people, a few hours a day on three days a week was all that was needed to make a very limited stock of goods available for sale. Besides, there was very limited spending money on the island with so few jobs and virtually no tourists to swell the turnover. For crofters like Peter Gray it was still worth the effort to make proper use of his land to grow at least potatoes and cabbage for his own use and oats to feed his hens and his cows. This meant that he had no need for cash to buy eggs, milk, butter or cheese so long as he and his wife Muriel were fit enough to produce their own. So a vital part of their needs for proteins, vitamins and calories was satisfied by their own labour. If he could also go fishing, either with his own boat or in a neighbour's, their balanced diet was complete. Weather permitting a fit crofter could feed well.

One key factor in this equation was the facility to mill the grain in order to produce those staples of all human diets, flour for bread or meal for porridge, oatcakes

or barley bannocks. At one time 'bere' bannocks were what all the pupils were expected to bring to school for their mid-day meal. Moreover a griddle was all that was needed to bake over an open peat fire. South Harrier had a mill with Scottie's home-made waterwheel but I wasn't aware of him using it to grind his grain for meal or flour, though I had seen his old grain mill with its quernstones in situ as I headed up the hill after Bonxies one day. I also took the opportunity later in the summer of 1955 to examine the old horizontal water-mills down by the shore at Hesti Geo, in the Hametoun, where several old boats lay. This was the only spot where the rocky shore allowed a small boat to be launched for fishing. The burn, which rose in the Daal and ran through the Hametoun between South Biggins, where the Isbisters lived, and the other crofthouses like Broadfoot, Breckans, Dykes, and Quinister, had just enough of a regular flow to make building water-powered mills feasible. The Second Edition of the Ordnance Survey 6″ map, dated 1902, shows five mills between the Mill Pond in the Daal and the sea.

If you follow the Daal Burn down past Steol (now ruined), there is a mill where it makes a short detour round 'Whirly Knowe', a rather mysterious knoll marked on some maps as 'Burnt Mound'. (I photographed this mill in quite good repair in the 1950s.) The stream, leaving South Biggins and the old Kirk on the right, then heads south-east over flat, reedy ground with no possibility of enough of a fall to produce any water-power, until it drops down to the shore at Hesti Geo, marked euphemistically on that map as 'Boat Harbour'. Here there were always the sad remains of some old boats, mere skeletons, but also one or two home-made boats lying in the 'noosts' which the islanders always built to protect their precious fishing boats over the winter. Noosts are simply boat-shaped hollows, open at the sea end, into which the boats were hauled and then tied down with ropes or cables lashed onto huge boulders to secure them against the winter gales. Below the noosts is just a suggestion of a landing place, a boulder beach of large stones. (The only proper sandy beach on the island is the seasonal beach at the head of Ham Voe which can disappear after a south-east gale, washed out into the deeper water until the steady action of calmer tides gradually washes the sand back again.) Here, just up the burn from the south landing place, there was enough 'head' of water to allow for two mills, one of which had survived remarkably intact. This water-mill is marked on the 1902 6″ Ordnance Survey map but was probably very much older than that. I remember as if it was yesterday the thrill I felt when I stooped down to discover a complete vertical tirl at the outflow and an almost perfect grain mill floor above.

It was a stone building, quite small and straddling the stream, with the roof intact and the walls sound and solid. My biggest surprise was the complete wooden grinding floor, with both upper and lower millstones in position, and looking almost as though ready for immediate use. It was all on a very small scale but beautifully built, although the wood-lined channel which guided the water from a small dam down into an opening, complete with stone lintel, in the wall of the mill, was in a poor state of repair and no longer serviceable for conducting water to the 'tirl'. It clearly hadn't been used for many years

and the wooden conduit, like a square box-shaped tube, was badly decayed. Luckily I knew what I was looking for from my acquaintance with Kenneth Williamson, who had been so helpful to me with information about migration and Bird Observatory work. He had made quite a name for himself in setting up the highly successful Observatory on Fair Isle. In 1948 Collins had published his book on the Faroes under the title 'Atlantic Islands', one of those books which had a major influence on my thinking about islands and the way of life of those who live on them, a book which could be said to be a model of its kind – authoritative, thoroughly researched, informative and spell-binding. Kenneth had lived in the Faroes as part of his wartime service in the R.A.F. and had married a Faroese wife, Esther. As a scientist he had made even better use of his time there than just acquiring a wife, by writing the definitive book on her homeland. 'Atlantic Islands' was typical of his enquiring mind and systematic approach to life. He had made a special study of Faroese horizontal water-mills and here was one almost exactly the same as those he described so vividly in the book. His excellent line drawings showing the working of the Faroese mills had intrigued me when I read the book in one of my school holidays from John Watson's. When I looked up my copy in the Manse, there on page 218 was an almost exact representation of the Foula mill in his drawing of his favourite horizontal water-mill in all the Faroes at Nidri a' Bo in Sudurøy.

What I also liked was his assessment of the value of this remarkable invention: "*The water-mill with the horizontal wheel is the most primitive power-mill in the world, and although much has been written about it, its*

The cornmill by the boat landing at Bankwell in the Hame Toun in 1954, with the remains of the wooden sluice which directed the flow of water onto the paddles of the tirl

*The grinding floor of the Bankwell Mill, as shown in full working order in the film 'The Edge of the World'
in 1936, still largely intact in 1954, with the wedges for the lightening tree for grinding coarse or fine meal,
still on the ledge to the left of the millstone, 1954*

origin, and the route or routes by which it came to North-West Europe, remain wrapped in the mists of antiquity. The genius who first conceived the idea of harnessing a stream to drive the rotary quern must be reckoned one of the greatest of forgotten human benefactors, for the emancipation from drudgery which followed its discovery was immense." He quotes the historian Strabo who records such a 'water-grinder' in King Mithridates' city of Pontus a hundred years B.C.; a city which was conquered by Pompey in 65 B.C., from which date the invention spread to Italy, Spain and France. The Vikings must have played some part in the spread north as they are found all over Norway and Sweden and in all the areas of the Norse occupation of the north-west of Britain. In 1814 Sir Walter Scott reckoned there were 500 mills in Shetland, Orkney and south through the Hebrides to the Isle of Man. I wondered how many there were left still in as good condition as this one below the old Kirk on Foula. Kenneth Williamson clearly valued highly the ones he found in the Faroes, but felt sure

they were all comparatively recent and so had also been introduced from Norway in their travel across Europe. As in Shetland they had replaced the old hand-querns which must have been such hard work and on a much smaller scale. H.B. Curwen published his 'Photographs of a Visit to Foula' in 1900, and Holbourn used some of his photographs in his book 'The Isle of Foula' (1938). He titles one picture of a horizontal water-mill 'The mill at Ham' but the background of hill slopes looks more like the Daal. Another built over a very reedy burn also has a steep hill in the background and is probably correctly identified as belonging to 'Steol croft'. There is a close-up photo of a tirl taken from below the outflow, which is very similar to the mill at Hesti Geo. But careful comparison of the stonework shows it is not the same building, so it is not clear which of the five mills they selected for a close-up of the horizontal waterwheel.

But there are also several pictures of hand querns in use, and one more detailed picture of a hand-quern with a lightening tree *"raised or lowered by turning"*, though

I fail to see how this could work. Maybe the inference is that the power-mill was a fairly recent introduction to Foula at the end of the 19th century; or it may be that as the water-mills were often owned by a small consortium of crofts, there were some crofts which still had no access to one or just preferred to stick to the old style. And there was only one water-powered mill shown outside the Hametoun, at South Harrier, the site of the only suitable stream. The rest of the crofters in the north of the isle had no choice, as there was no hydro power available, a sad loss.

Most waterwheels derive their power from the weight and speed of water dropping vertically onto the blades so that some sort of gearing is then required if heavy millstones are to be turned horizontally to grind the corn. For smaller mills, usually turning only one pair of stones, it had proved handier for the force of the water to be directed against horizontal wooden blades set into a vertical shaft, which then powered the stone without any need for gearing. On Foula some of the mills had these blades slightly slanted in order to maximize the force of a dropping flow of water. This called for skilled and accurate carpentry as these blades took the brunt of the force required to overcome the inertia of one very heavy stone against another. The vertical spindle, into which these horizontal wooden blades were slotted, was a solid wooden post, banded with metal top and bottom, and riding on an iron pin inserted into its base. The top of the post had an iron T-piece embedded into the upper mill-stone which was turned by the force of the water. The nether stone was bedded down onto the wooden floor with the post revolving in a hole carved in the middle. All this seemed to be more or less intact in the mill I was exploring down by the South Landing so that my first reaction was that here was a relic very well worth preserving as part of the island's history.

Best of all was that the 'lightening tree' was still intact and in place. This was a comparatively slender length of wood, resting on the cross-beam on which the base of the tirl rested, with a horizontal arm capable of levering up the base of the turning pole so as to lift it very slightly from its downward pressure on the lower grindstone. In this way, exerting upward pressure on the top of the lightening tree could alter the pressure which the grain

The tirl complete with horizontal paddles and the lightening tree in the foreground, 1954

was subjected to and so alter the coarseness of the meal. This was done by means of small wedges, several of which were in a neat pile on the wooden beam to the left of the grinding floor, ready to be inserted according to the needs of the miller, who thus had control of whether he was grinding coarse meal or finer flour.

In the Faroes the custom had been for a mill to belong to an owner but to be available free for others who wished to make use of it. I see no reason why such a system should not also have operated on Foula, where co-operation in most crofting activities seemed the order of the day. To me one of the most fascinating facts in Kenneth Williamson's account of the Faroese water-mills was that one of them was found on the island of Fugløy, meaning 'bird island', the exact counterpart in name of our island of Foula, and no doubt similarly named as a sanctuary for a significant population of seabirds. Horizontal water-mills of this type seem to have reached Shetland via Norway so that it seems more likely that the mills on Foula and a very similar one on Fair Isle, which I have also been lucky enough to examine, were based on a Norse design which was later copied in the Faroes. One quite unimportant fact appears in that the Faroese mills seem all to have turned anti-clockwise as part of the design, whereas at least one on Foula clearly turned clockwise by choice. Perhaps the miller, or at least the designer of the mill, was left-handed?

By April 1955 I had been on Foula one calendar year and in the course of my daily routine I was beginning to get a fair idea of how their subsistence method of crofting worked, as well as some fascinating glimpses into their past methods, which were just crying out to be examined and recorded. My second season of migration watching now involved much more detailed recording with such systems as bird-ringing with my Heligoland trap at Ham, and almost daily observation of the best patches of cover where small migrants could usually be found if the weather was right. So I was busier than ever both with field-work and paper-work in my efforts to keep some sort of semblance of an offshoot of the Fair Isle Bird Observatory going. School, church and library kept me busy enough on the professional front, which earned me my living. Now that I knew everybody much better and so had become familiar with individual needs and problems, there was also an increasing demand on my time both for spiritual and where possible practical help in liaison with the nurse, or any of the able-bodied few who were so frequently called upon for their services. There were also areas where new initiatives were clearly called for to try to improve in basic ways the services of

others outside our tiny community to help overcome the stress of overwork caused by the imbalance in the age structure of Foula's population. One of the first opportunities which came my way was an offer of help from a 'cottage industry' in the Highlands which had produced a comparatively cheap, small-scale tractor called the Croftmaster, specifically designed to suit both the pockets and the requirements of crofters in remote areas. I can't remember now how I heard about this venture, probably from discussion of crofters' problems at the annual Lay Missionaries Conference in Lerwick; but I do remember getting an immediate and generous reply from the entrepreneur who was running the firm. Surprisingly the reaction of most of the Foula families was sceptical, probably from a long history of animosity against the Shetland Island Council for what seemed like studied neglect of Foula's most pressing needs. There was undoubtedly, as indeed had been recorded by Holbourn in his book, a sad past history of exploitation of the islanders, who were dependent on fair treatment over shipment of sheep and cattle on boats provided by the dealers. They were in a position of power which often resulted in under-payment for stock which the dealers knew the crofters could not afford to ship back again if the market price offered was below the norm. Rumours were also rife on the island over the stated views of individual councillors that it would be far cheaper to re-house the whole population of Foula on the mainland than to subsidize their transport and housing needs on the island. There was a distinct attitude of victimization, coupled with a stoic determination to carry on the struggle to preserve their island home at all costs. So I wasn't altogether surprised that it was my immediate neighbours, the Beagries, who gladly took up the offer of the tractor. I had to admit when it arrived, complete with two-wheeled trailer, it was smaller and much slower on the road than we had anticipated, and looked almost like a Meccano toy with an engine, and sounded more like a motor-mower than a proper tractor. But for a long time it was the only four-wheeled vehicle on our roads and brought back at least half a dozen barrow-loads of peat on one journey from the peat banks, albeit at not much more than walking pace. To that extent I personally benefited though I still kept up my peat barrowing routine so as not to encroach on the Beagries' use of the Croftmaster for genuine croft work like ploughing and harrowing. And when I remembered all the letters I had written to clinch the deal, the time I had spent probably outweighed the time I saved. Island scribe seemed to be yet another duty of the Teacher-Missionary, which I usually tackled on wet, windy weekends.

Coming out of winter into the promise of spring was an inspiring experience, which I remember now especially vividly in just a few details. When leaving the house to pick up my wheelbarrow outside the back door one morning, I was amazed to see daffodil shoots appearing, long before I expected them, simply because they were planted along the foot of the south-facing gable end, where they were not only sheltered from the colder winds but had benefited from the extra warmth the stonework picked up from the spring sunshine. My vegetable patch was on the N.E. side of the house; good enough soil but just that bit colder so that not even the weeds were showing any signs of spring life even in April. During the blank days of winter I had discontinued my daily schedule of bird species, but by mid-March I was always on the look-out for any migrants arriving or seabirds returning to their nesting grounds. At first I had to be content merely that the snow had gone, as I relished milder air and softer winds, pushing my barrow along the road above the Mill Loch on my way to school in the morning. But then on the 20th March I was jerked into action once more with my daily routine of checking my species list, with the joyful return of the 'shalders'. I had recorded the last oystercatcher of the autumn on the 21st October, and then suddenly here they were back on the rigs of the Ham Toun, transforming the barren flats on either side of the road down to the pier into a battleground of gaudy displays and noisy piping parties. It was a welcome contrast to the drabness of land which had for so long been under a foot or more of snow. I was even moved to write a poem about it which must have captured something of my elation at the time as it was published in the 'New Shetlander' later that summer. The sighting of the first Bonxie over the breeding grounds, and then the Arctic skuas a few weeks later, heralded by the faithful 'Alan' sitting one day in May on the chimney pot of Leraback, set the scene for the long days of aerial battles and territorial disputes between the two species of skuas, which would create the background sound effects to weekend peat-cutting in early summer. It was a wonderful and very musical way to usher in the spring.

There was a break in my routine, and in my bird records, from the 27th March for three weeks when I took my first opportunity to go home to Edinburgh while the school holidays allowed. I was able to leave Norie at the Schoolhouse where I knew he would be well looked after, though I couldn't guarantee he wouldn't be spoiled by the children, with whom he was by now a firm favourite. As time was precious I had decided to fly, and as planes were few and far between in those days, it was not possible to get from Walls to Lerwick, and then Lerwick to Sumburgh by bus in time to fly out on the same day as I had crossed on the mailboat. So I had to spend the night in the Queen's Hotel in Lerwick, right on the harbour wall, and flew south to Edinburgh the next day.

My holiday was all a rather surreal experience. Everything was different. And yet at the same time everything was the same as before – except that the pace of life and my intake of sights and sounds and the throng of human contacts now scarcely seemed to allow me time to think or make decisions. Theoretically I had time to relax for a while from the hectic pressure of island life, and yet I still seemed to be overwhelmed by the futility of so much business. Although the gap since my last experience of 'normal' city life was comparatively short, I was able to understand the story the Holbourns had told me about one of the Gray sisters, from Dykes I think, who had been in hospital in Lerwick but for medical reasons had to be moved to Aberdeen to receive the right treatment. There the hospital was surrounded by trees quite close to the buildings and she was on the ground floor. She became at once noticeably worse and seemed unable to respond to her treatment, until an observant nurse detected what was wrong – she was terrified that the trees were going to fall on her. As soon as she was transferred back to the Gilbert Bain hospital in Lerwick she was on the mend, but in no way was she happy until she had got back to the world she knew of far horizons and open spaces on her beloved Foula. I too found myself thinking of Foula as home in a new way, as the place where I really belonged, where I could relax better and enjoy the company of friends with whom one shared so much common ground. What had I in common with shoppers and cinema-goers in Edinburgh's New Town, with the rush-hour hordes sitting mute in crowded trains isolated from their fellow travellers by a need to preserve their sanity by building barriers? I found that I too was resisting the effort to communicate with such an overwhelming number of potential contacts. On Foula we pined for company and felt an immediate bond with others who also loved our landscape, so limited, almost featureless, and yet so open and spacious. In Edinburgh I was surrounded, jostled, overwhelmed by so many people. I shared their environment in one sense but only by being caught up in its hectic pace. I had no real sense of sharing, as I felt with the islanders, a sense of our mutual dependence on and appreciation of so many things from the constant, never-ending wind, the noise of the sea, the smell of the peat, the unwritten law that one never met another human being without stopping to talk, to exchange a greeting and some gossip, to share one's humanity because it was all we had to enable us to cope with the harsh world of nature. Foula gave us our livelihood but also laid down clear conditions for our survival.

Family ties, the strongest bond in the world, made it lovely to be home for a break. For me especially there was the excitement of a new relationship, which had so far had to depend on an exchange of letters, which is not the best way of making one's long-term plans for the future. Three weeks doesn't last long, especially when it includes a visit to Oxford where Pat was working temporarily in her profession of psychiatric nurse. So before long I was home in Edinburgh again planning my return to Foula. Study of the timetables and my new-found knowledge of the local details led me to believe that I had a chance to complete the journey without an overnight stop. The daily flight from Edinburgh, via Aberdeen, Wick and Kirkwall airports, arrived too late to reach Walls in time for the mailboat, presuming of course that the weather was kind and none of the crew had 'the cold'. So it was an early train to Glasgow and an earlier direct flight to Sumburgh which did the trick. When P.I.'s bus rounded the corner by the store in Walls, I was hoping that my boat box was being filled with the order I had sent in advance for my weekly groceries. And so it was, for there was the *Island Lass* at the pier and Davie Gear's stately figure at the wheelhouse. We crossed on a moderate sea, on which my Dramamine

tablets worked their magic, and by late afternoon – well, perhaps it was really early evening; I can't remember – I was listening to Jim Gear's non-stop chatter about all the birds he had been recording for me while I was away, while his Aunty Mary was making a pot of tea in the Schoolhouse kitchen and setting a few of her freshly baked scones on a plate for me. Sitting close to my chair as though glued there by the sound of my voice was my faithful Norie. They had brought him down to the pier to meet the boat. Momentarily he had seemed confused by my sudden appearance back in his world, especially as he had never been on a boat and had no idea what they meant. Then suddenly the penny dropped and it was as though three weeks of frustration and pining for me had built up to a release, which he hardly knew how to express. However he certainly tried, tearing round the pier in a frenzy of yelps of welcome which brought tears to my eyes, and nearly knocked some of the crew into the water. So when we got back to familiar territory in the Schoolhouse kitchen, there was no way he was going to lose me again, and in fact for the next few days he was continually under my feet in his anxiety to keep close. The bond between us was now stronger than ever and I seemed to be completely forgiven for my perfidy, as is the way with dogs – which of course is why we love them so much. So with Norie by my side, I was well and truly home again, only fifteen hours after leaving my parents' home in Edinburgh. Suddenly Foula no longer seemed as remote and cut-off as my first long winter had led me to believe. The future looked friendly and full of promise.

Chapter 22: Highlights of Summer – and the End of the Dream

I settled back into the summer term on 19th April with every expectation of continuing in my role as Teacher-Lay Missionary on Foula for the foreseeable future. I had survived the worst winter they had experienced for many years and the prospect of my second summer on Foula was bright compared with my first one when so much was new and untried. I felt I was coping well with the school though the future of such a small number of pupils is always a problem. Children grow and have to move on when they reach Secondary school age, which has always been the greatest problem with remote islands, where communications were as unreliable as they were on Foula. Jim Gear was already twelve and Eric Isbister and Norman Beagrie only a year or two behind. Eric was going to be a problem with his family's history of liability to infection, a much more serious impediment to his progressing on to Lerwick than for the others, something I was going to have to deal with sooner or later, though I knew from the start that his father had already made up his mind – the boy was only going out to finish his education, staying at the Lerwick Hostel, over his dead body. I for one did not intend to oppose this decision, and secretly I felt that John Spence, the Director of Education would not take a strong line on it either. So there was the probability of some continuity there with the real probability that Eric would stay on at the Foula school till he was 16. In fact the prospect of having a highly intelligent and artistic teenager as a challenge was exciting rather than daunting. At the other end of the scale, little Sheila Umphray of Ham, was nearly five and would soon be eligible to start school. She was a shy and over cosseted child who had been rather isolated from other children and might take some time to adjust to school. She was the daughter of Mary who ran the croft of Ham in the absence of her husband Willie who, to earn enough money for the family, spent most of his time at his job in Glasgow. Sheila was not used therefore to taking orders from a man. But apart from personality problems, I foresaw that it would make a big difference to my organisation of the school timetable, for a five-year-old has totally different needs from those of the older children. Vina was the nearest in age, now nine and the brightest of

the whole bunch. Sheila would be like taking on a new class but without a new class teacher to cope. So far I had been lucky with five children close enough in age and capability to be taught in many respects as one class, though admittedly of very diverse ability. A single infant would change that scene, even if he or she was a good mixer and adaptable. From what I had seen of her, wee Sheila was anything but that. So I anticipated some problems at the start with her.

The church was still a challenge. To some extent I had had to adapt to the worshippers who came regularly enough every Sunday, as I could hardly expect them to adapt to me. Foula folk were seldom hypocritical and didn't pretend to be religious if they weren't. Those who came were sincere and lived by their faith. Those who had no faith just didn't come; but there was absolutely no animosity between us on those grounds. Foula of course had its factions and its family feuds like any very small community, but I had got to know where and with whom I needed to be tactful. There was always a role for the 'outsider' like me to play in pouring oil on troubled waters and if necessary to take the initiative in smoothing ruffled feathers – metaphors purposely chosen for an 'island of birds'! But most of those I had got to know were so robustly independent and sure of their opinions of their neighbours, that nothing I thought or said would have made that much difference anyway. I knew quite well that in any emergency or real need, there was always somebody ready to offer help or come to the rescue. And there were many examples of genuine Christian charity in their daily lives and relationships which involved real sacrifice of time and effort, especially in caring for the elderly. The obvious long-term problem for us all was that the average age was now so high. Where were the young and fit to come from to look after the older generation? In the past there had been a policy of using adoption as a means of bringing in a younger element into the community. Elisabeth Wiseman at Ham had been adopted, and was now in her forties and had integrated completely; but Donnie of Leraback, now in his late teens, had found great difficulty coping with being the only teenager in an ageing household. Apart from anything else an adopted child would always be an incomer and not an islander. In his case, where the four adults of the household ranged from 45 to 80, the original adoption had been far too late in their lives to avoid the feeling on the part of the adopted boy that he was there to provide free labour. His 'family' was already beginning to find it difficult to cope with many tasks around the house and croft so that the situation was ripe for misunderstanding by the incomer. So rebellion was only to be expected; and not surprisingly was seen as ingratitude. It was nobody's fault, except perhaps those who had arranged the adoption in the first place.

Naturally as 'the Meenister', such problems would arise as matters for discussion on my visits to crofts, and had I not had a full-time job as the schoolmaster as well, could have taken up a good deal of my time and energy. But time was of course far more limited for me than it had ever been before for any of my predecessors, though it was always gratifying when people chose to drop in on me for a chat or if they had a problem. As often as not this would be some mundane task that required a form to be filled in and submitted, to do with crofting regulations or tax or pension or whatever. The workings of bureaucracy were a closed book to most Foula folk and I was expected to know it all and have an answer to every query. Much of my own mail was to do with administrative matters regarding the church or the school or the Post Office or the telephone, liaison with the Holbourn family or the Shetland Island Council or the Library or the suppliers of food for our school dinners; and so on, and on, and on. It was still not uncommon for me to be up almost all night before a mailboat day if the weather looked promising, with a great pile of letters that had been put off a dozen times and at last just had to be written to catch that week's mail. I had opened the school in mid-April and ten weeks later I was mentally and physically exhausted from the pressures of the long daylight and the continuous demands on my time. There was no let-up, and there

John Henry back from two seasons away at the whaling in South Georgia, restoring the old croft house at Groups, aided by Harry Gear and Peter Ratter, summer 1954

John and Vida Henry and family in their new home at Groups in autumn 1959

was nobody else to fall back on. If I didn't cope with the paperwork I would be professionally culpable; if I didn't feed my hens or cut my peat or weed my garden, I might run short next winter. But when John Henry got back from 18 months away at the whaling in the Antarctic and South Georgia and needed to talk things over with regard to his and his family's future, that was surely the kind of thing I was there for and time just had to be found. Besides his wife Vida, who lived with her parents at the Schoolhouse while John was at sea, was a godsend to me, always willing to play the church organ for Sunday services. This was such a relief, as the hymns tended to be like dirges when Peter Gray was the only other person with the necessary musical skill – but at half speed. Bobby Isbister, the shopman, who composed his own songs, and played them with gusto on his own pedal organ, could have done it; but he was not a churchgoer.

John Henry had followed a popular course amongst Shetlanders in the 50s, but never an easy one for a married man, to sign up for a whole season's whaling activity on South Georgia, which meant over-wintering in the Antarctic. When he returned after 18 months of earning good wages, with little opportunity to spend them and plenty of incentive to save, he was in a far better position to take over a croft than if he had spent the equivalent time in Shetland. He had been allocated the tiny two-roomed house half way up the hill from the nurse's house, called Groups, and he set about improving it and building on a porch. Meanwhile he filled a place in the mailboat crew as a part-time job to earn cash and started planning his croft. He was a good craftsman but would have a lot to learn about Foula sheep for which Vida's knowledge, learned from Mima her mother, would be invaluable. John and Vida had married young, very young in John's case, but they could set up a home and expand their family more cheaply on Foula than anywhere else. What Foula needed was half a dozen such families to help balance the age structure of the population, to learn and preserve the old skills, and keep the school going. Old Mrs Henry down at North Biggins must have been delighted that her grandson (albeit born out of wedlock) had married her grand-daughter, eldest daughter of Mima (née Henry), wife of Davie Gear, skipper of the mailboat. So tightly were Foula families interwoven in their relationships. Their new cottage was just off my road to the school so I kept up with its progress, and one day would see James Andrew Gray helping with woodwork, another Harry Gear the postmaster up a ladder fitting a new chimney-pot. House-building demanded many skills but there were several crofters now living in houses either they or their fathers had built with their own hands, so there were usually tools for the borrowing and ready hands to help if it meant establishing the future of a new family.

On my visit south to Edinburgh I had organised a collection of second-hand clothing and household items of the sort that are regarded as cast-offs in the city but would have great value in a Foula winter, to be collected at one or two local churches and sent up by boat from Aberdeen. Two huge crates arrived with a fascinating assortment of clothes from everyday shirts, jerseys, underwear, socks and shoes, to fashionable fur-coats from Jenners, originally very expensive but now thoroughly dated, and being genuine fur, extremely warm. The Guild women unpacked and sorted it all out and priced the items according to Foula income levels, ridiculously cheap by Edinburgh standards but designed to be attractive to crofters, most of whom had virtually – or absolutely – no income. A day was fixed and a notice put up in the shop for a 'Great Summer Sale, to be held in the schoolyard – 'Bargains Galore'. (Mima, in her inimitable way would have said 'Galores of Bargains'.) We borrowed some trestles from the shed down at Ham and stretched ladders between them as makeshift stalls on which the goods could be laid out for inspection. The children were excused classroom work for the afternoon, but were given jobs manning the stalls. We were lucky with the day and it was dry with a soft wind for a change. Nearly everything we had was out on display or ready to be put out as items were sold. Only a few items, mostly kitchen utensils, were new, bought by generous donors for the occasion as likely to be useful to the crofter housewife. Long before opening time, folk started to arrive and soon

The 'Bargain Sale', mostly of second hand clothing, in the school playground, summer 1955. The 34 people in this photograph represent almost half the resident population at that time

it was going like a fair. There were folk from the furthest crofts North and South who hadn't been seen in the Ham Toun for years. Even Jeannie from Gravins just down the road was there, eyeing the fur coats and the price tickets. For many it must have been their first opportunity for many years to inspect what they were going to buy instead of having to depend on the illustrations in a catalogue. We had occasional travelling salesmen who would come across on the mailboat and spend a couple of days going door-to-door with a huge suitcase, selling household goods like towels and linen, kitchen ware and clothing. They always sold out, as the temptation of new goods was always irresistible when the only shop within reach, without making a major excursion to Lerwick, was Bobby Isbister's shop down by the pier, which sold only a very limited selection of foodstuffs and groceries. But a couple of suitcases did not go far at the doors of twenty-five houses, and there was often not much left for the last houses they reached. One had to admire the initiative of these traders, often of foreign origin, probably Indian, for they were well rewarded for their effort in terms of selling out almost all their stock. Besides as welcome visitors they must have had endless cups of tea and Black's biscuits on their rounds.

For the same reasons our sale was an extraordinary success and there was virtually nothing left at the end. Moreover we cleared almost £100 for the church and were able to send a glowing account of our appreciation back to the Edinburgh congregations who had responded so generously to my suggestion. To many Foula folk £100 would have represented a small fortune, and yet it was surprising to see so many five and ten-pound notes appearing from handbags when the chance to buy in person was offered. Perhaps with so little opportunity to spend money on Foula, I should not have been surprised that many crofters seemed to have more in the way of savings than I would have thought possible. For many households the old age pension was either the main or the sole source of cash income, such that the death of one elderly person in, say, a household of two pensioners, could create conditions of financial hardship or even crisis.

In spite of the comparative poverty of most of the inhabitants, and the great paucity of jobs or opportunities for earning cash, there were examples of great generosity and unselfish giving which were perhaps typical of people who knew the real meaning of being poor. One of the most dramatic was the collection I made for the Royal National Lifeboat Institute in summer 1955. I gathered that this was a fairly regular appeal in fishing communities where the presence of a local lifeboat service would be readily appreciated as a very meaningful service by a traditionally committed body of volunteers. Also there was always the Aith lifeboat which, very occasionally, might be called out but only in a time of real emergency – which often meant when the weather was too bad for the *Island Lass*, which was after all Foula's only lifeline for supplies and too valuable to risk in dangerous weather. She was seaworthy enough but, unlike most Shetland-built boats, not good at coping with really rough seas. She tended to bounce like a cork. The lifeboat could turn out in seas which would have swamped our mailboat, but of course she was two hours away and that extra time in an emergency could be crucial.

I guessed the response would be generous but I was still surprised when we collected over £130 from our 53 adult inhabitants, not counting children under 16 or those incapable of understanding what the appeal was a about. I sent off the money as requested to RNLI headquarters with a short note apologising that it was not more from a small community (I mentioned how many adults were potential contributors) but stressing that it was an expression of genuine appreciation of the lifeboat service from people who had had cause to be grateful from first-hand experience in the past. I got an astonishing reply back. It was from the Chief Executive who stated his sincere appreciation for our collection and said he thought I might be interested to know that, so far as he could ascertain, it was by far the highest per capita contribution to their funds of any community in the whole of the U.K. I wasn't surprised that the Foula folk had been generous, but Michael Powell's words of appreciation of their character sprang to mind. This was truly exceptional. I started to think of all the hundreds of far wealthier communities up and down our coastlines, whose inhabitants were equally well placed to appreciate and be grateful for their local lifeboat service, and most of whom would have had good jobs and reasonable incomes. This made me aware just how privileged I was to live with and enjoy the trust of such a remarkable body of people. I felt I wanted to sing their praises from my rooftop and tell the world how lucky I was. And at the risk of producing in them the sin of pride, I told them so from the pulpit the following Sunday. Several times after that I was told by members of the congregation of times past when the lifeboat had been called out and what a boon it was to them to know it was always there in an emergency. It had undoubtedly saved lives on occasions; but even so, I felt that this benefit the island received from their local lifeboat in no way diminished their astonishing expression of generosity as an example to others infinitely better off then they were. This accolade from the RNLI defined in at least one very positive and demonstrative way the virtue of a small, close-knit community.

Another day to remember that summer was the day of the annual school picnic. It was my responsibility to choose the day. The islanders always took such things seriously and as the families involved (who were all invited to join in) took a great deal of trouble baking and preparing for the event, the day had to be chosen well in advance. The place selected was on the green by 'the Biggins dyke', a beautiful place with a sheltering wall and a wonderful view across to Fitful Head in the South East and on a clear day to Fair Isle on the southern horizon. But it was also very exposed if a low came up to the north of us, bringing in wind and wet from the south east. However on the day I had chosen a huge ridge of high pressure extended right across Shetland, the sea lay round the South Ness with scarcely a ripple

and not a sign of the usual line of white water round the offshore skerries. The air was balmy and the views breath-taking. Women could be seen wending their way across from Dykes who had no children at the school but just didn't intend to be left out of a good party. Aggie Jean from South Biggins came complete with dogs; the Schoolhouse contingent with two of my five pupils, two parents and, most important, Mary Henry the school cook, plus former pupils Ken and Andy home from university – and all welcome and physically required both to carry and eventually to consume a veritable mountain of pancakes, scones, cakes and biscuits washed down with gallons of tea. Even 85-year-old Mrs Henry, Vina's great grand-mother from North Biggins, was able to walk that far, and sat herself down under the shelter of the wall to enjoy the gossip. So we all watched the children running three-legged races or throwing sticks for my indefatigable Norie, and filling the summer air with shrieks of delight. For all this, and quite undeserved, I seemed to get half the credit, having done none of the work but just because I had chosen the right day. This

Andy Gear home for vacation from Aberdeen University hands out cake at the annual school picnic to sisters Mary Henry and Bessie Ratter

The pupils and helpers from local crofts at the annual school picnic at the back of the Biggins dyke

was what being a 'good' teacher was all about, with a spot of luck thrown in. It also showed a community with a great capacity for getting the best out of life and enjoying it to the full when the opportunity offered. It was an afternoon to remember.

If I remember rightly there was one conspicuous absentee, Mrs Beagrie, my next door neighbour and mother of two of my pupils, Norman and Joyce. My guess would be that even after several years' residence, she was still too shy to feel at home with the island families. Besides she was a very conscientious mother and crofter, always busy about the croft and house, and still perhaps finding excuses not to socialize. That summer she decided that keeping the island's only bull was just one more responsibility than she wanted, with her husband out of the isle most of the year and fewer cows on the island. One by one the Foula crofters gave up keeping cows as they grew more infirm. So after all the immediate plans to get cows in calf had been satisfied, she recruited the help of two of the men with previous experience in butchering and the bull was slaughtered. Then the carcass had to be prepared for the massive

task of dividing up the meat for distribution to all who wanted to partake of the temporary surfeit of beef. She was landed with several days of intensive work in her kitchen with some help from those who could spare the time. Although there was the old tradition of curing mutton in various ways and in some crofts 'reestit' lamb could be seen hanging from a rafter, looking always as though it would be dry and tough to eat, beef was another story and was normally eaten fresh. I bought my share and very good it was; but beef had always been a very occasional part of my diet as it tended to exacerbate my problem of having an acid stomach.

When I went to Mornington that weekend for my Sunday lunch, Mrs Beagrie was making sausages, real, original sausages using the animal's lengthy intestinal tubing, duly washed out and cleaned for the purpose. It all looked so right, the perfect container, strong to handle and fill but tender and edible when cooked, and yards and yards of it for free, so to speak. She had three bowls of sausage fillings, one of minced prime beef mixed with some chopped onion and a little flour or breadcrumbs to give it the right texture; one for 'mealie' or 'white

191

puddins', made of oatmeal and dripping with some herbs for flavour; and one for 'fruitie puddins' where the oatmeal was enriched with dried fruit and peel to make it like a mincemeat sausage. I sampled them all and they were as individual and flavoursome as the best butchers in Edinburgh could supply. The only problem was that they had to be eaten as there was no refrigeration on the island. Some products like 'black puddins', made with oatmeal, meat and a generous quantity of blood mixed in, could be cooked and would keep a reasonable time in a cool larder, but for a week or two beef products were on everyone's menu.

Another excellent product from her kitchen was her cheese, which she made on a large cheese press, the result being what I called 'mousetrap' cheese, mellow cheddar- style cheese with a mature flavour and good keeping qualities which suited me admirably. So with my own supply of eggs from my five hens, giving me five eggs a day in the summer almost without fail, (and on one memorable day six!), my protein diet was assured and as pure and organic as one could ask for.

The sea round Foula teems with fish. The old definition of a Shetland crofter as a fisherman with a croft (as opposed to an Orkney man being a crofter with a boat) definitely applied to the Foula folk, except for the problem of Foula being an island without an all-weather harbour. Ham Voe on the map is just a tiny dent on the east coast, a short V-shaped inlet open to any south east swell, and in 1955 with only a short break-water for protection. On calm summer evenings boats would go out to 'da eela' and with luck and local knowledge good catches could be made of piltocks or saithe, mackerel or other species mostly with Shetland names I now cannot remember. The valuable fishing was for lobsters and for a while it paid quite well to invest in a set of lobster creels. However there was always competition from mainland boats, especially from Scalloway where a larger and safer harbour meant that bigger boats could be safely kept with which the Foula boats could not compete.

Occasionally one of the much larger fishing boats would come in to the Voe to repair torn nets, and it was possible with luck to stock up with some fish for the larder that way. I remember one such boat which came in with a huge cloud of seabirds at its stern, as the crew was cleaning part of their catch as they went. It was at a weekend and I was going down to the pier to leave my boat box ready for the Monday mail run. I was amazed at this unusual opportunity to watch at close quarters species I seldom got a chance to study at all, as most of the breeding places were either high on the hills or on the inaccessible west cliffs. Both species of skuas were there in good numbers, not pursuing other species like parasites which was their usual method of feeding under natural circumstances, but taking their food direct from the surface, either inside or close outside the harbour. The fish cleanings did not last long with such a throng of birds, mostly gulls but with fulmars also in good numbers. They were feeding in a way I had never seen fulmars feed before, grabbing and swallowing large gobbets of fish offal instead of the usual plankton on which they normally feed out at sea. Such was the feeding frenzy which had possessed them at this opportunistic feast, they paid scant attention to me standing bemused on the jetty, almost stunned by so much activity of perhaps a thousand birds wheeling right above my head and then swooping down and gorging themselves with food. Even the menacing Bonxies were there, too busy feeding direct to be a danger to the species they normally attacked as parasitic predators.

The only times I ever saw such numbers of skuas together was the Bachelors' Club of non-breeding Great Skuas which gathered all through the summer on the Mill Loch, bathing and preening in the fresh water. Some perhaps were the mates of breeding birds sitting on eggs or guarding young, but it was a communal activity with much calling and croaking to each other as they engaged in vigorous bathing activity, sometimes even lying on their backs and thrashing their wings on the surface, possibly to rid their feathers of parasites such as mites and feather-lice. It was the fascination of seeing a Bonxie lying on its back on the water, waggling its large webbed feet in the air that inspired me with the idea that only movie film would enable me to describe such actions photographically to my ornithological friends back in Edinburgh. And certainly a scene such as that round the fishing boat in the Voe was so full of colour and movement that nothing else except cine-film could do it justice. Thus was born an idea which eventually changed the course of my life.

In the meantime I was making good use of my Paxette 35mm still camera and building up a comprehensive collection of colour transparencies, though, as on that day at Ham Voe, I still hadn't mastered that basic rule for all aspiring photographers never to be without my camera. Life was so full and time so precious that allowing time for yet another activity was just too much. So I missed that opportunity and of course never saw that particular scene repeated. That in itself was frustrating, in contrast with the actual experience which was fulfilling and inspiring. As my fourth term as teacher drew to a close in June, I was suddenly brought up hard against the realisation that perhaps I had really bitten off more than I could chew. Life was so full and so wonderful that I was perhaps driving myself too hard for my own good, trying to cram a quart into a pint pot, especially when the long summer days allowed just too many opportunities to tackle too many projects, all in the same time frame.

Such are the pros and cons of small island life, endless conflicting loyalties and priorities, a rich and varied panoply of pains and pleasures, rewarding, enjoyable, frustrating, uplifting, all at the same time and to the same timetable. As a result I now had a problem. I had taken the job partly because my health had for long been my chief drawback, firstly in the army, and then under the pressure of university with exams and other trials. I was a born worrier. And, so the doctors told me, stress was what I must try to avoid if I was to cure myself of that 20th century affliction, the duodenal ulcer. It had started in the army, had plagued me through university where strict diets and far too many antacid tablets (Rennies were the fashion at the time) still hadn't kept the pain at bay. The challenge of my first job seemed to work for a while as I thrived in the boarding school atmosphere and the company of children. Then, to be honest, I had jumped at the chance of the Foula vacancy, partly with the romantic notion that 'getting away from it all' would be the most beneficial part of the isolation of a remote island. Instead I found I had put my head in a noose. I was trapped by my own enthusiasm for the job because it wasn't a job; it was about three jobs in one. I didn't even have a wife to share them with; well not yet. And although that was perhaps the most exciting prospect of all, it meant some big decisions about where to live. And what about her job? I was never very good at big decisions of that sort, especially where they involved other people. I knew I had found real fulfillment on Foula even if it was a very exacting and at times exasperating job and extremely hard work. But it did call for good health and a robust constitution; and that was what I had never had since leaving the army.

Now suddenly, after coping so well through that first winter, I was subject once more to those griping pains and all the miserable signs of an active ulcer. I remember so well Andy Gear, who had covered himself with glory as the first islander to have gone to university and graduated successfully at Aberdeen, coming home in the summer to Foula. This offered me a welcome break from island talk about the weather and the mailboat, and the weather and the sheep, and the weather… He found me temporarily

in my bed, suffering from the acute acidity which had so often come back to plague me when I least wanted it, and laid me low. Andy's mother Mima Gear had been my greatest support of all the islanders and he knew I had a strong sense of obligation to her as a wise counsellor in island affairs. They both agreed it was essential for me, if I was going to be of any use to the community in my job, to get the best possible advice about my health problems. And the best way to get that would be to go back to the hospital in Edinburgh which had diagnosed the trouble and prescribed the treatment. So as soon as the summer term was over, once again I had to leave my dog behind and go south, this time to seek a passport to return fit for the job, and with some reassurances that I could manage this weakness in my system in such a remote and testing environment as Foula. Without that prospect, not only were all my dreams for life on Foula endangered but the romance of my new relationship with Pat, which had originated from the idea of her coming to share the experience of Foula with me, was threatened if I proved not to be up to it.

I went south determined to succeed. There were no miracle cures in those days though everybody had their own pet theory about ulcers. But Zantac and the acid inhibitors had not yet been discovered and I had already tried nearly everything else. So I had yet more X-rays and barium 'meals' and the infamous acid test, which was one of the more horrible experiences of my life, and was warned that my acidity was acute and stubborn and not to be ignored. It could easily rupture; and a perforated ulcer could be fatal if not operated on within as short a time as possible. When I explained that the Aith lifeboat – the only really reliable transport from Foula to the mainland and the nearest hospital in Lerwick – would take two hours to get there and two hours back and then an hour by road across the mainland, the doctor said that was an unacceptable risk and would almost certainly prove fatal. His verdict was not the best road to a happy announcement of an engagement, nor was it the sort of news I wanted to impart to my elderly parents who were now retired pensioners sitting at home, worrying about their grown-up children. It was I suppose the unhappiest decision I have ever had to make. I felt like a deserter. I had just started on a long and exciting journey and was now turning back with a wonderful sunlit path beckoning me ahead into a dream future.

And who would take over and teach my precious pupils who had done so much to make my life meaningful and fulfilling with their infectious enthusiasm? Especially I thought of Eric Isbister, the shy boy with a gift for language and a real talent in art, but who was trapped by his lack of immunity to infection and would perhaps never leave the island for fear of the germs to which he had no resistance. He would never complete his education in Lerwick and would need all the skills his teacher on Foula could muster to see him through to achieving his undoubted potential. He was genuinely handicapped in a unique way through no fault of his own and now I was walking out on him. It seemed unforgivable. Once the agonizing decision to give in my notice on health grounds was made, I had many others to make. I am not sure to this day whether Pat's disappointment that the Foula dream was at an end wasn't tinged with a measure of relief. Foula had been the spark that brought us together but when that spark had gone out, we had lost something in our romance. Nevertheless we announced our engagement and looked to a different future. I saw the advertisement for an exciting job that in a quite different way was also right up my street, resident Warden at the Lerwick Hostel for school pupils from the islands. I put in a hasty application but, sad to say, the job went with a teaching post in the secondary school and my qualifications were in Classics and English. There was only one Classics vacancy at the Lerwick Secondary school and it had just recently been filled.

While I was still in Edinburgh, it was decided that a period of complete rest was the best starting point for my return to good health, and my mother who had long and bitter experience of my periodic bouts of pain and the strict diet which was supposed to cure it, took over the task with her usual loving care. But it was always a slow road and it took time to get back my energy and any enthusiasm for recovery. The idea of going back on my own, solely to the thankless task of packing up all my belongings and preparing the Manse for my successor was not an attractive one. So I recruited two of my oldest friends from bird-watching days, John Hyatt who had been my constant companion in every island adventure to date, and Ian Balfour Paul with whom I had made the schoolmaster's holiday of a lifetime to discover Scotland's ospreys in Speyside on our Coronation holiday in 1953. I offered them a conducted tour of Foula, promising them the best bird island of all, and they just couldn't refuse. Both were totally practical and supportive and with their help I felt I could face the task. So the three of us set off for Shetland in September 1955, only eighteen months after I had launched into the unknown to take up the appointment on Foula. I was not looking forward to it as I genuinely felt like a traitor, especially to the children and their parents at the school. Moreover I

knew that a replacement would not be easy to find and there was likely to be a hiatus at just the wrong time of the year with the autumn gales and then another uncertain winter in the offing. Our journey was much more typical than my spring return from Edinburgh which had gone so smoothly. We got to Walls to find no sign of the *Island Lass* and no prospect of a crossing on typical September days of equinoctial gales. So we put up in the only local accommodation we could find at a fisherman's hotel full of enthusiasts who regarded this time of the year as perfect for their piscatorial pursuits, with a good run of sea-trout reported locally. We hired the hotel's ancient hire car and visited some Shetland highspots, notably the famous woods at Kergord which give the lie to the normal view of the Shetlands as the 'treeless isles'. Several small experimental plantations in one of the most sheltered valleys available have at their centres small areas of quite substantial woodland trees, offering a real experience of what the atmosphere of a mature wood is like. As one walks to the edge the trees get steadily smaller until at the fringes they rise only to the height of the sheltering walls, and even there they are frayed and battered by the winter winds. From the outside these copses have a sculpted appearance, having indeed been shaped by the wind, with the exposed outer trees sheltering the inner ones, each successive layer benefiting from the protection until they can reach quite impressive proportions. Although rooks can be seen and many species of birds undoubtedly can benefit from the cover, especially hungry migrants newly arrived from the North Sea, commercially these woods are merely an interesting experiment which proves that woodland in Shetland is not a viable commercial proposition.

When we got back to the hotel we phoned the shop in Walls and were advised that they were planning to make the mail-run the next day. So in the morning we packed our bags and caught the bus down to Walls, taking care to have our sea-sickness tablets handy for the crossing. This was my seventh crossing on the mailboat and, with the help of the new generation of travel pills now available, I felt able to face the journeys with some confidence and if it was calm enough, even to look forward to the experience. As birdwatchers there was always the chance of spotting species like petrels and shearwaters on the crossing which were rarely seen from the island, and searching the surface for birds took one's mind off the possibility of feeling ill. Another possibility was sighting cetaceans on the journey or seals closer in to the island. From small boats when out fishing both

Grey and Common Seals were often seen at quite close quarters, and in the autumn I had seen quite large numbers either on the rocks or lying far below at the entrance to caves at the base of the cliffs, or hauled out in Ham Voe. Only once, while walking near the War Memorial above Ham Little, a pod of half a dozen Killer Whales, really close in so that their white markings and characteristic dorsal fins were all quite clear, gave me a real thrill of yet another new experience, this time of power and grace and a strange sense of dread. Their whole nature was as sinister as it was beautiful. They looked like killers.

The crossing from Walls had originally also inspired me with dread but of a different kind, the sheer misery of unavoidable nausea. Seasickness is a very real disadvantage for anyone with a passion for islands, and had been a major problem for me in my first year. Now it was ironic that I was just about over that hurdle but with only one more crossing on the *Island Lass* on the calendar of my immediate future.

Chapter 23: Farewell Fughley Island

On 14th September we did finally make the crossing and, with my two companions for moral support, I set about the unenviable task of packing up all my belongings and making the Manse habitable for whoever might turn out to be my successor. I had a fortnight to complete a myriad of jobs. One new self-imposed task was to make a movie film record of the island while I still had the opportunity. It might never be so easy, even though time was now so precious, but it would soften the blow of having to leave all this behind if I had as realistic a record to take with me as I could devise. The seed of the idea had long ago been sown by my Scoutmaster at Cargilfield, who had thrilled us by showing ourselves on the small screen in his study to the magic mechanical music of the purring cine projector. So I had splashed out on what to me was a much higher cost than my usual transparency film, three 100 ft rolls of Kodachrome 16mm movie film. This would give me 12 mins ready for projection with no further costs. Would this satisfy my new photographic ambition for the island, to record the birds and the people, the wind and the sea and the sky, all so full of life and the movement which my still photographs could never begin to capture?

We had stopped in Lerwick on the journey to call on Theo Kay who ran one of the most successful retail shops in Commercial Street. He was also that rare specialist, a 16mm film enthusiast, a hobby only for those with a good bank balance. He kindly lent me his 'spare' camera, a rather ancient Ensign, with the briefest instructions how to load the film and operate the mechanism. It had only one standard lens; but it was a fixed focus lens that did not require manual adjustment, whatever the subject, and so pretty well foolproof even for such a rank amateur as I was. It was ideal for my purpose; just point and shoot, leaving me only two things to think about – framing a well composed shot in the viewfinder and pressing the start button for the minimum time for a meaningful coverage of whatever movement was taking place. His advice was sound for someone in my situation, *"Remember it is a* movie *camera. Avoid too many static views or still subjects, but also too much camera movement which produces fuzzy pictures and tends to irritate the viewer"*. I had a lot to learn. The way I tried to put his advice into practice was to take shots like my two friends disappearing from sight down the steep footpath through the Uffshins at the South end, so that one moment they are seen poised 600 ft above the sea, and the next heading across a one-in-one slope; or a shot of Mima's washing flapping furiously in a stiff breeze on her washing line in the Schoolhouse yard; or Jim playing with his dog while his brother Ken rocks his infant nephew in a traditional Foula cradle. Life on Foula was all action and colour. All I had to do was design in my imagination a kaleidoscope of images which would, in a balanced way, give an accurate impression of life on Foula's 4000 acres for her community of 65 souls. It was a fascinating challenge and I was itching to get started, but the dreary task of packing up had to come first.

So the real impact of trying out the cine-film medium for my purpose came towards the end of September after my friends had left to go south. Life had been hectic. I scarcely had time to attend to the school where Ken Gear was gallantly filling the role of teacher and apparently managing very well. I planned before I left to visit every croft to say my farewells. Then one day a full gale was forecast but also some good autumn sunshine to give life to the scene. So I put the camera in my haversack and set off for the North end of the island. I was due to visit the North end crofts anyway to say goodbye, so I combined the film excursion with calls at Blowburn and South Harrier to visit the Mansons and the Umphrays for the last time. But the wind was really fresh and I had always wanted to see the Northern stacks, and especially the Gaada stack, in a heavy sea. First I breasted the ridge beyond the crofts and worked my way north to the cliff edge at Logat Head. Here one can find a viewpoint looking south west down the length of the North Bank, a vertical rock wall, from a point where the East Hoevdi juts out at the foot of Soberlie hill. Here I was about 300 ft above the sea, but the slopes above Soberlie, southwards, rose to over 700 ft for at least a mile of sheer cliffs. The sea was distraught, with spindrift blowing across a great Atlantic swell and huge rollers pounding in towards the base of the cliffs at an angle, so that each wave curled and rolled along the rock wall with a lift of countless tons of water twenty or thirty feet high. The distance between the crests of each of these giant waves was probably about a quarter of a mile, so that the whole scene had an amazing atmosphere of slow-motion about it. I wondered whether anyone watching such a scene on film might not feel that I had cheated by slowing down the film speed. But I had no need to try to add to the effect of such awesome power. There was no shelter and I was too concerned anyway to find a safe place to wedge myself in against the gusts so that I could concentrate on holding the camera steady for a long enough shot to make the impact I was looking for. I dug my shoulder into a crevice, braced my legs and framing the scene at the foot of the cliffs, pressed the button. Now I was joyfully aware that the incredible scene in my eye, pressed against the viewfinder, was being recorded at 16 frames every second. It was humbling but satisfying at the same time. I suddenly realised I could hardly hear the purr of the camera's motor running. It was silent film I was taking, and yet my senses were assailed by the roar of great waters, the whistle of wild gusts tearing at the grasses at the cliff face and, behind me, the sudden crash of immense waves against the stacks. I stopped filming and turned to look north. The whole surface of the ocean so far as the eye could see was white with blown spindrift, a confusion of wind, sea and sky. Closer and to my right, beyond the lacy patterns of the inshore white surf, a giant wave rose and surged right through the immense arch of the Gaada Stack. As I waited for the next wave to repeat the spectacle for my camera, I looked further out to sea where a patch of sunshine lit up a rainbow under a shower cloud. God's promise of rain seemed strangely incongruous in such a mad scene of Atlantic fury. The only promise that day was of a relentless, destructive force, which we had learnt to accept as inevitable whenever such a deep low-pressure system arrived from the west. The only comfort I could derive from the sense of subjection to the powers of nature was the sense of wonder that I had been given a mind able to appreciate the awful power of such a storm, and that I belonged to a species with enough ingenuity and technical know-how to enable me to capture it for others to learn from and be amazed by. As yet I knew very little about the subtleties of the process involved in making films of such phenomena, but the potential of what I hoped to have captured in the camera seemed to me far greater than any words I could write or sermons I could preach. This was my baptism in film. In those tense windswept moments, an ambition was born that was to stimulate me for forty years.

I must have been there for half an hour, to take just a three or four minute film sequence, before I could tear myself away to walk the long road home. There, in the peace of the Manse, I had only the roar of the gale in the chimney as evidence of the scenes I hoped I had captured as a keepsake of what I was leaving so soon. I was content I had seized this precious opportunity. Looking back on that day I feel sure that that was the seminal experience which converted me from a stills photographer to a film-maker. It wasn't until weeks later, when I started to edit the reels of tiny pictures, each frame less than the size of a standard postage stamp, that it really came home to me that I hadn't stopped taking 'still' pictures, but by the wonders of technology, forty of them to every foot of film, each frame one sixteenth of a second later than the last. Thus due to the natural ability of the human eye to retain each image for a sixteenth of a second (hence the minimum speed of 16 frames per second) was the wondrous illusion of continuous movement established. The pull-down time, when the projector's shutter obscured the blur as one still frame was replaced by the next, was in fact, a thirty-second of one second, just the same time allowed for the next picture on the screen to flash on the eye and be retained to cover the next black screen. And so on. Slow down this succession of bright pictures and black intervals by the smallest degree, and at once the screen flickered and spoilt the illusion. But all this came later and was a different kind of marvel for my as yet untrained eye. What I had seen through the camera viewfinder that evening had indeed been a thrilling and memorable experience; but as usual the humdrum necessities of daily life soon took over when I realised how much there was still left to do.

First came my work. There was of course nothing I could do towards finding a replacement for the school or the church responsibilities, where the respective authorities had their methods and standards of selection to be gone through. The Elders of the Kirk were men of genuine sincerity and conviction but not given to taking a lead or pushing themselves forward as shepherds of the flock. Humility is a great virtue but not given to solving crises. I suggested that if they didn't feel up to actually taking a service or giving a sermon, they could surely have some form of worship on Sundays, with suitable readings or hymns, as indeed they had done before in the absence of a missionary. The women of the Guild would help with the weekday sessions in the schoolroom which had become a traditional outlet as an enjoyable form of worship. It was hard for me to avoid a strong sense of guilt in all these stop-gap arrangements, as we all knew that it was going to take some time to find anyone at short notice willing to accept the challenge, especially with the autumn gales looming and a long winter ahead; just the time of year when they all needed spiritual help to face the isolation of island life with all its hardships.

I spent what time I could spare at the school in mid-September and was not surprised to find that Kenneth Gear, without any formal training as a teacher but simply by applying common sense and the inherited intelligence of his father, was continuing my policy of making full use of such aids as BBC Educational broadcasts and a good stock of text-books on most of the basic subjects to help him through. As it was only a year or so since he was in the school environment as a pupil, to be gainfully employed as a temporary teacher was a sufficient incentive for him to take the job seriously and put some considerable effort into making it a success. All this relieved my conscience and helped me to relax and leave him to get on with it while I completed the task of packing up my possessions. I couldn't help smiling at one job I had to undertake, packing into the wooden boxes in which I had brought them 18 months before, all those books I had thought would fill the long, tedious evenings of boredom in the

Shetland winter. Now, in the final few days of my life on Foula, more than ever before, I was aware of the pressure of the 'unforgiving minute'. In the life of a Teacher/ Missionary on a remote island, that minute just has to be "*filled with sixty seconds worth of distance run*", if one is to survive and to any degree, however inadequate, fulfil one's obligations to oneself, to the children and to the community to which one belongs.

Because Eric Isbister was now well integrated into the school and happy to make the journey north from his home every day without being dependent on me to take him from the Manse onwards, I was not as apprehensive about visiting South Biggins to say my farewells as I might have been a year earlier. I asked Bobby to play for me on his foot-pedal organ the song he had composed and played on a previous occasion, so that I would have it fresh in my memory after I left. The tune he had adopted almost note for note was that made popular by the American evangelist, Billy Graham, to the hymn 'To God be the Glory'. It was a catchy tune which tended to go round and round in one's head, so I needed the words to go with it. My reason for asking him to remind me of his composition was that the opening words were

Bobby Isbister, shopman and father of Eric; self-taught painter and musician

now so apposite to my own situation: "*Farewell Fugley Island, I am leaving thee now...*" (True to its Nordic origin, he had preserved the hard 'G' in his rendering of the name of the 'bird island' from the Norwegian word 'fugl', which also had the benefit of avoiding the juxtaposition of two vowels which would have been awkward in singing the first line.) In those days I had no tape recorder, and indeed portable recorders had hardly come within the reach of the amateur. So I made sure I had the notation and the phrasing correct, and I wrote down the words so that when I got home I could play an authentic version for myself and my friends. It was a rather sentimental song, envisaging the sort of sorrow I myself felt at the time at leaving the peace and serenity of the island, which I had scarcely any right to call my 'home', whereas Bobby had lived there all his life. What I could never really understand was why he wrote it in the first place, as the possibility of him voluntarily leaving the island seemed so remote as to be almost ridiculous. He confessed that it was entirely imaginary and that he wrote it as though being sung by a native forced, as in Powell's film 'The Edge of the World', to evacuate the island as had happened at St Kilda in 1930.

Like most of the islanders Bobby had been involved in the making of the film which had dominated island life for almost the whole of 1936. The film crew and the 'stars' had lived in a hutted camp behind the Haa, down at Ham Voe, for the whole of the summer; and then, beleaguered by stormy weather, much of the autumn as well. The film which was in all the press headlines about "*Filmstars Marooned*" long before it appeared on the nation's screens, achieved more and better publicity from Foula's fickle weather than any budget that Powell could muster would ever have provided. Many were the stories I was told by the islanders of their personal encounters with John Laurie or Finlay Currie, or especially Belle Chrystall or the other 'stars' whom Powell had assembled for his tour de force. Harry Gear especially remembered the harassed and over-worked camera crew who through inexperience in the face of such weather conditions, amassed 200,000 ft of 35mm movie film to tell the story and gave Powell the title for his racy book about the adventure – a 'must' for all Foula fans. But they still turned Powell's dream into a box office runaway success. Many of the islanders told me that they regarded "*the year that the film folk came*" as the key to Foula's survival for so long after St Kilda's demise. My own view was that it was undoubtedly a boost to their morale. St Kilda had failed and they had been chosen to tell the story, which established them as survivors, so

that long after the film folk left it was their own pride in their island and their unique communal way of life which were strong enough to withstand the buffetings of wild nature and a sceptical bureaucracy. I also had the satisfying and cheering impression that the authorities knew when they had met their match. Time after time, when it was a battle of wills, as for instance over their retaining their right to their own mailboat based on Foula and not one serving them from the mainland, they had always won in the end. It was the Viking blood in their veins which made the difference.

As I met them one by one – or two by two – during those last days, I found them generous in their understanding of my dilemma, sympathetic to my distress at having to leave, and genuinely concerned to wish me well in seeking better health. It was in fact quite revealing – something I had already become aware of from many conversations – how many Foula folk also suffered from chronic indigestion problems and all had their pet theories about the best remedy or diet. One name frequently mentioned as a reliable pick-me-up was Sanatogen, a form of medication claiming to bolster up the nervous system rather than the digestion, and one which I myself had never tried. Mima Gear and her sisters swore by it, especially as a tonic to offset the winter 'blues' or that run-down feeling when food supplies were difficult and diet restricted. The men were not immune either but much less ready to talk about it than the women, who perhaps carried more of the daily stress on their shoulders of the kind which causes indigestion. Although all were generally full of praise for the island nurse and the service she offered, especially in caring for the elderly, I got the distinct impression that normally she didn't have much say in what was the best remedy, as most of them were confident they already knew when it came to a case of indigestion.

One evening shortly before I was due to have my last crossing on the mailboat – one of the few things about the island I would not regret having to forego – I returned home to the Manse and found an envelope on my kitchen table. With it was a hand-written note which really bowled me over and did, in the privacy of my own home, reduce me to tears. It was a bundle of bank-notes and a short explanation that they had decided to make a collection as a kind of leaving present and an advance wedding present. Of course the news of my engagement in the summer to Pat, whom many of them had met on her visit in 1954, had gone the rounds of island gossip. What was so incredible was the knowledge that hardly any of them had any income at all except the very meagre old-age pension, which barely covered the very simplest of diets and nothing else, and that I was the only salaried member of the community, except perhaps the Postmaster. All this made this enormously generous present of £32 so touching. It was outrageous in one way but of course I had to accept it as the most wonderful thank-you I have ever had, or will ever have, in my whole life. I found it both humbling and overwhelming. One strange factor arose as a result. I simply did not know to whom to address any formal reply. My senior Elder? But it was not a church collection. The skipper of the mailboat? But they all knew how I hated going on the sea – and the Minister was always a Jonah anyway. There was no 'Parliament' on Foula as there had been on St Kilda, nor any ruling committee. I suspected Mima Gear was behind it as she and I saw eye-to-eye on more subjects than most of the islanders and she was in my view the 'matriarch' of the community, though there were several crofts who would not have agreed. But it was stated to be a gesture from the whole island and I answered it as such with as much gratitude as I knew how to put into words, and hoped it would be passed round to all concerned. I couldn't help thinking of dear old Betty Gray at her tiny house, North Harrier, on the footpath to the North end. She had so little going for her in her lonely life but was content enough with it to refuse the meagre increase in the old-age pension to which she was entitled. How on earth had she skimped and saved enough from her miniscule income (was it 10/- a week?) to be able to wish me well in monetary terms as I, who had so much going for my future in the south, deserted the sinking ship and left someone else to take her library books to help her fill her days with something to read. I almost began to wonder what my mother, one of the most charitable people I had ever known, would say I should do, as it was largely to abate the anxiety of my parents that I had reached the final decision to leave. Perhaps they would feel I should have accepted the risks and just stayed? But the die was now cast and my plans too fully implemented to reverse them now. It would however take me a long time to get over so many powerful regrets that I had put my own and my family's interests before those of these wonderful people. For the past eighteen months I had so much enjoyed getting to know them all, and, had I only been fitter for the job, I would have been so happy to continue sharing their joint enterprise in living on Foula.

I had many long thoughts during those final days on the island. Perhaps the most significant lesson I had learnt was the value of labour. To be fit to work and to enjoy whatever labour was your lot, either in employment or better still as self-employed, was life's greatest blessing. To be able to work and at the same time thereby to support yourself and your family, was in some ways a right but in others a privilege. It followed that those who had this privilege had a responsibility to those who did not, for reasons of disability or old age for instance, so that voluntary work done for the community or for one's neighbours, became not a way of earning merit or being considered generous, but rather a path of self-fulfilment with a goal of happiness both for one's own household but also the general welfare of the whole community. When this became an established tradition, not dependent on organised religion or primarily practised as an expression of one's faith, but as a valuable asset passed down the generations because it worked as a common-sense way of life, the result could be what I had enjoyed on Foula – a group of households who could co-exist in the face of all sorts of hardships, for whom survival was a much larger part of living than mere comfort or shallow enjoyment of leisure, and where the co-operation of every individual was essential to the success of the whole system. As a result, during my 18 months on Foula, I had never locked my door; I had never lost a thing; I had never seen any graffiti or vandalism, heard any swearing or foul language, seen anyone drunk, or been aware of any violence, domestic or otherwise, or any crime except perhaps possessing a shotgun without a licence. Could one say the same of any other human community? Moreover I had reached all my destinations without the use of any motorized transport, met no policeman, entered no pub, done virtually no shopping in person except a few basic necessities at Bobby Isbister's store, seen no film (there was no television), attended no concert or public entertainment as I used to do so regularly in the city, switched on no electricity in any shape or form for lighting or heating or mechanical aid – except the tuner on my battery radio and, very occasionally, the dynamo for the lights on my bicycle. And yet I had felt no sense of loss or deprivation. Though physical comforts and luxuries were few, the natural sights and sounds of everyday life, the joy of fresh clean air, the open bowl of the sky, the distant line of the horizon, the constant clamour of gulls and skuas, and the symphony of the tides and the weather, these were abundant compensation. And I always had my precious radio for the occasional luxury of listening to Beethoven, or more wistfully to Chopin. One of the few things I really did miss was a piano.

Only one thing I never got used to, the constant, unrelenting dominance of the wind which seemed like a daily reminder that you were an insignificant factor in an environment totally subservient to the surrounding ocean. The sea in turn gave me the joy of wide vistas and the endless changing colours and textures of the view across to mainland Shetland or out to the far horizons of the wide Atlantic. The pluses and minuses, the give and take of the natural world, the arrivals and departures of the migrant birds, the enhanced value and enjoyment of human contacts all the more meaningful for being few, all added meaning and significance to one's life, way beyond the noise and rush and uncaring business of the city for all its material comforts and shallow stimulations. But the wind remained a minus, an enemy to be fought, an irritation to be tholed, the one humbling factor I just learned to put up with but hated till the day I left.

Towards the end of September I watched the *Island Lass* chugging out of the Voe with several 6 ft rolls of wire netting tied down behind the wheelhouse, bound for Fair Isle as the residue of what I had used to build my Heligoland trap in the garden below Ham. I realised that the salty sea-air would probably take only a few years to turn my dream to rust. I could not foresee who else might have the time or energy to trap and ring a few migrant birds for the sake of scientific understanding of the marvels of migration. Although Fair Isle was beginning to attract small numbers of enthusiastic ornithologists to the Bird Observatory, Foula was altogether too difficult of access and lacking in facilities to offer a similar draw. I had proved that many migrants did reach it as a safe haven after long sea crossings, but the numbers were insignificant compared with Fair Isle. The reasons were obvious – no flashing lighthouses to attract the lost wanderers at night; and the whole of the mainland of Shetland offering a safe landing and the chance of food and shelter to lost migrants over the North Sea. And the more serious studies of the skuas and the cliff-nesting seabirds were in any case far more demanding than any full-time teacher could ever cope with. I had no doubt that in due course the true value of Foula as a nature reserve, a valuable asset to Scotland's heritage of wildlife treasures, would be appreciated and studied. But in the end I had to see that the greatest value of my all too brief stay on the island had been for myself, for my understanding of the marvels of the natural world and especially the magic beauty of birds. Birds are surely the most fascinating and mysterious examples of the wonderful system we call evolution, which has resulted in such variety and richness of forms and survival techniques as I had been

privileged to see and, to a very limited extent, study on Foula. But *"the proper study of mankind is man"* and I had had an opportunity to step back about a hundred years and experience a way of subsistence living that was gradually being eroded by the forces of so-called progress and the steady trend towards urbanization.

Of course I was too late to see the total dependence on the croft which must have made life so hard when the island's population was over 200. Then everything they needed for survival had to be grown or husbanded within the few acres of good land that could support crops of oats or barley or potatoes, and they had to achieve, whatever the weather, enough winter feed for their animals and stored protein for themselves to carry them through the long winter. When I arrived in the 1950s they still had most of the skills and some of the tools for that level of subsistence crofting, but the steady increase in the average age meant that without new blood and especially new families, with children prepared to call Foula 'home', there were just not enough able-bodied workers to carry the burdens of peat-cutting and harvesting required to enable them to get through each winter unaided. So I was witness to a rather valiant but clearly losing battle against the increasing work-load of smaller numbers, and the trials of advancing years. One factor shone through this picture of an island on the edge of change. In spite of a tough life and a restricted diet, they mostly lived to a good age. One of the things I managed to record on film, though only because she was unaware of the camera, was a shot of old Meggie Ratter of Punds wheeling home a heavy barrow of peats along the rough path between her peat banks and the road. So far as I remember she was 84; but she looked after her much older sister Jeannie who was still of very sound mind though no longer able to work outdoors. Several years after I left, we were reminded that she was to be 100 that winter. As I was at that time working a good deal with the BBC, I managed to get a special item included in the morning Scottish News programme about this special birthday of the oldest inhabitant of Scotland's remotest island community. I sent her congratulations and we played part of the 'Foula Reel' for her over the airwaves. We had warned her to listen in, and as a thank you she knitted me a pair of woollen socks in soft Shetland wool which were always known in my family thereafter as my 'hundred-year-old socks'. What a character! She died the following year.

I also kept in touch with the Women's Guild, who were always looking for outlets to sell their knitted goods, and especially with Jeannie's neighbour Edith Gray of Dykes, who was probably the best knitter of the traditional Fair Isle patterns – or rather the special Foula versions of traditional motifs and 'go-betweens'. Her speciality was knitting in the natural colours of the wool which on Foula varied from white through grey and fawn to the deep brown 'moorit' sheep (very like the St Kilda Soay sheep in colour) and finally black. Edith had knitted me one jersey of that type before I left; but a couple of years later I ordered two very small children's cardigans in the bright dyes which she blended into her patterns with great skill and good taste, for my two nieces when they were one and three years old. I had often watched her knitting such garments on my visits to Dykes, never once referring to any pattern guide or book but carrying on a conversation while her fingers appeared to be on automatic pilot, clicking away at full speed with three colours going at once, and the wool carried over on the reverse side to reappear as required by the intricate variations of the chosen pattern, and never a mistake to be corrected or a single stitch out of place. Now such knitting is extremely rare as so much is done on knitting machines. Even the famous 'Fair Isle made in Fair Isle' label – to protect their brand from all the thousands of imitations of similar but not authentic patterns that were

*Edith Gray of Dykes, crofter
and hand-knitter extraordinary,
aged 76 in 1993*

appearing for the market – no longer carries the claim 'Hand knitted'. Over twenty years later when I made a film in Fair Isle, I recorded on film the lightning fast fingers of a Fair Isle knitter repeating the performance but in traditional Fair Isle themes, so fast that the needles are just a blur and the pattern is produced almost by instinct as the three coloured balls of wool rapidly disappear into the pattern. Magic!

In early October 1955, I finally came to the end of my attempt to live the insular life amongst these wonderful people. I brought the school records up to date and preached my last sermon from the pulpit in the Kirk. I have the notes still of my preparation for that service and of my announcement the previous Sunday that, weather and mailboat permitting, I would be taking my last service that day and there was no word so far of anyone to take my place. I talked about human life as being full of changes, some of which we knew would please us while others would inevitably cause us distress. St Paul's words, "*Set your affections on things above and not on things on the earth*", was a way of protecting ourselves from the changing fortunes of life. I mentioned some of the sad changes we had seen since I had come in April 1954 and how lucky we were to have such an awe-inspiring setting for our lives. It made the passing of old friends seem just part of the greater plan of nature so that our mourning was more for ourselves than for them. It seems to me interesting now to note that I took as an example the keeping of a dog as a deliberate choice that many of us make, even though we know we shall outlive the dog and so subject ourselves to the distress of losing a 'friend' in due course. The joy of sharing that relationship outweighs the sadness of the loss.

Those thoughts I have recalled only with the help of my sermon notes which I still have, brief headings only as I always spoke in the pulpit from the heart and never from a script. The dog theme would have meant so much more to the Schoolhouse family, following earnest discussion over whether I should leave Norie behind where he 'belonged' and was happy, or should I take him with me to an unfamiliar and possibly, to him, a very frightening world. The consensus was that he would probably miss me more than he would miss Foula so that taking him would be best for both of us. Besides, the bond between us after more than a year was so deep that I couldn't have coped without his companionship to offset the wrench of leaving Foula. And so on that final Monday morning while Harry was sealing up the mailbags in the Post Office for the weekly collection, as declared in the window as 'Mondays 10.20', I was busy

down at the pier making sure that both Norie and I had taken our travel pills – in his case half a sedative tablet. There's a shot in that first film I ever made, taken as the mailboat slid round the end of the pier and headed for the open sea, of Mima with her dogs and some of the youngest children waving good-bye, a scene I could never look at without a lump in my throat and a tear in my eye. It was a momentous day for Norie in particular and his first taste of so many strange and sometimes terrifying experiences – the bumping and bouncing on the floor of Peter Isbister's bus under my seat on the way across to Lerwick; the incarceration in the dog pound below decks, where I had to leave him for most of the overnight sea journey to Aberdeen before I went down to rescue him, and a seriously over-worked tail, on arrival. Worst of all from his point of view was the long train journey with so many unfamiliar sounds and smells while he lay quiet, but clearly very anxious, as close to my feet as he could manage. Luckily the Edinburgh suburb where he underwent his early acclimatization training was fairly quiet because traffic terrified him at first. Luckily too his instinct was to cower as far from the road or up the bank as possible, an instinct which proved extremely useful many times when passing juggernauts might otherwise have panicked him into their path. Norie immediately became my link with Foula. His name (the second part of Tammy Norie, the Shetland name for a puffin and the nickname of the menfolk of Foula) was the introduction to many a conversation about 'the island of birds'. The joke that he was named so because he was always "*puffin' and pantin'*" soon wore thin. But Foula as a topic of conversation never did, and I gradually found that everywhere I went, with or without my Foula dog, as soon as the word got around where I had been for the past eighteen months, there was a universal and genuine interest in remote island communities and how they lived.

As I took up my old connections with such organisations as the Scottish Ornithologists' Club and the Fair Isle Bird Observatory Trust, there was a curiosity about Foula which always seemed to translate into a request for a talk or preferably a slide lecture. For this I had a good general collection of slides of the scenery, the birds and the way of life. At that time colour transparencies were a comparatively new method of illustrating a talk. An island, as a closed finite subject, is the ideal topic for a model lecture long enough to be interesting, not so long as to be boring. I must have given my lecture on Foula a hundred times over the ensuing years so that talking about my experience on

Foula became almost a way of life. More important for me was how much it helped me to get over the sense of anti-climax. There had been some publicity for my venture in the Edinburgh papers when I left for Shetland in 1954, and I had sent the Evening News several articles with photographs of my experiences and especially the wildlife for their weekly Nature column. All that of course fizzled out when I returned, so I grasped every opportunity to make a success of some aspect of my adventure to offset the sense of bitter disappointment and personal failure. The best opportunity came when by sheer chance an unexpected vacancy arose in the staff of my father's school. He had retired and appointed a paid Headmaster after moving the school to Melville House, a 17th century mansion in Fife, after the lease on Dalhousie Castle, my home for twenty-one years, had expired. Although I was now returning in a sense to what I had once been used to, living in a noisy, busy community of 60 pupils and 12 staff, it was an abrupt change from my solo existence on Foula and it took some time to adjust. Often my thoughts, especially on windy nights, were far north under that wonderfully black, starry sky with those distant lights from passing fishing boats or from the Shetland mainland, twinkling across the water. I had to admit it was pleasant to be back in wooded countryside again and to have some shelter when out bird-watching. In 1955 when winter came with a substantial snowfall, my thoughts turned at once to Foula with memories of our ordeals at Christmas in 1954. So when I went back to my parents' home in Edinburgh for the Christmas holidays I decided to send off a parcel of all the sorts of goodies which Bobby Isbister never stocked in his shop and which I knew would be a treat for the children and a welcome change for their very restricted diet. So far as I can remember I tried to send something for all the children but addressed the large parcel to the Schoolhouse. I wasn't home for the school holidays in time to pack it up and commit it to the post before 25th December, but I knew they would celebrate at Old Yule anyway, so it was enough to dispatch it before 1st January to arrive by the 6th. It was I suppose a sort of gesture of compensation for my departure, a sop to my conscience, a hopelessly inadequate token of thanks for all their kindness and generosity to me especially the previous Christmas.

I cannot now remember, and I kept no diary of it, but I guess it was the following winter that I received a strange parcel just before Christmas. It must have intrigued the Post Office sorting offices for it was simply a hessian sack, sewn up with string at the neck and containing with the flimsiest of packing materials a fully feathered dead goose. I can just picture what had happened. There was always a gaggle of domestic geese around the Schoolhouse, so much part of the scene that one paid little attention to them, but they must have formed a significant proportion of the Gears' annual home-grown protein. One Sunday evening, Mima, bless her, had decided that I needed a reminder of my time on Foula, and had caught up one of her precious geese. Instead of putting it in the lambing-shed for the night, she had wrung its neck and popped it into a sack for Harry to take down to the pier with the mails on Monday morning. Just like that – and so typical of her generous spirit. My mother was delighted and highly amused at the packing, but not quite so amused when she realised the bird still had to be drawn, cleaned and plucked. Delving back into her girlhood days as the daughter in the big house on the Turnworth Estate in Dorset, she knew all the tricks of country cooking and had the bird ready for the oven in no time. In her later years she would take the Foula goose to the butcher to be plucked and prepared. By that time, the ceremony of Mima's goose was well established in the Mylne household and became an annual family event. The generosity of the gesture was not lost on us when one considered all the work which had gone into feeding and caring for their precious birds. Thanks to the green pastures of the valley of the Ham Burn (and the fact that there are no foxes on Foula,) the bird was always plump and tender, with enough fat on it to roast an ox; but never as plump and sumptuous as the infamous Whooper Swan of Christmas 1954.

I stayed on the staff of Dalhousie School for a year. Of course I missed Foula in many ways as the experience had changed so many of my values and interests. I was however lucky in that life in a busy boarding school is very full and demanding. I loved the atmosphere and the boys were the usual mixture of insufferable and attractive, difficult and rewarding, likeable and sometimes even lovable, so that I hadn't the time or energy left to think about what I was missing. Sadly the change in my plans and future prospects had a fatal effect on my rather short-lived relationship with Pat. She lived in the Lodge at the top of the entrance drive to the school which was of course how we had first met. It should have provided every opportunity for a successful outcome, but somehow the romance of the idea of a shared life on the island proved to have been an essential component of the dream we had built up, admittedly mostly at long-range through letters. So I had yet another loss and disappointment to cope with when she called it all off, and I had the galling task of returning several early wedding presents the staff at the school had clubbed together to give us. At such times a devoted dog is an amazing comfort to one's distress. Norie, as a tangible link with the island, was even more than that.

There was another link with Foula, however, which was to prove of real significance for my future plans. Already my collection of colour transparencies had improved my photographic skills and provided me with the means of sharing my experience with many audiences. At first this was on a voluntary basis as I quickly discovered there was an almost never-ending demand for filling the winter meetings of dozens of small clubs, societies of every kind with some form of light entertainment. Most would offer a cup of tea and a biscuit; some would reimburse travel expenses; a few would present a small cheque or a book token. Only years later did I discover the lecture agencies and speakers earning astonishing fees to huge audiences. I had started my career as a lecturer with an enthusiastic audience of islanders one evening in the Foula schoolroom after I acquired a small but remarkably effective DC projector which I ran off Harry's Post Office batteries. It was the first such show most of them had ever seen. Simply seeing people they knew on the screen was the source of more astonishment and often uncontrollable merriment than I ever experienced anywhere else.

My first-ever movie film was of course even more of an event when I finally got the precious 300 ft of 16mm Kodachrome edited, titled and introduced with a few informative map shots to show where Foula was and how to get there. I achieved all this through a valuable contact in the street in Edinburgh where my parents lived, my home in the school holidays. Eric Lucey was a neighbour, a scientist, a boffin, and an enthusiast. Luckily for me he ran a small Film Unit in the Department of Genetics in Edinburgh University with just enough editing equipment to allow me to produce a 15 minute silent film. My original 300 ft at 16 frames a second (the old silent speed for movies) only lasted for 12½ minutes if one used every frame, so there was very little wastage. It was very amateurish but brought the whole story to life. The first showings were to some of the branches of the Scottish Ornithologists' Club (SOC) and not surprisingly the first of these was in St Andrews, the nearest to Melville House where I was teaching. It was there that in 1956 I met my future wife Margaret. She was on the staff of the Physical Education Department of the university as a coach for the women students, with special qualifications in fencing. What drew us together

initially therefore was our common interest in birds and bird-watching, but Margaret must very soon have realised that islands were part of my psyche and just had to be accepted as an obsession.

The film was made for several reasons. First a lifelong fascination with moving pictures all through my boyhood – from Felix the Cat home movie cartoons, to Walt Disney with 'Snow White', the first full-length animated film the highlight of a whole summer holiday. Though Charlie Chaplin and Laurel and Hardy kept my brother and I entertained on frequent visits to our local cinema, there was something even more magic about the purring sound of the little home movie projector showing a family 8mm film taken by the father of one of our friends from a wealthier family than our own. Second was my fervent desire to take away with me from the Foula experience a personal record, not just of stills, but of the constant movement of sea and sky, birds and people, wind and water, which made up the Foula scene. The result was a success but on a very small, low-key level. Yet it was enough to trigger a whole series of events which, coupled with some extraordinarily fortuitous circumstances led to a complete change in the direction of my professional career. As a result of that very tentative beginning, I changed from being a dedicated teacher to a lifelong wildlife film-maker. Unlike many others who went to sunny Africa where the weather was almost always on the photographer's side, I stuck to the British Isles and mostly Scotland, and therein largely on Scottish islands. The weather was enemy No. 1 but that meant far less competition, simply because conditions were often so frustrating and difficult or even quite impossible.

All this must be the subject of another book, 35 years of film-making, 25 of them as a free-lance, covering many wonderful locations and preserving records of several Scottish islands and one Norwegian one, each with a different story to be told of both human and wildlife communities. Foula was the turning point which opened a whole new chapter in my life. In 1956 I was temporarily back in teaching but already planning my first return visit to the island as part of a six-week stretch of island-visiting, to gain proper experience of the Scottish bird observatories and my own study of bird migration patterns across the North Sea. I was back on Foula again in 1959 to make a BBC Scotland radio programme; a 45 minute audio portrait of the island. Thereafter other islands demanded my time, notably St Kilda, where I made four films over the years as part of my work with the National Trust for Scotland. I ended my career with two major projects. First was an expedition to Karlsøy, a beautiful island in the Norwegian fjords, north of Tromsø and well into the Arctic Circle; and the second was a return three-week visit to Foula in 1993. This, 38 years after I left, enabled me to chart the astonishing changes that had taken place, a reflection in miniature of the huge changes in our way of life in Britain as a whole. I was privileged to have witnessed the end of subsistence crofting as a way of life and the extension of the welfare state and the cash economy to even the remotest parts of the British Isles. Now we are faced with global threats in climate change on a scale of impending catastrophe that the human spirit seems incapable of grasping, and so may not find answers in time to solve. I have developed a theory that in small communities with intelligible statistics there may lie, not just answers to our current energy problems, but also a method of demonstrating to both public and politicians, social and technical solutions we can all comprehend. Small really is beautiful; but time is very short. We must explore every avenue that may help us to grasp survival before it is too late.

Fishing boat HF190 – drawing by Eric Isbister

Norwegian fishing boat H016 – drawing by Eric Isbister

Index of Crofts and Residents as in 1954

Bibliography

There are very few books devoted solely to Foula:

Gear, Sheila, *Foula, Island West of the Sun*, Robert Hale, London, 1983
Gear, Sheila, *The Flora of Foula*, Waterstones, 2008
Martin, Simon, *The Other Titanic*, David & Charles, 1980
Powell, Michael, *200,000 ft. on Foula*, Faber & Faber, London, 1938
Stoughton Holbourn, Ian B., *The Isle of Foula*, Johnson & Greig, Lerwick, 1938

Other publications, or books with only a chapter devoted to Foula:

Curwen, H.B., *Photographs of a Visit to Foula*, 1900
Fisher, James, *The Fulmar*, New Naturalist, Collins, 1954
Fisher James and Lockley, R.M., *Seabirds,* Collins, 1954
Haswell-Smith, Hamish, *An Island Odyssey,* Canongate Books Ltd., Edinburgh, 1999 (p. 127)
Henley, John, *Living at the Edge of the World*, The Guardian, 2 February 2008 (p. 5)
Isbister, R.W., *Tales of Foula*, The Shetland Times, 1970
Svensson, Roland, Lonely Islands, Rabén & Sjögren/Vi, Stockholm, 1954 (Chapter 2, p. 42, "Isle of Shadows")
The Foula School Centenary – booklet, by Education Committee, Shetland Islands Council, 1979
Wildlife of Scotland – the Bird Islands, Macmillan London Ltd., 1979 (pp. 116–121)

Websites

http://en.wikipedia.org/wiki/Foula
www.foulaheritage.org.uk
www.windandsun.co.uk/Projects/foula.htm (*Foula's sustainable energy project and electricity supply system based on the new school – hydro/solar/aero and diesel back-up*)
www.northlinkferries.co.uk/Shetland Pages/shetland.html (*transport details and aerial views round the cliffs*)
www.cycharters.co.uk/foula.html (*daytrips to Foula and circumnavigation*)

General Index

Index of Bird Species

Arctic Skua (Scooty Alan) 25, 38, 39, 40, 50, 51, 74, 75, 76, 183
Arctic Tern (Tirrick) 41, 51

Barred Warbler 113
Blackbird 38, 51, 116
Blackcap 113
Black Guillemot (Tystie) 25, 51, 157
Black Redstart 38

Chiffchaff 113
Curlew (Whaup) 51

Dunlin 51

Eider (Dunter) 51, 75

Fieldfare 116
Fulmar (Maalie) 11, 18, 25, 40, 45, 51, 109, 111

Gannet (Solan) 25
Garden Warbler 50, 113
Glaucous Gull (Iceland Scorie) 83, 84
Goldcrest 116, 117
Great Skua (Bonxie) 11, 17, 25, 38, 40, 50, 51, 75, 76, 77, 83, 176
Greylag Goose 40
Guillemot (Loom longie) 40, 51, 109

House Martin 40
House Sparrow 38, 116

Kestrel 113
Kittiwake (Pirie Maa) 40, 51, 176

Lapwing 50
Leach's Petrel 86
Lesser Grey Shrike 96, 97
Lesser Whitethroat 48, 113

Manx Shearwater (Lyrie) 25, 85, 110, 111
Merlin 113, 158

Oystercatcher (Shalder) 51, 157, 183
Puffin (Tammy Norie) 40, 51, 76, 77, 81, 109
Purple Sandpiper 25

Raven (Corbie) 81, 82
Razorbill (Sea Craa) 40, 51, 109
Red-backed Shrike 90, 91
Red-throated Diver (Raingoose) 25, 51, 90
Redwing 25, 38, 116
Reed Bunting 38
Ringed Plover (Sandy Loo) 51, 90
Robin 25, 113

Scarlet Grosbeak 113
Shag (Scarf) 25, 41, 51
Short-eared Owl 50
Skylark 51, 75
Snipe (Snippik) 22, 38
Snow Bunting (Snaa Fool) 40, 113
Song Thrush 116
Starling 24, 38, 51, 97, 116
Storm Petrel (Oily Mootie) 85, 86
Swallow 7

Teal 51
Turtle Dove 113
Twite (Lintie) 24, 38, 116

Water-rail 38
Wheatear 40
Whitethroat 48
White Wagtail 113
Whimbrel (Pirie Whaup) 51
Whooper Swan 139
Wigeon 51
Willow Warbler 113
Wood Sandpiper 90
Wren (Shetland/Fair Isle) 25, 40, 116

Yellow Wagtail 113

The Mill Loch in summer is the scene of the gathering of non-breeding Great Skuas, for social bathing and preening

The hen bird does more of the incubation on the nest, but both birds will vigorously defend the territory against all intruders – including especially bird-watchers!

Acknowledgements

My principal debt is to the people of Foula who made me so welcome in the 1950s and made my stay on the island so memorable. I owe special thanks to Eric Isbister, one of my former pupils at the school, for keeping me up to date with island news and answering so many questions from his incredible memory of Foula families, personalities and events. My thanks too to Sheila Gear for the inspiration I derived from her wonderful book, published in 1988, 'Foula, Island West of the Sun', with a wealth of background knowledge of crofting life derived from personal experience. My principal debt of gratitude however must go to David Wilson, bookseller and collector of remote island memorabilia, especially from Foula and St Kilda, whose unique collection of press cuttings, news items and references was put freely at my disposal and provided a generous and specialised source of material for this book.

Finally the Islands Book Trust, under the inspired leadership and enthusiasm of John Randall, have seen the project through and converted my aim of recording a vital stage in the past life of the island from a dream into a positive step towards its continued future. The survival of Foula and its gallant community can still be a reality and a lesson for all mankind. A second book in my story will describe how dramatic changes on Foula in recent years can provide, on a credible scale, answers for human communities and their chances of survival against the enormous challenges of climate change and food and energy provision for human needs in our immediate future.

Snow in Shetland is rare, but can occur as late as April, as in this view of the Kame and Mebbifield from a National Trust for Scotland spring cruise, of the massive West cliffs of stratified old red sandstone